ARCTIC OCEAN

Queen Elizabeth Islands

Baffin Island

D0116062

ND
rk)

ALASKA
(to U.S.)

Aleutian Islands (to U.S.)

urile Islands
o Russ. Fed.)

PACIFIC OCEAN

CANADA

ST. PIERRE
& MIQUELON
(to France)

UNITED STATES
OF AMERICA

ATLANTIC OCEAN

MIDWAY ISLANDS
(to U.S.)

BERMUDA
(to U.K.)

PUERTO RICO (to U.S.)

Guadelupe
(to Mexico)

DOMINICAN REPUBLIC

BRITISH VIRGIN ISLANDS (to U.K.)

TURKS & CAICOS ISLANDS (to U.K.)

VIRGIN ISLANDS (to U.S.)

CAYMAN ISLANDS
(to U.K.)

ANGUILLA (to U.K.)

BAHAMAS

ST. KITTS & NEVIS

Hawaii
(to U.S.)

ANTIGUA & BARBUDA

HONDURAS
BELIZE

CUBA

MONTSERRAT (to U.K.)

Revillagigedo
Islands
(to Mexico)

JAMAICA

GUADELOUPE (to France)

WAKE ISLAND
(to U.S.)

NAVASSA I.
(to U.S.)

HAITI

DOMINICA

JOHNSTON ATOLL (to U.S.)

CURAÇAO
(to Neth.)

MARTINIQUE (to France)

MARSHALL
ISLANDS

GUATEMALA
EL SALVADOR

ARUBA
(to Neth.)

ST. LUCIA

WALLIS & FUTUNA
(to France)

KINGMAN REEF (to U.S.)

NICARAGUA
COSTA RICA

BARBADOS

ST. VINCENT & THE GRENADINES

PALMYRA ATOLL (to U.S.)

CLIPPERTON ISLAND
(to French Polynesia)

PANAMA

VENEZUELA

GRENADA

TRINIDAD & TOBAGO

BAKER &
HOWLAND
ISLANDS
(to U.S.)

NAURU

JARVIS ISLAND
(to U.S.)

COLOMBIA

FRENCH GUIANA
(to France)

Galapagos Islands
(to Ecuador)

KIRIBATI

GUYANA
SURINAME

ECUADOR

TOKELAU
(to N.Z.)

B R A Z I L

TUVALU

SOLOMON
ISLANDS

SAMOA

COOK
ISLANDS
(to N.Z.)

PERU

PACIFIC OCEAN

FRENCH POLYNESIA
(to France)

VANUATU

BOLIVIA

NEW
CALEDONIA
(to France)

FIJI

TONGA

PARAGUAY

NIUE (to N.Z.)

San Felix Island
(to Chile)

RAL SEA ISLANDS
Australia)

AMERICAN
SAMOA
(to U.S.)

PITCAIRN
ISLANDS
(to U.K.)

NORFOLK ISLAND
(to Australia)

Easter Island
(to Chile)

Sala y Gomez
(to Chile)

San Ambrosia
Island
(to Chile)

CHILE

Lord Howe Island
(to Australia)

Kermadec Island
(to N.Z.)

ARGENTINA

URUGUAY

Juan Fernandez Island
(to Chile)

NEW
ZEALAND

Chatham Island
(to N.Z.)

Bounty Island
(to N.Z.)

Campbell Island
(to N.Z.)

FALKLAND ISLANDS
(to U.K.)

Macquarie Island (to Australia)

CHILE

SOUTH GEORGIA &
SOUTH SANDWICH ISLANDS
(to U.K.)

ANTARCTICA

Continental key

NORTH AMERICA pages 2-23	EUROPE pages 46-73
SOUTH AMERICA pages 24-33	ASIA pages 74-99
AFRICA pages 34-45	AUSTRALASIA & OCEANIA pages 100-109

MEXICO

CHILDREN'S
WORLD
ATLAS

WITHDRAWN

Consultant

Dr. Kathleen Baker

Senior Lecturer in Geography, King's College London (retired)
Senior Visiting Fellow, London South Bank University

Written by

Simon Adams • Mary Atkinson • Sarah Phillips • John Woodward

A Dorling Kindersley Book

LONDON, NEW YORK, MUNICH, MELBOURNE, AND DELHI

Project editors Lucy Hurst, Sadie Smith,
Shaila Awan, Amber Tokeley
Art editors Joe Conneally, Sheila Collins,
Rebecca Johns, Simon Oon, Andrew Nash
Senior editor Fran Jones
Senior art editor Floyd Sayers
Managing editor Andrew Macintyre
Managing art editor Jane Thomas
Picture research Carolyn Clerkin, Brenda Clynch
DK Pictures Sarah Mills
Production Jenny Jacoby
DTP designer Siu Yin Ho
Senior cartographic editor Simon Mumford
Cartographer Ed Merritt
Digital Cartography Encompass Graphics Limited
Satellite images Rob Stokes
3D globes Planetary Visions Ltd., London

THIS EDITION
Editor Jessamy Wood
Art editors Mark Lloyd, Katie Knutton
Senior editor Rob Houston
Senior art editor Carol Davis
Managing editor Linda Esposito
Managing art editor Jim Green
Picture research Myriam Mégharbi
Production editor Marc Staples
Print production Charlotte Oliver
Senior cartographic editor Simon Mumford
Satellite images Ed Merritt
3D Globes Planetary Visions Ltd., London
US editor Stephanie Pliakas

First published in the United States in 2003.
This revised edition published in the United States in 2011 by
DK Publishing, 375 Hudson Street, New York, New York 10014.
Copyright © 2003, 2008, 2011 Dorling Kindersley Limited

10 9 8 7 6 5 4 3 2 1
003 – 179338 – Jun/11

Published in Great Britain by Dorling Kindersley Limited.

A catalogue record for this book is available from the Library of Congress.

ISBN: 978-0-7566-7584-4

Colour reproduction by Colourscan, Singapore, and MDP, UK
Printed and bound by Star Standard Industries Ltd, Singapore

Discover more at
www.dk.com

Contents

Active Planet

EARTH IS A DYNAMIC PLANET that is always changing its form. Heat generated by nuclear reactions deep below the surface creates hugely powerful currents that keep Earth's rocks on the move, triggering earthquakes and volcanic eruptions. Meanwhile, solar energy striking the planet in different ways creates currents in the air, driving the atmospheric turmoil of the weather. This changes with the seasons and from place to place, creating an enormous range of climates and habitats for the most dynamic element of all—life.

Earth formed from iron-rich asteroids that smashed together to build the planet. Early in its history it melted, allowing the heavy iron to sink and create a metallic core. The core is surrounded by lighter rock, with the lightest forming Earth's crust. Most of the water on the planet lies in huge oceans, and above them is the layer of air that forms the atmosphere.

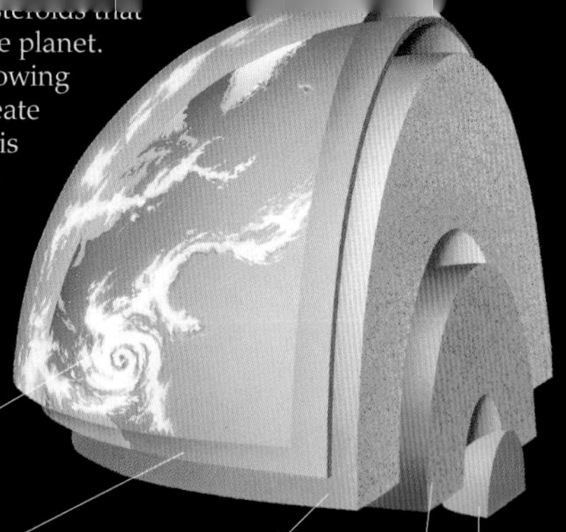

Lower atmosphere, 10 miles (16 km) thick

Crust, 5–45 miles (8–70 km) thick

Mantle, 1,800 miles (2,900 km) thick

Liquid outer core, 1,400 miles (2,250 km) thick

Solid inner core, 1,515 miles (2,440 km) across

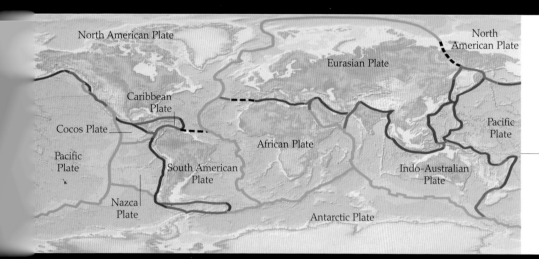

THE PLATES OF EARTH'S CRUST

Heat generated deep within the planet creates currents in the mobile mantle rock beneath the crust. These currents drag some sections of the cool, brittle crust apart while pushing other parts together, fracturing the crust into separate plates. The biggest of these span oceans and continents, but there are many smaller plates. At their boundaries the plates may be diverging (pulling apart), converging (pushing together), or sliding past each other at transform faults.

Plate labels on map:
- North American Plate
- Eurasian Plate
- North American Plate
- Caribbean Plate
- Cocos Plate
- Pacific Plate
- African Plate
- Pacific Plate
- South American Plate
- Indo-Australian Plate
- Nazca Plate
- Antarctic Plate

Key to map

———	Transform fault	········	Divergent boundary
– – –	Uncertain boundary	———	Convergent boundary

WHERE MOVING PLATES MEET

The boundaries between the plates are volcanic earthquake zones. The plates move very slowly, pulling apart at divergent boundaries. This allows hot rock below to melt, erupt, and cool to form new crust – especially at the spreading rifts that form mid-ocean ridges. Meanwhile, at convergent boundaries, one plate slides beneath another, pushing up mountain ranges and making volcanoes erupt. Other volcanoes erupt over hot spots in the mantle below the crust.

1. Continental crust, much thicker than oceanic crust
2. Broad basin formed near uplifted area
3. Ancient converging boundary, now inactive
4. Mountains created when plate boundary was active
5. Oceanic crust formed from heavy basalt rock
6. Upper mantle, mostly solid but very hot
7. Mantle, solid but mobile owing to heat currents
8. Spreading rift forming a mid-ocean ridge
9. Hot-spot volcano erupting over mantle plume
10. Ocean trench marking convergent plate boundary
11. Volcano erupting over convergent boundary
12. Earthquake zone—one plate grinding under another
13. Plates pulling apart, creating a rift valley

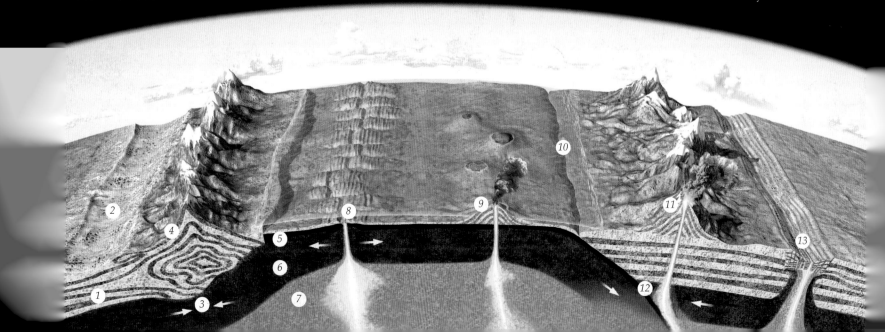

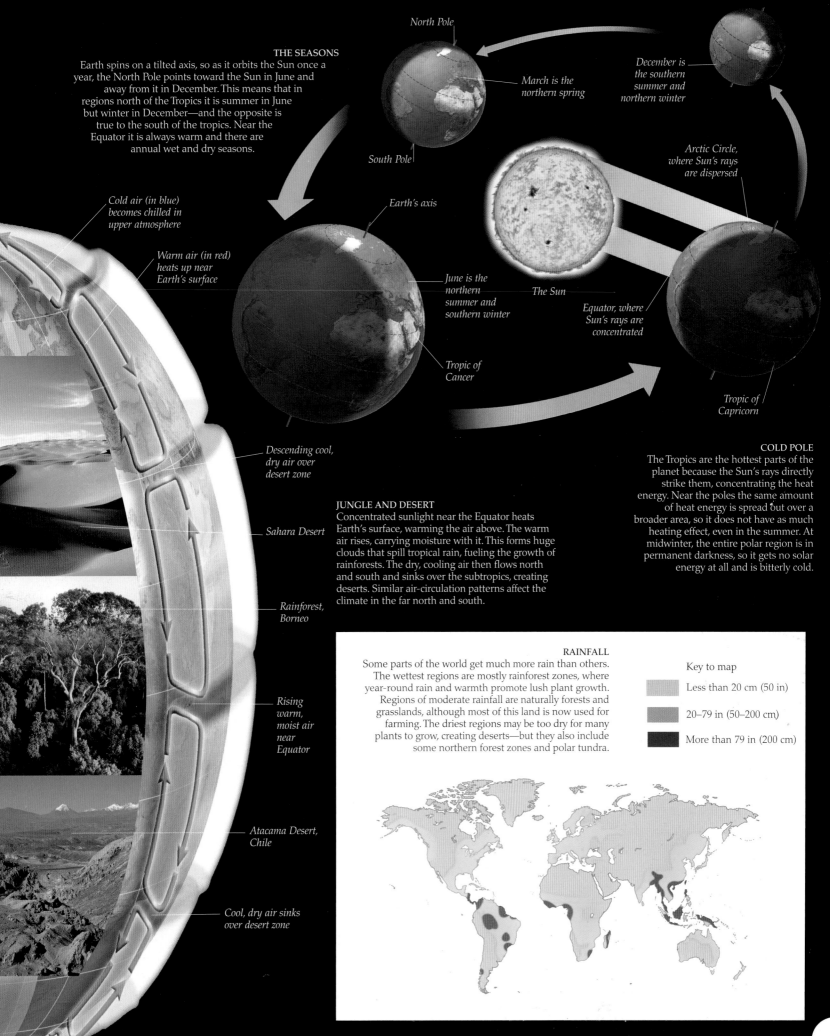

THE SEASONS

Earth spins on a tilted axis, so as it orbits the Sun once a year, the North Pole points toward the Sun in June and away from it in December. This means that in regions north of the Tropics it is summer in June but winter in December—and the opposite is true to the south of the tropics. Near the Equator it is always warm and there are annual wet and dry seasons.

North Pole

March is the northern spring

December is the southern summer and northern winter

South Pole

Arctic Circle, where Sun's rays are dispersed

Cold air (in blue) becomes chilled in upper atmosphere

Earth's axis

Warm air (in red) heats up near Earth's surface

June is the northern summer and southern winter

The Sun

Equator, where Sun's rays are concentrated

Tropic of Cancer

Tropic of Capricorn

Descending cool, dry air over desert zone

Sahara Desert

Rainforest, Borneo

Rising warm, moist air near Equator

Atacama Desert, Chile

Cool, dry air sinks over desert zone

JUNGLE AND DESERT

Concentrated sunlight near the Equator heats Earth's surface, warming the air above. The warm air rises, carrying moisture with it. This forms huge clouds that spill tropical rain, fueling the growth of rainforests. The dry, cooling air then flows north and south and sinks over the subtropics, creating deserts. Similar air-circulation patterns affect the climate in the far north and south.

COLD POLE

The Tropics are the hottest parts of the planet because the Sun's rays directly strike them, concentrating the heat energy. Near the poles the same amount of heat energy is spread out over a broader area, so it does not have as much heating effect, even in the summer. At midwinter, the entire polar region is in permanent darkness, so it gets no solar energy at all and is bitterly cold.

RAINFALL

Some parts of the world get much more rain than others. The wettest regions are mostly rainforest zones, where year-round rain and warmth promote lush plant growth. Regions of moderate rainfall are naturally forests and grasslands, although most of this land is now used for farming. The driest regions may be too dry for many plants to grow, creating deserts—but they also include some northern forest zones and polar tundra.

Key to map

Less than 20 cm (50 in)

20–79 in (50–200 cm)

More than 79 in (200 cm)

Planet People

THE NUMBER OF PEOPLE ON THE PLANET has quadrupled since 1900. A lot of this growth has taken place in the developing world, which is now home to more than 80 percent of the population. Many of these people are very poor and do not enjoy the living conditions that most citizens of the developed world take for granted. This is changing, however, especially in nations such as China, India, and Brazil. Here, new technology and international trade are fueling rapid economic growth that is transforming how people live. But as more of the planet's people demand more of its scarce resources, there may be some difficult challenges ahead.

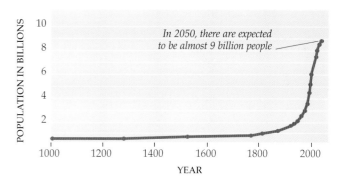

In 2050, there are expected to be almost 9 billion people

POPULATION INCREASE
For centuries, the number of people on the planet stayed the same, at roughly 300 million. But since the 1750s, better living conditions and health care have allowed more babies to survive, causing a population explosion. In only 60 years from 1950, the population soared from 2.5 billion to 6.8 billion. It will keep growing, but probably not quite so fast.

POPULATION DENSITY
On this map the area of each part of the world is adjusted to reflect the number of people who live there. For example, Japan's population of 128 million is much bigger than that of Australia, with 22 million, so it is shown much larger here despite being a smaller country. More people live in Nigeria—153 million—than in all of Russia. But the nations with the biggest populations by far are India and China, each with far more than 1 billion citizens.

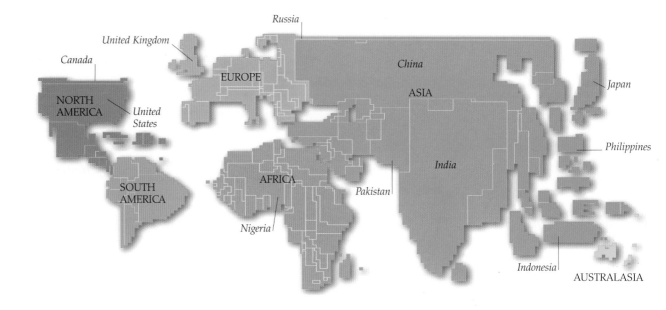

FAMILY SIZE
All over the world, some women have more children than others, but the average varies from continent to continent. European women have 1.5 children on average, so two families may have three children between them. This is much fewer than in Africa, where the population is growing faster despite higher death rates among children. Worldwide, the average is 2.6—more than enough to replace both parents.

AFRICA	ASIA	SOUTH AMERICA	NORTH AMERICA	AUSTRALASIA	EUROPE
4.6 children per woman	2.3 children per woman	2.2 children per woman	2 children per woman	1.8 children per woman	1.5 children per woman

BIRTH AND DEATH RATES
If the birth rate is the same as the death rate, the population stays the same. But in most countries, the birth rate is higher. In Niger, west Africa, there are 50.6 births but only 13.1 deaths per 1,000 people, and the population is growing at 4 percent a year. Brazil's population is also growing, with 14.2 births compared to 6.5 deaths. By contrast, Lithuania has a shrinking population, with 9.9 births outweighed by 13.8 deaths.

A country with few young people is said to have an aging population. But these school children in Burundi, east Africa, are part of a youthful population, with fewer elder people. Both situations can cause problems.

NIGER
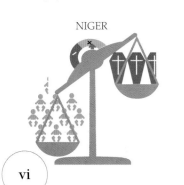

BRAZIL

LITHUANIA

CITY POPULATIONS

As populations grow, people tend to move from the country to a city to find work. Today one third of the world's people live in cities, which grow bigger every year. Some are colossal, like Tokyo, Japan—the largest city in Asia. The other cities shown here are the most populous on each continent. They are vibrant centErs of civilization, but some cities are fringed by sprawling shantytowns, where poor people live in makeshift shacks with no public health services or clean water.

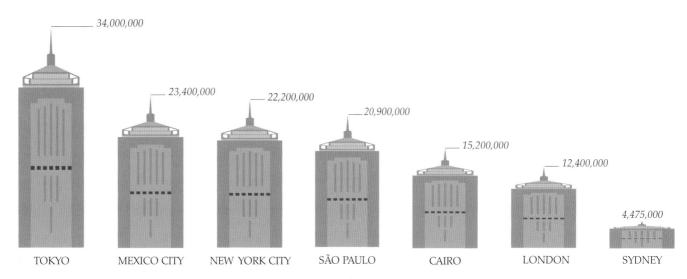

34,000,000 — TOKYO

23,400,000 — MEXICO CITY

22,200,000 — NEW YORK CITY

20,900,000 — SÃO PAULO

15,200,000 — CAIRO

12,400,000 — LONDON

4,475,000 — SYDNEY

LANGUAGES

These are the 10 most common languages worldwide, sized in proportion to the number of native speakers. Chinese outstrips the others because China has such a huge population. But Spanish comes next because it is the main language of many Latin American countries, such as Mexico. English is almost as common, thanks mostly to it being the language of the United States. It is also used as an international language for trade.

HINDI ARABIC SPANISH CHINESE ENGLISH PORTUGUESE RUSSIAN JAPANESE BENGALI GERMAN

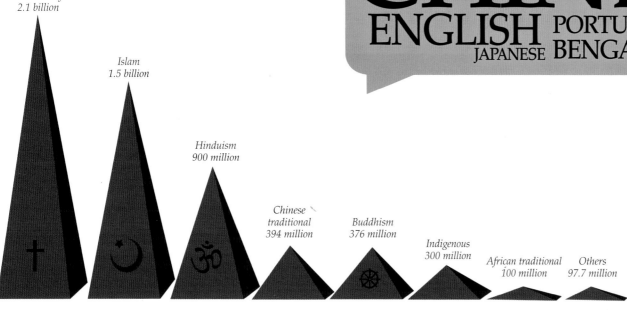

Christianity
2.1 billion

Islam
1.5 billion

Hinduism
900 million

Chinese traditional
394 million

Buddhism
376 million

Indigenous
300 million

African traditional
100 million

Others
97.7 million

Others

Sikhism	23 million
Juche	19 million
Spiritism	15 million
Judaism	14 million
Baha'i	7 million
Jainism	4.2 million
Shinto	4 million
Cao Đái	4 million
Zoroastrianism	2.6 million
Tenrikyo	2 million
Neo-Paganism	1 million
Unitarian Universalism	800,000
Rastafarianism	600,000
Scientology	500,000

RELIGIONS AND BELIEFS

Almost three fourths of the world's population are followers of Christianity, Islam, Hinduism, or Buddhism. But many people follow other faiths, especially in China, where the traditional folk religion, Shenism, is practiced by almost one third of the huge population. The "indigenous" and "African traditional religions" data points are both groupings of different, but similar, religions. Others are listed at the far right, in order of popularity.

ONLINE ACCESS

Over the 10 years, the Internet has become a vital tool for global business, education, and politics, so the more people who can use it, the better. These charts show the percentage of people with Internet access both worldwide and in particular regions. North America, Australia, and Europe lead the field, but the number of Internet users is growing fastest in the Middle East and Africa.

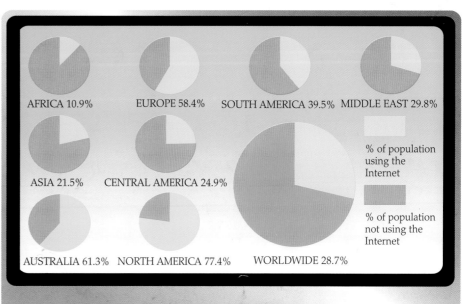

AFRICA 10.9%   EUROPE 58.4%   SOUTH AMERICA 39.5%   MIDDLE EAST 29.8%

ASIA 21.5%   CENTRAL AMERICA 24.9%

% of population using the Internet

% of population not using the Internet

AUSTRALIA 61.3%   NORTH AMERICA 77.4%   WORLDWIDE 28.7%

PLANET PEOPLE

WEALTH

A country's wealth is usually measured in terms of the money it earns divided by the number of its citizens living both at home and overseas. This is called its gross national product (GNP) per capita. Qatar in the Middle East has huge wealth generated by exports of oil and natural gas, and since it has a small population, its GNP per capita is very high. Burundi in east Africa has only one thirtieth of the income of Qatar divided between seven times as many people, so its GNP per capita is very low.

| Burundi $135 | Bolivia $1,457 | Lithuania $11,871 | Japan $38,207 | Canada $41,729 | Norway $87,068 | Qatar $93,201 |

BUSIEST AIRPORTS

Air travel has expanded hugely since the 1950s, when international air travel was a luxury enjoyed by a few wealthy people known as the "jet set." Today, flying is often the most economical way to travel, as well as the quickest. This is reflected in the vast number of passengers who pass through the world's airports as they travel for business or pleasure. The busiest airport is Hartsfield-Jackson International Airport in Atlanta, Georgia, with more than 90 million people arriving and departing each year.

AIRBUS A380

The growth in air travel has led to the development of giant airliners such as the Airbus A380. When it entered service in 2007, this was the world's largest passenger plane, capable of carrying up to 853 people. The first commercial jet airliner, the Comet 1, had seats for only 44 passengers at the most.

HARTSFIELD-JACKSON, ATLANTA, GEORGIA — 90,039,280

HEATHROW, LONDON, U.K. — 67,056,379

TOKYO, JAPAN — 66,754,829

KINGSFORD SMITH, SYDNEY, AUSTRALIA — 32,900,000

GUARULHOS, SÃO PAULO, BRAZIL — 20,400,304

TAMBO, JO'BURG, RSA — 18,400,000

TRADE

Although air freight is an important part of international trade, about 80 percent of cargo by weight is transported by sea. This adds up to around 8.8 billion tons of freight. A lot of this is transported in containers carried by more than 4,700 container ships. The busiest shipping routes link Europe and North America with the Middle East and Far East, with ports such as Singapore, Shanghai (China), Dubai (U.A.E.), and Rotterdam (Netherlands) handling most of the trade.

Traffic in millions of tonnes

| 400+ |
| 300–400 |
| 200–300 |
| 100–200 |
| 20–100 |
| 10–20 |
| 5–10 |

Mapping the World

ABOUT THE ATLAS

This atlas is divided into six continental sections—North America, South America, Africa, Europe, Asia, and Australasia and Oceania. Each country—or group of countries—then has its own map that shows cities, towns, and main geographical features such as rivers, lakes, and mountain ranges. Photographs and text provide detailed information about life in that country—its people, traditions, politics, and economy. Each continental section has a different colored border to help you locate that section. There is also a gazetteer (place-name index) and an index to help you access information.

MAP LOCATER

This map shows, in red, the location of each country, part of a country, or group of countries in relation to the entire planet. There is a locater for each map in the book.

MAP COLORS

The colors shown on the maps are built up from numerous satellite photographs and reflect the true colors of the land, averaged over the seasons. Certain colors give clues to what the land is like—whether it is forested or farmland, mountains or desert.

Land appearing sandy tends to be desert, semidesert, or scrub

Mountainous desert looks like this, with shadows on the sandy background color

Pale green is usually grassland or cropland

Darker greens usually indicate woodland or pasture

White shows land under permanent cover by snow and ice

Central Asia

```
0 km        100        200
0 miles           100        200
```

FOREIGN NAMES

Features on the maps are generally labeled in the language of that country. For example, you will see:

Lake on English-speaking countries
Lago on Spanish-speaking countries
Lac on French-speaking countries

However, if a feature is wellknown or mentioned in the main text on the page, it will appear there in English so that readers can easily find it.

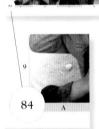

9

84   A

USING THE GRID REFERENCES

The letters and numbers around the outside of the page form a grid to help you find places on the map. For example, to find Kabul, look up its name in the gazetteer (pp. 112–133) and you'll find the reference 85 J7. The first number is the page and the letter and number refer to the square made by following up or down from J and across from 7 to form J7.

SCALE

Each map features a scale that shows how distances on the map relate to kilometers and miles. The scale guide can be used to see how big a country is. Not all maps in the book are drawn to the same scale.

KEY TO MAP SYMBOLS

BORDERS

	International border: Border between countries which is mutually recognized.
	State border: Border used in some large countries to show internal divisions.
	Disputed border: Border used in practice, but not mutually agreed between two countries.
●●●●●●	Claimed border: Border which is not mutually recognized – where territory belonging to one country is claimed by another.
×-×-×	Ceasefire line
▪ ▪ ▪ ▪	Undefined boundary

PHYSICAL FEATURES

△	Mountain
▽	Depression
▲	Volcano
✕	Pass/Tunnel

DRAINAGE FEATURES

	Major river
	Minor river
	Seasonal river
┼	Dam
	Canal
│	Waterfall
	Seasonal lake

MISCELLANEOUS FEATURES

◇	Site of interest
⌇⌇⌇	Ancient wall

COMMUNICATIONS

▭▭▭	Highway
	Major road
	Minor road
	Rail
✈	Airport

TOWNS & CITIES

◉	More than 500,000
◉	100,000 – 500,000
○	50,000 – 100,000
○	Less than 50,000
●	National capital
◉	Internal administrative capital
◉	Polar research station

LATITUDE & LONGITUDE

	Equator
– – – –	Tropics/Circles

NAMES

REGIONS

FRANCE	Country
JERSEY (to UK)	Dependent territory
KANSAS	Administrative region
Dordogne	Cultural region

TOWNS & CITIES

PARIS	National capital
SAN JUAN	Dependent territory capital city
Seattle	
Limón	Other towns & cities
Genk	
San José	

NAMES *continued*

PHYSICAL

Andes	Landscape features
Ardennes	
Balearic Islands	Island group
Majorca	Island
Lake Baikal	Lake/River /Canal
PACIFIC OCEAN	
Gulf of Mexico	Sea features
Bay of Campeche	
Chile Rise	Undersea feature

OTHER FEATURES

Tropic of Cancer	Graticule text

NORTH AMERICA

The North American continent extends from the frozen wastes of Arctic Canada to the Caribbean islands and the tropical jungles of Panama. It is politically dominated by the United States, the richest nation on Earth, yet life in countries such as Mexico and Nicaragua is still a struggle. The data below is arranged in order of each nation's size.

Canada
- 3,855,103 sq miles
  9,984,670 sq km
- 33,600,000
- Ottawa
- English, French, Chinese, Italian, German, Ukrainian, Portuguese, Inuktitut, Cree

Mexico
- 758,449 sq miles
  1,964,375 sq km
- 110,000,000
- Mexico City
- Spanish, Nahuatl, Mayan, Zapotec, Mixtec, Otomi, Totonac, Tzotzil, Tzeltal

Honduras
- 43,278 sq miles
  112,090 sq km
- 7,470,000
- Tegucigalpa
- Spanish, Garífuna (Carib), English Creole

United States of America
- 3,794,100 sq miles
  9,826,675 sq km
- 315,000,000
- Washington, DC
- English, Spanish, Chinese, French, German, Tagalog, Vietnamese, Italian, Korean, Russian, Polish

Nicaragua
- 50,336 sq miles
  130,370 sq km
- 5,740,000
- Managua
- Spanish, English Creole, Miskito

The warm waters and glorious beaches of the Caribbean make islands like St. Lucia magnets for tourists. The wealth they bring is vital to the local economy.

Cuba
- 42,803 sq miles
  110,860 sq km
- 11,200,000
- Havana
- Spanish

Panama
- 29,120 sq miles
  75,420 sq km
- 3,450,000
- Panama City
- English Creole, Spanish, Amerindian languages, Chibchan languages

Dominican Republic
- 18,792 sq miles
  48,670 sq km
- 10,100,000
- Santo Domingo
- Spanish, French Creole

Guatemala
- 42,042 sq miles
  108,889 sq km
- 14,000,000
- Guatemala City
- Quiché, Mam, Kakchiquel, Kekchí, Spanish

Haiti
- 10,714 sq miles
  27,750 sq km
- 10,000,000
- Port-au-Prince
- French Creole, French

Costa Rica
- 19,730 sq miles
  51,100 sq km
- 4,580,000
- San José
- Spanish, English Creole, Bribri, Cabecar

Belize
- 8,867 sq miles
  22,966 sq km
- 306,800
- Belmopan
- English Creole, Spanish, English, Mayan, Garifuna (Carib)

The Statue of Liberty in New York Harbor is a potent symbol of freedom, especially for political refugees to the United States who arrived by ship.

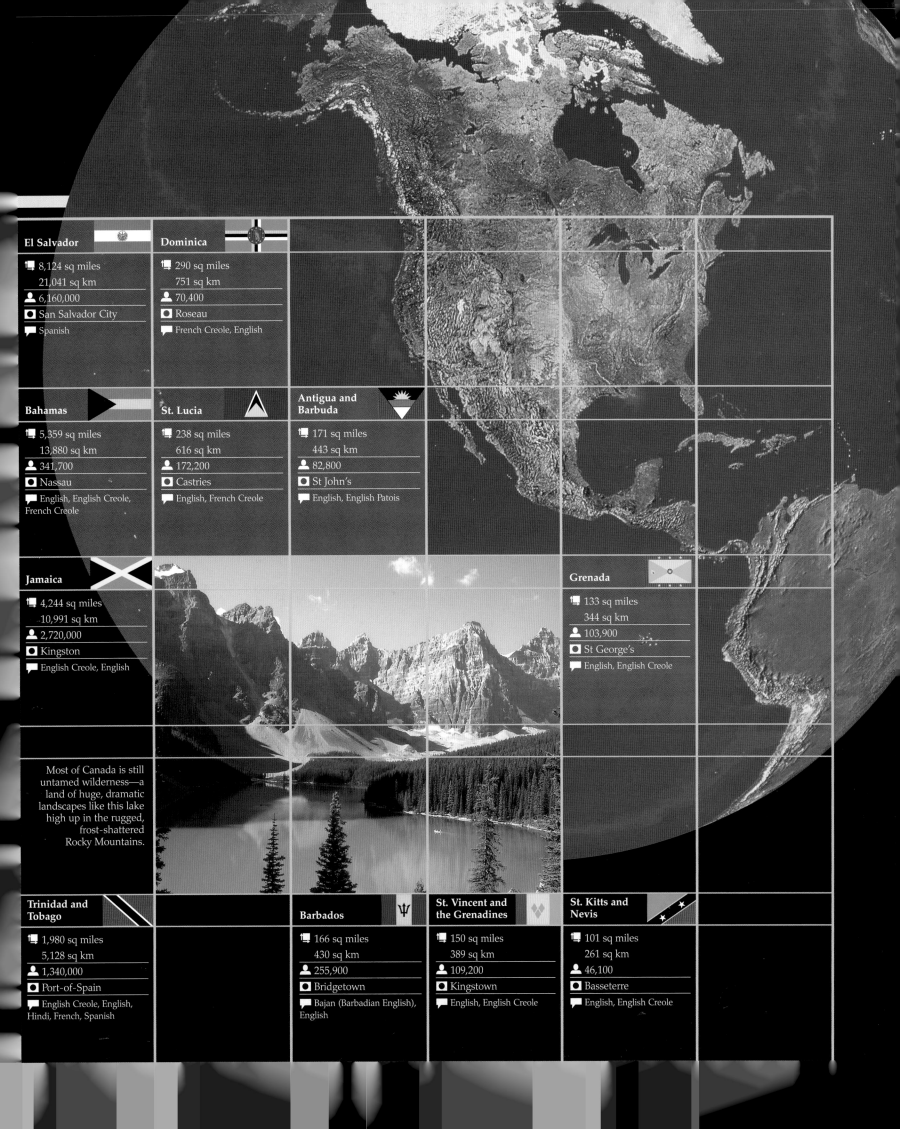

El Salvador

- 8,124 sq miles
  21,041 sq km
- 6,160,000
- San Salvador City
- Spanish

Dominica

- 290 sq miles
  751 sq km
- 70,400
- Roseau
- French Creole, English

Bahamas

- 5,359 sq miles
  13,880 sq km
- 341,700
- Nassau
- English, English Creole,
  French Creole

St. Lucia

- 238 sq miles
  616 sq km
- 172,200
- Castries
- English, French Creole

Antigua and Barbuda

- 171 sq miles
  443 sq km
- 82,800
- St John's
- English, English Patois

Jamaica

- 4,244 sq miles
  10,991 sq km
- 2,720,000
- Kingston
- English Creole, English

Grenada

- 133 sq miles
  344 sq km
- 103,900
- St George's
- English, English Creole

Most of Canada is still untamed wilderness—a land of huge, dramatic landscapes like this lake high up in the rugged, frost-shattered Rocky Mountains.

Trinidad and Tobago

- 1,980 sq miles
  5,128 sq km
- 1,340,000
- Port-of-Spain
- English Creole, English,
  Hindi, French, Spanish

Barbados

- 166 sq miles
  430 sq km
- 255,900
- Bridgetown
- Bajan (Barbadian English),
  English

St. Vincent and the Grenadines

- 150 sq miles
  389 sq km
- 109,200
- Kingstown
- English, English Creole

St. Kitts and Nevis

- 101 sq miles
  261 sq km
- 46,100
- Basseterre
- English, English Creole

Western Canada and Alaska

CANADA IS A HUGE COUNTRY and its western half stretches from the flat prairies in the east to the towering Rocky Mountains in the west, and from the relatively mild south to the permanently frozen area north of the Arctic Circle. Harsh conditions throughout most of the region mean that most of the population is concentrated in cities in the south, such as Vancouver, Calgary, and Winnipeg. The Prairies—once a vast expanse of grassland—are now mostly used for growing wheat on huge mechanized farms. Oil and natural gas are found there, too. These natural resources are also important in Alaska, a part of the United States. The majority of Alaska's people moved there to work in these lucrative industries.

FORESTRY
Large parts of western Canada are covered in forests, and lumbering is a major part of the local economy. The trees are used to make buildings, furniture, and paper. In the past, entire forests of trees were cleared, but now sustainable methods, such as selective cutting and replanting, are practiced.

Felled trees transported down a river near Vancouver

TOTEM POLES
The native peoples of British Columbia use totem poles to record their clan histories. Each carved and painted totem describes a real or mythical event and often features animals that the clan has a close connection with, such as the eagle (left).

DOGSLED RACING
The state sport of Alaska is dogsled racing. Here, competitors take part in the annual Iditarod Trail Great Sled Race, a gruelling run across the rugged landscape for drivers and their teams of dogs.

VANCOUVER
This city's vibrant cultural mix is typical of Canada's diversity. Many South Asian, Chinese, as well as other ethnic groups live here and reflect Vancouver's historic role as a destination for migrants. Hosting the 2010 Winter Olympics raised its profile and its bustling economy, mild climate, and cultural links make it an attractive place to live.

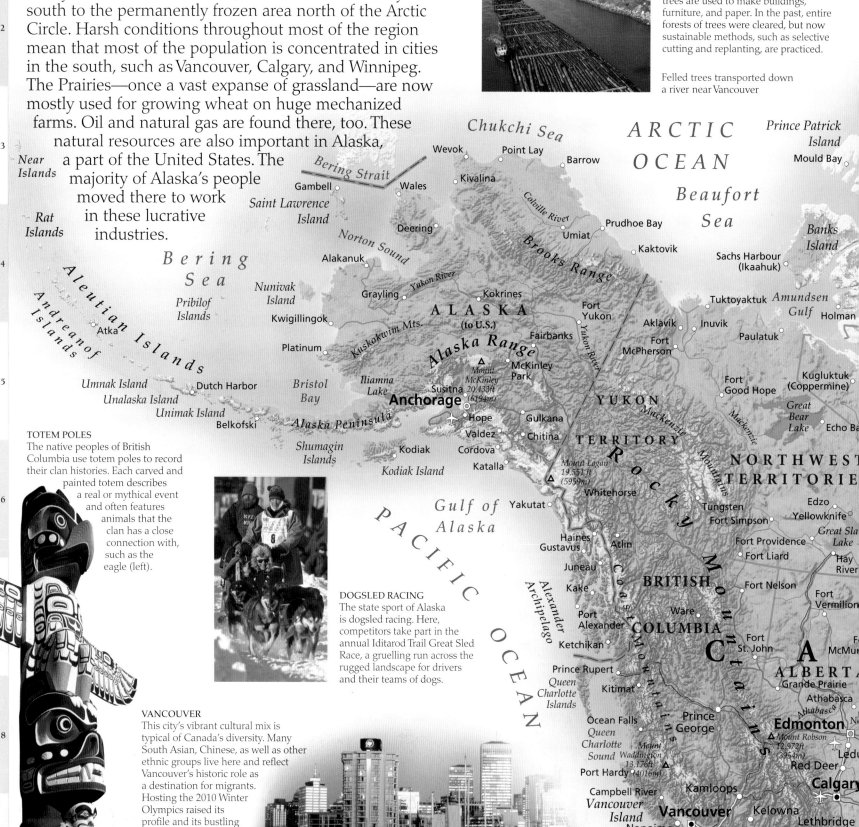

4

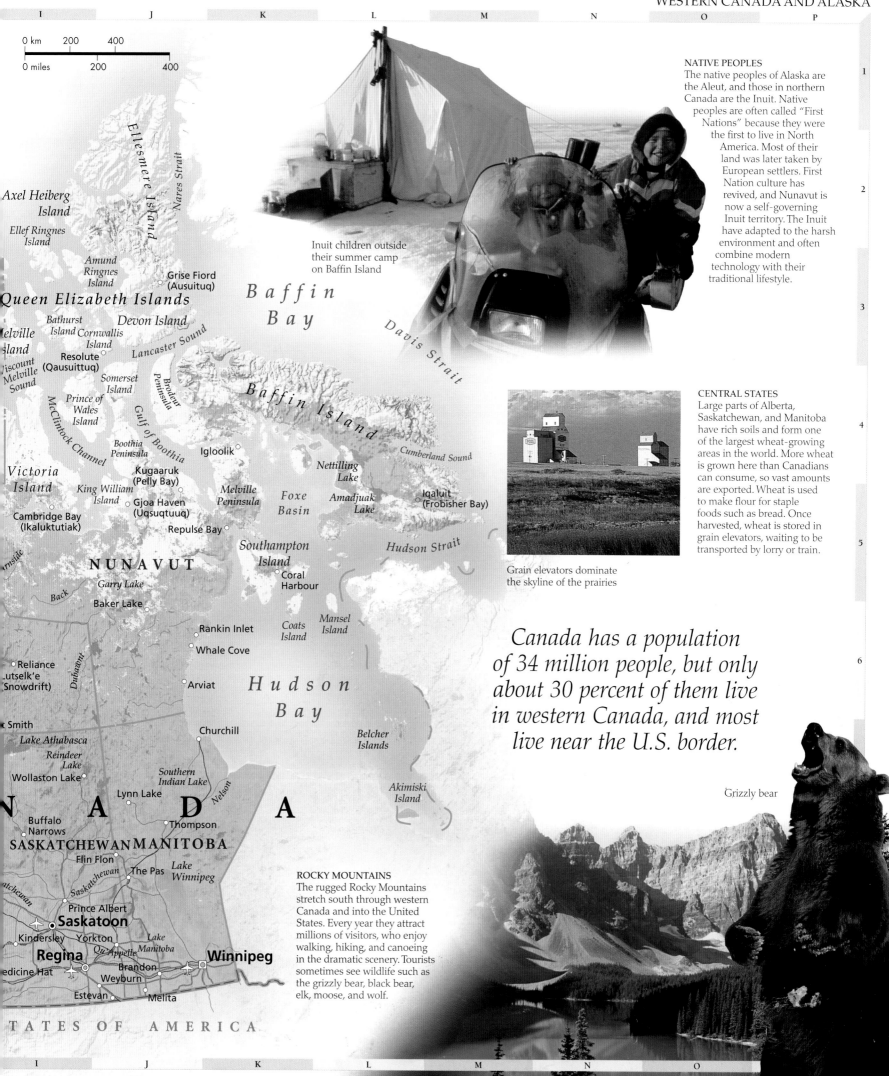

0 km   200   400

0 miles   200   400

Axel Heiberg Island

Ellef Ringnes Island

Ellesmere Island

Nares Strait

Amund Ringnes Island

Grise Fiord
(Ausuituq)

Queen Elizabeth Islands

*B a f f i n
B a y*

Bathurst Island *Devon Island*

elville sland *Cornwallis Island*

Resolute
(Qausuittuq)

Lancaster Sound

iscount Melville Sound

Somerset Island

Broder Peninsula

B a f f i n   I s l a n d

Davis Strait

Prince of Wales Island

Gulf of Boothia

McClintock Channel

Boothia Peninsula

Igloolik

Cumberland Sound

Victoria Island

Kugaaruk
(Pelly Bay)

Nettling Lake

King William Island

Gjoa Haven
(Uqsuqtuuq)

Melville Peninsula

Foxe Basin

Amadjuak Lake

Iqaluit
(Frobisher Bay)

Cambridge Bay
(Ikaluktutiak)

Repulse Bay

Southampton Island

Hudson Strait

Coral
Harbour

rnside

N U N A V U T

Back

Garry Lake

Baker Lake

Rankin Inlet

Coats Island

Mansel Island

Whale Cove

Reliance
utselk'e
Snowdrift)

Dubawnt

Arviat

*H u d s o n
B a y*

Smith

Lake Athabasca

Churchill

Belcher Islands

Reindeer Lake

Southern Indian Lake

Nelson

Akimiski Island

Wollaston Lake

Lynn Lake

N   A   D   A

Buffalo
Narrows

Thompson

SASKATCHEWAN MANITOBA

Flin Flon

Lake Winnipeg

atchewan

The Pas

Saskatchewan

Prince Albert

Saskatoon

Kindersley   Yorkton

Lake Manitoba

Regina

Qu Appette

Winnipeg

edicine Hat

Brandon

Weyburn

Estevan   Melita

T A T E S   O F   A M E R I C A

NATIVE PEOPLES

The native peoples of Alaska are the Aleut, and those in northern Canada are the Inuit. Native peoples are often called "First Nations" because they were the first to live in North America. Most of their land was later taken by European settlers. First Nation culture has revived, and Nunavut is now a self-governing Inuit territory. The Inuit have adapted to the harsh environment and often combine modern technology with their traditional lifestyle.

Inuit children outside their summer camp on Baffin Island

CENTRAL STATES

Large parts of Alberta, Saskatchewan, and Manitoba have rich soils and form one of the largest wheat-growing areas in the world. More wheat is grown here than Canadians can consume, so vast amounts are exported. Wheat is used to make flour for staple foods such as bread. Once harvested, wheat is stored in grain elevators, waiting to be transported by lorry or train.

Grain elevators dominate the skyline of the prairies

Canada has a population of 34 million people, but only about 30 percent of them live in western Canada, and most live near the U.S. border.

Grizzly bear

ROCKY MOUNTAINS

The rugged Rocky Mountains stretch south through western Canada and into the United States. Every year they attract millions of visitors, who enjoy walking, hiking, and canoeing in the dramatic scenery. Tourists sometimes see wildlife such as the grizzly bear, black bear, elk, moose, and wolf.

Eastern Canada

THE MOST INDUSTRIALIZED AND HEAVILY populated parts of Canada are in the east. Ottawa, the capital, is located here, along with other important cities, such as Toronto, Montreal, and Québec. Some of the earliest settlers were French, and many people speak French as their first language. The Great Lakes—the largest system of lakes in the world—and the St. Lawrence Seaway link the interior to the coast. The most easterly parts of Canada, the Atlantic Provinces, have rugged coastlines and dramatic scenery. However, soils are thin and commercial agriculture is limited to a few areas. Fishing used to be the main activity, but fish stocks have been so depleted that few people are now employed in the industry, despite recent environmental efforts to rebuild the stocks. A growing oil and gas industry and new high-tech businesses are attracting younger workers, although many people still migrate to the bustling cities farther west.

Canadians have a high life expectancy—the average person lives to be 80 years old.

Maple sap collected from cuts in the tree trunk

MAPLE SYRUP
The maple trees of Québec and Ontario are tapped for maple syrup, a major export—and a popular topping on pancakes for Canadians. The maple leaf is the national symbol of Canada and features on the nation's flag.

TORONTO
Toronto is Canada's most important economic center. Located on Lake Ontario, close to the U.S. border, it is not only an industrial and commercial centre but is also home to a wide diversity of ethnic and cultural groups. The Canadian National (CN) tower, which dominates the Toronto skyline, is the world's tallest tower, and locals and tourists can get an impressive view of the city and Lake Ontario from the top.

CN Tower

ICE HOCKEY
Sports and leisure are important to Canadians. A popular sport is ice hockey, which thousands of people play or watch enthusiastically. Teams of skaters use long, curved sticks to try to get a hard rubber disk—called a puck—into the opposing team's goal. Both the men's and women's national ice hockey teams won gold medals at the Vancouver 2010 Winter Olympics.

Charles Island

Ungava Peninsu

Ivujivik

Inukjuak (Port Harrison)

Hudson Bay

Fort Severn

Belcher Islands

Peawanuk

James Bay

Akimiski Island

Sandy Lake

Winisk

Attawapiskat

C A N

Attawapiskat

Fort Albany

O N T A R I O

Albany

Moosonee

Rivière de Ruper

Lac Seul

Armstrong

Kenora

Dryden

Lake of the Woods

Lake Nipigon

Longlac

Hearst

Moose

Harricana

Fort Frances

Atikokan

Nipigon

Marathon

Kapuskasing

Cochrane

Amos

Réserv Gou

Thunder Bay

Tip Top Mountain △ 2100ft (640m)

Timmins

Foleyet

Kirkland Lake

Rouyn-Noranda

Val-d'Or

Wawa

Lake Superior

Sault Ste. Marie

Sudbury

North Bay

Pembroke

Gatine Hull

OTTAWA

Manitoulin Island

Georgian Bay

Lake Huron

Midland

Kingston

Peterborough

Brampton

Kitchener

Sarnia

Hamilton

Oshawa

Toronto

Lake Ontar

St. Catharines

London

Niagara Falls

Windsor

Leamington

Lake Erie

UNITED STATES OF AMERICA

Q

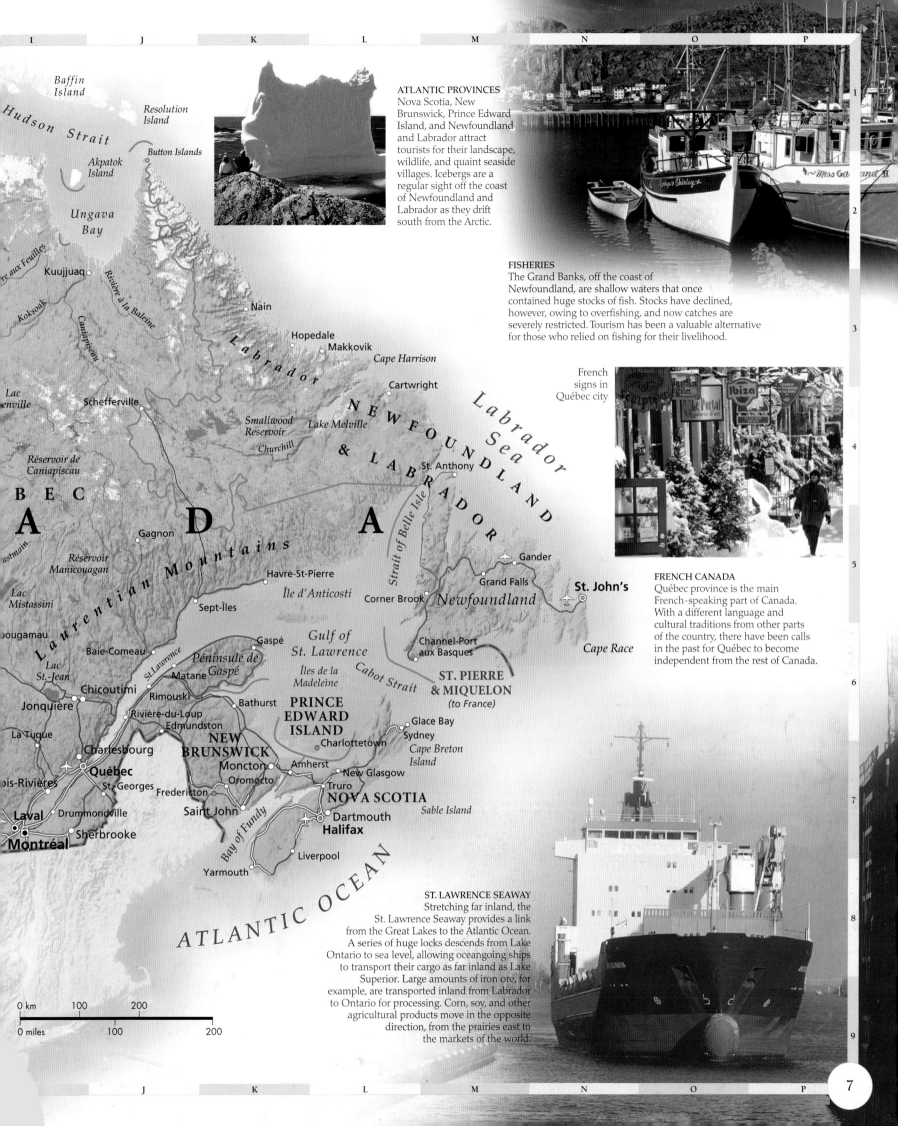

Baffin
Island

Resolution
Island

Hudson Strait

Button Islands

Akpatok
Island

Ungava
Bay

Kuujjuaq

Rivière à la Baleine

Koksoak

Caniapiscau

Nain

Hopedale

Makkovik

Cape Harrison

Cartwright

Labrador

Lac
enville

Schefferville

Smallwood
Reservoir

Lake Melville

Churchill

NEWFOUNDLAND

&

LABRADOR

Labrador Sea

St. Anthony

Strait of Belle Isle

Réservoir de
Caniapiscau

B E C

A

D

A

Gagnon

Réservoir
Manicouagan

Laurentian Mountains

Havre-St-Pierre

Gander

Grand Falls

St. John's

Lac
Mistassini

Sept-Îles

Île d'Anticosti

Corner Brook

Newfoundland

ougamau

Baie-Comeau

Gaspé

Gulf of
St. Lawrence

Channel-Port
aux Basques

Cape Race

Lac
St.-Jean

Chicoutimi

Matane

St. Lawrence

Péninsule de
Gaspé

Îles de la
Madeleine

Cabot Strait

ST. PIERRE
& MIQUELON
(to France)

Jonquière

Rimouski

Rivière-du-Loup

Bathurst

La Tuque

Edmundston

PRINCE
EDWARD
ISLAND

Glace Bay

Sydney

Charlesbourg

NEW
BRUNSWICK

Charlottetown

Cape Breton
Island

ois-Rivières

Québec

St-Georges

Frederitcton

Moncton

Oromocto

Amherst

New Glasgow

Laval

Drummondville

Saint John

Truro

NOVA SCOTIA

Sable Island

Sherbrooke

Dartmouth

Montréal

Bay of Fundy

Halifax

Liverpool

Yarmouth

ATLANTIC OCEAN

ATLANTIC PROVINCES
Nova Scotia, New Brunswick, Prince Edward Island, and Newfoundland and Labrador attract tourists for their landscape, wildlife, and quaint seaside villages. Icebergs are a regular sight off the coast of Newfoundland and Labrador as they drift south from the Arctic.

FISHERIES
The Grand Banks, off the coast of Newfoundland, are shallow waters that once contained huge stocks of fish. Stocks have declined, however, owing to overfishing, and now catches are severely restricted. Tourism has been a valuable alternative for those who relied on fishing for their livelihood.

French signs in Québec city

FRENCH CANADA
Québec province is the main French-speaking part of Canada. With a different language and cultural traditions from other parts of the country, there have been calls in the past for Québec to become independent from the rest of Canada.

ST. LAWRENCE SEAWAY
Stretching far inland, the St. Lawrence Seaway provides a link from the Great Lakes to the Atlantic Ocean. A series of huge locks descends from Lake Ontario to sea level, allowing oceangoing ships to transport their cargo as far inland as Lake Superior. Large amounts of iron ore, for example, are transported inland from Labrador to Ontario for processing. Corn, soy, and other agricultural products move in the opposite direction, from the prairies east to the markets of the world.

0 km   100   200
0 miles   100   200

U.S.A.: Northeast

THE NORTHEASTERN UNITED STATES is a heavily populated area that is steeped in history. This is traditionally the main immigration point into the United States, with the Statue of Liberty lighting the way for those arriving into New York City by boat. People from all over the world have settled in this region to live and work, creating a "melting pot" of cultures and ethnic groups. Important historical events, such as the signing of the Declaration of Independence and the Constitution, took place in Philadelphia, Pennsylvania. These documents set the foundations for American life today. It is also here that the capital and center of government were established. Today, while industry and agriculture are still important, finance and commerce are the driving forces of the economy.

The White House in Washington, D.C. has been home to every president except George Washington, whom the city is named after.

THRIVING CITY
New York is the largest city in the U.S. Historically it grew because it has a good harbor and sits at the mouth of the Hudson River. Immigrants from overseas flooded into the city in the 19th and 20th centuries, boosting its population and economy. Today, it is the main financial center, not just of the U.S.A., but of the world.

Lake Ontario

Hudson River

New York City

Appalachian Mountains

PITTSBURGH
Once a major steel-manufacturing centre with a polluted environment, Pittsburgh, Pennsylvania, is now a thriving financial center with a large number of corporate headquarters. Bridges span the three rivers that run through the city, connecting the core downtown area (above) to the suburbs.

CENTRE OF GOVERNMENT
All three branches of the federal government, the executive, legislative, and judicial, reside in Washington, D.C. The United States Congress (the legislative branch) meets here in the Capitol building. Many of the city's residents work for the government.

Capitol building, the seat of government

CANADA

ONTARIO

St. Lawrence

Ogdensburg

Adirondack Mountains

Watertown
Boonville

App

Lake Ontario
Oswego
Mohawk Ri

Niagara Falls
Lockport
Rochester
Newark
Syracuse
Utica

Niagara Falls
Buffalo
Avon
Dansville
NEW YORK
Oneonta
Ithaca
Catski Mounta

Hamburg

Lake Erie
Dunkirk
Jamestown
Allegheny Plateau
Elmira
Binghamton

Erie
Warren
Mansfield
Sayre

Meadville
Wilcox
Scranton
Wilkes Barre
Milford
Middletow

Mercer
Allegheny River
Du Bois
Lock Haven
Milton
Stroudsberg

OHIO
Butler
State College
Appalachian Mountains

Indiana
PENNSYLVANIA
Allentow

Aliquippa
Pittsburgh
Altoona
Harrisburg
Reading
Trenton

Washington
Carlisle
Lancaster
Philadelphia

Bedford
York
Wilmington
Cherry Hill

Uniontown
Hagerstown
Aberdeen
Vineland

Cumberland
Towson
N

WEST VIRGINIA
Oakland
Baltimore
Columbia

Annapolis
DELAWAR

VIRGINIA
WASHINGTON, D.C.

Cambridge
Ocean City

MARYLAND
Salisbur

Chesapeake Bay

CRANBERRIES

The northeast U.S. is a major cranberry-growing region. Cranberries grow in flooded bogs, and once harvested—often with high-tech equipment (above)—they can be eaten in pies and sauces.

MAINE

Although Maine is a large state, it is relatively sparsely populated. Early settlers were attracted to its coastline, and fishing communities gradually developed. To this day, fishing remains an important activity, while colorful foliage attracts tourists in the fall.

Maine (above), famous for its clam chowder and lobsters (right)

THANKSGIVING

The first Thanksgiving was held in 1621 as a gesture of friendship between American Indians and the Pilgrims after the Pilgrims' first successful harvest. Americans honor this tradition every November by gathering with family and friends to give thanks for life's blessings and to share a meal.

HIGHER EDUCATION

A large number of universities are located in this region, including two of the most famous—Harvard (above) and Yale. As well as studying, students enjoy a full campus life, including taking part in sport. Links between industry and education are strong, so many high-tech companies have been established here.

Tourists can take an elevator to the top of the Statue of Liberty

NEW YORK CITY

The center of U.S. commerce and business is New York City. People living here have a fast-paced lifestyle, and many travel by train or bus from the suburbs to work in the towering high-rise office buildings of Manhattan. People traveling by boat across the harbor pass the Statue of Liberty, a huge monument that represents freedom and opportunity to Americans.

Map labels

Madawaska
Presque Isle
Mars Hill
Houlton
NEW BRUNSWICK
Mount Katahdin 5266ft (1605m)
Moosehead Lake
Jackman
Lincoln
Calais
Milo
Machias
MAINE
Penobscot River
Bangor
Millbridge
Searsport
Bay of Fundy
Waterville
QUÉBEC
Newport
VERMONT
Bar Harbor
Mount Desert Island
ttsburgh
Lake Champlain
Burlington
Berlin
Augusta
Camden
Montpelier
NEW HAMPSHIRE
Mount Washington 6289ft (1917m)
Lewiston
Bath
Chelsea
Gulf of Maine
Rutland
Laconia
Portland
Green Mountains
Connecticut River
Lebanon
Biddeford
Glens Falls
Concord
Rochester
Hillsboro
Portsmouth
enectady
Manchester
Troy
Nashua
Lawrence
Albany
Lowell
Pittsfield
Greenfield
ATLANTIC OCEAN
Worcester
Boston
MASSACHUSETTS
Provincetown
Cape Cod
Springfield
Pawtucket
Orleans
Windsor
Providence
Hartford
Warwick
New Bedford
CONNECTICUT
RHODE ISLAND
Martha's Vineyard
Waterbury
Nantucket
Nantucket Island
Groton
nkers
New Haven
Bridgeport
Stamford
aterson
New York
Long Island
ewark
Middletown
RSEY
antic City
Bristol
ngston
Hudson River

0 km 50 100 150
0 miles 50 100 150

U.S.A.: South

0 km 50 100 150 200
0 miles 50 100 150 200

THE SOUTHERN STATES of the U.S.A. have a varied landscape and an interesting mix of people, both culturally and economically. Some areas of the region are poor, especially the Appalachian Mountain communities, while other parts, such as the Florida coast, are wealthy and attract many people from other states and countries. The cultural mix includes people of Latin American origin, African-Americans, Cajuns (French-Canadians), and European Americans, giving rise to diverse music styles, dialects, pastimes, and food. While coal mining in the Appalachian Mountains has declined in recent years, agriculture is still important, as are tourism and industry. Tourism is especially important in Florida and in New Orleans, Louisiana, near the mouth of the mighty Mississippi River.

COTTON CROPS
Cotton was once the main crop of the South and was grown by African-American slaves. Today, cotton is still important for the economy of the region and is grown in large fields and harvested with huge machinery. Cotton has many uses, primarily as the raw material for textiles.

The Mississippi is the largest river in North America and the third largest in the world.

Cotton pod, or boll

MUSICAL ORIGINS
The southern U.S.A. is famous for its music, most of which reflects the cultural mix of the region. New Orleans and other parts of Louisiana are the birthplaces of jazz and Cajun music, while bluegrass and country have origins in Nashville and Memphis, Tennessee. These music styles started here, but quickly spread throughout the country and developed even further in the cities.

Jazz musician on Bourbon Street, New Orleans

Chef holding a skillet of jambalaya, a Cajun dish

CAJUN CULTURE
The Cajuns in this region are French-speaking people who were expelled from Canada in the 1700s. They mixed with other cultures in Louisiana, but their French influence can be seen in the music, food, and place names, such as Lafayette.

FLORIDA EVERGLADES
The increasing population of Florida means that the Everglades, swampy plains inhabited by alligators and other wildlife, are under threat as land is needed for houses and farms. However, the Everglades National Park protects part of this important ecosystem.

Mississippi River Delta

Cincinnati
Newport
INDIANA
Louisville
Evansville
Frankfor
Owensboro
Lexington
Henderson
Elizabethtown
Richmonc
Paducah
KENTUCKY
Somerset
Hopkinsville
Bowling Green
Kentucky Lake
Green River
Clarksville
Union City
Cookeville
Nashville
Franklin
Murfreesboro
MISSOURI
Rogers
Bull Shoals Lake
Mountain Home
Pocahontas
Fayetteville
Walnut Ridge
Blytheville
Dyersburg
Boston Mountains
TENNESSEE
Fort Smith
ARKANSAS
Jonesboro
Jackson
Lawrenceburg
Columbia
Maryvi
Clevela
Russellville
Searcy
West Memphis
Memphis
Chattanooga
North Little Rock
Forrest City
Corinth
Florence
Huntsville
Dalto
Ouachita Mountains
Little Rock
Holly Springs
Decatur
Scottsboro
Hot Springs
Benton
Tupelo
Hamilton
Cullman
Rome
Pine Bluff
Clarksdale
Grenada
Anniston
Marietta
Gadsden
Atlanta
Red River
Texarkana
Camden
Greenwood
Columbus
Tuscaloosa
Birmingham
El Dorado
Greenville
MISSISSIPPI
Alexander City
Griff
Shreveport
Bastrop
Yazoo City
ALABAMA
Opelika
Ruston
Monroe
Canton
Demopolis
Phenix City
Bossier City
Tallulah
Clinton
Meridian
Prattville
Columbus
LOUISIANA
Vicksburg
Jackson
Montgomery
Natchitoches
Red River
Troy
Alba
Natchez
Brookhaven
Laurel
Andalusia
Alexandria
Hattiesburg
Ozark
De Ridder
McComb
Brewton
Dothan
Bainbride
Bogalusa
Prichard
Crestview
Lake Seminole
Opelousas
Baton Rouge
Mobile
Lake Charles
Lafayette
Gulfport
Fort Walton Beach
Tallahasse
New Iberia
Biloxi
Pensacola
Panama City
Metairie
New Orleans
Morgan City
Houma
Chandeleur Islands
Cape San Blas
Venice
Apalach Bay
Gulf of Mexico

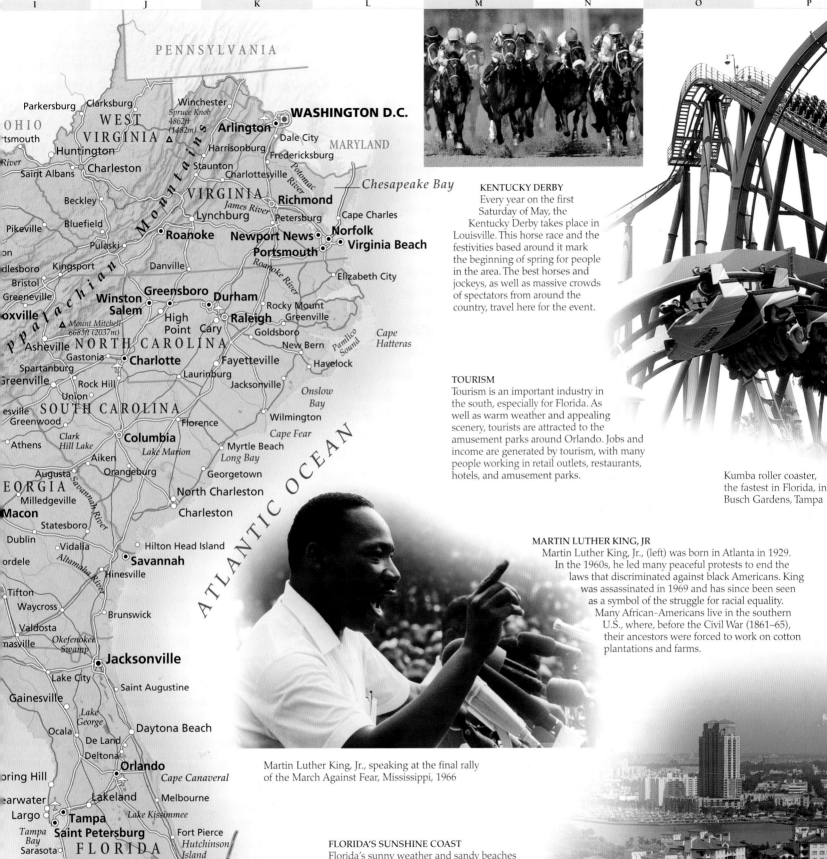

PENNSYLVANIA

Parkersburg • Clarksburg • Winchester • Dale City
WEST VIRGINIA Spruce Knob 4862ft (1482m) • **Arlington** • **WASHINGTON D.C.**
OHIO • Huntington • Saint Albans • Charleston • Harrisonburg • Staunton • Fredericksburg **MARYLAND**
Beckley • Charlottesville • *Potomac River* • *Chesapeake Bay*
Pikeville • Bluefield • **VIRGINIA** • *James River* • **Richmond**
Roanoke • Lynchburg • Petersburg • Cape Charles
Kingsport • Danville • *Roanoke River* • **Newport News** • **Norfolk**
Bristol • Pulaski • **Portsmouth** • **Virginia Beach**
Greeneville • Elizabeth City
Winston Salem • **Greensboro** • **Durham**
Knoxville • Mount Mitchell 6683ft (2037m) • High Point • **Raleigh** • Rocky Mount • Greenville
Asheville • **NORTH CAROLINA** • Cary • Goldsboro
Gastonia • **Charlotte** • Fayetteville • New Bern • *Pamlico Sound* • *Cape Hatteras*
Spartanburg • Rock Hill • Laurinburg • Jacksonville • *Onslow Bay*
Greenville • Union • **SOUTH CAROLINA** • Wilmington
Greenwood • Florence • *Cape Fear*
Athens • *Clark Hill Lake* • **Columbia** • Myrtle Beach • *Long Bay*
Augusta • Aiken • *Lake Marion* • Georgetown
Orangeburg
GEORGIA • **North Charleston**
Milledgeville • *Savannah River* • **Charleston**
Macon • Statesboro
Dublin • Vidalia • Hilton Head Island
Cordele • *Altamaha River* • **Savannah**
Tifton • Hinesville
Waycross • Brunswick
Valdosta • *Okefenokee Swamp*
Thomasville • **Jacksonville**
Lake City • Saint Augustine
Gainesville • *Lake George*
Ocala • Daytona Beach
De Land • Deltona
Spring Hill • **Orlando** • *Cape Canaveral*
Clearwater • Lakeland • Melbourne
Largo • **Tampa** • *Lake Kissimmee*
Tampa Bay • **Saint Petersburg** • Fort Pierce
Sarasota • **FLORIDA** • *Hutchinson Island*
Port Charlotte • *Lake Okeechobee* • West Palm Beach
Charlotte Harbor • Boca Raton
Fort Myers • Pompano Beach
Big Cypress Swamp • **Fort Lauderdale**
Naples • Miami Beach
The Everglades • **Miami**
Cape Sable
Florida Bay • Key Largo
Key West • *Florida Keys* • *Straits of Florida*

ATLANTIC OCEAN

KENTUCKY DERBY
Every year on the first Saturday of May, the Kentucky Derby takes place in Louisville. This horse race and the festivities based around it mark the beginning of spring for people in the area. The best horses and jockeys, as well as massive crowds of spectators from around the country, travel here for the event.

TOURISM
Tourism is an important industry in the south, especially for Florida. As well as warm weather and appealing scenery, tourists are attracted to the amusement parks around Orlando. Jobs and income are generated by tourism, with many people working in retail outlets, restaurants, hotels, and amusement parks.

Kumba roller coaster, the fastest in Florida, in Busch Gardens, Tampa

MARTIN LUTHER KING, JR
Martin Luther King, Jr., (left) was born in Atlanta in 1929. In the 1960s, he led many peaceful protests to end the laws that discriminated against black Americans. King was assassinated in 1969 and has since been seen as a symbol of the struggle for racial equality. Many African-Americans live in the southern U.S., where, before the Civil War (1861–65), their ancestors were forced to work on cotton plantations and farms.

Martin Luther King, Jr., speaking at the final rally of the March Against Fear, Mississippi, 1966

FLORIDA'S SUNSHINE COAST
Florida's sunny weather and sandy beaches have traditionally attracted many retired people, many of whom live in apartments along the coast in resorts such as Miami Beach (right). Florida also attracts young people, especially to the vibrant city of Miami, where many immigrants from Central America, Cuba, and other Caribbean islands live, and Spanish is spoken by half the population. The Florida Keys, an island chain in the south of the peninsula, is also popular with tourists, and contains sone of the largest living coral formations in North America.

U.S.A.: Midwest

THE AMERICAN MIDWEST is dominated by the Great Plains, once the home of cattle ranches, cowboys, and Native American peoples. However, the discovery of gold in South Dakota brought a rush of settlers to the area. This, combined with a decline in buffalo numbers, led to the eventual displacement of the Native Americans from the Plains. The area is prone to dramatic weather—tornadoes, blizzards, and hot summers. To the west, vast areas of farmland generate more wheat and corn than anywhere else in the world. East of the Mississippi River, the landscape varies and, although farming is important, this is the industrial center of the country. Cities such as Chicago (Illinois), Detroit (Michigan), and Cleveland (Ohio) are major manufacturing centers.

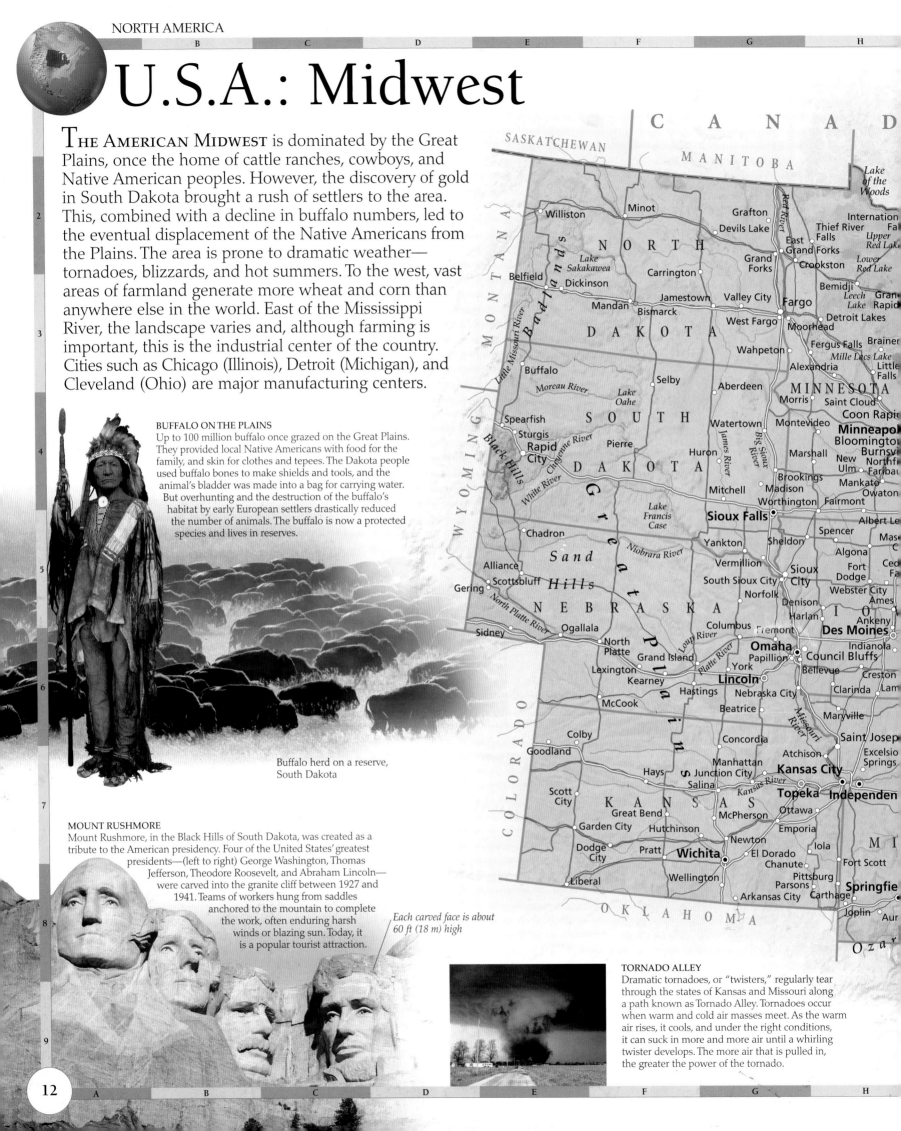

BUFFALO ON THE PLAINS
Up to 100 million buffalo once grazed on the Great Plains. They provided local Native Americans with food for the family, and skin for clothes and tepees. The Dakota people used buffalo bones to make shields and tools, and the animal's bladder was made into a bag for carrying water. But overhunting and the destruction of the buffalo's habitat by early European settlers drastically reduced the number of animals. The buffalo is now a protected species and lives in reserves.

Buffalo herd on a reserve, South Dakota

MOUNT RUSHMORE
Mount Rushmore, in the Black Hills of South Dakota, was created as a tribute to the American presidency. Four of the United States' greatest presidents—(left to right) George Washington, Thomas Jefferson, Theodore Roosevelt, and Abraham Lincoln—were carved into the granite cliff between 1927 and 1941. Teams of workers hung from saddles anchored to the mountain to complete the work, often enduring harsh winds or blazing sun. Today, it is a popular tourist attraction.

Each carved face is about 60 ft (18 m) high

TORNADO ALLEY
Dramatic tornadoes, or "twisters," regularly tear through the states of Kansas and Missouri along a path known as Tornado Alley. Tornadoes occur when warm and cold air masses meet. As the warm air rises, it cools, and under the right conditions, it can suck in more and more air until a whirling twister develops. The more air that is pulled in, the greater the power of the tornado.

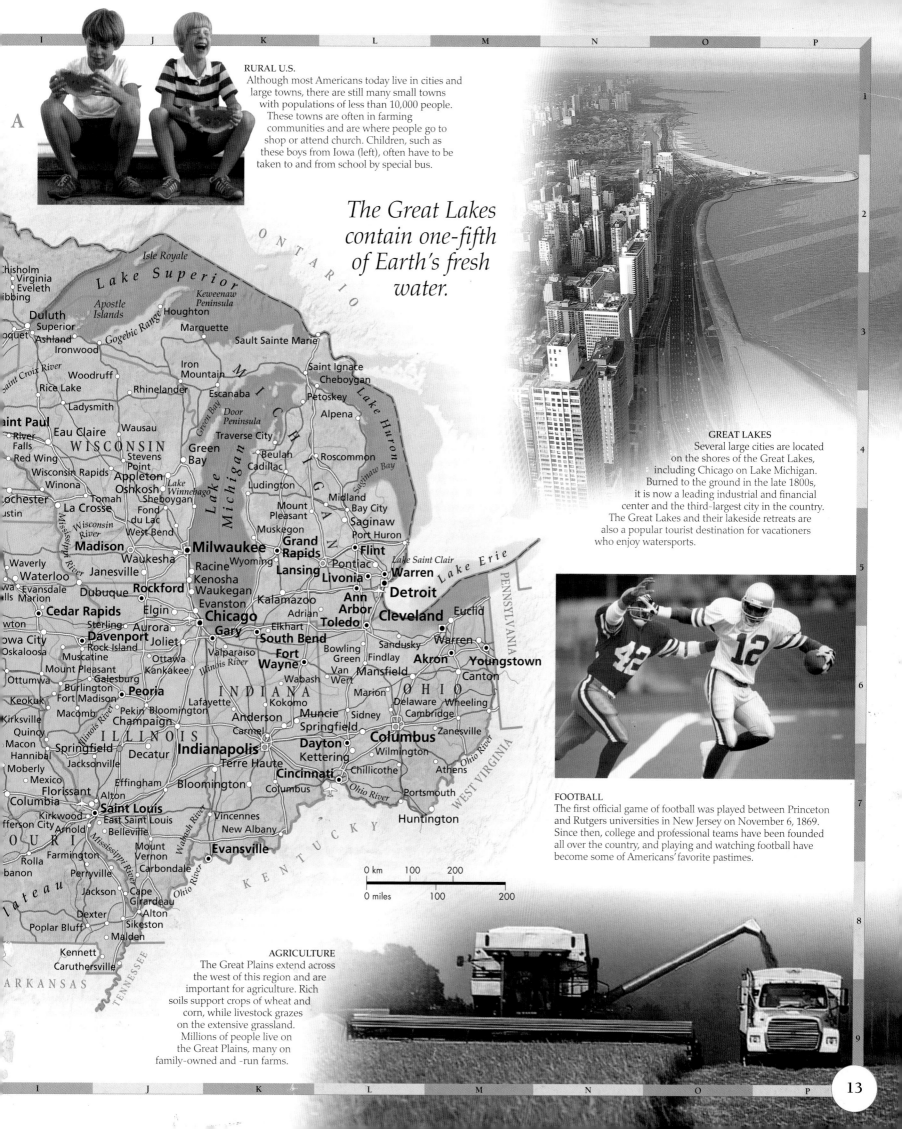

RURAL U.S.
Although most Americans today live in cities and large towns, there are still many small towns with populations of less than 10,000 people. These towns are often in farming communities and are where people go to shop or attend church. Children, such as these boys from Iowa (left), often have to be taken to and from school by special bus.

The Great Lakes contain one-fifth of Earth's fresh water.

GREAT LAKES
Several large cities are located on the shores of the Great Lakes, including Chicago on Lake Michigan. Burned to the ground in the late 1800s, it is now a leading industrial and financial center and the third-largest city in the country. The Great Lakes and their lakeside retreats are also a popular tourist destination for vacationers who enjoy watersports.

FOOTBALL
The first official game of football was played between Princeton and Rutgers universities in New Jersey on November 6, 1869. Since then, college and professional teams have been founded all over the country, and playing and watching football have become some of Americans' favorite pastimes.

AGRICULTURE
The Great Plains extend across the west of this region and are important for agriculture. Rich soils support crops of wheat and corn, while livestock grazes on the extensive grassland. Millions of people live on the Great Plains, many on family-owned and -run farms.

0 km 100 200
0 miles 100 200

U.S.A.: West

THE ROCKY MOUNTAINS separate the coastal region from the drier inland states. Fast-growing cities in California, such as San Francisco, Los Angeles, and San Diego, hug the Pacific coast and have attracted many migrants because of good job opportunities. Inland, blazing deserts and towering mountains provide some of the most dramatic landscapes in the country. National parks, such as Yellowstone in northwestern Wyoming and Montana, and Yosemite in central California, protect some of these wilderness areas. Farther east, the foothills of the Rockies give way to vast plains grazed by large herds of cattle.

NORTHERN FORESTS
The coastal areas of Oregon and Washington contain large forests. These produce economically important timber, but a lot of land is also left in its natural state and is popular with hikers. Most people here live in large cities like Seattle, Washington, and in the fertile inland valleys.

CALIFORNIA AGRICULTURE
California is warm, fertile, and well irrigated, ideal for agriculture. Grapes are an important crop north of San Francisco in the Napa Valley. Farther south, citrus crops such as oranges also flourish. Premium farming land is under threat, however, as the population expands.

The Native American name for Death Valley is Tomesha, which means "land where the ground is on fire."

LOS ANGELES
This sprawling city—the second largest in the U.S.—is home to migrants from all over the world as well as other states in the country. Sandwiched between the coast and the mountains, the city has major air-pollution problems. This mostly arises from the exhaust fumes from the high number of cars used by commuters on the city's highways.

I **J** **K** **L** **M** **N** **O** **P**

0 km 100 200 300
0 miles 100 200 300

A D A A

ALBERTA   SASKATCHEWAN

eka
hitefish   Shelby   Havre   Milk River   Malta
Kalispell   △ Baldy Mountain   Fort Peck
Flathead   6624ft   Lake
Lake   (2019m)   Missouri River   Sidney
issoula   Helena   Great Falls   Glendive
          Boulder   M O N T A N A
Orchard Homes   Lewistown
Anaconda   Yellowstone River   Miles City
Butte   Billings
Pioneer   Bozeman   Livingston   Laurel
Mountains   Bighorn River   Powder River   Little Missouri River
Dillon
                                        Sheridan
          Cody   Powell   Gillette
                 Cloud Peak
                 13,166ft (4013m)
Rexburg   Worland
I D A H O Idaho Falls   W Y O M I N G
          Blackfoot
Snake River Plain Pocatello
in Falls American Falls   Lander   Riverton   Douglas
Burley   Reservoir   Casper
          Bear   Wheatland
          Lake   Rawlins   Laramie Mountains   Torrington
Brigham City Logan Green River
Ogden   Evanston Rock Springs   Cheyenne
Great   Bountiful   Laramie
Salt Lake Magna Salt Lake City
Great   Sandy City   Steamboat   Fort Collins Sterling
Salt Lake Orem   Vernal   Craig Springs Greeley
Desert   Provo   Loveland Fort Morgan
Utah   Longmont Brighton
Lake   Boulder
          Price   Broomfield Denver
                 Grand   Lakewood Aurora
U T A H   Junction Mount Elbert Littleton Englewood
                 14,432ft (4399m)
evier   Richfield   Pikes Peak   C O L O R A D O
Lake   Moab   14,108ft Colorado Springs
        Montrose Gunnison (4300m) Pueblo
        Mount Ellen △   Canon City   Lamar
Cedar City 11,522ft   Uncompahgre △ San Juan La Junta
        (3512m)   Peak 14,308ft Mountains Rio Grande
Saint George Lake   (4361m) Alamosa
        Powell   Durango
A R I Z O N A   N E W   M E X I C O   OKLAHOMA

N O R T H   D A K O T A
S O U T H   D A K O T A
N E B R A S K A
K A N S A S

CATTLE RANCHES
Many people who live in Montana, Wyoming, Utah, and Colorado work in the booming farming and mining industries. A lot of the land on these foothills and plains is grazed by cattle on huge ranches, established originally to provide food for the flourishing east coast. Modern cowboys may use horses, trucks, or even helicopters to watch over the cattle.

DEATH VALLEY
The driest place in the U.S. is Death Valley, which also holds the highest recorded temperature in North America of 135°F (57°C). Although seemingly inhospitable, its canyons, rock formations, and sudden spring blooms make it popular with tourists.

COLORADO
The Rocky Mountains cut through this region. The stunning terrain and the light, dry snow that falls here support the skiing industry in Colorado. Resorts such as Aspen are popular with Americans as well as overseas visitors.

YELLOWSTONE
The first national park in the world, Yellowstone was established in 1827 in Wyoming and Montana to protect the abundant wildlife and hydrothermal activity. The United States now has more than 350 national parks, which attract millions of visitors every year.

Tourists watching the Old Faithful geyser, Yellowstone National Park

Silicon, an element, is used in many computer products

EARTHQUAKES
San Francisco, California suffers from frequent earthquakes owing to its location on the San Andreas fault line. Modern skyscrapers are designed to withstand tremors, but many houses, especially those on typically steep streets, are still at risk.

SILICON VALLEY
The area between Palo Alto and San Jose has been nicknamed "Silicon Valley" because of the many companies engaged in high-technology research and manufacturing here. It is the center of the world's computer industry.

U.S.A.: Southwest

THE SOUTHWEST is an area of huge contrasts. A lot of Oklahoma and Texas consists of flat, rolling grasslands and huge farms, while both Arizona and New Mexico are hot, arid, and mountainous, with vast canyons and river valleys carving their way through the land. Since the discovery of oil in 1901, Texas has become the country's top oil producer with Houston as the center of the billion-dollar industry. Tourism is also important to the southwest, with visitors flocking to see the Grand Canyon, the Painted Desert, and other natural wonders. Buildings here reflect the mix of Hispanic, Native American, European American, and modern American cultures.

HOT PLACE TO LIVE
The climate across much of the southwest is hot and dry, with summer temperatures often reaching 38°C (100°F). Although water can be scarce, many people have a swimming pool in their garden so they can cool off.

Suburbs of Phoenix, Arizona

DESERT LIFE
The saguaro cactus can reach up to 50 ft (15 m) tall, grow as many as 40 branches, and live for 200 years. Cacti, yucca, and other plants have all adapted to the hot, dry desert conditions found in the Southwest. So, too, have many animals, including the deadly rattlesnake.

Saguaro cacti in the Sonoran Desert

(Map of U.S.A. Southwest)

UTAH · NEVADA · CALIFORNIA · ARIZONA · NEW MEXICO · MEXICO · COLORADO

Lake Powell · San Juan River · Page · Shiprock · Aztec · Farmington · Bloomfield · Wheeler Pe 13,15 (4011 · Lake Mead · Grand Canyon · Tuba City · Coconino Plateau · Chuska Mountains · Colorado Plateau · Los Alamos · Espanol · San Juan Mountains · Kingman · Humphreys Peak 12,365ft (3851m) · Painted Desert · Gallup · Santa Fe · Rocky · Hualapai Peak 8419ft (2566m) · Sanders · Grants · Corrales · Albuquerque · Lake Havasu City · Sedona · Flagstaff · Prescott · Holbrook · Mountains · Belen · Vau · ARIZONA · Show Low · Willard · Wickenburg · Socorro · Glendale · Scottsdale · NEW ME · Signal Peak 4879ft (1487m) · Phoenix · Mesa · Globe · San Carlos · Elephant Butte Reservoir · Black Range · Rio Grande · Yuma · Casa Grande · Eloy · Clifton · Alamogordo · Sacramento Mount · Somerton · Gila River · Sonoran Desert · Safford · Ajo · Las Cruces · Organ Peak 8871ft (2704m) · Tucson · Willcox · Deming · Sierra Vista · Benson · Nogales · Bisbee · El Paso · Douglas · Fabens · MEXICO

0 km 50 100 150 200
0 miles 50 100 150 200

THE GRAND CANYON
The Grand Canyon in northern Arizona is one of the natural wonders of the world. This incredibly deep gorge was slowly cut out of the rock, beginning 6 million years ago, by the Colorado River. People can hike around its edge or venture down into the canyon to camp for the night.

NATIVE-AMERICAN CULTURES
Native Americans, including Navajo, Hopi, and Apache, used to live across the Southwest but are now concentrated in reservations set up by the U.S. government. The largest of these is in Arizona and New Mexico and is home to the Navajo people. The Navajo farm the land and produce crafts, such as the woven blanket wrapped around these Navajo children.

Kachina doll made by the Hopi

ADOBE HOUSES
Traditional homes of the Pueblo peoples of the Southwest were made from adobe bricks of sun-baked earth and straw covered with plaster. Dwellings had a flat roof and smooth walls. Modern adobe-style buildings can still be seen in the Southwest but are often made of concrete and then painted to look like adobe. Here, a woman demonstrates baking bread in an adobe oven.

Astronaut leaving the Space Shuttle by means of a manned manouvering unit (MMU)

NASA
Houston, Texas, is the centre of the United States space program. After a rocket has blasted off from Cape Canaveral in Florida, its journey is controlled by the National Aeronautics and Space Administration (NASA) in Houston. Astronauts are also trained at the center, and new space technology is developed here.

The Grand Canyon is up to 1 mile (1.6 km) deep, 18 miles (29 km) wide, and 217 miles (349 km) long.

SPANISH INFLUENCE
Close to Mexico and Central America, the southwestern states have long been settled by Hispanic people, whose influence can be seen—and heard—throughout the Southwest. Spanish is widely spoken, and the Roman Catholic religion that the Spanish brought is evident in the churches scattered here.

OIL FIELDS
The oil industry has provided Texas with a lot of its wealth. Oil lies deep underground and is brought up to the surface by huge oil jacks, also known as nodding donkeys.

Mexico

ONCE HOME TO THE GREAT Aztec and Mayan civilizations and then the focus of Spanish conquistadors who came in search of wealth, Mexico today reflects its colorful past through its culture and architecture. The majority of Mexicans is mestizo (mixed race)—of Spanish and native Indian descent. Mexico City, the site of the ancient Aztec capital, is today one of the largest cities in the world, with a population of more than 16 million. Despite oil and natural gas reserves and a plentiful supply of labor, large numbers of Mexicans are still poor, especially in rural areas and urban slums.

ALONG THE BORDER
In 1994, Mexico signed the North American Free Trade Agreement (NAFTA), which effectively bound its economy to that of the U.S. A large industrial area has developed along the Mexican border with the U.S., and many American companies have relocated south of the border to benefit from the lower labor costs.

DAY OF THE DEAD
One of the biggest festivals in Mexico is the Day of the Dead. It is believed that once a year the souls of the dead can come back and visit their loved ones. In celebration of this, special food is prepared to welcome the souls, and offerings of flowers, candles, and incense are made at gravesides.

LIFE IN THE CITY
Mexico City is the political, economic, and cultural hub of the country and is home to some 16 million people. Its location, in a basin surrounded by mountains, means that expansion is difficult. Air pollution from factories and cars cannot escape, so on most days a thick layer of smog builds up over the city. Attempts to deal with the pollution, including banning cars from some areas, have had limited success.

The volcano Popocatépetl is the highest peak around the city

Mexico City is contained within a ring of mountains

WORKING ON THE LAND
Agriculture employs 6.5 million people—about one eighth of Mexico's work force. However, only 12 percent of the land is suitable for farming because it is so mountainous and dry. The peasant communities of the south rely on farming for their food, while communities in the north are more industrialized. Here, the agave plant is being harvested near the town of Tequila.

Map labels:
UNITED STATES OF
Mexicali · Tijuana · Rosarito · San Luis · Ensenada · Colorado River · Desierto de Altar · Sierra San Pedro Mártir · Ciudad Juárez · Rio Grande del Norte · Rio Bravo del Norte · Nogales · Agua Prieta · Samalayuca · Cananea · Caborca · Magdalena · Rio Bavispe · Nuevo Casas Grandes · El Sueco · Ojinaga · Cumpas · San Pedro de la Cueva · Rio Conchos · Isla Ángel de la Guarda · El Sáuz · Hermosillo · Chihuahua · Delicias · Isla Tiburón · Cuauhtémoc · Ciudad Camargo · Baja California · Empalme · Guaymas · Esperanza · San Francisco del Oro · Jiménez · Isla Guadalupe · Bahía Sebastián Vizcaíno · Isla Cedros · Guerrero Negro · Ciudad Obregón · Navojoa · Hidalgo del Parral · Santa Barbara · Huatabampo · San Ignacio · San Blas · Gómez Pala · Gulf of California · Sierra Madre Occidental · Loreto · Los Mochis · Guasave · Guamúchil · Culiacán · M E · Sierra de la Giganta · Navolato · Durango · Bahía de La Paz · El Dorado · Isla Magdalena · Isla Santa Margarita · La Paz · Tropic of Cancer · Santa Genoveva 7894ft (2406m) · Miraflores · Mazatlán · Escuinapa · PACIFIC OCEAN · Acaponeta · Tuxpa · Tepic · Islas Marías · Puerto Vallarta · Manzan

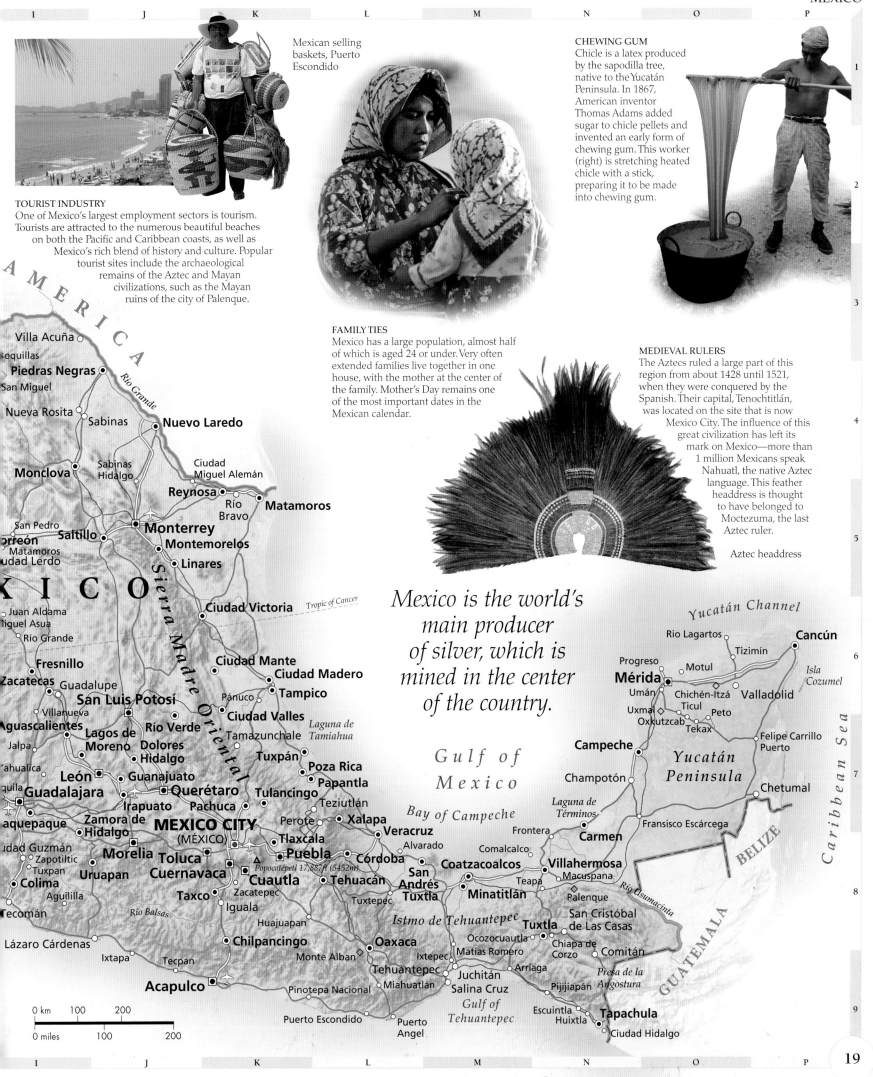

Mexican selling baskets, Puerto Escondido

TOURIST INDUSTRY

One of Mexico's largest employment sectors is tourism. Tourists are attracted to the numerous beautiful beaches on both the Pacific and Caribbean coasts, as well as Mexico's rich blend of history and culture. Popular tourist sites include the archaeological remains of the Aztec and Mayan civilizations, such as the Mayan ruins of the city of Palenque.

CHEWING GUM

Chicle is a latex produced by the sapodilla tree, native to the Yucatán Peninsula. In 1867, American inventor Thomas Adams added sugar to chicle pellets and invented an early form of chewing gum. This worker (right) is stretching heated chicle with a stick, preparing it to be made into chewing gum.

FAMILY TIES

Mexico has a large population, almost half of which is aged 24 or under. Very often extended families live together in one house, with the mother at the center of the family. Mother's Day remains one of the most important dates in the Mexican calendar.

MEDIEVAL RULERS

The Aztecs ruled a large part of this region from about 1428 until 1521, when they were conquered by the Spanish. Their capital, Tenochtitlán, was located on the site that is now Mexico City. The influence of this great civilization has left its mark on Mexico—more than 1 million Mexicans speak Nahuatl, the native Aztec language. This feather headdress is thought to have belonged to Moctezuma, the last Aztec ruler.

Aztec headdress

Mexico is the world's main producer of silver, which is mined in the center of the country.

AMERICA

MEXICO

Sierra Madre Oriental

Villa Acuña
oquillas
Piedras Negras
San Miguel
Río Grande
Nueva Rosita
Sabinas
Nuevo Laredo
Sabinas Hidalgo
Ciudad Miguel Alemán
Monclova
Reynosa
Río Bravo
Matamoros
San Pedro
orreón **Saltillo** **Monterrey**
Matamoros
udad Lerdo **Montemorelos**
Linares

Juan Aldama
liguel Asua
Río Grande
Ciudad Victoria *Tropic of Cancer*
Fresnillo
Ciudad Mante
Zacatecas Guadalupe
Ciudad Madero
San Luis Potosí
Pánuco **Tampico**
Villanueva
Ciudad Valles
Aguascalientes
Lagos de Moreno **Río Verde**
Tamazunchale *Laguna de Tamiahua*
Jalpa
Dolores
ahualica **Hidalgo**
Tuxpán
León **Guanajuato**
Poza Rica
quila **Papantla**
Guadalajara **Querétaro** **Tulancingo**
Irapuato Pachuca Teziutlán
aquepaque **Zamora de** Perote
Hidalgo **MEXICO CITY** **Xalapa**
(MÉXICO) *Bay of Campeche*
udad Guzmán **Tlaxcala** **Veracruz**
Morelia **Toluca** **Puebla** Alvarado
Zapotiltic **Córdoba**
Tuxpan **Cuernavaca** **Cuautla** **Tehuacán** **San**
Colima **Uruapan** Zacatepec **Andrés**
Aguililla **Taxco** **Tuxtla**
Iguala Tuxtepec
Tecomán *Río Balsas*
Huajuapan
Chilpancingo
Ixtapa **Oaxaca**
Tecpan Monte Alban
Acapulco Ixtepec
Tehuantepec
Pinotepa Nacional Miahuatlán
Puerto Escondido Puerto
Angel

Popocatépetl 17,887ft (5452m)

Coatzacoalcos
Comalcalco
Villahermosa
Teapa Macuspana
Palenque
Río Usumacinta
Minatitlán
San Cristóbal de Las Casas
Tuxtla
Ocozocuautla Chiapa de Corzo **Comitán**
Matías Romero
Arriaga *Presa de la Angostura*
Juchitán Pijijiapán
Salina Cruz
Gulf of Tehuantepec
Escuintla **Tapachula**
Huixtla
Ciudad Hidalgo

Gulf of Mexico

Yucatán Channel
Río Lagartos Tizimín **Cancún**
Progreso Motul *Isla Cozumel*
Mérida Chichén-Itzá
Umán Ticul **Valladolid**
Uxmal Peto
Oxkutzcab Tekax
Campeche *Yucatán*
Champotón *Peninsula*
Laguna de Términos
Frontera Felipe Carrillo Puerto
Carmen Chetumal
Fransisco Escárcega
Caribbean Sea

BELIZE
GUATEMALA

Istmo de Tehuantepec

0 km 100 200
0 miles 100 200

Central America

Lake Nicaragua is the only freshwater lake in the world that contains sharks.

VOLCANOES, EARTHQUAKES, and hurricanes threaten the livelihoods of people in the seven countries of Central America. People here have also struggled with poverty and civil war. In more recent years, however, peace and economic recovery have offered hope, and education is now free in all countries. Remains of the ancient Mayan civilization that flourished until the 1500s, when the Spanish invaded, can be seen throughout the region. Large numbers of the native population died after the invasion, mostly from disease. Today, Spanish is the main language of the region.

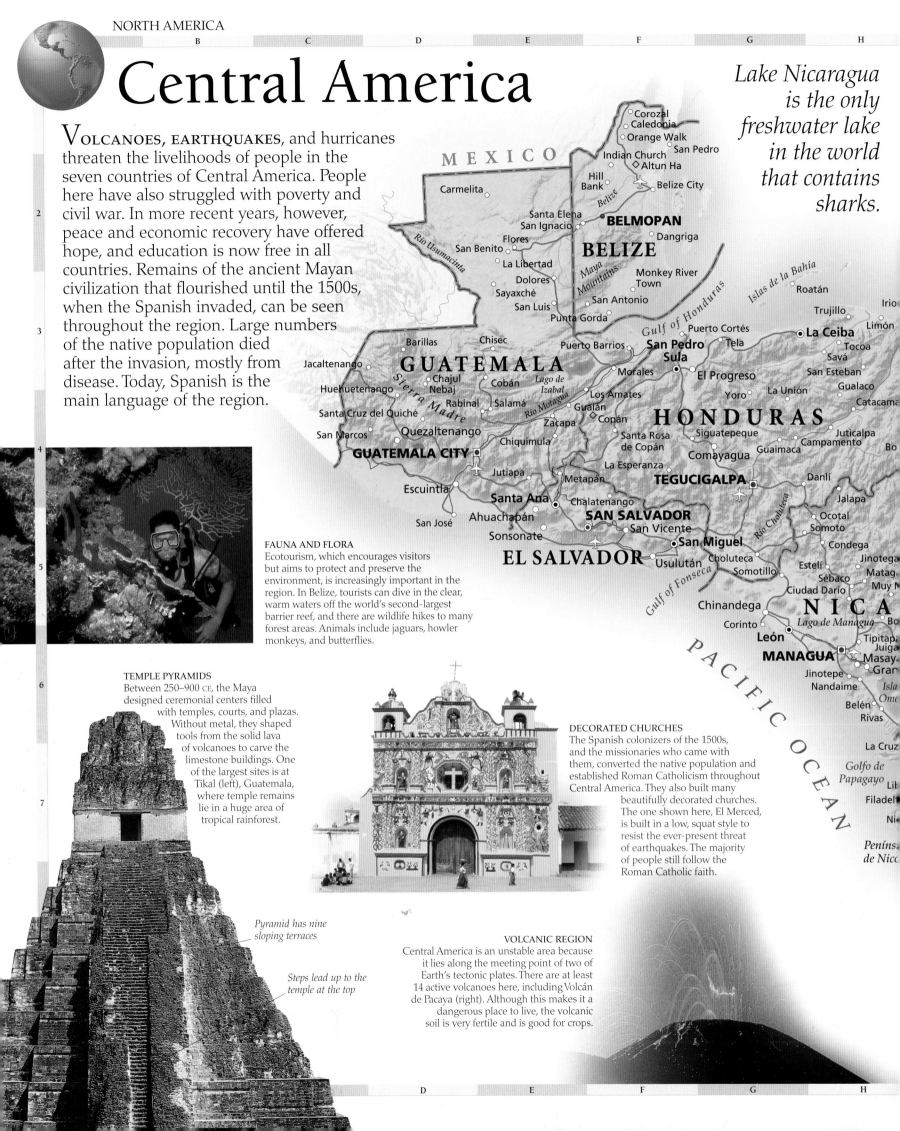

MEXICO

Corozal
Caledonia
Orange Walk
Indian Church
Hill Bank
Carmelita
San Pedro
Altun Ha
Belize City

Santa Elena
San Ignacio
Flores
San Benito
La Libertad
Dolores
Sayaxché
San Luis
Punta Gorda

BELMOPAN
Dangriga
BELIZE
Monkey River Town
San Antonio

Río Usumacinta

Maya Mountains

Gulf of Honduras
Puerto Cortés
Puerto Barrios
San Pedro Sula
Tela
Islas de la Bahía
Roatán
Trujillo
Irio
Limón

Barillas
Chisec
Jacaltenango
GUATEMALA
Chajul
Nebaj
Cobán
Lago de Izabal
Morales
Los Amates
Gualán
La Ceiba
Tocoa
Savá
San Esteban
Gualaco
Catacama

Huehuetenango
Rabinal
Salamá
Río Motagua
Zacapa
Copán
El Progreso
Yoro
La Unión

Santa Cruz del Quiché
San Marcos
Quezaltenango
Chiquimula
Copán
HONDURAS
Santa Rosa de Copán
Siguatepeque
Guaimaca
Comayagua
Juticalpa
Campamento
Bo

GUATEMALA CITY
Jutiapa
La Esperanza
TEGUCIGALPA
Danlí

Escuintla
Metapán
Santa Ana
Chalatenango
Jalapa

Ahuachapán
San José
SAN SALVADOR
San Vicente
Ocotal
Somoto

Sonsonate
EL SALVADOR
Usulután
San Miguel
Choluteca
Somotillo
Río Choluteca
Condega
Jinotega
Estelí
Matag
Muy

Chinandega
Gulf of Fonseca
Sébaco
Ciudad Darío
NICA
Bo

Corinto
Lago de Managua
León
Tipitap
Juiga

MANAGUA
Jinotepe
Nandaime
Masay
Gran
Isla Ome

Belén
Rivas

PACIFIC OCEAN

La Cruz

Golfo de Papagayo
Lib
Filadel
Ni

Peníns
de Nic

FAUNA AND FLORA
Ecotourism, which encourages visitors but aims to protect and preserve the environment, is increasingly important in the region. In Belize, tourists can dive in the clear, warm waters off the world's second-largest barrier reef, and there are wildlife hikes to many forest areas. Animals include jaguars, howler monkeys, and butterflies.

TEMPLE PYRAMIDS
Between 250–900 CE, the Maya designed ceremonial centers filled with temples, courts, and plazas. Without metal, they shaped tools from the solid lava of volcanoes to carve the limestone buildings. One of the largest sites is at Tikal (left), Guatemala, where temple remains lie in a huge area of tropical rainforest.

Pyramid has nine sloping terraces

Steps lead up to the temple at the top

DECORATED CHURCHES
The Spanish colonizers of the 1500s, and the missionaries who came with them, converted the native population and established Roman Catholicism throughout Central America. They also built many beautifully decorated churches. The one shown here, El Merced, is built in a low, squat style to resist the ever-present threat of earthquakes. The majority of people still follow the Roman Catholic faith.

VOLCANIC REGION
Central America is an unstable area because it lies along the meeting point of two of Earth's tectonic plates. There are at least 14 active volcanoes here, including Volcán de Pacaya (right). Although this makes it a dangerous place to live, the volcanic soil is very fertile and is good for crops.

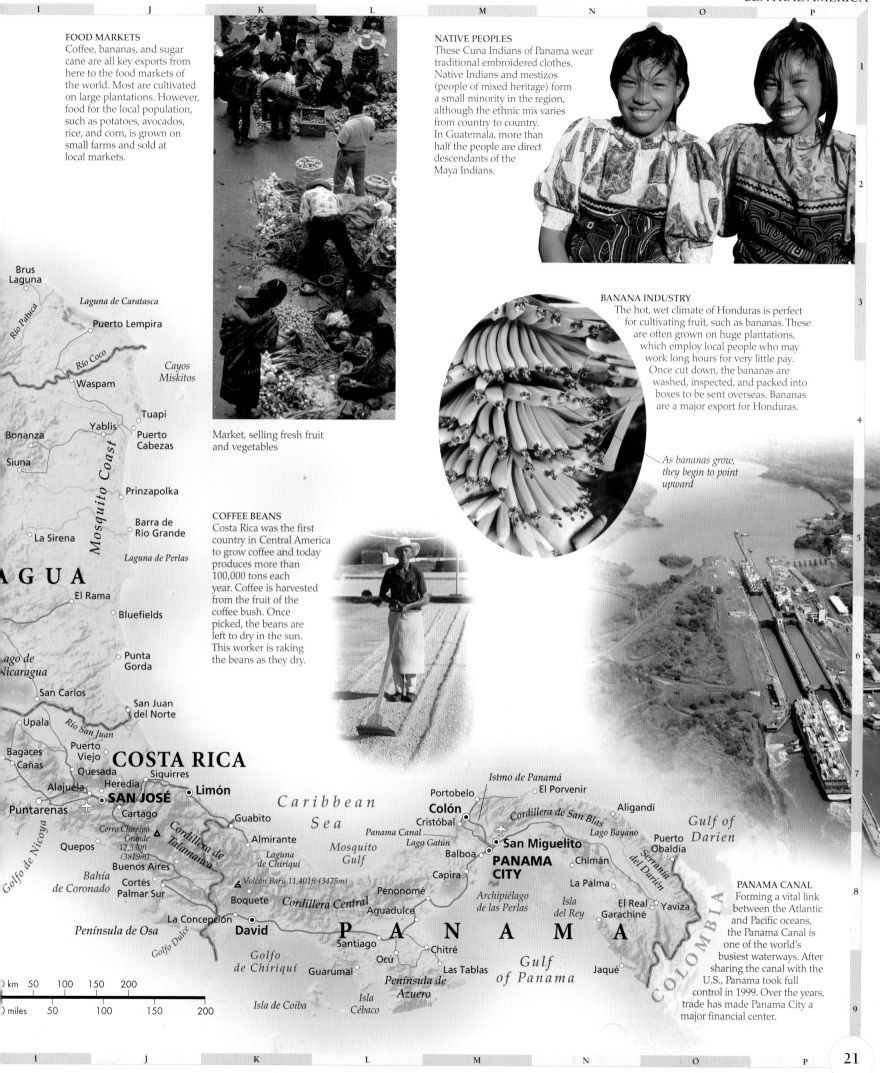

FOOD MARKETS

Coffee, bananas, and sugar cane are all key exports from here to the food markets of the world. Most are cultivated on large plantations. However, food for the local population, such as potatoes, avocados, rice, and corn, is grown on small farms and sold at local markets.

Market, selling fresh fruit and vegetables

NATIVE PEOPLES

These Cuna Indians of Panama wear traditional embroidered clothes. Native Indians and mestizos (people of mixed heritage) form a small minority in the region, although the ethnic mix varies from country to country. In Guatemala, more than half the people are direct descendants of the Maya Indians.

BANANA INDUSTRY

The hot, wet climate of Honduras is perfect for cultivating fruit, such as bananas. These are often grown on huge plantations, which employ local people who may work long hours for very little pay. Once cut down, the bananas are washed, inspected, and packed into boxes to be sent overseas. Bananas are a major export for Honduras.

As bananas grow, they begin to point upward

COFFEE BEANS

Costa Rica was the first country in Central America to grow coffee and today produces more than 100,000 tons each year. Coffee is harvested from the fruit of the coffee bush. Once picked, the beans are left to dry in the sun. This worker is raking the beans as they dry.

PANAMA CANAL

Forming a vital link between the Atlantic and Pacific oceans, the Panama Canal is one of the world's busiest waterways. After sharing the canal with the U.S., Panama took full control in 1999. Over the years, trade has made Panama City a major financial center.

Brus Laguna
Laguna de Caratasca
Río Patuca
Puerto Lempira
Río Coco
Cayos Miskitos
Waspam
Tuapi
Yablis
Puerto Cabezas
Bonanza
Siuna
Prinzapolka
La Sirena
Barra de Río Grande
Mosquito Coast
Laguna de Perlas
AGUA
El Rama
Bluefields
ago de Nicaragua
Punta Gorda
San Carlos
San Juan del Norte
Upala
Río San Juan
Bagaces
Cañas
Puerto Viejo
COSTA RICA
Quesada
Siquirres
Alajuela
Heredia
SAN JOSÉ
Limón
Puntarenas
Cartago
Cerro Chirripó Grande 12,530ft (3819m)
Cordillera de Talamanca
Quepos
Buenos Aires
Bahía de Coronado
Cortés
Palmar Sur
Boquete
La Concepción
David
Península de Osa
Golfo Dulce
PANAMA
Golfo de Nicoya
Guabito
Almirante
Laguna de Chiriquí
Mosquito Gulf
Volcán Barú 11,401ft (3475m)
Cordillera Central
Santiago
Golfo de Chiriquí
Guarumal
Ocú
Península de Azuero
Isla de Coiba
Isla Cébaco

Caribbean Sea
Istmo de Panamá
Portobelo
El Porvenir
Colón
Cristóbal
Cordillera de San Blas
Aligandí
Panama Canal
Lago Bayano
Lago Gatún
Balboa
San Miguelito
PANAMA CITY
Chimán
Capira
La Palma
Penonomé
Aguadulce
Archipiélago de las Perlas
Isla del Rey
El Real
Garachiné
Yaviza
Puerto Obaldía
Serranía del Darién
Gulf of Darien
Chitré
Las Tablas
Gulf of Panama
Jaqué
COLOMBIA

km 50 100 150 200
miles 50 100 150 200

The Caribbean

THIS REGION CONSISTS of thousands of islands stretching from Cuba in the west to Trinidad and Tobago in the southeast. European colonists wanted control of the islands in the 1500s, but the diseases they brought wiped out most of the local Carib and Arawak peoples. African slaves, imported to work on plantations, replaced local peoples, and today most of the population are descended from those Africans. English, Spanish, and French are spoken in different countries, depending on which European power claimed the territory. Tourism and agriculture are major sources of employment.

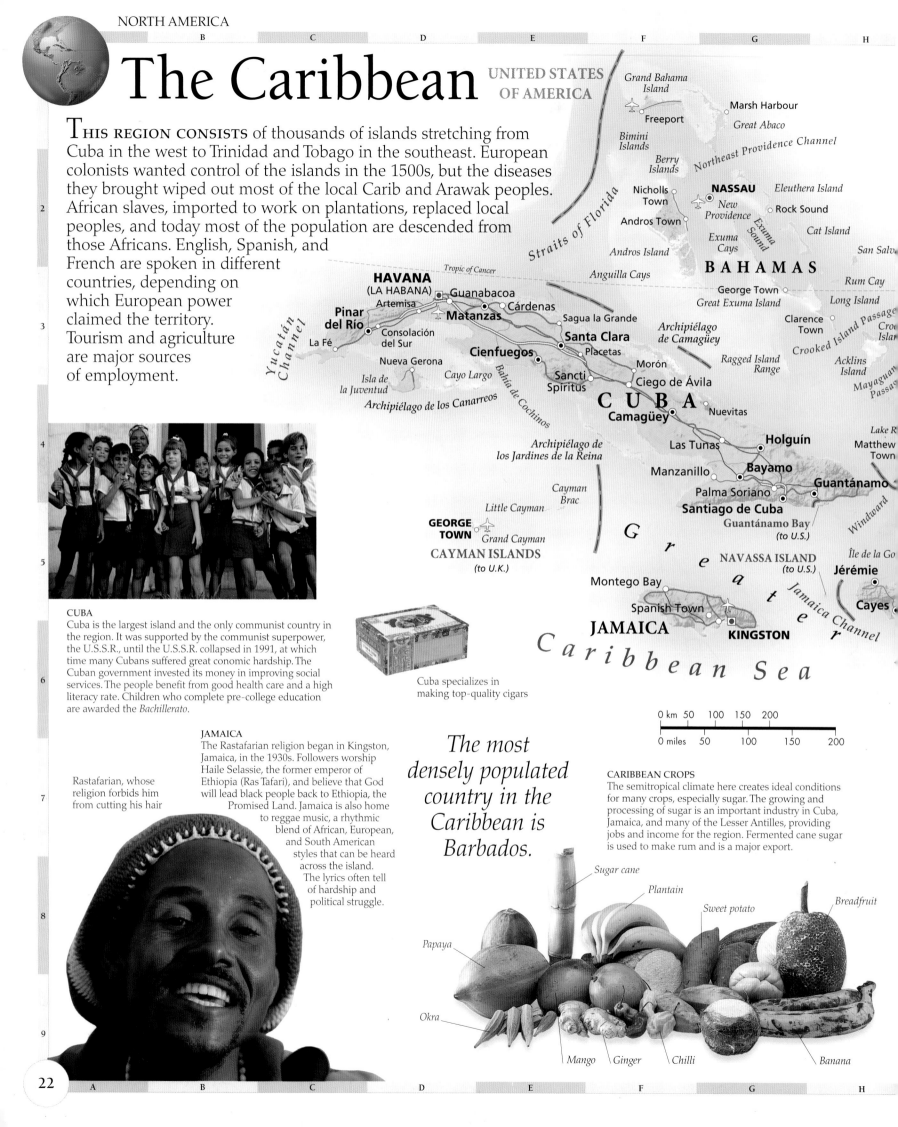

CUBA
Cuba is the largest island and the only communist country in the region. It was supported by the communist superpower, the U.S.S.R., until the U.S.S.R. collapsed in 1991, at which time many Cubans suffered great economic hardship. The Cuban government invested its money in improving social services. The people benefit from good health care and a high literacy rate. Children who complete pre-college education are awarded the *Bachillerato*.

Cuba specializes in making top-quality cigars

JAMAICA
The Rastafarian religion began in Kingston, Jamaica, in the 1930s. Followers worship Haile Selassie, the former emperor of Ethiopia (Ras Tafari), and believe that God will lead black people back to Ethiopia, the Promised Land. Jamaica is also home to reggae music, a rhythmic blend of African, European, and South American styles that can be heard across the island. The lyrics often tell of hardship and political struggle.

Rastafarian, whose religion forbids him from cutting his hair

The most densely populated country in the Caribbean is Barbados.

CARIBBEAN CROPS
The semitropical climate here creates ideal conditions for many crops, especially sugar. The growing and processing of sugar is an important industry in Cuba, Jamaica, and many of the Lesser Antilles, providing jobs and income for the region. Fermented cane sugar is used to make rum and is a major export.

Sugar cane
Plantain
Sweet potato
Breadfruit
Papaya
Okra
Mango
Ginger
Chilli
Banana

UNITED STATES OF AMERICA

Grand Bahama Island
Freeport
Marsh Harbour
Great Abaco
Bimini Islands
Berry Islands
Northeast Providence Channel
Nicholls Town
NASSAU
Eleuthera Island
New Providence
Rock Sound
Andros Town
Cat Island
Straits of Florida
Exuma Cays
Exuma Sound
San Salv
Andros Island
Tropic of Cancer
Anguilla Cays
BAHAMAS
Rum Cay
George Town
Great Exuma Island
Long Island
HAVANA (LA HABANA)
Guanabacoa
Artemisa
Cárdenas
Pinar del Río
Matanzas
Sagua la Grande
Clarence Town
Cro
Islan
Consolación del Sur
Santa Clara
Archipiélago de Camagüey
Crooked Island Passage
La Fé
Cienfuegos
Placetas
Acklins Island
Nueva Gerona
Cayo Largo
Morón
Ragged Island Range
Yucatán Channel
Isla de la Juventud
Sancti Spíritus
Ciego de Ávila
Mayaguan
Passa
Archipiélago de los Canarreos
Bahía de Cochinos
CUBA
Camagüey
Nuevitas
Archipiélago de los Jardines de la Reina
Las Tunas
Holguín
Lake R
Matthew Town
Cayman Brac
Manzanillo
Bayamo
Guantánamo
Little Cayman
Palma Soriano
Santiago de Cuba
GEORGE TOWN
Grand Cayman
Guantánamo Bay (to U.S.)
Windward
CAYMAN ISLANDS (to U.K.)
G
NAVASSA ISLAND (to U.S.)
Île de la Go
Montego Bay
r
e
Jérémie
Spanish Town
a
Jamaica Channel
Cayes
JAMAICA
KINGSTON
t
e
r
Caribbean Sea

0 km 50 100 150 200
0 miles 50 100 150 200

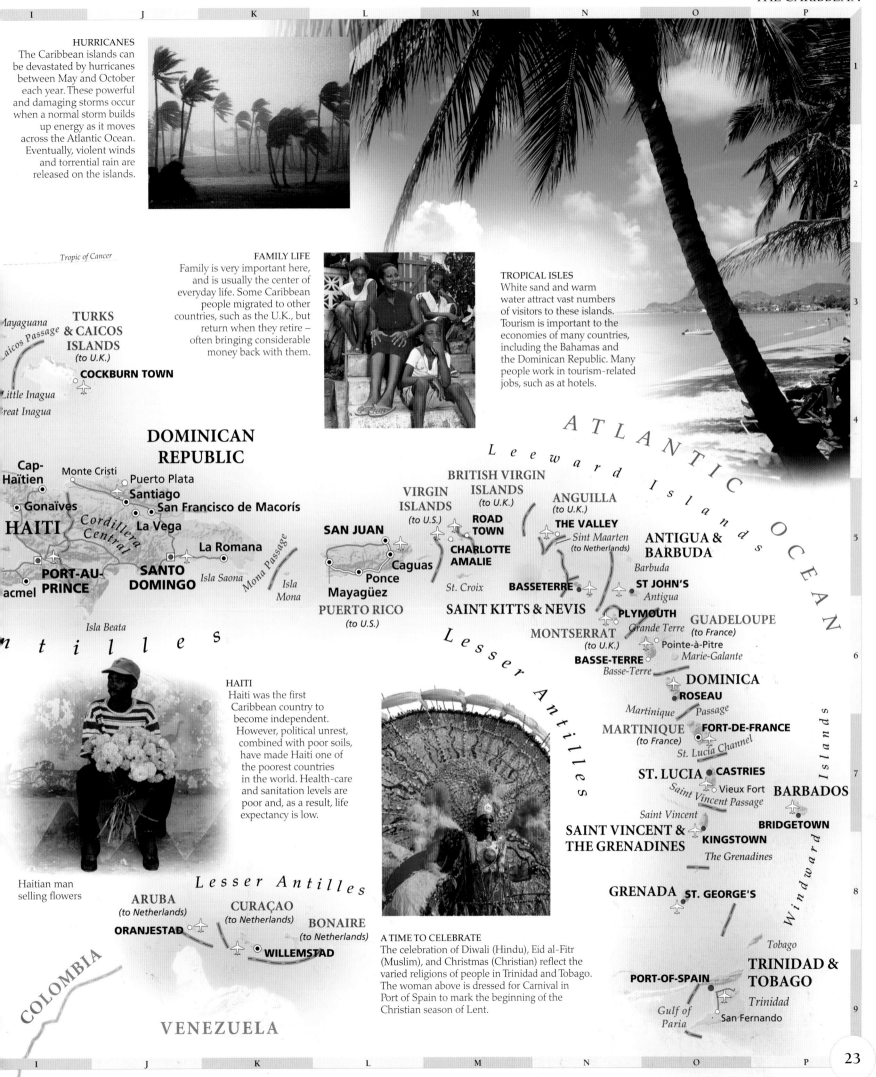

HURRICANES
The Caribbean islands can be devastated by hurricanes between May and October each year. These powerful and damaging storms occur when a normal storm builds up energy as it moves across the Atlantic Ocean. Eventually, violent winds and torrential rain are released on the islands.

FAMILY LIFE
Family is very important here, and is usually the center of everyday life. Some Caribbean people migrated to other countries, such as the U.K., but return when they retire – often bringing considerable money back with them.

TROPICAL ISLES
White sand and warm water attract vast numbers of visitors to these islands. Tourism is important to the economies of many countries, including the Bahamas and the Dominican Republic. Many people work in tourism-related jobs, such as at hotels.

Tropic of Cancer

Mayaguana

Caicos Passage

TURKS & CAICOS ISLANDS
(to U.K.)
COCKBURN TOWN

Little Inagua

Great Inagua

ATLANTIC OCEAN

Leeward Islands

DOMINICAN REPUBLIC

Cap-Haïtien
Monte Cristi
Puerto Plata
Santiago
San Francisco de Macorís
Gonaïves
Cordillera Central
La Vega
HAITI
La Romana

BRITISH VIRGIN ISLANDS
(to U.K.)

VIRGIN ISLANDS
(to U.S.)

SAN JUAN

ROAD TOWN

ANGUILLA
(to U.K.)

THE VALLEY

Sint Maarten (to Netherlands)

CHARLOTTE AMALIE

ANTIGUA & BARBUDA
Barbuda

PORT-AU-PRINCE
acmel
SANTO DOMINGO
Isla Saona
Mona Passage
Isla Mona

Caguas
Ponce
Mayagüez
PUERTO RICO
(to U.S.)

St. Croix

BASSETERRE

ST JOHN'S
Antigua

SAINT KITTS & NEVIS

PLYMOUTH

Isla Beata

ntilles

Lesser Antilles

MONTSERRAT
(to U.K.)

GUADELOUPE
Grande Terre *(to France)*
Pointe-à-Pitre

BASSE-TERRE
Basse-Terre
Marie-Galante

DOMINICA
ROSEAU

Martinique Passage

HAITI
Haiti was the first Caribbean country to become independent. However, political unrest, combined with poor soils, have made Haiti one of the poorest countries in the world. Health-care and sanitation levels are poor and, as a result, life expectancy is low.

MARTINIQUE
(to France)
FORT-DE-FRANCE

St. Lucia Channel

ST. LUCIA **CASTRIES**
Vieux Fort
Saint Vincent Passage

BARBADOS

Saint Vincent

BRIDGETOWN

SAINT VINCENT & THE GRENADINES
KINGSTOWN

The Grenadines

Haitian man selling flowers

Lesser Antilles

ARUBA
(to Netherlands)
CURAÇAO
(to Netherlands)
BONAIRE
(to Netherlands)
ORANJESTAD
WILLEMSTAD

GRENADA **ST. GEORGE'S**

Tobago

Windward Islands

A TIME TO CELEBRATE
The celebration of Diwali (Hindu), Eid al-Fitr (Muslim), and Christmas (Christian) reflect the varied religions of people in Trinidad and Tobago. The woman above is dressed for Carnival in Port of Spain to mark the beginning of the Christian season of Lent.

PORT-OF-SPAIN

TRINIDAD & TOBAGO
Trinidad

Gulf of Paria
San Fernando

COLOMBIA

VENEZUELA

SOUTH AMERICA

Although South America is much poorer than its northern neighbor, it is rich in natural resources. Its mineral wealth led to its invasion by the Portuguese and Spanish in the 1500s, and their languages and culture still shape the lives of the people here. The nations below are listed in order of area, headed by Brazil—the world's fifth-largest country.

Brazil
- 3,287,612 sq miles
  8,514,877 sq km
- 194,000,000
- Brasília
- Portuguese, German, Italian, Spanish, Polish, Japanese, Amerindian languages

Venezuela
- 352,144 sq miles
  912,050 sq km
- 28,600,000
- Caracas
- Spanish, Amerindian languages

Bolivia
- 424,164 sq miles
  1,098,581 sq km
- 9,860,000
- La Paz
- Aymara, Quechua, Spanish

Chile
- 291,933 sq miles
  756,102 sq km
- 17,000,000
- Santiago
- Spanish, Amerindian languages

Latin American culture is world famous, thanks to its infectious music and dance. Here a couple in Buenos Aires, Argentina, demonstrates the art of the tango.

Argentina
- 1,073,518 sq miles
  2,780,400 sq km
- 40,300,000
- Buenos Aires
- Spanish, Italian, Amerindian languages

Paraguay
- 157,048 sq miles
  406,752 sq km
- 6,350,000
- Asunción
- Guaraní, Spanish, German

Ecuador
- 109,484 sq miles
  283,561 sq km
- 13,600,000
- Quito
- Spanish, Quechua, other Amerindian languages

Peru
- 496,225 sq miles
  1,285,216 sq km
- 29,200,000
- Lima
- Spanish, Quechua, Aymara

Guyana
- 83,000 sq miles
  214,969 sq km
- 762,500
- Georgetown
- English Creole, Hindi, Tamil, Amerindian languages, English

Uruguay
- 68,037 sq miles
  176,215 sq km
- 3,360,000
- Montevideo
- Spanish

Colombia
- 439,737 sq miles
  1,138,914 sq km
- 45,700,000
- Bogotá
- Spanish, Wayuu, Páez, and other Amerindian languages

Soccer is a national passion in Brazil. Most of these barefoot boys on Ipanema beach, Rio de Janeiro, will be dreaming of playing for Brazil in the World Cup.

Suriname
- 63,251 sq miles
  163,820 sq km
- 519,700
- Paramaribo
- Sranan (creole), Dutch, Javanese, Sarnami Hindi, Saramaccan (creole), Chinese, Carib

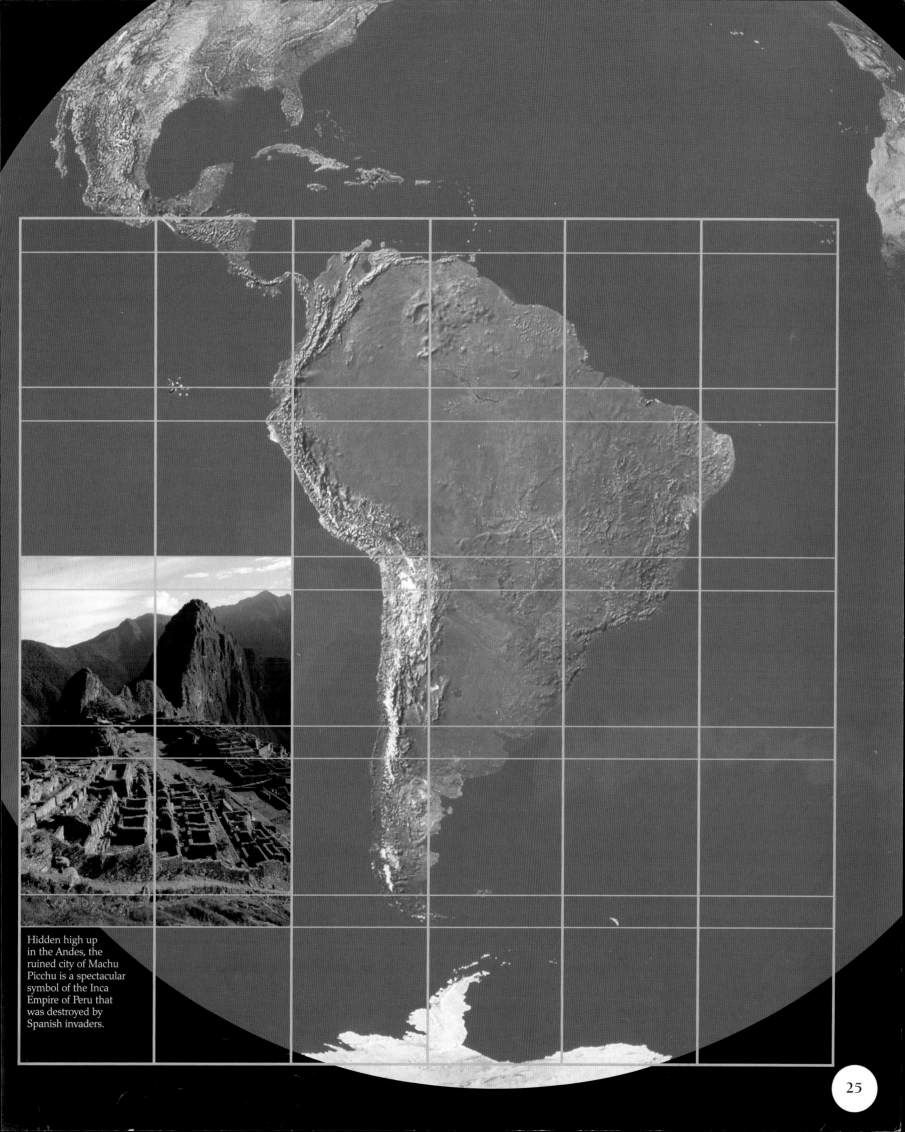

Hidden high up in the Andes, the ruined city of Machu Picchu is a spectacular symbol of the Inca Empire of Peru that was destroyed by Spanish invaders.

Northwest South America

High mountains and plateaus, dense tropical rainforests, and coastal swamps are found in this region. In the 1500s, promises of untold riches attracted the Spanish to the countries here. They found the vast empire of the Inca, which stretched from what is now Peru into northern Colombia. To the north and east, other colonizers—Dutch, English, and French—arrived. Today, although the countries are independent—with the exception of French Guiana—Spanish remains the main language. The population is mostly a mix of native peoples and Europeans, except along the Caribbean coast where descendants of former African slaves live.

ANDES MOUNTAINS

The Andes, the world's longest mountain chain, extends 4,505 miles (7,250 km) down the western edge of South America. Barley, wheat, and potatoes grow well in highland areas and are cultivated on the terraced hillsides.

FRENCH GUIANA

French Guiana is the only remaining colony in South America and is governed by France. Tropical forests cover more than four fifths of its land. In 1968, the European Space Agency established a launch site on the coast in Kourou, which is still used today.

CARACAS

Venezuela's population is growing rapidly, and more than 88 percent of the people now live in cities. The oil industry brings in considerable wealth, but many people are still poor. Although Caracas, Venezuela's capital city, is an important financial center, it has many shantytowns.

Map labels

ATLANTIC OCEAN

PACIFIC OCEAN

Caribbean Sea

CAYENNE
Ouanary
St.-Georges
Camopi
Grand-Santi
FRENCH GUIANA
(to France)
Sinnamary
Kourou
St.-Laurent-du-Maroni
PARAMARIBO
Tumuc-Humac Mountains
(claimed by Suriname)
New Amsterdam
Totness
Apoera
SURINAME
Orealla
Courantyne
GEORGETOWN
Charity
Matthews Ridge
Aurora
Linden
Essequibo River
(claimed by Suriname)
Peters Mine
Kamarang
GUYANA
Lethem
Kurupukari
(Venezuela claims all of Guyana west of Essequibo River)

Tobago
TRINIDAD & TOBAGO
Trinidad
Isla Blanquilla
Isla de Margarita
Porlamar
La Asunción
Carúpano
Cumaná
Puerto La Cruz
Barcelona
Maturín
Anaco
Tucupita
Ciudad Guayana
Upata
El Callao
El Dorado
Angel Falls
Pakaraima Mountains
Guiana Highlands

CARACAS
Maracay
Valencia
Valle de la Pascua
El Tigre
Ciudad Bolívar
Embalse de Guri
Río Caroní
VENEZUELA
San Fernando
Llanos
Río Caura
BRAZIL
Guiana

Coro
Punto Fijo
Maracaibo
Cabimas
Ciudad Ojeda
Barquisimeto
Acarigua
Guanare
Barinas
Valera
El Vigía
Mérida
San Cristóbal
Río Apure
Río Arauca
Río Meta
Puerto Carreño
Río Orinoco
Puerto Ayacucho

Santa Marta
Riohacha
Barranquilla
Soledad
Cartagena
Sincelejo
Montería
Gulf of Darién
PANAMA
Dabeiba
Puerto López
Valledupar
Bucaramanga
Barrancabermeja
Cúcuta
Aguachica
Río Cauca
Yarumal
Caucasia
Bello
Medellín
Manizales
Pereira
Armenia
Tuluá
Quibdó
Nuquí
Cordillera Central
Tunja
Sogamoso
Yopal
Zipaquirá
BOGOTÁ
Villavicencio
San José del Guaviare
Río Meta
COLOMBIA
Río Guaviare
Puerto Inírida
Río Vaupés
Mitú
Río Apaporis

Palmira
Cali
Popayán
Pasto
Buenaventura
Ibagué
Neiva
Garzón
Pitalito
Florencia
Mocoa
Tumaco
Esmeraldas
Santo Domingo de los Colorados
Ibarra
Tulcán
QUITO
Ambato
Riobamba
ECUADOR
Manta
Portoviejo
Guayaquil
Milagro
Cuenca
Machala
Equator
Amazonia
Río Caquetá
Río Putumayo
Río Napo
Iquitos
Río Pastaza

ANGEL FALLS

Each year, thousands of tourists visit the spectacular Angel Falls on the Churún River in eastern Venezuela. They were spotted by an American pilot, Jimmy Angel, in 1935 and were later named after him. The water drops for 807 m (2,648 ft), making Angel Falls the highest uninterrupted waterfall in the world.

The railroad from Lima climbs 15,807 ft (4,818 m) into the Andes and is the highest in the world.

THE INCA

The Inca first lived in the mountainous area near Cusco in Peru. By the time of the Spanish invasion, the Inca Empire extended north into southern Colombia and south through Bolivia and into Argentina and Chile. The Quechua Indians were the most powerful group in the empire, and Quechua was the official language. The Quechua and Aymara peoples now live on the high plains of the Andes.

Quechua woman in Peru

LIFE ON THE HIGH PLAINS

The Altiplano is a cold plateau at high altitude between two ranges of the Andes Mountains in southwest Bolivia and southern Peru. The native peoples who live here graze sheep and llamas on the windy plains. They have usually retained their own language and customs.

MACHU PICCHU

The conquering Spaniards never found the remains of this important Inca city—it stayed a secret until Hiram Bingham, an American archaeologist and explorer, discovered its ruins hidden in the forest in 1911. Situated on a high ridge northwest of Cusco, Peru, this magnificent ruined city covers 5 sq miles (13 sq km), and has small houses, temples, and staircases built around a central square.

MINERALS

Many countries in this area have extensive reserves of gold, silver, copper, and gems. Colombia produces more than half the world's emeralds. The Inca made good use of these resources and created many beautiful golden objects, such as this llama.

LAKE TITICACA

At 12,507 ft (3,812 m), Lake Titicaca is the highest navigable lake in the world. It is also South America's largest lake. The Uru people live here in houses built on huge floating reed islands. They grow potatoes, hunt birds, and catch fish, using boats made from tightly bundled reeds.

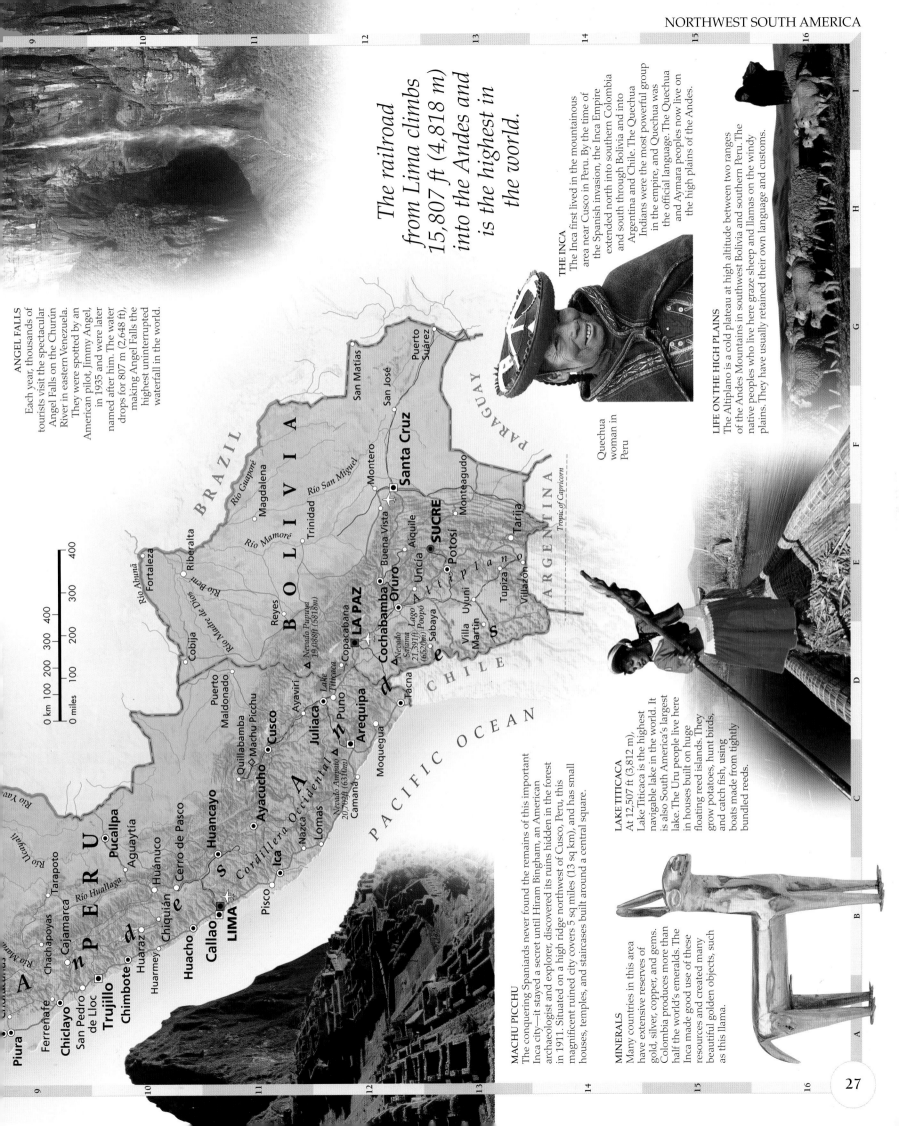

Map labels:

BRAZIL · BOLIVIA · PARAGUAY · ARGENTINA · CHILE · PERU

Andes · Cordillera Occidental · Nazca · Altiplano

Piura · Ferreñafe · Chiclayo · San Pedro de Lloc · Trujillo · Chimbote · Huaraz · Huarmey · Chiquián · Huacho · Callao · LIMA · Pisco · Ica · Lomas · Camaná · Moquegua · Tacna · Arequipa · Puno · Juliaca · Ayacucho · Huancayo · Cerro de Pasco · Huánuco · Pucallpa · Aguaytía · Tarapoto · Chachapoyas · Cajamarca · Quillabamba · Machu Picchu · Cusco · Ayaviri

Lake Titicaca · Copacabana · LA PAZ · Cochabamba · Oruro · Uncía · Potosí · SUCRE · Aiquile · Buena Vista · Santa Cruz · Montero · Trinidad · Magdalena · Riberalta · Fortaleza · Cobija · Reyes · Puerto Maldonado · San Matías · San José · Puerto Suárez · Monteagudo · Tarija · Tupiza · Villazón · Villa Martín · Sabaya · Uyuni

Río Yavarí · Río Mayo · Río Huallaga · Río Ucayali · Río Madre de Dios · Río Abuná · Río Beni · Río Mamoré · Río Guaporé · Río San Miguel

Nevado Ampato 20,709ft (6310m) · Nevado Sajama 21,391ft (6520m) · Nevado Payuya 19,088ft (5818m) · Lago Poopó · Tropic of Capricorn

PACIFIC OCEAN

0 km 100 200 300 400
0 miles 100 200 300 400

Brazil

THE VIBRANT CULTURE OF BRAZIL—with its fusion of music and dance—reflects the rich mix of its ethnic groups. The country also boasts immense natural resources with well-developed mining and manufacturing industries. Brazil grows all of its own food and exports large quantities of coffee, sugar cane, soybeans, oranges, and cotton. However, the wealth is not evenly distributed, with some people living in luxury, most struggling with poverty. São Paulo is home to almost 10 million people, but poverty and lack of housing means that many live in shantytowns without running water or sanitation. Brazil was colonized in the 1500s by the Portuguese, who established their language and Roman Catholic faith. It remains a deeply Catholic country with a strong emphasis on family life.

COFFEE
Brazil produces about one fourth of the world's coffee, which is grown on large plantations in the states of Paraná and São Paulo. However, because world coffee prices go up and down so much, Brazilians are now growing other crops for export, too.

AMAZON RAINFOREST
Covering more than one third of Brazil, the rainforest is home to a huge variety of animal and plant life. At one time, more than 5 million native Indians also lived here, but now only about 200,000 remain. Over the years, vast areas of forest have been cut down to provide timber for export, make way for farmland, or mine minerals such as gold, silver, and iron. The Kaxinawa Indians (left) still cultivate root vegetables as a food crop.

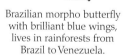

Brazilian morpho butterfly with brilliant blue wings, lives in rainforests from Brazil to Venezuela.

BRASÍLIA
Brasília replaced Rio de Janeiro as Brazil's capital in 1960 as part of a program to develop the interior of the country. Situated on land that was once rainforest, the city is laid out in the shape of an airplane. Government buildings are in the "cockpit," and residential areas are in the "wings."

SOCCER FANS
Brazilians are passionate about football, which is played everywhere from beaches to shantytowns. There is fervent support for the national team, which has won the World Cup more times than any other country, most recently in 2002.

PEOPLE OF BRAZIL
Brazilians come from a variety of different ethnic groups, including descendants of the original native Indians, Portuguese colonizers, African slaves brought over to work in the sugar plantations, and European migrants.

VENEZUELA
COLOMBIA
Guiana Highland
Uraricoera
Boa Vista
Caracaraí
Roraima
Pico da Neblina 9888ft (3014m)
Equator
Represa Balbina
Rio Negro
Rio Japurá
Rio Içá
Tefé
Amazon
Manaus
Coari
Rio Javari
Rio Juruá
Rio Purus
Rio Madeira
Amazon Basin
Humaitá
Japiim
Feijó
B R
Acre
Rio Abunã
Porto Velho
Rondônia
PERU
BOLIVIA
Chapada dos Parecis
Guaporé
Vilhena

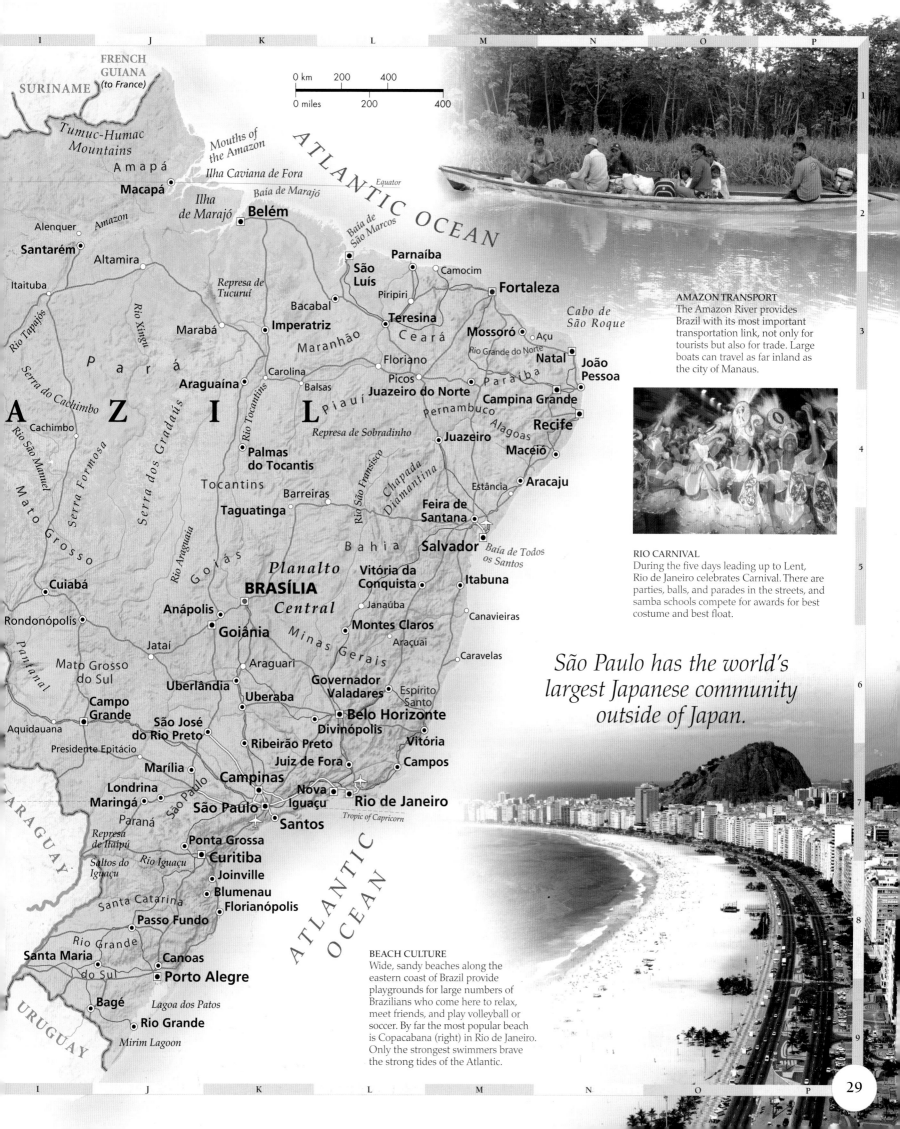

SURINAME

FRENCH GUIANA
(to France)

Tumuc-Humac Mountains

Amapá

Macapá

Alenquer

Amazon

Santarém

Itaituba

Altamira

Rio Tapajós

Rio Xingu

Serra do Cachimbo

Cachimbo

P a r á

Rio São Manuel

Serra Formosa

Mato Grosso

Serra dos Gradaús

Rio Tocantins

A Z I L

Rio Araguaia

Goiás

Mouths of the Amazon

Ilha Caviana de Fora

Equator

ATLANTIC OCEAN

Baía de Marajó

Ilha de Marajó

Belém

Baía de São Marcos

Marabá

Imperatriz

Araguaína

Carolina

Balsas

Palmas do Tocantis

Represa de Tucuruí

Bacabal

São Luís

Teresina

Parnaíba

Camocim

Piripiri

Floriano

Picos

Juazeiro do Norte

Maranhão

C e a r á

Fortaleza

Cabo de São Roque

Mossoró

Açu

Rio Grande do Norte

Natal

João Pessoa

Campina Grande

P i a u í

Represa de Sobradinho

Rio São Fransisco

Juazeiro

Pernambuco

Alagoas

Recife

Maceió

Cuiabá

Rondonópolis

Pantanal

Mato Grosso do Sul

Aquidauana

Campo Grande

Presidente Epitácio

Jataí

Anápolis

Goiânia

Araguari

Uberlândia

Uberaba

São José do Rio Preto

Ribeirão Preto

Marília

Londrina

Maringá

Paraná

Represa de Itaipú

Saltos do Iguaçu

Rio Iguaçu

Taguatinga

Barreiras

B a h i a

Planalto

BRASÍLIA

Central

Chapada Diamantina

Feira de Santana

Salvador

Baía de Todos os Santos

Vitória da Conquista

Itabuna

Janaúba

Montes Claros

Araçuai

Canavieiras

Caravelas

Minas Gerais

Estância

Aracaju

Governador Valadares

Espírito Santo

Belo Horizonte

Divinópolis

Vitória

São Paulo

Campinas

Nova Iguaçu

São Paulo

Santos

Juiz de Fora

Campos

Rio de Janeiro

Tropic of Capricorn

Ponta Grossa

Curitiba

Joinville

Blumenau

Florianópolis

Santa Catarina

Passo Fundo

ATLANTIC OCEAN

Santa Maria

Rio Grande

Canoas

do Sul

Porto Alegre

Bagé

Lagoa dos Patos

Rio Grande

Mirim Lagoon

URUGUAY

ARAGUAY

0 km   200   400

0 miles   200   400

AMAZON TRANSPORT
The Amazon River provides Brazil with its most important transportation link, not only for tourists but also for trade. Large boats can travel as far inland as the city of Manaus.

RIO CARNIVAL
During the five days leading up to Lent, Rio de Janeiro celebrates Carnival. There are parties, balls, and parades in the streets, and samba schools compete for awards for best costume and best float.

São Paulo has the world's largest Japanese community outside of Japan.

BEACH CULTURE
Wide, sandy beaches along the eastern coast of Brazil provide playgrounds for large numbers of Brazilians who come here to relax, meet friends, and play volleyball or soccer. By far the most popular beach is Copacabana (right) in Rio de Janeiro. Only the strongest swimmers brave the strong tides of the Atlantic.

Southern South America

TOWERING MOUNTAINS, vast grassy plains, and hot deserts create a very diverse geographical landscape. The four countries in this region—Chile, Paraguay, Uruguay, and Argentina—were once Spanish colonies but gained their independence in the early 1800s. Each country has an elected government, but their economies remain fragile. Most of the population speak Spanish and are mestizo—of mixed Spanish and native Indian descent—except for Argentina, where up to 97 percent are descended from Europeans.

Mix of Colonial Spanish, Italian, and Art Deco styles of architecture shows Montevideo's rich history

ITAIPÚ DAM
The enormous Itaipú Dam on the Paraná River in Paraguay is one of the world's largest hydroelectric projects. It can generate 90 percent of the electricity that Paraguay needs, as well as large amounts for export.

URUGUAY'S CAPITAL
The capital of Uruguay, Montevideo, is home to almost half the country's population. It is also the main port and economic center. This lively capital lies on the east bank of the Río de la Plata and is a popular vacation resort because of its white sandy beaches.

ATACAMA DESERT
Sandwiched between the high Andes and the ocean, the Atacama Desert in northern Chile is one of the hottest and driest areas in the world. Rain hardly ever falls here. This harsh landscape, however, is rich in copper deposits.

CHILEAN EDUCATION
Chile has a relatively high literacy rate (ability to read and write). This may be because between the ages of 6 and 18, education is both free and compulsory.

Map labels

BRAZIL

BOLIVIA

PARAGUAY
Capitán Pablo Lagerenza
General Eugenio A.Garay
Mariscal Estigarribia
Fuerte Olimpo
Pedro Juan Caballero
Concepción
Las Lomitas
Coronel Oviedo
Villarrica
Caazapá
Yuty
San Juan Bautista
ASUNCIÓN
Formosa
Pilar
Paraguay

Ciudad del Este
Eldorado
Encarnación
Posadas
Rosario
Rivera
Artigas
Tacuarembó

URUGUAY
Paysandú
Salto
Mercedes
Florida
Trinidad
BUENOS AIRES
La Plata
Chuy
Melo
Mirim Lagoon

Tropic of Capricorn

Corrientes
Santo Tomé
Mercedes
Goya
Monte Caseros
Concordia
Gualeguaychú
Dolores
Zárate
Paraná
Rosario
Pergamino
Junín
Rufino
Realicó

CHILE

PERU

Arica
Iquique
Lagunas
Tocopilla
Mejillones
Antofagasta
Taltal
Chañaral
Caldera
Copiapó
Vallenar
Domeyko
Calama
Chuquicamata
La Quiaca
Cordillera Occidental
Atacama Desert

San Ramón de la Nueva Orán
San Salvador de Jujuy
Salta
Metan
Cafayate
Nevado de Chañi 20,341ft (6200m)
Cerro Galan 21,654ft (6600m)
San Miguel de Tucumán
Santiago del Estero
Frías
Añatuya
Río Salado
Reconquista
Vera
Resistencia
Rafaela
Laguna Mar Chiquita
Santa Fe

La Rioja
Deán Funes
Jesús María
Córdoba
Villa María
San Luis
Villa Mercedes
San Rafael

Cerro Ojos del Salado 22,572ft (6880m)
La Serena
Coquimbo
Ovalle
Illapel
Salamanca
La Ligua
La Calera
Viña del Mar
Valparaíso
San Antonio
Rancagua
Pichilemu
Curicó
Monte Patria
Cerro Aconcagua 22,835ft (6960m)
San Juan
Mendoza
Godoy Cruz
SANTIAGO

Río Bermejo
Pilcomayo
Paraná

Uruguay

P A M P A S
A N D E S

DANCING THE TANGO
Popular around the world today, the tango originated in the slums of Buenos Aires in the late 1800s. This passionate dance with its characteristic rhythm is accompanied by music on a type of accordion known as a *bandoneón*, together with the piano and violin.

Chile has a large concentration of astronomical observatories because of its exceptionally clear skies.

BUENOS AIRES
More than one third of Argentina's population lives in or around the capital, Buenos Aires. A thriving port on the River Plate estuary, it is the largest city in Argentina. The colorful La Boca neighborhood, with its painted walls, is home to the descendants of Italian immigrants.

Gaucho herding cattle in the Pampas region

PAMPAS
Vast treeless plains called the Pampas—which means "flat" in Spanish—cover most of southern and western Argentina. The Pampas are used to grow grain and raise cattle. Gauchos—Argentinian cowboys—work on large ranches, or estancias.

WINES FROM CHILE
About 90 percent of Chileans live in the central region, where the rich soil is ideal for a wide range of agriculture. Vines were brought to Chile by the Spaniards, and the country now has an important winemaking industry that exports wine all over the world.

ANDES WEATHER
The Andes stretch the entire length of South America, and this has a major effect on the weather. As westerly air from the Pacific Ocean rises over the mountains, its moisture can fall as rain and snow. By the time it reaches the eastern side, the air is much drier and the landscape is more arid.

0 km 200 400
0 miles 200 400

PACIFIC OCEAN

ATLANTIC OCEAN

ARGENTINA

CHILE

Patagonia

Dolores
Mar del Plata
Necochea
Tandil
Balcarce
Azul
Coronel Dorrego
Tres Arroyos
Olavarría
Bahía Blanca
Santa Rosa
Lauquen
Viedma
Punta Alta
Bahía Blanca
Choele Choel
San Antonio Oeste
Río Negro
Golfo San Matías
Península Valdés
Golfo Nuevo
Rawson
Cipolletti
Neuquén
Zapala
San Carlos de Bariloche
Lago Nahuel Huapí
Maquinchao
Trelew
Río Chubut
Paso de Indios
Lago Musters
Golfo San Jorge
Comodoro Rivadavia
Caleta Olivia
Puerto Deseado
Río Deseado
Puerto San Julián
Sarmiento
Lago Buenos Aires
Río Chico
Perito Moreno
Esquel
Río Bío Bío
Loncoche
Valdivia
Osorno
Puerto Varas
Puerto Montt
Ancud
Castro
Isla de Chiloé
Golfo Corcovado
Archipiélago de los Chonos
Golfo de Penas
Puerto Aisén
Coihaique
Chile Chico
Cochrane
Cerro San Valentín 13,314ft (4058m)
Isla Wellington
Cerro Melimoyu 10,007ft (3050m)
Cerro Paine 8760ft (2670m)
Río Santa Cruz
El Calafate
Puerto Natales
Río Gallegos
Bahía Grande
Strait of Magellan
Porvenir
Punta Arenas
Tierra del Fuego
Ushuaia
Beagle Channel
Cape Horn (Cabo de Hornos)
Isla de los Estados
Talcahuano
Chillán
Concepción
Los Angeles
Temuco
Lebu
Santa Rosa
Coronel

Atlantic Ocean

THE WORLD'S SECOND-LARGEST OCEAN, the Atlantic separates the Americas from Europe and Africa. The Atlantic is the world's youngest ocean, starting to form about 180 million years ago, as the continental plates began to separate. This movement continues today, as the oceanic plates that meet at the Mid-Atlantic Ridge continue to pull apart. The Atlantic is a major source of fish but, due to overfishing, stocks are now low. Many shipping routes cross the Atlantic, and pollution is an international problem as ships dump chemicals and waste. There are substantial reserves of oil and gas in the Gulf of Mexico, off the coast of west Africa, and in the north Atlantic.

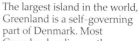

GREENLAND
The largest island in the world, Greenland is a self-governing part of Denmark. Most Greenlanders live on the southwest coast. Mostly Inuit, with some Danish-Norwegian influences, they make their living by seal hunting, fishing, and fur trapping.

Fishing for halibut

TOURISM
The volcanic islands and black beaches of the eastern Atlantic, especially the Canaries (left), Madeira, and the Azores, are popular with tourists, who are attracted to the scenery and subtropical climate.

WARM CURRENTS
The Gulf Stream flows up the east coast of North America and across the Atlantic. It brings warm water and a mild climate to northern Europe, which would otherwise be cooler.

Mid-Atlantic Ridge

Tristan da Cunha island

At the center of the ridge is a valley at least 10 miles (16 km) wide

UNDERWATER MOUNTAINS
The Mid-Atlantic Ridge is a huge underwater mountain chain that runs the entire length of the Atlantic. It was formed by magma that oozed up from the sea bed, cooled to create solid rock, and gradually built up to form a ridge. Some peaks are so high that they break the surface to form volcanic islands, such as the country of Iceland.

ATLANTIC FISHING INDUSTRY
The Atlantic Ocean contains more than half of the world's total stock of fish. Herring, anchovy, sardine, cod, flounder, and tuna are among the most important fish found here. However, overfishing, especially of cod and tuna, has caused a significant decline in numbers.

WHALES
Many whales live in the Atlantic, migrating from summer feeding grounds in the cold polar regions to warmer waters in the Caribbean for the winter. They give birth and mate again before returning north.

Humpback whale breaching

FALKLANDS
Set in the windy south Atlantic off the coast of Argentina, the Falkland Islands belong to the U.K. but are also claimed by Argentina. Fishing and sheep farming are important. The land is rocky, mountainous, boggy, and almost treeless.

NORTH AMERICA

BERMUD (to U.K

Gulf of Mexico

Hatteras Plain

Greater Antilles

Puerto Rico Trench

Caribbean Sea

Guatemala Basin

Colombian Basin

Lesser Antille

Panama Basin

Galápagos Islands (to Ecuador)

SOUTH

Peru-Chile Trench

Peru Basin

PACIFIC OCEAN

Andes

Chile Basin

Peru-Chile Trench

Chile Rise

GREENLAND
(to Denmark)

Labrador
Sea

Denmark Strait

ICELAND
REYKJAVIK

FAEROE ISLANDS
(to Denmark)

Labrador
Basin

Reykjanes
Basin

Iceland
Basin

British
Isles

North
Sea

Baltic Sea

Charlie-Gibbs Fracture Zone

Rockall Bank

EUROPE

Newfoundland

Grand Banks of
Newfoundland

Newfoundland
Basin

Azores
(to Portugal)

Bay of
Biscay

Alps

Mediterranean Sea

Bermuda
Rise

Sohm
Plain

East Azores Fracture Zone

Atlas Mountains

Madeira
(to Portugal)

Great Meteor
Tablemount

Canary Islands
(to Spain)

Sahara

Sargasso
Sea

Madeira
Plain

ares
ain

Cape Verde
Plain

Kane Fracture Zone

Cape Verde
Basin

PRAIA
CAPE
VERDE

Sahel

ATLANTIC

Doldrums Fracture Zone

Sierra
Leone
Rise

Sierra
Leone
Basin

AFRICA

Demerara
Plain

OCEAN

Guinea
Basin

Gulf of
Guinea

Amazon
Fan

Mid-

Ascension Fracture Zone

AMERICA

Ceará Plain

Fernando de
Noronha
(to Brazil)

Pernambuco
Plain

ASCENSION ISLAND
(to St. Helena)

Brazil
Basin

Angola
Basin

ST. HELENA
(to U.K.)

Vitória
Seamount

Ilha da
Trindade
(to Brazil)

Zubov
Seamount

Santos
Plateau

Walvis Ridge

Orange Fan

Rio Grande
Rise

Cape
Basin

Cape of
Good Hope

Argentine

TRISTAN DA CUNHA
(to St. Helena)

Gulf of San Matías

Basin

Gough Fracture Zone

Gough Island
(to Tristan da Cunha)

Gulf of San Jorge

FALKLAND ISLANDS
(to U.K.)

Zapiola Ridge

Scotia
Sea

SOUTH SANDWICH
ISLANDS
(to U.K.)

BOUVET
ISLAND
(to Norway)

Cape
Horn

SOUTH GEORGIA
(to U.K.)

Drake Passage

SOUTHERN OCEAN

East Scotia
Basin

Mineral-rich waters
in the Blue Lagoon,
Iceland, are said to
be beneficial to
people's health

ICELAND

Iceland is situated in the north Atlantic on
the Mid-Atlantic Ridge. As a result, it has at
least 20 active volcanoes and suffers from
frequent earthquakes. There are numerous
thermal springs with boiling mud lakes and
geysers. Water from hot springs (above) is
used to provide hot water and heat for a
large proportion of Iceland's population,
most of whom live on the coast. The
warm Gulf Stream ensures that
the country's ports stay
icefree in the winter.

The Atlantic
covers one fifth
of Earth's
surface.

ICEBERGS

Icebergs in the Atlantic Ocean
are formed when ice sheets and
glaciers reach the ocean. Parts
break off and start to drift, driven
by winds and currents.

AFRICA

Covering one fifth of the world's land area, Africa has a rapidly growing population. Many of its 52 nations—listed below in order of size—are desperately poor. This is partly due to hostile climates, especially in and around the vast Sahara desert, but also because of a history of political turmoil, ethnic tennsion or conflict and, in some countries, war. Despite this, African culture is among the most vibrant on Earth.

Sudan
- 967,500 sq miles
- 2,505,813 sq km
- 42,300,000
- Khartoum
- Arabic, Dinka, Nuer, Nubian, Beja, Zande, Bari, Fur, Shilluk, Lotuko

Chad
- 495,755 sq miles
- 1,284,000 sq km
- 11,200,000
- N'Djamena
- French, Sara, Arabic, Maba

Ethiopia
- 426,373 sq miles
- 1,104,300 sq km
- 82,800,000
- Addis Ababa
- Amharic, Tigrinya, Galla, Sidamo, Somali, English, Arabic (Oromu)

Namibia
- 318,261 sq miles
- 824,292 sq km
- 2,170,000
- Windhoek
- Ovambo, Kavango, English, Bergdama, German, Afrikaans

Madagascar
- 226,658 sq miles
- 587,041 sq km
- 19,600,000
- Antananarivo
- Malagasy, French

Zimbabwe
- 150,872 sq miles
- 390,757 sq km
- 12,500,000
- Harare
- Shona, isiNdebele, English

Algeria
- 919,595 sq miles
- 2,381,741 sq km
- 34,900,000
- Algiers
- Arabic, Tamazight (Berber: Kabyle, Shawia, Tamashek), French

Niger
- 489,191 sq miles
- 1,267,000 sq km
- 15,300,000
- Niamey
- Hausa, Djerma, Fula, Tuareg, Teda, French

Mauritania
- 397,955 sq miles
- 1,030,700 sq km
- 3,290,000
- Nouakchott
- Hassaniyah Arabic, Wolof, French

Mozambique
- 308,642 sq miles
- 799,380 sq km
- 22,900,000
- Maputo
- Makua, Xitsonga, Sena, Lomwe, Portuguese

Botswana
- 224,607 sq miles
- 581,730 sq km
- 1,950,000
- Gaborone
- Setswana, English, Shona, San, Khoikhoi, isiNdebele

Ivory Coast
- 124,504 sq miles
- 322,463 sq km
- 21,100,000
- Yamoussoukro
- Akan, French, Kru, Voltaïque

Congo, Dem Rep of
- 905,355 sq miles
- 2,344,858 sq km
- 66,000,000
- Kinshasa
- Kiswahili, Tshiluba, Kikongo, Lingala, French

Angola
- 481,354 sq miles
- 1,246,700 sq km
- 18,500,000
- Luanda
- Portuguese, Umbundu, Kimbundu, Kikongo

Egypt
- 386,662 sq miles
- 1,001,450 sq km
- 83,000,000
- Cairo
- Arabic, French, English, Berber

Zambia
- 290,587 sq miles
- 752,618 sq km
- 12,900,000
- Lusaka
- Bemba, Tongan, Nyanja, Lozi, Lala-Bisa, Nsenga, English

Kenya
- 224,081 sq miles
- 580,367 sq km
- 39,800,000
- Nairobi
- Kiswahili, English, Kikuyu, Luo, Kalenjin, Kamba

Burkina Faso
- 105,869 sq miles
- 274,200 sq km
- 15,800,000
- Ouagadougou
- Mossi, Fulani, French, Tuareg, Diyula, Songhai

Congo, Republic of
- 905,355 sq miles
- 2,344,858 sq km
- 3,680,000
- Brazzaville
- Kikongo, Teke, Lingala, French

Mali
- 478,841 sq miles
- 1,240,192 sq km
- 13,000,000
- Bamako
- Bambara, Fula, Senufo, Soninke, French

Tanzania
- 365,755 sq miles
- 947,300 sq km
- 43,700,000
- Dodoma
- Kiswahili, Sukuma, Kichagga, Nyamwezi, Hehe, Makonde, Yao, Sandawe, English

Somalia
- 246,201 sq miles
- 637,657 sq km
- 9,130,000
- Mogadishu
- Somali, Arabic, English, Italian

Cameroon
- 183,568 sq miles
- 475,440 sq km
- 19,500,000
- Yaoundé
- Bamileke, Fang, Fula, French, English

Gabon
- 103,347 sq miles
- 267,667 sq km
- 1,470,000
- Libreville
- Fang, French, Punu, Sira, Nzebi, Mpongwe

Libya
- 679,362 sq miles
- 1,759,540 sq km
- 6,420,000
- Tripoli
- Arabic, Tuareg

South Africa
- 470,693 sq miles
- 1,219,090 sq km
- 50,100,000
- Tshwane
- English, isiZulu, isiXhosa, Afrikaans, Sepedi, Setswana, Sesotho, Xitsonga, siSwati, Tshivenda, isiNdebele

Nigeria
- 356,669 sq miles
- 923,768 sq km
- 155,000,000
- Abuja
- Hausa, English, Yoruba, Igbo

Central African Republic
- 240,535 sq miles
- 622,984 sq km
- 4,420,000
- Bangui
- Sango, Banda, Gbaya, French

Morocco
- 172,414 sq miles
- 446,550 sq km
- 32,000,000
- Rabat
- Arabic, Tamazight (Berber), French, Spanish

Guinea
- 94,926 sq miles
- 245,857 sq km
- 10,100,000
- Conakry
- Pulaar, Malinké, Sousou, French

Uganda

- 93,065 sq miles
  241,038 sq km
- 32,700,000
- Kampala
- Luganda, Nkole, Chiga, Lango, Acholi, Teso, Lugbara, English

Eritrea

- 45,406 sq miles
  117,600 sq km
- 5,070,000
- Asmara
- Tigrinya, English, Tigre, Afar, Arabic, Saho, Bilen, Kunama, Nara, Hedareb

Ghana

- 92,098 sq miles
  238,533 sq km
- 23,800,000
- Accra
- Twi-Fanti, Ewe, Ga, Adangbe, Gurma, Dagomba (Dagbani)

Benin

- 112,622 sq km
  43,484 sq miles
- 8,940,000
- Porto-Novo
- Fon, Bariba, Yorùbá, Adja, Houeda, Somba, French

Guinea-Bissau

- 13,948 sq miles
  36,125 sq km
- 1,610,000
- Bissau
- Portuguese Creole, Balante, Fula, Malinké, Portuguese

Senegal

- 75,955 sq miles
  196,722 sq km
- 12,500,000
- Dakar
- Wolof, Pulaar, Serer, Diyula, Mandinka, Malinké, Soninke, French

Liberia

- 43,000 sq miles
  111,369 sq km
- 3,960,000
- Monrovia
- Kpelle, Vai, Bassa, Kru, Grebo, Kissi, Gola, Loma, English

Lesotho

- 11,720 sq miles
  30,355 sq km
- 2,070,000
- Maseru
- English, Sesotho, isiZulu

Rwanda

- 10,169 sq miles
  26,338 sq km
- 10,000,000
- Kigali
- Kinyarwanda, French, Kiswahili, English

Gambia

- 4,361 sq miles
  11,295 sq km
- 1,710,000
- Banjul
- Mandinka, Fula, Wolof, Jola, Soninke, English

Mauritius

- 788 sq miles
  2,040 sq km
- 1,290,000
- Port Louis
- French Creole, Hindi, Urdu, Tamil, Chinese, English, French

Tunisia

- 63,170 sq miles
  163,610 sq km
- 10,300,000
- Tunis
- Arabic, French

Sierra Leone

- 27,699 sq miles
  71,740 sq km
- 5,700,000
- Freetown
- Mende, Temne, Krio, English

Equatorial Guinea

- 10,831 sq miles
  28,051 sq km
- 676,300
- Malabo
- Spanish, Fang, Bubi, French

Djibouti

- 23,200 sq km
  8,958 sq miles
- 864,200
- Djibouti City
- Somali, Afar, French, Arabic

Cape Verde

- 1,557 sq miles
  4,033 sq km
- 505,600
- Praia
- Portuguese Creole, Portuguese

São Tomé and Príncipe

- 372 sq miles
  964 sq km
- 162,800
- São Tomé
- Portuguese Creole, Portuguese

Malawi

- 45,747 sq miles
  118,484 sq km
- 5,300,000
- Lilongwe
- Chewa, Lomwe, Yao

Togo

- 21,925 sq miles
  56,785 sq km
- 6,620,000
- Lomé
- Ewe, Kabye, Gurma

Burundi

- 10,745 sq miles
  27,830 sq km
- 8,300,000
- Bujumbura
- Kirundi, French, Kiswahili

Swaziland

- 17,364 sq km
  6,704 sq miles
- 1,180,000
- Mbabane
- English, siSwati, isiZulu

Comoros

- 863 sq miles
  2,235 sq km
- 676,000
- Moroni
- Arabic, Comorian, French

Northwest Africa

FOUR COUNTRIES, plus the disputed area of Western Sahara, make up this part of Africa. Algeria, Libya, and Tunisia have rich supplies of oil and natural gas that boost their economies. Morocco relies on tourism, phosphates used for chemicals and fertilizer, and agriculture. In the fertile valleys of the Atlas Mountains, farmers grow grapes, citrus fruit, dates, and olives. The area also attracts tourists to its colorful markets, historical sites, and sandy beaches. The Sahara Desert dominates the region, especially in Algeria and Libya.

SUN AND SEA
Many tourists visit Tunisia and Morocco each year to enjoy the warm climate and sandy beaches. Tourism provides jobs for the local people and brings much-needed income.

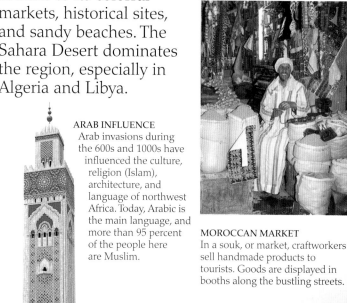

ARAB INFLUENCE
Arab invasions during the 600s and 1000s have influenced the culture, religion (Islam), architecture, and language of northwest Africa. Today, Arabic is the main language, and more than 95 percent of the people here are Muslim.

MOROCCAN MARKET
In a souk, or market, craftworkers sell handmade products to tourists. Goods are displayed in booths along the bustling streets.

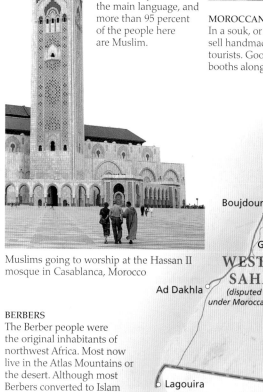

Muslims going to worship at the Hassan II mosque in Casablanca, Morocco

BERBERS
The Berber people were the original inhabitants of northwest Africa. Most now live in the Atlas Mountains or the desert. Although most Berbers converted to Islam when the Arabs arrived, they kept their own language and way of life. In 2001, Algeria recognized Berber (Tamazight) as an official language.

Berber woman working the land in the Atlas Mountains

Map labels

ATLANTIC OCEAN

Strait of Gibraltar
GIBRALTAR (to U.K.)
Tizi Ouzou
ALGIERS (ALGER)
Chlef
Ceuta (to Spain)
Tangier
Tetouan
Melilla (to Spain)
Oran
Blida
Ksar-el-Kebir
Chefchaouen
Mostaganem
Salé
Kénitra
Fès
Oujda
Sidi Bel Abbès
RABAT
Casablanca
Mohammedia
Jerada
Tlemcen
Djelfa
El-Jadida
Hauts Plateaux
Chott ech Chergui
Khouribga
Beni-Mellal
Atlas Saharien
Laghouat
Safi
Atlas Mountains
Essaouira
Marrakech
Er-Rachidia
Figuig
Ghardaïa
MOROCCO
Ouarzazate
Béchar
Agadir
Grand Erg Occidental
Tiznit
El Goléa
Hamada du Dra
A L G E R[IA]
Tan-Tan
Plateau du Tademaït
LAÂYOUNE
Tindouf
Adrar
I-n-Salah
Smara
El Mahbas
Boujdour
Bou Craa
Erg Iguîdi
Reggane
Galtat-Zemmour
MAURITANIA
WESTERN SAHARA
(disputed territory under Moroccan occupation)
Ad Dakhla
Erg Chech
S[ahara]
Tropic of Cancer
Tanezrouft
Lagouira
M A L I

DATE PALMS

Dates are an important crop for Algeria and Tunisia. Date palms are often grown at oases, where water lies close to the surface of the desert. Here, the clusters of dates are shown ripening beneath polyethylene. Leaves from the trees can be used for thatch and the trunk is cut for timber.

ANCIENT RUINS

Phoenicians, Romans, and Greeks from ancient times have all left their marks on this part of Africa. Today, tourists come to admire the historical sites along the coast. These ruins of Carthage, near Tunis, date from 146 BCE, when Romans laid waste to this city. The Romans went on to control all of the north African coast.

The pits from dates can be roasted and ground to make a traditional date coffee.

Ruins of a Roman bath in Carthage

SURVIVAL IN THE SAHARA

The Sahara Desert covers almost one third of Africa and is an inhospitable place to live, with high daytime temperatures and freezing nights. The Tuareg are nomads and call the desert home. Traditionally, they raise camels for transportation and to provide meat, milk, and hides. Many Tuareg now live in mountain areas or dwell in cities.

Tuareg nomads in the Sahara carry salt to trade in markets

0 km 100 200

0 miles 100 200

Libyan oil field

LIBYAN OIL RESOURCES

The discovery of oil and gas in 1959 brought considerable wealth to Libya, and oil and gas currently make up 95 percent of the country's exports. As a result, Libya's cities have grown as people have moved from rural areas to find work in the oil industry. Some of the money from oil is spent on better health care and education for Libyans.

Map labels

Mediterranean Sea
Bizerte
Annaba
Carthage
TUNIS
étif
Constantine
Sousse
Batna
Kairouan
Kasserine
Mahdia
iskra
Chott Melghir
Gafsa
Sfax
Tozeur
Golfe de Gabès
Chott el Jerid
Gabès
Île de Jerba
TRIPOLI (ṬARĀBULUS)
Al Baydā'
Darnah
El Oued
Médenine
Zuwārah
Al Marj
Ṭubruq
Touggourt
TUNISIA
Az Zāwiyah
Al Khums
Benghazi (Banghāzī)
Al Jabal al Akhdar
Ouargla
Yafran
Gharyān
Miṣrātah
Gulf of Sirte (Khalīj Surt)
Cyrenaica
Nālūt
Ajdābiyā
Surt
Wādī al Ḥamīm
Grand Erg Oriental
Marsā al Burayqah
Al Jaghbūb
Tripolitania
Marādah
Jālū
A
Waddān
Great Sand Sea
LIBYA
Bordj Omar Driss
Birāk
Tiguentourine
Sabhā
Awbārī
Fezzan
Ramlat Rabyānah
Libyan
Tassili-n-Ajjer
Zawīlah
Al 'Uwaynāt
Al Kufrah
Desert
Tropic of Cancer
h
a
r
a
Djanet
Idhán Murzuq
Ahaggar
Tahat 9573ft (2918m)
Picco Bette 7500ft (2286m)
Tamanrasset
CHAD
NIGER
SUDAN
EGYPT
37

Northeast Africa

THIS REGION, KNOWN AS the Horn of Africa, contains the oldest civilizations in the continent and some of its poorest countries. The borders that divide the countries today were mostly created by colonial rulers in the last 100 years. Pastoral nomads with their herds of animals often cross these borders in search of pastures. Most people still live in the countryside and farm the land, but many people now live in cities. Tourism and agriculture are important sources of income for Egypt and Kenya, two of the richest and fastest-growing countries in the region. Elsewhere, tribal rivalries and disputes over land and resources have sometimes erupted into full-scale wars and these, together with droughts and poverty, have blighted the lives of millions of people in the region.

NILE RIVER
The Nile is the world's longest river. It flows north from Burundi running along the Tanzania–Rwanda border, then through Uganda, Sudan, and Egypt to the coast. Most of Egypt's population lives around the valley and delta of the Nile, which provides the region's water. The river also provides irrigation for local crops, such as cotton.

SUEZ CANAL
The Suez Canal, opened in 1869, is one of the world's longest and most important artificial waterways. It links the Mediterranean Sea with the Gulf of Suez and the Red Sea, providing a crucial shortcut from Europe to India and east Asia. The tolls from the canal are a large source of income for Egypt.

LOSING FARMLAND
As the population grows in Ethiopia, forests are cut down for firewood or to cultivate new areas for food crops. The soil, no longer held firm by the trees, is easily blown or washed away, and valuable farmland is lost.

Plowing fields in Ethiopia

ABU SIMBEL
Tourists come to Egypt to see the pyramids in Giza and the temples along the Nile River, such as these two built in Abu Simbel, south of Aswan. Tourism brings in money to preserve these historical sites.

Map labels

Mediterranean Sea

Red Sea

Gulf of Aden

Danakil Desert

ERITREA — ASMARA

DJIBOUTI

Massawa, Zula, Teseney, Mek'ele, Mayc'ew, Lalibela, Gonder, Tana Hayk', Blue Nile, Gedaref, Kassala, Khashm el Girba, Haiya, Suakin, Tokar, Port Sudan, Akeb, Obock, Caluula

SUDAN — KHARTOUM

Omdurman, Wad Medani, El Obeid, Sennar, Shendi, Ed Damer, Atbara, Abu Hamed, Shereik, Merowe, Argo, Dongola, Ed Debba, Delgo, Akasha, Wadi Halfa, Sodiri, Umm Ruwaba, Er Rahad

Nubian Desert

Wadi Howar, Wadi Muqaddam, Wadi Oko

Darfur — Umm Buru, Kebkabiya, El Fasher, Nyala, El Geneina

CHAD

LIBYA

EGYPT

CAIRO, Alexandria, Port Said, Dumyât, Al Ismā'īlīyah, Suez, Az Zagāzīg, Giza, Beni Suef, Al Minya, Mallawī, Asyūt, Sawhāj, Akhmim, Qinā, Luxor, Isnā, Idfū, Aswān, Al 'Alamayn, Sidi Barāni, Siwah, Bawiti, Qasr Faráfra, El Khárga

Sinai, Gebel Mûsa 7497ft (2285m)

Gulf of Suez, Suez Canal, Nile Delta, Hurghada

Saharā al Gharbiya (Western Desert), Gilf Kebir Plateau

Great Sand Sea

Qattara Depression −436ft (−133m)

Jabal al 'Uwaynāt 6257ft (1907m)

Lake Nasser, Aswan Dam

(administered by Egypt), (administered by Sudan)

El'Atrun

Tropic of Cancer

Water makes up almost one fifth of the surface area of Uganda.

RELIGIOUS BELIEFS
The Ethiopian Orthodox Tewahedo Church has existed since the 300s CE. It is a branch of the Coptic Church and mixes Christian beliefs, such as Catholic saints, with some traditional African spiritual beliefs.

Coptic cross

TEA IN KENYA
Kenya is an important world producer of tea, which is grown on plantations in the highland areas (such as this one below). High rainfall here ensures good crops. Coffee is also a valuable export.

Kenyan workers carefully select tea leaves for picking.

CAIRO
The largest city in Africa is Cairo, the capital of Egypt, with a population of more than 15 million. Here, Arab, African, and European influences exist alongside more traditional Egyptian customs.

Busy street bazaar in Cairo

SUDANESE DINKA
There are more than 500 different tribes in Sudan, who speak more than 100 languages and dialects. Like many tribal people here, the Dinka are nomadic—their cattle graze on the plains east of the Nile. Cattle are central to their lives—young Dinka men officially become adults with an initiation ceremony in which they are given an ox of their own.

Young Dinka man

MOUNTAIN GORILLAS
The Volcanoes National Park in Rwanda is one of the few places where you can still see a mountain gorilla (right) in the wild. These animals are threatened with extinction because of poachers and the destruction of their habitat. Tanzania and Kenya also have many important game reserves that preserve the wildlife of the savanna.

0 km   100   200   300   400
0 miles   100   200   400

West Africa

0 km 100   200   300   400
0 miles   100   200   300   400

Dramatically different climates and landscapes influence life in west Africa. In the hot, dry north, it is difficult to grow crops. Only oases in the Sahara Desert and seasonal rainfall in the Sahel make crop-growing possible. To the south, the climate is warm and wet, and crops such as cocoa and coffee are grown on large plantations. This region also has many valuable minerals. Despite these rich resources, most countries are poor. Since independence from colonial powers, there has been a lot of political unrest, often sparked by poverty and tribal rivalries in the region. West Africa is also divided by religion, with Islam dominant in the north and Christianity in the south.

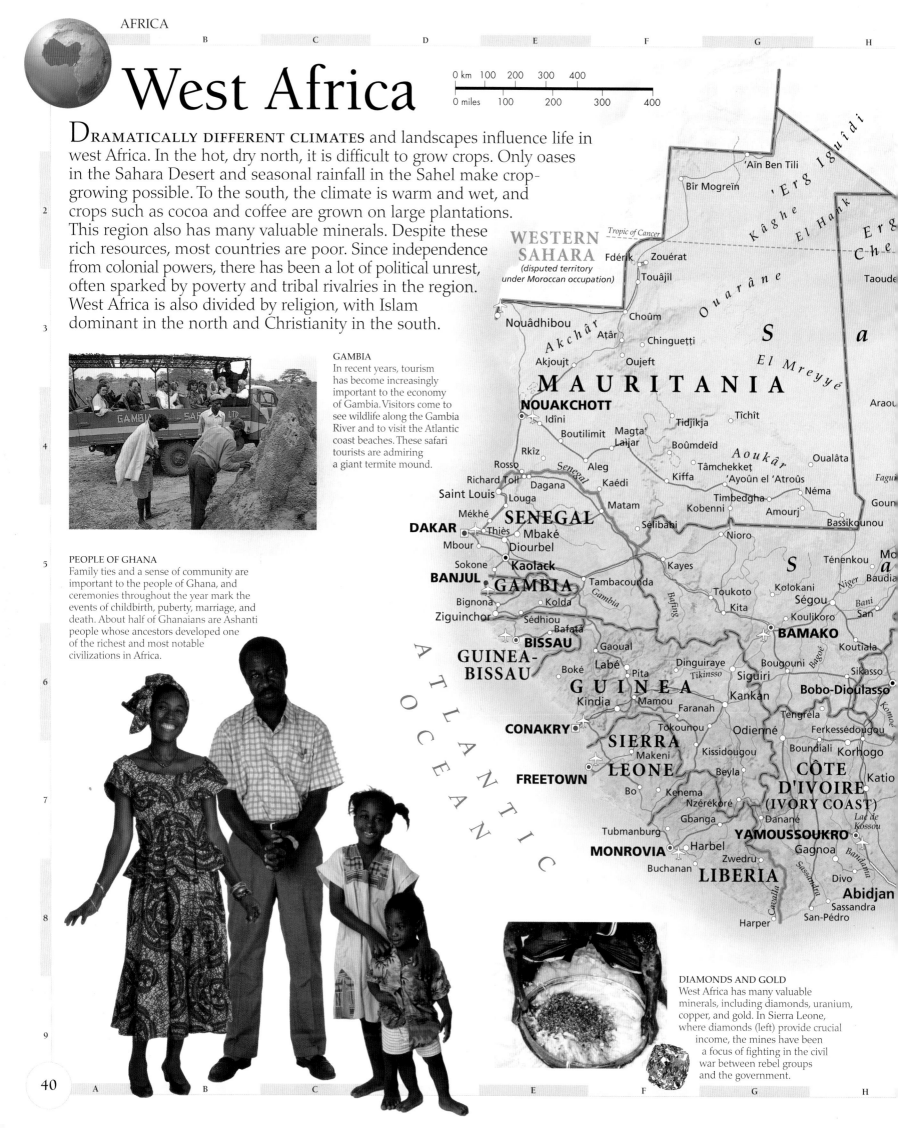

GAMBIA
In recent years, tourism has become increasingly important to the economy of Gambia. Visitors come to see wildlife along the Gambia River and to visit the Atlantic coast beaches. These safari tourists are admiring a giant termite mound.

PEOPLE OF GHANA
Family ties and a sense of community are important to the people of Ghana, and ceremonies throughout the year mark the events of childbirth, puberty, marriage, and death. About half of Ghanaians are Ashanti people whose ancestors developed one of the richest and most notable civilizations in Africa.

DIAMONDS AND GOLD
West Africa has many valuable minerals, including diamonds, uranium, copper, and gold. In Sierra Leone, where diamonds (left) provide crucial income, the mines have been a focus of fighting in the civil war between rebel groups and the government.

WESTERN SAHARA
(disputed territory under Moroccan occupation)

Tropic of Cancer

'Aïn Ben Tili
Bîr Mogreïn
'Erg Iguîdi
Kâghe
El Hank
Erg
Che

Fdérik   Zouérat
Touâjîl
Taoude

Nouâdhibou   Choûm
Ouarâne
S   a

Akchâr   Aṭâr   Chinguetti
Akjoujt   Oujeft
El Mreyyé
Arao

MAURITANIA
NOUAKCHOTT
Idîni
Tîchît
Tidjîkja
Boutilimit   Magta'   Lajjar   Boûmdeïd   Âoukâr   Oualâta
Rkîz
Rosso   Aleg   Tâmchekket   'Ayoûn el 'Atroûs   Fagui
Richard Toll   Dagana   Kaédi   Kiffa   Néma   Goun
Saint Louis   Louga   Matam   Timbedgha   Bassikounou
Mékhé   SENEGAL   Kobenni   Amourj
DAKAR   Thiès   Mbaké   Sélibâbi   Nioro
Mbour   Diourbel   Kayes   S   a
Sokone   Kaolack   Ténenkou   Mo
BANJUL   GAMBIA   Tambacounda   Kolokani   Niger   Baudia
Bignona   Kolda   Toukoto   Ségou   Bani
Ziguinchor   Sédhiou   Kita   Koulikoro   San
Bafaṭá   BAMAKO   Koutiala
BISSAU   Gaoual   Bougouni   Bagoé   Sikasso
GUINEA-   Boké   Labé   Dinguiraye   Siguiri   Bobo-Dioulasso
BISSAU   Pita   Tikinsso   Kankan   Komoé
GUINEA   Mamou   Faranah   Tengréla   Ferkessédougou
CONAKRY   Kindia   Tokounou   Odienné   Boundiali   Korhogo
SIERRA   Makeni   Kissidougou   CÔTE
FREETOWN   LEONE   Beyla   D'IVOIRE   Katio
Bo   Kenema   (IVORY COAST)
Nzérékoré   Danané   Lac de Kossou
Gbanga   Gagnoa   Bandama
Tubmanburg   YAMOUSSOUKRO
MONROVIA   Harbel   Divo
Zwedru   Sassandra   Abidjan
Buchanan   LIBERIA   Sassandra
Harper   San-Pédro   Cavalla

ATLANTIC OCEAN

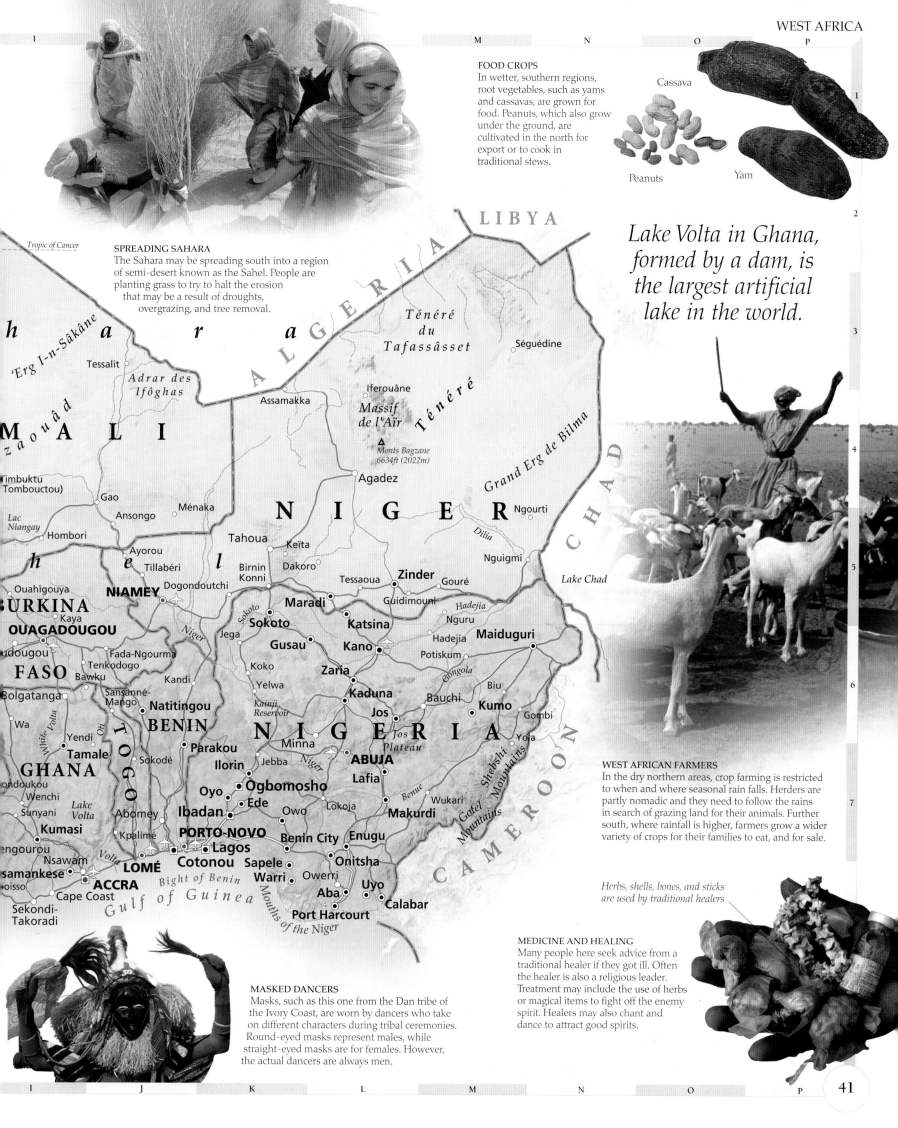

FOOD CROPS
In wetter, southern regions, root vegetables, such as yams and cassavas, are grown for food. Peanuts, which also grow under the ground, are cultivated in the north for export or to cook in traditional stews.

Cassava

Peanuts

Yam

SPREADING SAHARA
The Sahara may be spreading south into a region of semi-desert known as the Sahel. People are planting grass to try to halt the erosion that may be a result of droughts, overgrazing, and tree removal.

Lake Volta in Ghana, formed by a dam, is the largest artificial lake in the world.

WEST AFRICAN FARMERS
In the dry northern areas, crop farming is restricted to when and where seasonal rain falls. Herders are partly nomadic and they need to follow the rains in search of grazing land for their animals. Further south, where rainfall is higher, farmers grow a wider variety of crops for their families to eat, and for sale.

Herbs, shells, bones, and sticks are used by traditional healers

MEDICINE AND HEALING
Many people here seek advice from a traditional healer if they got ill. Often the healer is also a religious leader. Treatment may include the use of herbs or magical items to fight off the enemy spirit. Healers may also chant and dance to attract good spirits.

MASKED DANCERS
Masks, such as this one from the Dan tribe of the Ivory Coast, are worn by dancers who take on different characters during tribal ceremonies. Round-eyed masks represent males, while straight-eyed masks are for females. However, the actual dancers are always men.

41

Central Africa

ALL EIGHT COUNTRIES IN central Africa were European colonies with a painful history of slavery. Since the 1960s, independence has brought them mixed success. Rich mineral deposits and the discovery of offshore oil reserves have provided income for Cameroon, Congo, and Gabon, while civil war and repressive governments have damaged other countries in the region. These include Chad and the Central African Republic, two of the world's poorest countries.

Although the north is mostly arid, Africa's largest tropical rainforest dominates the south, with the powerful Congo River linking the interior with the coast. The tiny, volcanic country of São Tomé and Príncipe lies off the coast of Gabon.

RELIGIOUS BELIEFS
Although Christianity is the main religion here, many people also follow traditional beliefs. These suggest that natural objects, such as mountains and rivers, have spirits. Masks, like this Bambuku head, are sometimes used to scare off evil spirits.

VILLAGE LIFE
Most people in rural areas live in villages or small towns. Some grow crops, such as cotton or cassava, for sale, but many exist by growing food just for their family.

Mud-brick home

FISHING IN LAKE CHAD
Lake Chad is an important source of food, but it is shrinking at an alarming rate. A shallow lake, it is now only about 6.5–13 ft (2–4 m) deep on average. Its surface area has also reduced, due to droughts and the demand for water to irrigate the land.

PEOPLE OF CHAD
With almost half the country lying in the arid Sahara Desert, more than 70 percent of Chadians work on farmland near the Chari River in the south. Across Chad there are large numbers of ethnic groups, speaking more than 100 languages. Women here live an average of only 50 years and have 6.2 children.

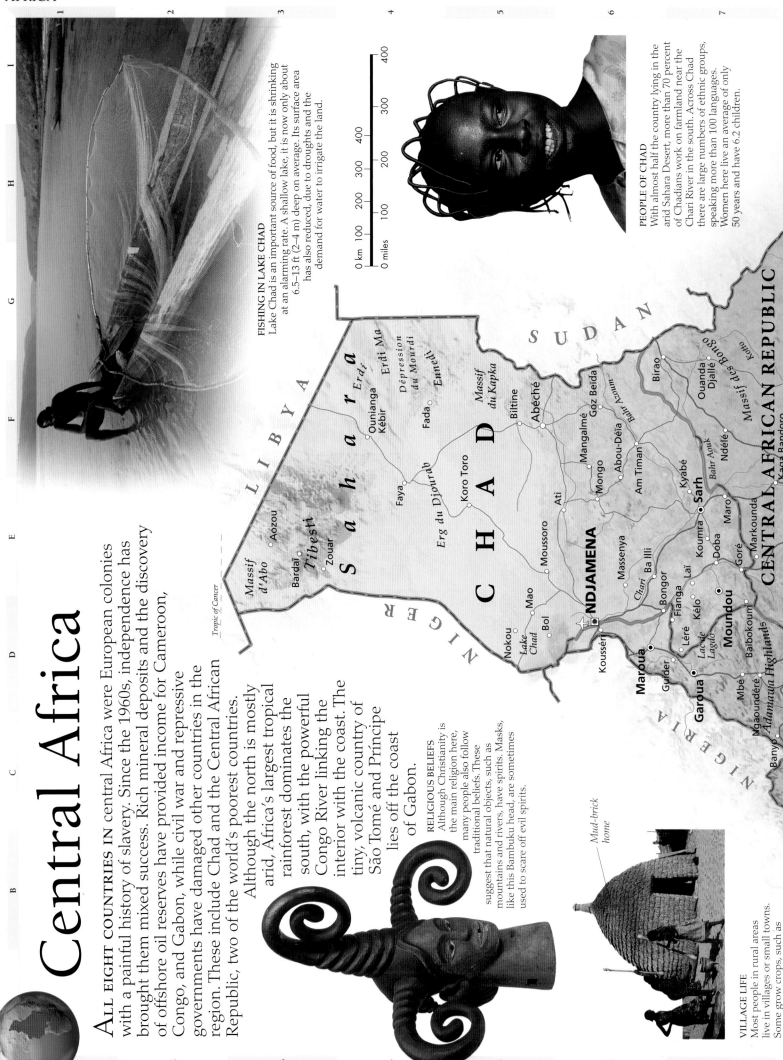

0 km 100   200   300   400
0 miles   100   200   300   400

SUDAN

LIBYA

NIGER

NIGERIA

CHAD

CENTRAL AFRICAN REPUBLIC

CAMEROON

ANGOLA

Tropic of Cancer

S a h a r a

Erdi

Erdi Ma

Dépression du Mourdi

Ennedi

Tibesti

Massif d'Abo

Aozou

Bardaï

Zouar

Massif du Kapka

Biltine

Abéché

Ounianga Kébir

Fada

Faya

Koro Toro

Erg du Djourab

Goz Beida

Mangalmé

Mongo

Abou-Déïa

Am Timan

Bahr Azoum

Birao

Ouanda Djallé

Massif des Bongo

Komo

Ati

Moussoro

Kyabé

Sarh

Bahr Aouk

Ndélé

Bria

Ippy

Bambari

Alindao

Dembia

Bangassou

Djéma

Banu

Obo

Nokou

Lake Chad

Bol

Mao

Massenya

Ba Illi

Bongor

Fianga

Laï

Goré

Doba

Koumra

Maro

Markounda

Bossangoa

Kaga Bandoro

Dékoa

Sibut

Grimari

Bakala

Damara

(Oubangui)

Ubangi

MOUNDOU

Kélo

Léré

Lac de Lagdo

Baïbokoum

Bossembélé

Bouar

Baoro

Bossangoa

NDJAMENA

Koussér

Maroua

Guider

Garoua

Mbé

Ngaoundéré

Adamawa Highlands

Djérem

Bertoua

Berbérati

Banyo

Foumban

Bafoussam

Bamenda

Nkongsamba

Kumba

Douala

Chari

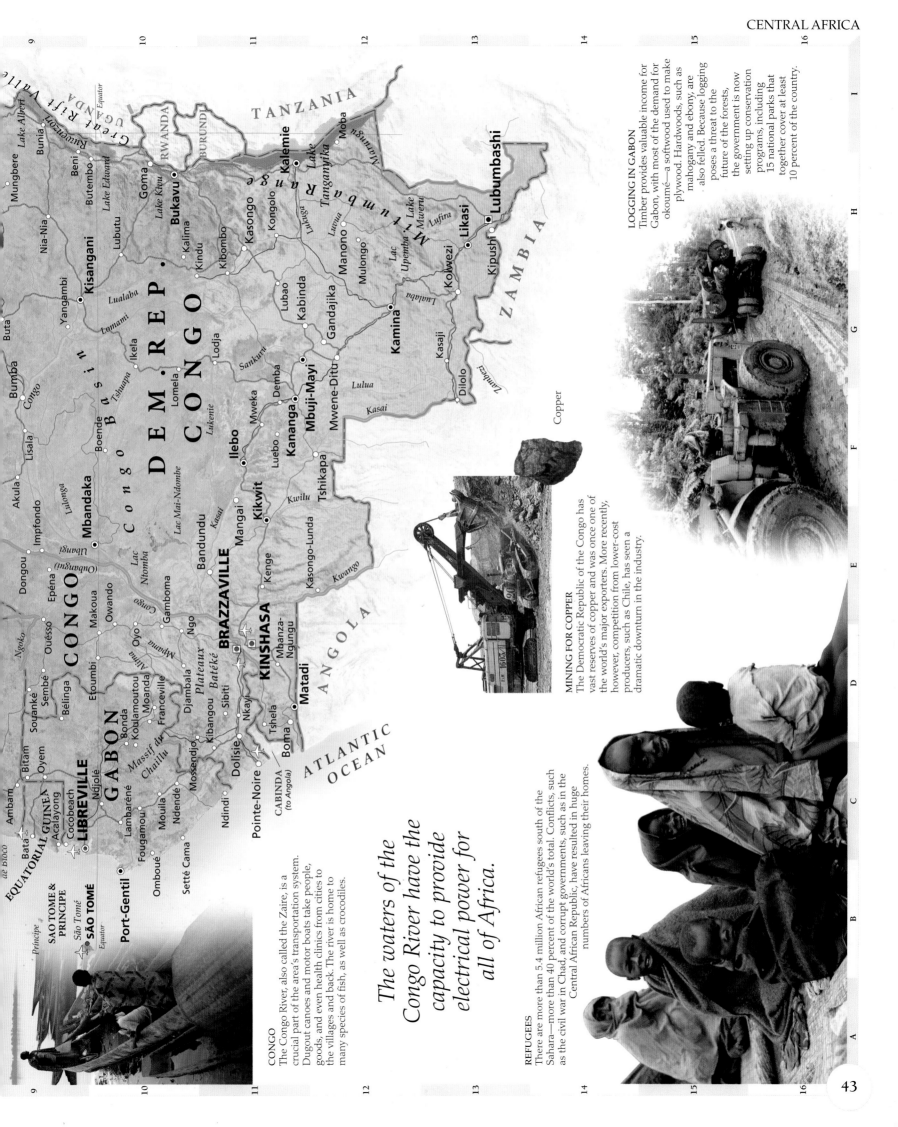

Map labels

TANZANIA

UGANDA

RWANDA

BURUNDI

ZAMBIA

ANGOLA

CABINDA (to Angola)

GABON

CONGO

DEM. REP. CONGO

EQUATORIAL GUINEA

SAO TOME & PRINCIPE

ATLANTIC OCEAN

Great Rift Valley

Ruwenzori

Lake Albert

Lake Edward

Lake Kivu

Lake Tanganyika

Lake Mweru

Lac Upemba

Lake Rukwa

Mitumba Range

Mungbere, Bunia, Beni, Butembo, Nia-Nia, Goma, Bukavu, Kalemie, Moba, Lubutu, Kisangani, Kalima, Kindu, Kongolo, Kasongo, Kongolo, Manono, Mulongo, Likasi, Kolwezi, Lubumbashi, Kipushi

Yangambi, Buta, Bumba, Lisala, Akula, Lualaba, Lomami, Ikela, Lomela, Lodja, Demba, Kamina, Kasaji, Dilolo

Mbandaka, Boende, Lukenie, Mangai, Ilebo, Mweka, Kananga, Mbuji-Mayi, Mwene-Ditu, Gandajika, Kabinda, Lubao

Impfondo, Dongou, Epéna, Makoua, Owando, Oyo, Bandundu, Kikwit, Kenge, Kwilu, Tshikapa, Luebo, Kasongo-Lunda

Ouésso, Sembé, Souanké, Etoumbi, Gambona, Ngo, Djambala, Sibiti, Nkayi, Mbanza-Ngungu, KINSHASA, BRAZZAVILLE, Matadi, Boma, Dolisie, Pointe-Noire, Tshela

Bitam, Oyem, Bélinga, Koulamoutou, Moanda, Franceville, Mouila, Lambaréné, Ndjolé, LIBREVILLE, Cocobeach, Bata, Ambam, Acalayong

Port-Gentil, Omboué, Fougamou, Ndendé, Mossendjo, Kibangou, Ndindi, Setté Cama

SÃO TOMÉ, São Tomé, Príncipe, Equator

Congo, Lualaba, Lomami, Sankuru, Kasai, Lulua, Zambezi, Lukuga, Luvua, Aufira, Marungu, Kwango, Kwilu, Ntomba, Lac Mai-Ndombe, Lac Tumba, Lac Ntomba, Ubangi, Sangha, Ngoko, Ivindo, Ogooué (Ogowe), Massif du Chaillu, Plateaux Batéké

CONGO
The Congo River, also called the Zaire, is a crucial part of the area's transportation system. Dugout canoes and motor boats take people, goods, and even health clinics from cities to the villages and back. The river is home to many species of fish, as well as crocodiles.

The waters of the Congo River have the capacity to provide electrical power for all of Africa.

REFUGEES
There are more than 5.4 million African refugees south of the Sahara—more than 40 percent of the world's total. Conflicts, such as the civil war in Chad, and corrupt governments, such as in the Central African Republic, have resulted in huge numbers of Africans leaving their homes.

MINING FOR COPPER
The Democratic Republic of the Congo has vast reserves of copper and was once one of the world's major exporters. More recently, however, competition from lower-cost producers, such as Chile, has seen a dramatic downturn in the industry.

Copper

LOGGING IN GABON
Timber provides valuable income for Gabon, with most of the demand for okoumé—a softwood used to make plywood. Hardwoods, such as mahogany and ebony, are also felled. Because logging poses a threat to the future of the forests, the government is now setting up conservation programs, including 15 national parks that together cover at least 10 percent of the country.

Southern Africa

FROM THE DRAMATIC Namib and Kalahari deserts in the west to the tropical forests in the north, southern Africa is a region of contrasts. Oil, diamonds, gold, and other precious metals are all mined here. There are huge inland plains that are home to a variety of wildlife and large areas devoted to agriculture. But flooding and droughts, together with civil unrest, have hampered development so that, despite an abundance of natural resources, many countries remain poor.

SAN BUSHMEN
One of the few groups of hunter-gatherers left in Africa, the San people roam the Kalahari Desert. Also known as Bush people, many San are now changing to a more settled life, often working on cattle ranches.

San hunter using a poison-tipped arrow

The Okavango River does not run out to the ocean like most rivers, but runs inland into the Kalahari Desert.

Tunnels transport water between dams

Dams are marked in black

LESOTHO
Water is a valuable resource in southern Africa, and Lesotho makes good use of its mountainous land and numerous rivers. The Highlands Water Project uses dams and tunnels to transport water to neighboring South Africa.

JOHANNESBURG, SOUTH AFRICA
With a population of more than 7.5 million, Johannesburg is the fourth-largest city in Africa after Cairo, Lagos, and Kinshasa. Many people have moved here from the surrounding countryside in search of work.

GOLD MINING
Gold, first discovered near Johannesburg in 1886, brought a great deal of wealth to the region. South Africa currently produces about 12 percent of the world's gold.

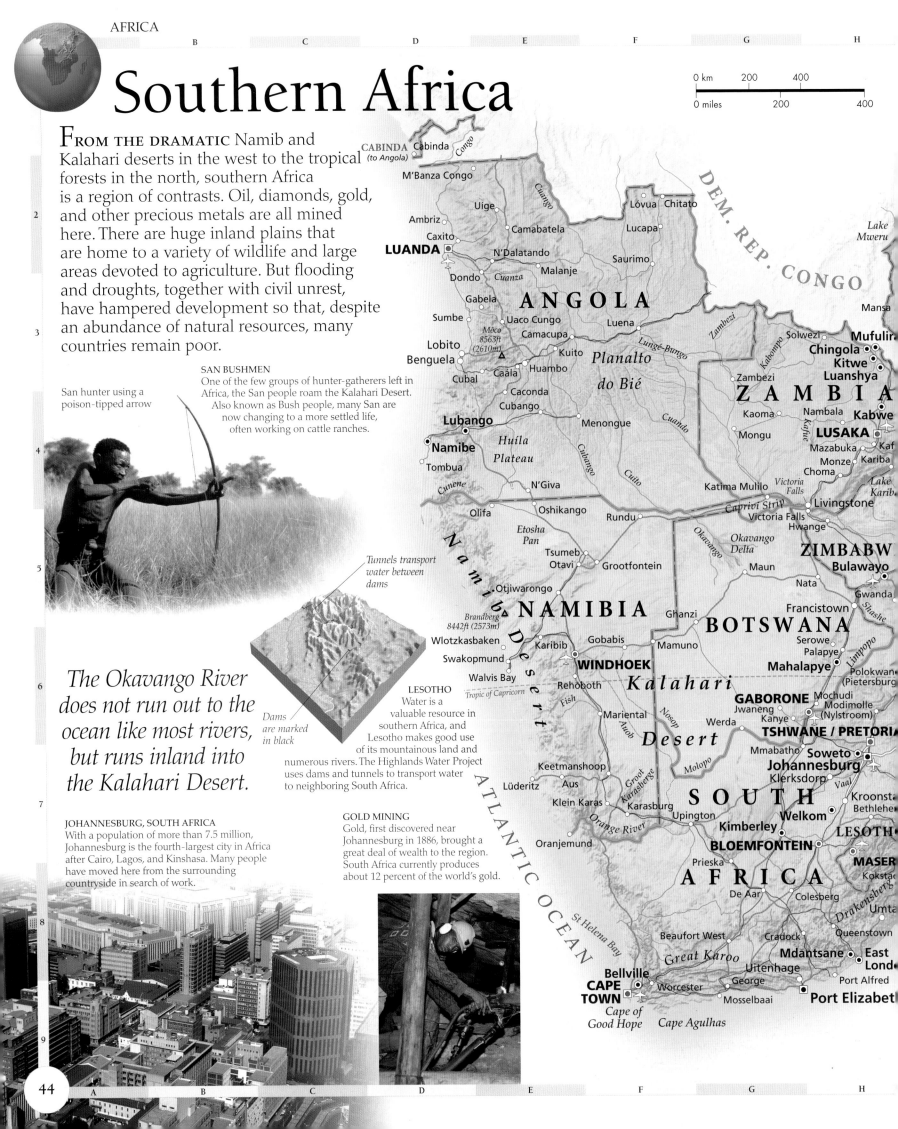

0 km   200   400
0 miles   200   400

CABINDA (to Angola) — Cabinda — Congo
M'Banza Congo
Uíge — Lóvua — Chitato
Ambriz — Camabatela — Lucapa
Caxito — N'Dalatando — Saurimo
LUANDA — Mansa
Dondo — *Cuanza* — Malanje
Gabela — Cuango
Sumbe — Uaco Cungo — Luena — Solwezi — **Mufulir**
Lobito — Môco 8563ft (2610m) — Camacupa — **Chingola**
Benguela — Kuito — *Planalto do Bié* — Zambezi — **Kitwe**
Cubal — Caála — Huambo — **Luanshya**
Caconda — **Z A M B I A**
Cubango — Kaoma — Nambala — **Kabwe**
Lubango — Menongue — Mongu — **LUSAKA**
Huíla Plateau — *Cuando* — Mazabuka — Kaf
Namibe — Monze — Kariba
Tombua — Katima Mulilo — *Victoria Falls* — Choma
Cunene — N'Giva — *Victoria Falls* — *Lake Karib*
Olifa — Oshikango — Rundu — Victoria Falls — **Livingstone**
Etosha Pan — *Caprivi Strip* — Hwange
Tsumeb — *Okavango Delta* — **ZIMBABW**
Otavi — Grootfontein — Maun — **Bulawayo**
Otjiwarongo — Nata — Gwanda
Brandberg 8442ft (2573m) — **N A M I B I A** — Ghanzi — Francistown — *Shashe*
Wlotzkasbaken — Gobabis — **B O T S W A N A**
Karibib — Mamuno — Serowe
Swakopmund — **WINDHOEK** — Palapye — *Limpopo*
Walvis Bay — Rehoboth — *Kalahari* — **Mahalapye** — Polokwan (Pietersburg)
Tropic of Capricorn — *Fish* — *Desert* — **GABORONE** — Mochudi Modimolle (Nylstroom)
Mariental — Jwaneng — Kanye — **TSHWANE / PRETORI**
Keetmanshoop — *Nosop* — Werda — Mmabatho — **Soweto**
Auob — **Johannesburg**
Lüderitz — Aus — *Groot Karasberge* — *Molopo* — Klerksdorp
Klein Karas — Karasburg — **S O U T H** — Kroonsta
Upington — Bethlehe
Oranjemund — *Orange River* — Welkom
Kimberley — **LESOTH**
BLOEMFONTEIN — **MASER**
Prieska — **A F R I C A** — Kokstad
De Aar — Colesberg — *Drakensberg* — Umta
Beaufort West — Cradock — Queenstown
Great Karoo — **Mdantsane** — East Lond
Bellville — Uitenhage — George — Port Alfred
CAPE TOWN — Worcester — *St Helena Bay* — Mosselbaai — **Port Elizabet**
Cape of Good Hope — *Cape Agulhas*
ATLANTIC OCEAN
DEM. REP. CONGO
Lake Mweru

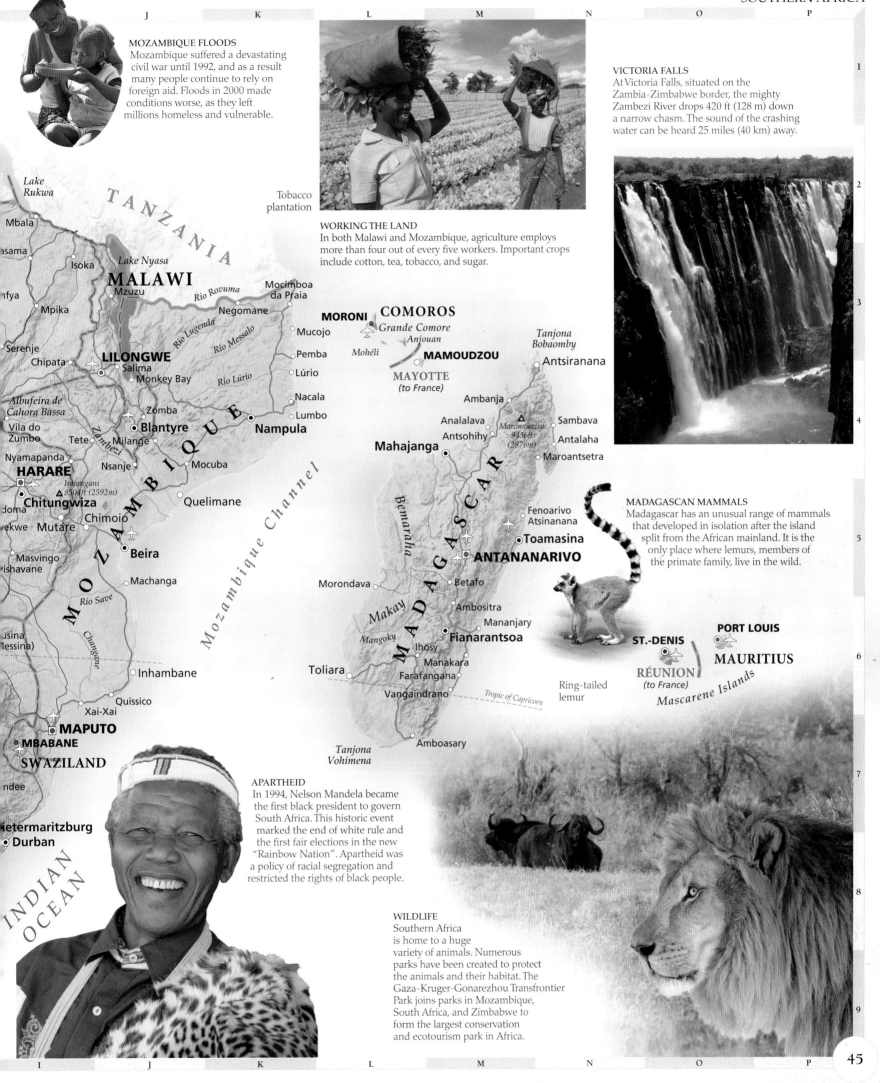

MOZAMBIQUE FLOODS
Mozambique suffered a devastating civil war until 1992, and as a result many people continue to rely on foreign aid. Floods in 2000 made conditions worse, as they left millions homeless and vulnerable.

Tobacco plantation

WORKING THE LAND
In both Malawi and Mozambique, agriculture employs more than four out of every five workers. Important crops include cotton, tea, tobacco, and sugar.

VICTORIA FALLS
At Victoria Falls, situated on the Zambia-Zimbabwe border, the mighty Zambezi River drops 420 ft (128 m) down a narrow chasm. The sound of the crashing water can be heard 25 miles (40 km) away.

MADAGASCAN MAMMALS
Madagascar has an unusual range of mammals that developed in isolation after the island split from the African mainland. It is the only place where lemurs, members of the primate family, live in the wild.

Ring-tailed lemur

APARTHEID
In 1994, Nelson Mandela became the first black president to govern South Africa. This historic event marked the end of white rule and the first fair elections in the new "Rainbow Nation". Apartheid was a policy of racial segregation and restricted the rights of black people.

WILDLIFE
Southern Africa is home to a huge variety of animals. Numerous parks have been created to protect the animals and their habitat. The Gaza-Kruger-Gonarezhou Transfrontier Park joins parks in Mozambique, South Africa, and Zimbabwe to form the largest conservation and ecotourism park in Africa.

45

EUROPE

Separated from Asia by the ridge of the Ural Mountains, Europe is a continent of very different nations, listed below in order of their land area. Each nation has its own language and culture, but they share a 2,000-year-old history of civilization that has inspired some of the world's greatest political ideas, works of art, and innovations in technology.

Russian Federation
🏳 6,601,668 sq miles
17,098,242 sq km
👤 141,000,000
🏛 Moscow
💬 Russian, Tatar, Ukrainian, Chuvash, various other national languages

Germany
🏳 137,847 sq miles
357,022 sq km
👤 82,200,000
🏛 Berlin
💬 German, Turkish

United Kingdom
🏳 94,058 sq miles
243,610 sq km
👤 61,600,000
🏛 London
💬 English, Welsh, Scottish Gaelic, Irish Gaelic

Iceland
🏳 39,769 sq miles
103,000 sq km
👤 322,700
🏛 Reykjavík
💬 Icelandic

Serbia
🏳 29,913 sq miles
77,474 sq km
👤 7,750,000
🏛 Belgrade
💬 Serbian, Hungarian (Magyar)

Bosnia and Herzegovina
🏳 19,767 sq miles
51,197 sq km
👤 3,770,000
🏛 Sarajevo
💬 Bosnian, Serbian, Croatian

France
🏳 248,429 sq miles
643,427 sq km
👤 62,300,000
🏛 Paris
💬 French, Provençal, German, Breton, Catalan, Basque

Finland
🏳 130,559 sq miles
338,145 sq km
👤 5,330,000
🏛 Helsinki
💬 Finnish, Swedish, Sami

Romania
🏳 92,043 sq miles
238,391sq km
👤 21,300,000
🏛 Bucharest
💬 Romanian, Hungarian (Magyar), Romany, German

Hungary
🏳 35,918 sq miles
93,028 sq km
👤 9,990,000
🏛 Budapest
💬 Hungarian (Magyar)

Ireland
🏳 27,133 sq miles
70,273 sq km
👤 4,520,000
🏛 Dublin
💬 English, Irish Gaelic

Slovakia
🏳 18,933 sq miles
49,035 sq km
👤 5,410,000
🏛 Bratislava
💬 Slovak, Hungarian (Magyar), Czech

Ukraine
🏳 233,032 sq miles
603,550 sq km
👤 45,700,000
🏛 Kiev
💬 Ukrainian, Russian, Tatar

Norway
🏳 125,021 sq miles
323,802 sq km
👤 4,810,000
🏛 Oslo
💬 Norwegian (Bokmål, "book language," and Nynorsk," new Norsk"), Sami

Belarus
🏳 180,155 sq miles
207,600 sq km
👤 9,630,000
🏛 Minsk
💬 Belarussian, Russian

Portugal
🏳 35,556 sq miles
92,090 sq km
👤 10,700,000
🏛 Lisbon
💬 Portuguese

Lithuania
🏳 25,212 sq miles
65,300 sq km
👤 3,290,000
🏛 Vilnius
💬 Lithuanian, Russian

Estonia
🏳 17,463 sq miles
45,228 sq km
👤 1,340,000
🏛 Tallinn
💬 Estonian, Russian

Spain
🏳 195,124 sq miles
505,370 sq km
👤 44,900,000
🏛 Madrid
💬 Spanish, Catalan, Galician, Basque

Poland
🏳 120,728 sq miles
312,685 sq km
👤 38,100,000
🏛 Warsaw
💬 Polish

Greece
🏳 50,949 sq miles
131,957 sq km
👤 11,200,000
🏛 Athens
💬 Greek, Turkish, Macedonian, Albanian

Austria
🏳 32,383 sq miles
83,871 sq km
👤 8,360,000
🏛 Vienna
💬 German, Croatian, Slovenian, Hungarian (Magyar)

Latvia
🏳 24,938 sq miles
64,589 sq km
👤 2,250,000
🏛 Riga
💬 Latvian, Russian

Denmark
🏳 16,639 sq miles
43,094 sq km
👤 5,470,000
🏛 Copenhagen
💬 Danish

Sweden
🏳 173,860 sq miles
450,295 sq km
👤 9,250,000
🏛 Stockholm
💬 Swedish, Finnish, Sami

Italy
🏳 116,348 sq miles
301,340 sq km
👤 59,900,000
🏛 Rome
💬 Italian, German, French, Rhaeto-Romanic, Sardinian

Bulgaria
🏳 42,811 sq miles
110,879 sq km
👤 7,540,000
🏛 Sofia
💬 Bulgarian, Turkish, Romany

Czech Republic
🏳 30,451 sq miles
78,867 sq km
👤 10,400,000
🏛 Prague
💬 Czech, Slovak, Hungarian (Magyar)

Croatia
🏳 21,851 sq miles
56,594 sq km
👤 4,420,000
🏛 Zagreb
💬 Croatian

Netherlands
🏳 16,040 sq miles
41,543 sq km
👤 16,600,000
🏛 Amsterdam
💬 Dutch, Frisian

Switzerland
- 🗺 15,937 sq miles
  41,277 sq km
- 👤 7,570,000
- ⬛ Bern
- 💬 German, Swiss-German, French, Italian, Romansh

Slovenia
- 🗺 7,827 sq miles
  20,273 sq km
- 👤 2,020,000
- ⬛ Ljubljana
- 💬 Slovenian

Moldova
- 🗺 13,070 sq miles
  33,851 sq km
- 👤 3,600,000
- ⬛ Chisinau
- 💬 Moldovan, Ukrainian, Russian

Montenegro
- 🗺 5,333 sq miles
  13,812 sq km
- 👤 624,200
- ⬛ Podgorica
- 💬 Montenegrin, Serbian, Albanian, Bosnian, Croatian

Belgium
- 🗺 11,787 sq miles
  30,528 sq km
- 👤 10,600,000
- ⬛ Brussels
- 💬 Dutch, French, German

The cathedral dome of Santa Maria del Fiore dominates the skyline of Florence, Italy—one of the world's most beautiful cities.

Albania
- 🗺 11,100 sq miles
  28,748 sq km
- 👤 3,160,000
- ⬛ Tirana
- 💬 Albanian, Greek

Kosovo
- 🗺 4,203 sq miles
  10,887 sq km
- 👤 2,100,000
- ⬛ Pristina
- 💬 Albanian, Serbian, Bosnian, Gorani, Romany, Turkish

Luxembourg
- 🗺 998 sq miles
  2,586 sq km
- 👤 486,200
- ⬛ Luxembourg
- 💬 Luxembourgish, German, French

Malta
- 🗺 122 sq miles
  316 sq km
- 👤 408,700
- ⬛ Valletta
- 💬 Maltese, English

San Marino
- 🗺 24 sq miles
  61 sq km
- 👤 31,400
- ⬛ San Marino
- 💬 Italian

Vatican City
- 🗺 0.17 sq miles
  0.44 sq km
- 👤 800
- ⬛ Vatican City
- 💬 Italian, Latin

Macedonia
- 🗺 9,928 sq miles
  25,713 sq km
- 👤 2,040,000
- ⬛ Skopje
- 💬 Macedonian, Albanian, Turkish, Romany, Serbian

Cyprus
- 🗺 3,572 sq miles
  9,251 sq km
- 👤 871,000
- ⬛ Nicosia
- 💬 Greek, Turkish

Andorra
- 🗺 181 sq miles
  468 sq km
- 👤 82,200
- ⬛ Andorra la Vella
- 💬 Spanish, Catalan, French, Portuguese

Liechtenstein
- 🗺 62 sq miles
  160 sq km
- 👤 35,000
- ⬛ Vaduz
- 💬 German, Alemannisch dialect, Italian

Monaco
- 🗺 0.77 sq miles
  2 sq km
- 👤 32,000
- ⬛ Monaco
- 💬 French, Italian, Monégasque, English

Scandinavia and Finland

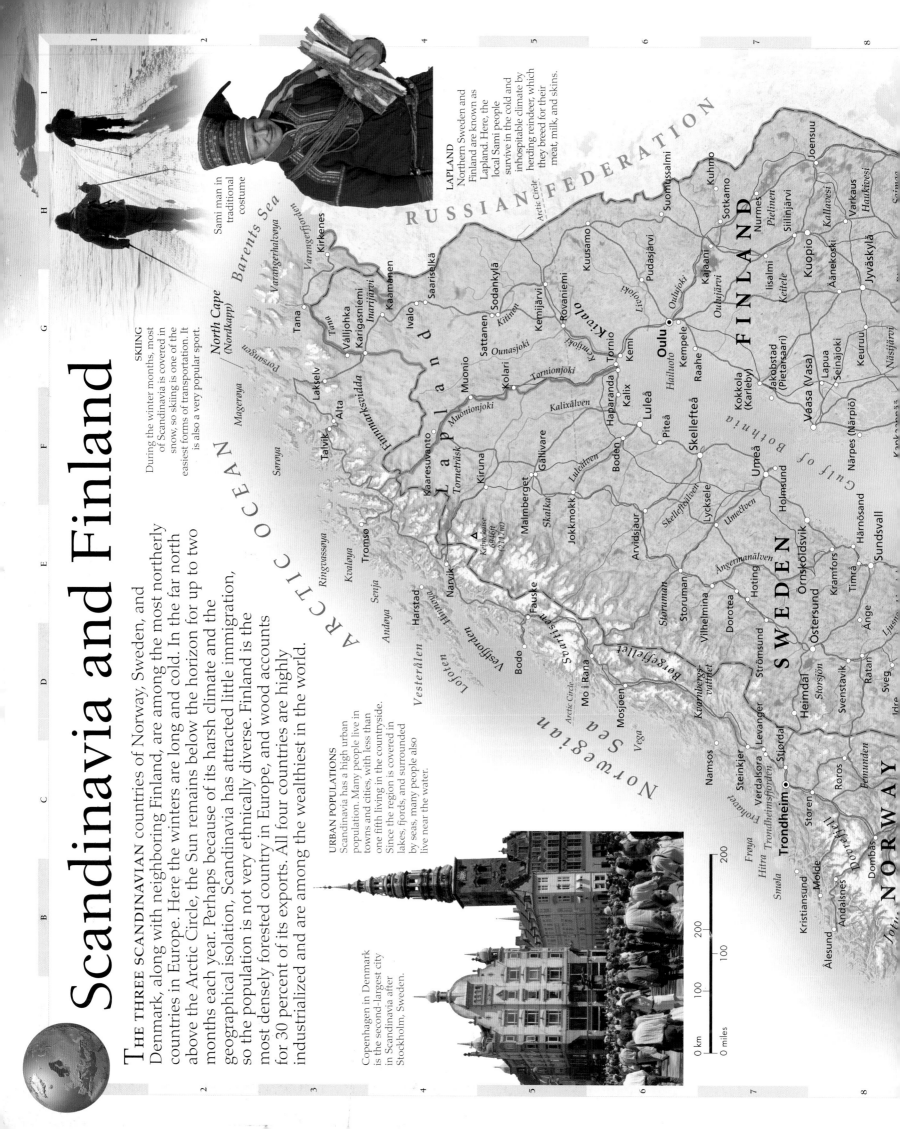

THE THREE SCANDINAVIAN countries of Norway, Sweden, and Denmark, along with neighboring Finland, are among the most northerly countries in Europe. Here the winters are long and cold. In the far north above the Arctic Circle, the Sun remains below the horizon for up to two months each year. Perhaps because of its harsh climate and the geographical isolation, Scandinavia has attracted little immigration, so the population is not very ethnically diverse. Finland is the most densely forested country in Europe, and wood accounts for 30 percent of its exports. All four countries are highly industrialized and are among the wealthiest in the world.

SKIING
During the winter months, most of Scandinavia is covered in snow, so skiing is one of the easiest forms of transportation. It is also a very popular sport.

LAPLAND
Northern Sweden and Finland are known as Lapland. Here, the local Sami people survive in the cold and inhospitable climate by herding reindeer, which they breed for their meat, milk, and skins.

Sami man in traditional costume

URBAN POPULATIONS
Scandinavia has a high urban population. Many people live in towns and cities, with less than one fifth living in the countryside. Since the region is covered in lakes, fjords, and surrounded by seas, many people also live near the water.

Copenhagen in Denmark is the second-largest city in Scandinavia after Stockholm, Sweden.

RUSSIAN FEDERATION

FINLAND

SWEDEN

NORWAY

Barents Sea

ARCTIC OCEAN

Norwegian Sea

Gulf of Bothnia

Lapland

Kiruna

Arctic Circle

North Cape (Nordkapp)

Kirkenes

Tana

Vardø

Váljohka

Karigasniemi

Kaamanen

Ivalo

Saariselkä

Sodankylä

Kittinen

Rovaniemi

Kuusamo

Pudasjärvi

Suomussalmi

Kuhmo

Sotkamo

Joensuu

Nurmes

Pielinen

Siilinjärvi

Varkaus

Haukivesi

Kallavesi

Kuopio

Äänekoski

Jyväskylä

Näsijärvi

Keuruu

Seinäjoki

Lapua

Vaasa (Vasa)

Närpes (Närpiö)

Jakobstad (Pietarsaari)

Kokkola (Karleby)

Raahe

Kempele

Oulu

Oulujärvi

Oulujoki

Kajaani

Iisalmi

Keitele

Lieksa

Kiantajärvi

Kiiminki

Kemijärvi

Kemijoki

Kemi

Tornio

Haparanda

Kalix

Luleå

Piteå

Skellefteå

Umeå

Holmsund

Härnösand

Sundsvall

Timrå

Kramfors

Örnsköldsvik

Hoting

Dorotea

Vilhelmina

Strömsund

Östersund

Ange

Ljusnan

Ratan

Sveg

Idre

Storsjön

Svenstavik

Storjord

Levanger

Verdalsøra

Steinkjer

Namsos

Trondheim

Stjørdal

Heimdal

Storen

Røros

Femunden

Dombås

Dovrefjell

Jotunheimen

Åndalsnes

Molde

Kristiansund

Smøla

Hitra

Frøya

Froan

Trondheimsfjorden

Mosjøen

Mo i Rana

Vega

Borgefjellet

Storuman

Sorsele

Arvidsjaur

Skellefteälven

Lycksele

Umeälven

Ångermanälven

Kvarnbergsvattnet

Jokkmokk

Gällivare

Malmberget

Skalka

Boden

Kalixälven

Luleälven

Kebnekaise 6946 ft (2117 m)

Kaaresuvanto

Torneträsk

Muonionjoki

Muonio

Kolari

Tornionjoki

Pajala

Karesuando

Narvik

Fauske

Bodø

Vestfjorden

Saltfjellet

Lofoten

Vesterålen

Hamarøy

Andøya

Senja

Harstad

Tromsø

Kvaløya

Ringvassøya

Soroya

Magerøya

Finnmarksvidda

Alta

Talvik

Lakselv

Porsangen

Varangerhalvøya

Varangerfjorden

Kvænangen

Kautokeino

Kilpisjärvi

Inarijärvi

Inari

Ounasjoki

Sattanen

Kiistala

F I N L A N D

L a p l a n d

0 km 100 200

0 miles 100 200

INDUSTRIAL STRENGTH

Manufacturing is an important source of employment and wealth throughout Scandinavia. Many of the goods produced, such as cars in Sweden, electronic goods in Denmark (above), and cell phones in Finland, are exported all over the world. In Denmark, many people also work in agriculture, fish processing, and brewing.

NORWEGIAN FJORDS

The west coast of Norway has thousands of deep inlets—known as fjords—gouged out of the mountains by glaciers during the last ice age and then flooded by the sea. The fjords run inland between high mountains and make favorite destinations for cruise ships bringing tourists to admire the stunning scenery.

THE SAUNA

The sauna, or steam bath, was invented in Finland about 1,000 years ago as a way of cleaning and relaxing the body. After a hot sauna, many Finns cool off by plunging into an icy pool (below) or a snowdrift.

BUILDING WITH WOOD

Most of Norway and Sweden—and two thirds of Finland—is covered by dense forests of birch, pine, spruce, and other trees. Finland has more than 16 times more forested land per person than the European average. Many people in the region work in forestry, producing wood for the construction and furniture industries. This great natural resource is also used to build homes and churches, such as this medieval stave church (left) in Norway.

SAVING THE ENVIRONMENT

The people of Scandinavia are very environmentally conscious and recycle as many household items as they can. Strict national laws protect the environment from industrial waste and pollution, although there is growing concern about the levels of pollution in the Baltic Sea.

Kouvola
Kotka
Lahti
Riihimäki
Porvoo
HELSINKI
Hyvinkää
Hämeenlinna
Vantaa
Espoo
Gulf of Finland
Rauma
Salo
Turku
(Åbo)
Hanko
(Hangö)
Åland
Ålands Hav

Söderhamn
Gävle
Sandviken
Tierp
Norrtälje
Uppsala
Täby
STOCKHOLM
Sala
Avesta
Mättnen
Sollentuna
Södertälje
Leksand
Falun
Nora
Västerås
Hjälmaren
Nyköping
Rättvik
Bollnäs
Ludvika
Borlänge
Ludvika
Karlstad
Örebro
Norrköping
Linköping
Gotland
Visby
Mora
Malung
Klarälven
Filipstad
Säffle
Mariestad
Askersund
Vättern
Oskarshamn
Borgholm
Öland
Åmål
Lidköping
Vänern
Jönköping
Växjö
Kalmar
Boras
Mölndal
Kungsbacka
Varberg
Ljungby
Karlskrona
Uddevalla
Mellerud
Gothenburg
(Göteborg)
Halmstad
Laholm
Kristianstad
Hanöbukten
Lillehammer
Gol
Gjøvik
Hamar
Mjøsa
OSLO
Lillestrøm
Moss
Helsingborg
Lund
Ronne
Bornholm
Eidfjord
Geilo
Hønefoss
Sandvika
Drammen
Horten
Sarpsborg
Fredrikstad
Strömstad
Helsingør
Malmö
Møn
Falster
Haukeligrend
Kongsberg
Porsgrunn
Arendal
Helsingborg
Sjælland
Slagelse
Nykøbing
Hardanger-
fjorden
Hardangervidda
Setesdal
Kristiansand
Lolland
Moi
Evje
Liknes
North
Sea
Skagerrak
Hjørring
Aalborg
Hobro
Viborg
Arhus
DENMARK
COPENHAGEN
(KØBENHAVN)
Fyn
Storebælt
Setesdal
Bergen
Leirvik
Haugesund
Sandnes
Stavanger
Boknafjorden
Ringkøbing
Fjord
Holstebro
Esbjerg
Rømø
Varde
Kolding
Odense
Slagelse
GERMANY
Jutland
(Jylland)
Kattegat
Randers
Læsø

Baltic Sea

9
10
11
12
13
14
15
16

A B C D E F G H I

49

The British Isles

FOR SUCH A SMALL GROUP OF ISLANDS, the British Isles has a very rich history. This is evident from its legacy of ancient ruins, medieval castles, dramatic cathedrals, and grand country houses. Once a leading industrial and colonial power, British monarchs ruled an empire that circled the globe. As a result, English is still widely spoken around the world. Today, many traditional industries, such as shipbuilding, mining, and engineering, have declined, and the emphasis is now on banking and insurance, as well as pharmaceuticals. The British Isles consists of two countries: the United Kingdom of Great Britain and Northern Ireland (the U.K.), and the Republic of Ireland.

Wales has more than 200 castles.

SCOTLAND
Scotland and England united as a single country in 1707. Today, however, Scotland is a self-governing part of the U.K., with its own parliament and distinct legal and educational systems. Edinburgh, above, is a popular city with a magnificent castle. Each summer, the city hosts an international arts festival.

IRELAND
Tourists visit Ireland, attracted by its unspoiled countryside and lively cities, such as Dublin (left). Once part of Great Britain, Ireland gained independence in 1922. In 2005–2007, it had one of the fastest-growing economies in Europe, but its economy shrank along with Europe's in 2008–2010.

HORSE BREEDING
Lush pastures and a mild climate have encouraged the breeding of thoroughbred racehorses in Ireland. Stud farms here raise some of the finest racehorses in the world.

Irish horse and rider on a training run

NORTH SEA ENERGY
Beneath the shallow seas around Great Britain, there are supplies of oil and natural gas. Oil rigs bring oil and gas to the surface, where it is pumped by pipeline to be refined on the mainland. Production has declined and supplies are now running low, but more distant reserves still wait to be exploited. However, few businesses are willing to take on further costly exploration.

MONEY MATTERS
The City of London is the U.K.'s financial center. Before the banking crash of 2008, more than 500 banks had offices there. Lloyd's Insurance Building (right) is one of the city's most distinctive skyscrapers. Built of steel and glass, it has elevators on the outside.

Map labels

ATLANTIC OCEAN

Shetland Islands
Unst
Yell
Fetlar
Mainland
Lerwick
Fair Isle

Orkney Islands
Sanday
Kirkwall
Mainland
Hoy
John o'Groats

North Sea

Thurso
Wick
Stornoway
Isle of Lewis
Harris
North Uist
South Uist
Barra
St. Kilda
Outer Hebrides
The Minch
The Little Minch
Ullapool
Isle of Skye
Stromeferry
Mallaig
Rhum
Eigg
Coll
Tiree
Isle of Mull
Inner Hebrides
Jura
Islay
Firth of Lorn
Oban
Fort William
Ben Nevis △ 4406ft (1343m)
Loch Ness
Loch Lomond
Inverness
Aviemore
Moray Firth
Elgin
Spey
North West Highlands
Ben Hope △ 3041ft (927m)
Grampian Mountains
SCOTLAND
Dee
Fraserburgh
Peterhead
Aberdeen
Montrose
Arbroath
Dundee
St. Andrews
Forfar
Tay
Perth
Firth of Tay
Firth of Forth
Dunfermline
Edinburgh
Berwick-upon-Tweed
Stirling
Forth
Clyde
Glasgow
Hamilton
Paisley
East Kilbride
Greenock
Kilmarnock
Prestwick
Ayr
Isle of Arran
Kintyre
Southern Uplands
Dumfries
Galashiels
Hawick
Cheviot Hills
Stranraer
Carlisle
Penrith
Lake District
Workington
Whitehaven
Barrow-in-Furness
Kendal
Lancaster
Pennines
Hawick

NORTHERN IRELAND
Coleraine
Londonderry
Strabane
Stranorlar
Donegal
Donegal Bay
Sligo
Colloney
Boyle
Castlebar
Lower Lough Erne
Upper Lough Erne
Enniskillen
Cavan
Omagh
Newtownabbey
Belfast
Bangor
Downpatrick
Newry
Armagh
Portadown
Lough Neagh
Dundalk
Ardee

UNITED KINGDOM
ISLE OF MAN
DOUGLAS
Newcastle upon Tyne
South Shields
Sunderland
Durham
Hartlepool
Middlesbrough
Northallerton
Whitby
Scarborough
Bridlington
Darlington
Tees
Ribble
Ouse
Harrogate
Northorpe
York
Beverley
Leeds

EUROPE

LONDON

The capital of the U.K. is London, a sprawling city on the banks of the River Thames. It is the political and financial center of the country, as well as home to more than 8 million people. One of its most recent attractions is the London Eye—a giant ferris wheel, 443 ft (135 m) high.

Each pod is almost completely see-through, giving the occupants a view of the whole city beneath them when it reaches the top

BRITISH LANDMARKS

Tourism is a major industry in Britain. Visitors come from all over the world to see the many churches, castles, and ancient monuments, such as Stonehenge (above), and to admire the pretty villages. Many also come for the theaters, galleries, and stores in Britain's vibrant cities.

Stonehenge in southern England was built from about 3000 BCE onward.

WALES

Wales was formally united with England in 1536 but retains its own language and traditions. Welsh is widely spoken in some areas, and public signs appear in both Welsh and English. Coal mining and steel production were once important in the south, but both have declined. Rugby is the national sport.

MULTICULTURAL SOCIETY

Britain once controlled a world empire, with colonies in every continent. Many people—from the Indian subcontinent, Africa, and the Caribbean in particular—came here and brought their cultures with them. Today, about 1 in 12 British people is from an ethnic minority but is integrated into British life.

Wales plays Scotland in rugby at the Millennium Stadium, Cardiff

Map labels

North Sea

Irish Sea

Celtic Sea

Atlantic Ocean

St. George's Channel

English Channel

IRELAND

DUBLIN
Lucan
Dún Laoghaire
Arklow
Wicklow Mountains
Carlow
Kilkenny
Wexford
Newbridge
Port Laoise
Athlone
Tullamore
Nenagh
Loughrea
Galway
Galway Bay
Ennis
Limerick
Clonmel
Waterford
Youghal
Cork
Cashel
Mallow
Tralee
Killarney
Abbeyfeale
Rathkeale
Bantry
Bantry Bay
Dingle Bay
Lough Corrib
Lough Derg
Munster
Leinster
Shannon
Blackwater
Barrow
Liffey

WALES
Cardiff
Swansea
Newport
Llanelli
Carmarthen
Haverfordwest
Milford Haven
Fishguard
Aberystwyth
Cardigan Bay
Tywyn
Barmouth
Bangor
Holyhead
Anglesey
Snowdonia
Cambrian Mountains
Brecon Beacons
Port Talbot
Wye
Severn

ENGLAND
Liverpool
Birkenhead
Manchester
Sheffield
Doncaster
Chester
Crewe
Stoke-on-Trent
Stafford
Shrewsbury
Wolverhampton
Birmingham
Kidderminster
Worcester
Coventry
Nuneaton
Leicester
Derby
Nottingham
Mersey
Trent
Lincoln
Louth
Skegness
Boston
The Wash
King's Lynn
Norwich
Great Yarmouth
Lowestoft
Ipswich
Felixstowe
Harwich
Colchester
Southend-on-Sea
Margate
Canterbury
Dover
Folkestone
Hastings
Eastbourne
Brighton
Hove
Channel Tunnel
Maidstone
Crawley
Croydon
LONDON
Watford
St. Albans
Woking
Guildford
Reading
Windsor
Luton
Bedford
Stevenage
Harlow
Cambridge
Newmarket
Peterborough
The Fens
Kettering
Northampton
Milton Keynes
Oxford
Swindon
Cotswold Hills
Cheltenham
Gloucester
Bristol
Bath
Weston-super-Mare
Bristol Channel
Andover
Winchester
Salisbury
Stonehenge
Southampton
Eastleigh
Portsmouth
Havant
Bournemouth
Poole
Newport
Isle of Wight
Weymouth
Lyme Bay
Bridport
Yeovil
Taunton
Exeter
Exmoor
Exmouth
Tiverton
Barnstaple
Bideford
Ilfracombe
Dartmoor
Torquay
Plymouth
Saltash
Newquay
St. Austell
Bodmin
Truro
Falmouth
Penzance
Land's End
Isles of Scilly
Thames
Avon
Exe
Tamar

CHANNEL ISLANDS
(to U.K.)
ST. PETER PORT
Guernsey
Alderney
Sark
Jersey
ST. HELIER

Scale

0 km   50   100
0 miles   50   100

The Low Countries

THE NETHERLANDS, BELGIUM, AND LUXEMBOURG are known as the Low Countries because the land is so flat and lowlying. In the case of the Netherlands, most of the land is below sea level—*Netherlands* is Dutch for "under lands." The three countries are among the richest in Europe, and while farming still plays an important part, they all have strong modern economies based on manufacturing and trade. Luxembourg in particular is known as a tax haven and is a major center for international finance. Their location at the mouth of the Rhine River and other major European rivers places the three countries at the heart of western European trade and politics—all three were founding members of the European Economic Community (now the European Union, or EU), established in 1957.

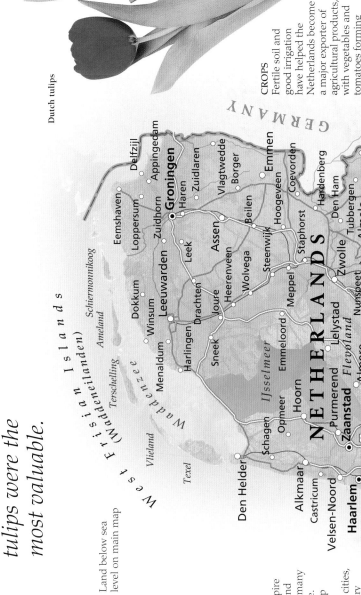

ROTTERDAM, NETHERLANDS
Every year, more than 30,000 ocean-going ships and 110,000 barges call at the port of Rotterdam. Lying at the mouth of the Rhine River, this port is the largest in the world and is where huge container ships from all over the world load or unload their cargoes. The smaller barges help transport goods farther inland. With the port's ultra-modern Vessel Traffic Service (VTS), it's possible to track ships on a radar screen up to 37 miles, (60 km) off the coast and 25 miles (40 km) inland.

Dutch tulips

CROPS
Fertile soil and good irrigation have helped the Netherlands become a major exporter of agricultural products, with vegetables and tomatoes forming important crops. It is also famous for its bulbs and cut flowers, notably tulips.

Tulips were introduced to the Netherlands from Turkey in 1562. Black tulips were the most valuable.

Land below sea level on main map

RECLAIMING THE LAND
Over the centuries, the Dutch have reclaimed land from the sea. They did this by building huge dykes, or dams, to keep out the sea and then draining the surface water into canals. Windmills originally pumped out the water, but electric pumps are now used.

DUTCH PEOPLE
The Dutch once ruled a vast empire in Indonesia, the Caribbean, and South America. As a result, many nationalities now live here. Ethnic minorities make up about 20 percent of the population and in some cities, the majority of elementary schoolchildren have a non-Dutch background.

GERMANY

NETHERLANDS

West Frisian Islands (Waddeneilanden)

Waddenzee

IJsselmeer

Flevoland

Texel

Vlieland

Terschelling

Ameland

Schiermonnikoog

Delfzijl
Appingedam
Groningen
Haren
Zuidlaren
Vlagtwedde
Borger
Emmen
Coevorden
Eemshaven
Loppersum
Zuidhorn
Hardenberg
Leek
Assen
Beilen
Den Ham
Hoogeveen
Tubbergen
Almelo
Staphorst
Zwolle
Rijssen
Deventer
Goor
Hengelo
Enschede
Zutphen
Eemshaven
Winsum
Dokkum
Drachten
Heerenveen
Wolvega
Steenwijk
Meppel
Leeuwarden
Sneek
Joure
Menaldum
Harlingen
Emmeloord
Lelystad
Nunspeet
Vaassen
Apeldoorn
Amersfoort
Baarn
Zeewolde
Almere
Hoorn
Purmerend
Zaanstad
Hilversum
Sassenheim
Opmeer
Amstelveen
Schagen
Den Helder
Alkmaar
Castricum
Velsen-Noord
Haarlem
AMSTERDAM
Noordwijk aan Zee
Leiden

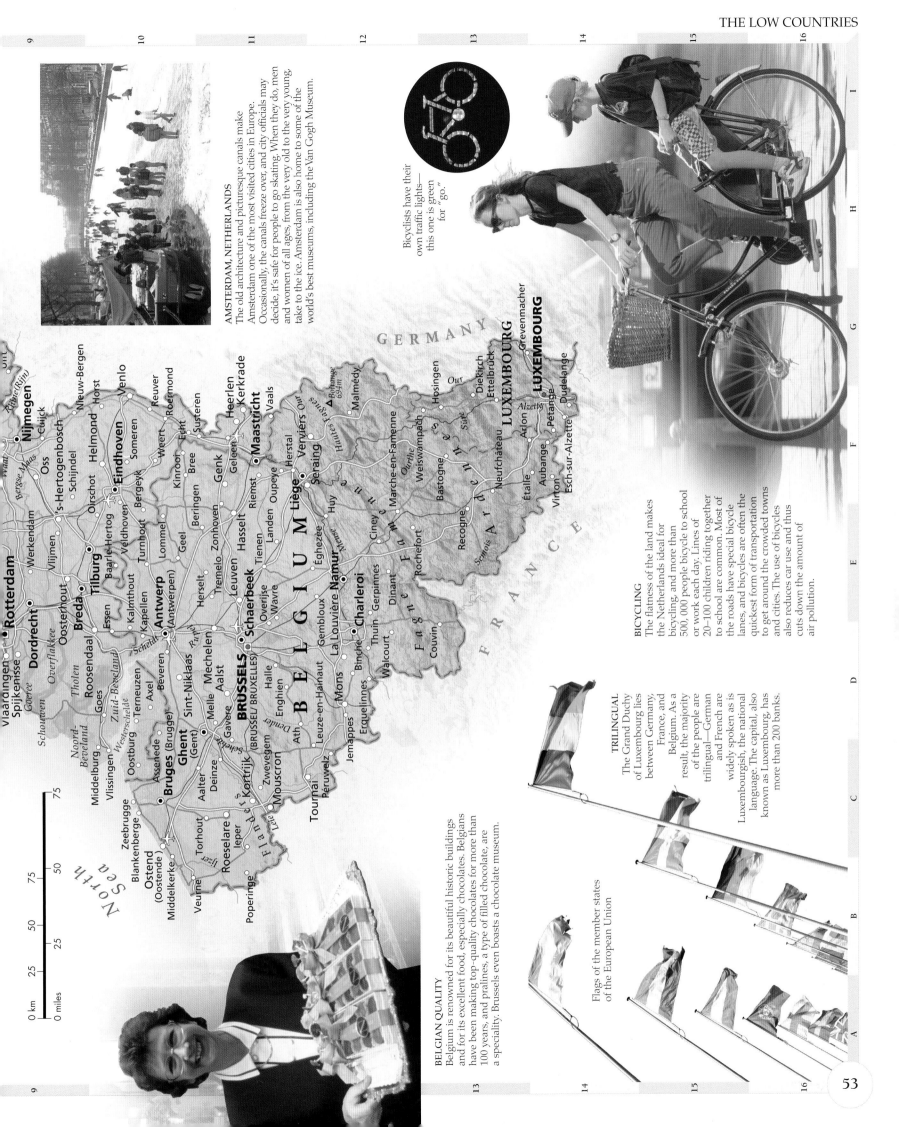

AMSTERDAM, NETHERLANDS

The old architecture and picturesque canals make Amsterdam one of the most visited cities in Europe. Occasionally, the canals freeze over, and city officials may decide, it's safe for people to go skating. When they do, men and women of all ages, from the very old to the very young, take to the ice. Amsterdam is also home to some of the world's best museums, including the Van Gogh Museum.

Bicyclists have their own traffic lights—this one is green for "go."

BICYCLING

The flatness of the land makes the Netherlands ideal for bicycling, and more than 500,000 people bicycle to school or work each day. Lines of 20–100 children riding together to school are common. Most of the roads have special bicycle lanes, and bicycles are often the quickest form of transportation to get around the crowded towns and cities. The use of bicycles also reduces car use and thus cuts down the amount of air pollution.

TRILINGUAL

The Grand Duchy of Luxembourg lies between Germany, France, and Belgium. As a result, the majority of the people are trilingual—German and French are widely spoken as is Luxembourgish, the national language. The capital, also known as Luxembourg, has more than 200 banks.

Flags of the member states of the European Union

BELGIAN QUALITY

Belgium is renowned for its beautiful historic buildings and for its excellent food, especially chocolates. Belgians have been making top-quality chocolates for more than 100 years, and pralines, a type of filled chocolate, are a speciality. Brussels even boasts a chocolate museum.

North Sea

0 km   25   50   75
0 miles   25   50   75

GERMANY

FRANCE

LUXEMBOURG

BELGIUM

France

IN DIRECT CONTRAST TO ITS mostly rural landscape, France is a modern nation, with most people now living in towns and cities. It has flourishing industries and is the fifth-richest economy in the world after the U.S.A., Japan, Germany, and the U.K. A country of varied scenery, from gently rolling farmland in the north to a stretch of dry, warm Mediterranean coast in the south, France also shares two mountain ranges—the Pyrenees and the Alps. Each of the 22 regions within France, which includes the island of Corsica, has its own distinct identity and culture. The tiny countries of Andorra and Monaco lie next to France.

Boules, the national game of France, is still played in village squares around the country.

NUCLEAR POWER

Three fourths of France's electricity is produced by nuclear power plants (above), making the country largely self-sufficient in energy and one of the main producers of nuclear power in Europe. Hydroelectric plants are also an important source of power.

HIGH-SPEED TRAVEL

France has Europe's fastest train, the TGV—*train à grande vitesse*—which travels at up to 186 mph (300 kph) during normal services. In 2007, a modified TGV even set a speed record for conventional trains of 357.2 mph (574.8 kph). The TGV network connects Paris with all of the country's major cities, which makes it easier to commute or visit relatives. It also extends to Germany, Italy, Belgium, Switzerland, and through the Channel Tunnel to Great Britain.

STREETS OF PARIS

Tourists flock to Paris to visit its world-famous museums and art galleries, shop in its elegant stores, and soak up its vibrant atmosphere. Montmartre, which overlooks the city, is famous for its artists. Close by, in the Place du Tertre (above), visitors can have their portraits painted.

BELGIUM
GERMANY
LUX.
SWITZERLAND

F R A N C E

ATLANTIC OCEAN

English Channel

CHANNEL ISLANDS (to U.K.)

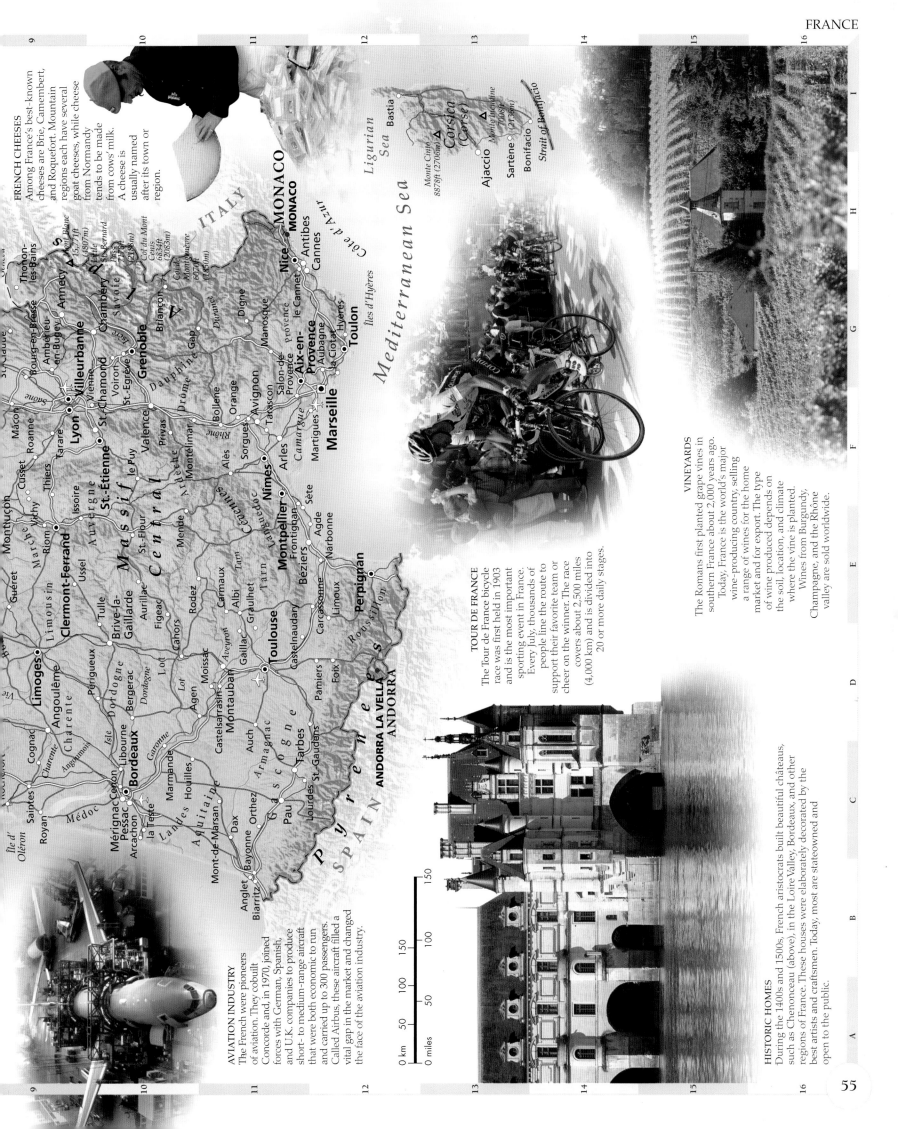

FRENCH CHEESES

Among France's best-known cheeses are Brie, Camembert, and Roquefort. Mountain regions each have several goat cheeses, while cheese from Normandy tends to be made from cows' milk. A cheese is usually named after its town or region.

VINEYARDS

The Romans first planted grape vines in southern France about 2,000 years ago. Today, France is the world's major wine-producing country, selling a range of wines for the home market and for export. The type of wine produced depends on the soil, location, and climate where the vine is planted. Wines from Burgundy, Champagne, and the Rhône valley are sold worldwide.

TOUR DE FRANCE

The Tour de France bicycle race was first held in 1903 and is the most important sporting event in France. Every July, thousands of people line the route to support their favorite team or cheer on the winner. The race covers about 2,500 miles (4,000 km) and is divided into 20 or more daily stages.

AVIATION INDUSTRY

The French were pioneers of aviation. They cobuilt Concorde and, in 1970, joined forces with German, Spanish, and U.K. companies to produce short- to medium-range aircraft that were both economic to run and carried up to 300 passengers. Called Airbus, these aircraft filled a vital gap in the market and changed the face of the aviation industry.

HISTORIC HOMES

During the 1400s and 1500s, French aristocrats built beautiful châteaus, such as Chenonceau (above), in the Loire Valley, Bordeaux, and other regions of France. These houses were elaborately decorated by the best artists and craftsmen. Today, most are stateowned and open to the public.

Germany and the Alpine States

LYING AT THE HEART OF EUROPE, Germany is one of the world's wealthiest nations. It is also Europe's leading industrial power. To its south lie the Alpine states of Switzerland, Austria, Liechtenstein, and Slovenia. The region is famed for its beautiful Alpine scenery, mountains, and lakes. German is the main language in all but Slovenia. However, each of the five countries has its own distinct history, culture, and national identity. In fact, since 1815, Switzerland has been recognized as a neutral nation and has stayed out of all of the wars that have affected Europe.

THE JOY OF UNIFICATION
After World War II, Germany was divided, with a U.S.-backed capitalist state in the west and a Russian-backed state in the east. Built in 1961, the Berlin Wall was 96 miles (155 km) long and was designed to stop East Germans from leaving for a better life in the West. The wall divided Berlin and separated families, friends, and a nation for 28 years. When Germany was unified (reunited) in 1990, the wall was demolished.

Celebrations at Brandenburg Gate mark the tenth anniversary of the fall of the Berlin Wall.

GENEVA
Geneva lies on the shores of Lake Geneva, Europe's largest Alpine lake. This orderly city is a global center for banking and finance. It is also a base for many international organizations, such as the Red Cross.

The Swiss speak German, French, Italian, and Romansh.

GERMAN INDUSTRY
With its coal and iron mines, the Ruhr Valley was once the powerhouse of the German economy. Today's industry ranges from engineering to high-tech goods. Quality assembly and design make Germany the third-largest car producer in the world.

FOOD AND DRINK
The annual Munich *Oktoberfest* is Germany's biggest beer festival. Entertainment includes parades and music.

Map labels

POLAND

BELGIUM

NETHERLANDS

DENMARK

Baltic Sea

BERLIN

GERMANY

Frankfurt an der Oder
Guben
Cottbus
Görlitz
Zittau
Löbau
Bautzen
Hoyerswerda
Senftenberg
Finsterwalde
Dresden
Pirna
Lübbenau
Lübben
Spree
Eisenhüttenstadt
Chemnitz
Zwickau
Plauen
Hof
Ore Mts. (Erzgebirge)
Marktredwitz
Mündberg
Kronach
Coburg
Lichtenfels
Schweinfurt
Eberswalde-Finow
Bad Freienwalde
Bernau
Ludwigsfelde
Potsdam
Leipzig
Riesa
Döbeln
Hainichen
Gera
Jena
Weimar
Erfurt
Gotha
Suhl
Saalfeld
Bad Hersfeld
Hünfeld
Fulda
Frankfurt am Main
Wetzlar
Gießen
Marburg an der Lahn
Koblenz
Boppard
Neuwied
Mainz
Wiesbaden
Offenbach
Angermünde
Prenzlau
Pasewalk
Neustrelitz
Oranienburg
Neuruppin
Wittenberge
Perleberg
Brandenburg
Magdeburg
Schönebeck
Dessau
Bernburg
Halle
Halle-Neustadt
Eisleben
Nordhausen
Northeim
Göttingen
Kassel
Melsungen
Marsberg
Warburg
Paderborn
Siegen
Olpe
Wuppertal
Solingen
Leverkusen
Cologne (Köln)
Bonn
Aachen
Düren
Alsdorf
Neubrandenburg
Waren
Müritz
Teterow
Malchin
Demmin
Anklam
Wolgast
Greifswald
Pomeranian Bay
Rügen
Sassnitz
Bergen
Stralsund
Warnemünde
Rostock
Güstrow
Parchim
Schwerin
Wismar
Ludwigslust
Dannenberg
Uelzen
Salzwedel
Stendal
Wolfsburg
Braunschweig
Salzgitter
Hildesheim
Peine
Hannover
Minden
Herford
Bielefeld
Gütersloh
Hamm
Ahlen
Dortmund
Bochum
Essen
Recklinghausen
Duisburg
Krefeld
Düsseldorf
Mönchengladbach
Oberhausen
Dülmen
Münster
Rheine
Osnabrück
Lingen
Cloppenburg
Delmenhorst
Oldenburg
Bremen
Bremerhaven
Wilhelmshaven
Emden
Leer
Weener
Norden
Nordhorn
East Frisian Islands (Ostfriesische Inseln)
Ems
Weser
Seesen
Celle
Soltau
Verden
Bassum
Diepholz
Lüneburg
Winsen
Rosengarten
Scheessel
Stade
Elmshorn
Itzehoe
Heide
Husum
Cuxhaven
Helgoland Bay
Westerland
North Frisian Islands (Nordfriesische Inseln)
Schleswig-Holstein
Kiel Canal
Neumünster
Rendsburg
Schleswig
Kappeln
Flensburg
Kiel
Kieler Bucht
Fehmarn
Fehmarn Belt
Puttgarden
Oldenburg
Eutin
Lübeck
Norderstedt
Hamburg
Boizenburg
Elbe
Saale
Havel
Lahn
Rhine
Eifel
Hunsrück
Rheinisches Schiefergebirge
Westerwald
Vogelsberg
Rhön
Thuringian Forest (Thüringer Wald)
Lausitz (Lužica)
Oderhaff
Mecklenburger Bucht
Bitburg
Wittlich
Blankenheim
Bocholt
Nordhorn
Oder

Map labels

SLOVAKIA

HUNGARY

CROATIA

CZECH REPUBLIC

VIENNA (WIEN)

Mistelbach an der Zaya
Hollabrunn
Tulln
Traiskirchen
Neusiedler See
Perchtoldsdorf
Bad Vöslau
Eisenstadt
Sankt Pölten
Wiener Neustadt
Zwettl
Linz
Hauzenberg
Wels
Steyr
Enns
Mürzzuschlag
Leoben
Graz
Murska Sobota
Maribor
Ptuj
Drava
Mur
Judenburg
Wolfsberg
AUSTRIA
Salzburg
Bad Ischl
Ebensee
Liezen
Vöcklabruck
Ried im Innkreis
Velenje
Celje
Trbovlje
Novo Mesto
Krško
Kočevje
Klagenfurt
Villach
Jesenice
Kranj
LJUBLJANA
Nova Gorica
Koper
Postojna
Totmin
SLOVENIA
Gulf of Istra
Gulf of Venice

Passau
Deggendorf
Straubing
Regensburg
Regenstauf
Schwandorf
Landshut
Pocking
Munich (München)
Rosenheim
Schwaz
Innsbruck
Brenner Pass 4508ft (1374m)
Plöcken Pass 4452ft (1357m)
Ingolstadt
Donauwörth
Augsburg
Mindelheim
Kempten
Kaufbeuren
Memmingen
Füssen
Bregenz
VADUZ
LIECHTENSTEIN
Chur
St. Moritz
ITALY
Bellinzona
Locarno
Lugano
Lake Maggiore

Nuremberg (Nürnberg)
Fürth
Weissenburg
Aalen
Göppingen
Heidenheim an der Brenz
Ulm
Neu-Ulm
Reutlingen
Stuttgart
Ludwigsburg
Sinsheim
Heidelberg
Mannheim
Schwenningen
Villingen
Rottweil
Konstanz
Lake Constance
Singen
Friedrichshafen
Sankt Gallen
Zürich
Winterthur
Schaffhausen
Bülach
Zug
Schwyz
Heilbronn
Pforzheim
Karlsruhe
Baden-Baden
Offenburg
Kehl
Lahr
Emmendingen
Freiburg im Breisgau
Bad Krozingen
Müllheim
Lörrach
Basel
Biel
BERN
Thun
Luzern
Brig
Sion
Monthey
Geneva (Genève)
Lausanne
Neuchâtel
La Chaux-de-Fonds
Onex
SWITZERLAND
FRANCE
Great Saint Bernard Pass 8100ft (2469m)
Simplon Pass 6578ft (2005m)

Merzig
Neunkirchen
Saarbrücken
Neustadt an der Weinstrasse

Side text

SWISS WATCHES
The Swiss invented the first wristwatch, the first quartz watch, and the first waterresistant watch. With their worldwide reputation for quality and style, watches make up the country's third-largest export.

SLOVENIA
After centuries of rule by overlords, Slovenia became independent in 1991. Although the population is only 2 million, the national culture is strong. The famous Lipizzaner show horses are named after the Slovenian farm where they were first bred.

VIENNA, AUSTRIA
Vienna is a city of baroque buildings, palaces, and famous concert halls. Grand balls with traditional waltzes are still common. These are a reminder of when the city was the center of the Austro-Hungarian Empire, which controlled large parts of east and central Europe.

The opera ball in Vienna

The high and graceful stride of the Lipizzaner horses makes them excel in competitions.

ALPS
The Alps run from southeast France and spread eastwardsthrough Switzerland and northern Italy into Austria and Slovenia. A popular tourist destination, the Alps are famous for dramatic scenery and winter sports.

Spain and Portugal

THE COUNTRIES OF SPAIN AND PORTUGAL share an area of land called the Iberian Peninsula. In the north, this land is cut off from the rest of Europe by the Pyrenees Mountains, while to the south, it is separated from Africa by the Strait of Gibraltar. The region was once ruled by Islamic people from north Africa known as Moors. Evidence of their occupation can still be seen in buildings in the cities of Andalucía. The Moors were eventually defeated in 1492, and for a while, Portugal came under Spanish control, as did most of Europe. During the 1900s, both countries were ruled by brutal dictatorships that were overthrown in the 1970s. They are now modern democracies.

Spanish families tend to eat dinner late, at around 9 PM. So after school, children eat a snack called a merienda.

HARVESTING CORK
Cork is made from the outer bark of the evergreen cork oak tree. The bark is carefully stripped off, flattened, laid out in sheets, and then left to dry. Cork is used for many products, such as stoppers for wine bottles, mats, and tiles. Portugal is the world's leading exporter of cork.

LISBON
Portugal's capital city is Lisbon, which is situated at the mouth of the Tagus River on a series of steep hills and valleys. In 1755, two thirds of the city was completely destroyed by an earthquake and tidal wave but was rebuilt with beautiful squares and public buildings. Many explorers have set sail from Lisbon in their quest to find new lands.

Trams are a feature of Lisbon streets and a popular form of transportation for both locals and tourists.

FISHING
Spain and Portugal have well-developed fishing industries, with large-scale fleets and many smaller local fleets. However, overfishing along Portugal's coast and in the north Atlantic has put many people's livelihoods at risk. A huge oil spill off the coast of Galicia in 2002 also affected fish stocks, but the Portuguese government and thousands of volunteers restored beaches to their former beauty.

A Coruña (La Coruña) · Ferrol · Betanzos · Laracha · Santa Comba · Cabo Fisterra · Outes · Muros · Santiago · Ribeira · Lalín · Chantada · Pontevedra · O Carballiño · Marín · Ourense (Orense) · Vigo · Ponteareas · Xinzo de Limia · Viana do Castelo · Ponte da Barca · Póvoa de Varzim · Braga · Guimarães · Vila do Conde · Vila Real · Matosinhos · Porto (Oporto) · Vila Nova de Gaia · Douro · Lamego · Ovar · São João da Madeira · Albergaria-a-Velha · Aveiro · Viseu · Ílhavo · Alto da Torre 6539ft (1993m) · Guarda · Coimbra · Covilhã · Figueira da Foz · Serra da Estrela · Leiria · Castelo Branco · Tomar · Tagus · Entroncamento · Abrantes · Peniche · Caldas da Rainha · Santarém · Torres Vedras · Portalegre · Coruche · Sintra · LISBON (LISBOA) · Cascais · Estremoz · Elvas · Almada · Barreiro · Évora · Serra d'Ossa · Setúbal · Alcácer do Sal · Baía de Setúbal · Sines · Beja · Ourique · Cortegana · Nerva · Valverde del Camino · La Algaba · Algarve · Lepe · Portimão · Ayamonte · Cabo de São Vicente · Faro · Isla Cristina · Huelva · Lagos · Tavira · Olhão · Gulf of Cadiz (Golfo de Cádiz) · Lebrija · Las Cabezas de San Juan · Cádiz · San Fernando · Jerez de la Frontera · Ubrique · Costa de la Luz · Barbate de Franco · Algeciras · Strait of Gibraltar · GIBRALTAR (to U.K.) · Ceuta (to Spain) · MOROCCO

Gijon (Xixón) · Costa Ver · Luarca · Avilés · Villaviciosa · Llan · Pravia · Tineo · Oviedo · Mieres del Camin · Asturias · Cantabria · Pola de Lena · Cabañaquinta · Galicia · Lugo · Cordillera Cantábrica · Monforte · Ponferrada · León · Astorga · Castilla-León · Benavente · Palencia · Bragança · Embalse de Ricobayo · Valladolid · Chaves · Zamora · Toro · Duero · Medina del Campo · Embalse de Almendra · Salamanca · Sego · Ciudad-Rodrigo · Ávila · Béjar · Sistema Central · Sierra de Gredos · Plasencia · Talavera de la Reina · Coria · Embalse de Valdecañas · Embalse de Alcántara · Cáceres · Trujillo · Herrera del Duque · Extremadura · Mérida · Villanueva de la Serena · Don Benito · Puertolla · Badajoz · Castuera · Almendralejo · Zafra · Villafranca de los Barros · Pozoblanco · Azuaga · Jeréz de los Caballeros · Sierra Morena · Córdoba · Montoro · Guadalquivir · Bujala · Palma del Río · Alcauc · Carmona · Ecija · Andalucía · Seville (Sevilla) · Osuna · Lucena · Dos Hermanas · Archidona · Antequera · Olvera · Álora · Mála · Coín · Ronda · Fuengirola · Jerez de la Frontera · Marbella · Costa del S · Estepona

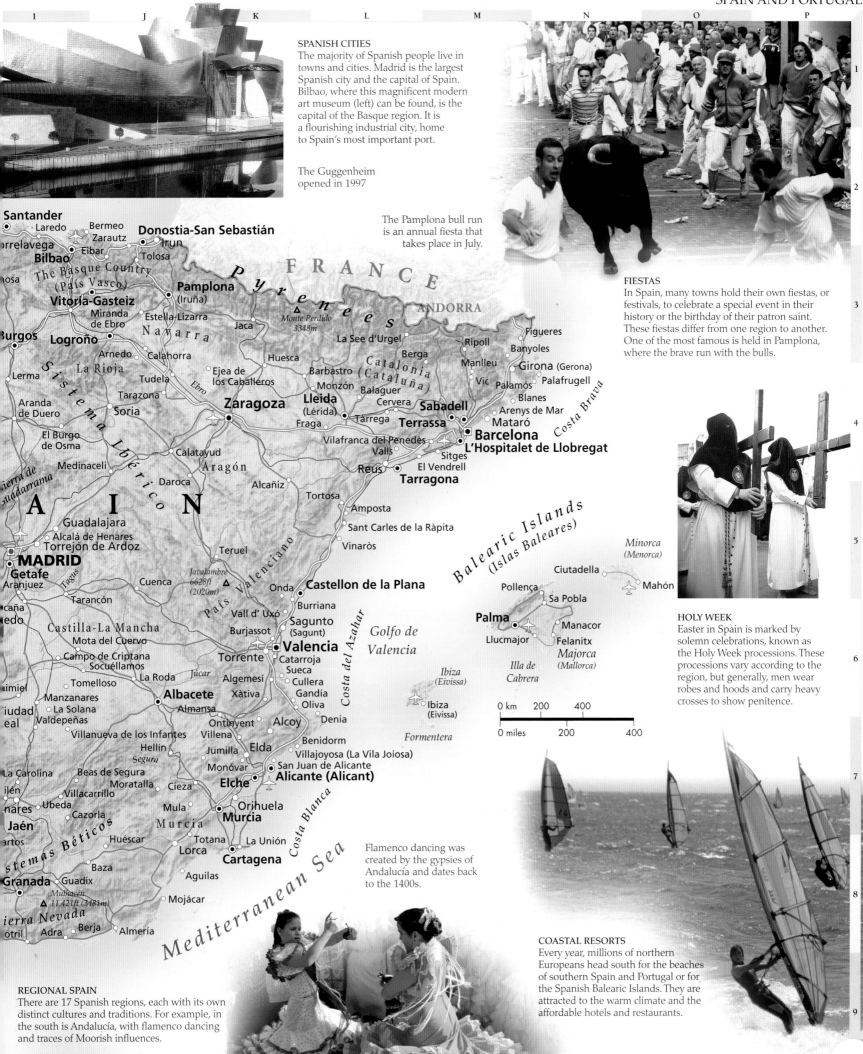

SPANISH CITIES

The majority of Spanish people live in towns and cities. Madrid is the largest Spanish city and the capital of Spain. Bilbao, where this magnificent modern art museum (left) can be found, is the capital of the Basque region. It is a flourishing industrial city, home to Spain's most important port.

The Guggenheim opened in 1997

The Pamplona bull run is an annual fiesta that takes place in July.

FIESTAS

In Spain, many towns hold their own fiestas, or festivals, to celebrate a special event in their history or the birthday of their patron saint. These fiestas differ from one region to another. One of the most famous is held in Pamplona, where the brave run with the bulls.

HOLY WEEK

Easter in Spain is marked by solemn celebrations, known as the Holy Week processions. These processions vary according to the region, but generally, men wear robes and hoods and carry heavy crosses to show penitence.

COASTAL RESORTS

Every year, millions of northern Europeans head south for the beaches of southern Spain and Portugal or for the Spanish Balearic Islands. They are attracted to the warm climate and the affordable hotels and restaurants.

Flamenco dancing was created by the gypsies of Andalucía and dates back to the 1400s.

REGIONAL SPAIN

There are 17 Spanish regions, each with its own distinct cultures and traditions. For example, in the south is Andalucía, with flamenco dancing and traces of Moorish influences.

Santander
Laredo
Bermeo
Zarautz
orrelavega
Eibar
Donostia-San Sebastián
Irun
Tolosa
Bilbao
The Basque Country
(País Vasco)
Vitoria-Gasteiz
Pamplona
(Iruña)
Miranda
de Ebro
Estella-Lizarra
Jaca
Navarra
Monte Perdido
3348m
ANDORRA
FRANCE
Pyrenees
Burgos
Logroño
Arnedo
Calahorra
Huesca
La See d'Urgel
Ripoll
Figueres
Banyoles
Berga
Manlleu
Girona (Gerona)
La Rioja
Ejea de
los Caballeros
Barbastro
Monzón
Balaguer
Vic
Palamós
Palafrugell
Lerma
Aranda
de Duero
Soria
Tarazona
Tudela
Zaragoza
Cervera
Blanes
El Burgo
de Osma
Catalonia
(Cataluña)
Lleida
(Lérida)
Fraga
Tàrrega
Sabadell
Arenys de Mar
Costa Brava
Medinaceli
Calatayud
Terrassa
Mataró
Daroca
Aragón
Vilafranca del Penedès
Barcelona
L'Hospitalet de Llobregat
ierra de
uadarrama
Guadalajara
Alcalá de Henares
Torrejón de Ardoz
Alcañiz
Valls
Reus
Sitges
El Vendrell
AIN
Tortosa
Tarragona
MADRID
Getafe
Teruel
Javalambre
6628ft
(2020m)
Amposta
Sant Carles de la Ràpita
Vinaròs
Balearic Islands
(Islas Baleares)
Minorca
(Menorca)
Aranjuez
aña
edo
Cuenca
Onda
Castellon de la Plana
Ciutadella
Mahón
Tarancón
Burriana
Vall d' Uxó
Sagunto
(Sagunt)
Golfo de
Valencia
Pollença
Sa Pobla
Castilla-La Mancha
Mota del Cuervo
Burjassot
Palma
Manacor
Campo de Criptana
Socuéllamos
La Roda
Torrente
Valencia
Catarroja
Sueca
Llucmajor
Felanitx
Majorca
(Mallorca)
imiel
Tomelloso
Júcar
Algemesí
Cullera
Gandía
Costa del Azahar
Ibiza
(Eivissa)
Illa de
Cabrera
iudad
eal
Manzanares
La Solana
Valdepeñas
Albacete
Almansa
Xàtiva
Oliva
Denia
Ibiza
(Eivissa)
Villanueva de los Infantes
Ontinyent
Villena
Alcoy
Formentera
Hellín
Jumilla
Elda
Benidorm
Villajoyosa (La Vila Joíosa)
La Carolina
Beas de Segura
Moratalla
Monóvar
San Juan de Alicante
Segura
ilén
ares
Villacarrillo
Cieza
Mula
Elche
Alicante (Alicant)
Ubeda
Cazorla
Murcia
Orihuela
Murcia
Costa Blanca
Jaén
Sistemas Béticos
Huéscar
Totana
La Unión
artos
Lorca
Cartagena
Baza
Aguilas
Mediterranean Sea
Granada
Guadix
Mulhacén
11,421ft (3481m)
Mojácar
ierra Nevada
otril
Adra
Berja
Almería

0 km   200   400
0 miles   200   400

Italy

THE BOOT-SHAPED COUNTRY of Italy stretches from the mountainous north down to the Mediterranean Sea. For most of its history, Italy consisted of city-states—such as Florence and Venice—and was united only in 1870. Regional differences in Italy are huge, as each region has its own cuisine, customs, and dialect and is geographically quite distinct. As a result, many Italians identify themselves first by region and then by country. The largest division, however, is between the rich north and the poorer south—a rugged region with several active volcanoes and the occasional severe earthquake. The mainland of Italy includes two tiny independent states—San Marino and Vatican City.

Vatican City has a permanent population of only about 800 people, although more than 3,000 come to work in the city-state each day.

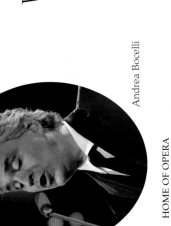

Andrea Bocelli

Carnival masks

HOME OF OPERA
The idea of setting drama to music originated in Italy during the 1500s. Since then, Italian composers, such as Rossini, Verdi, and Puccini, have made opera the most popular musical form in Italy. Many cities have their own opera houses.

COLISEUM
One of Rome's greatest sights is the Coliseum, which opened in 80 CE. Deadly gladiatorial combats and animal fights were staged here before crowds of up to 55,000 people.

The oval-shaped Colosseum stood at 620 ft (189 m) high.

CITY OF CANALS
The beautiful city of Venice is made up of 118 islands, 177 canals, and 400 bridges. The only way to get around is to walk or take a boat: a *vaporetto*, *motoscafo*, or *motonave*. The most distinctive boat, however, is the gondola. Each year, in the days before Ash Wednesday, Venice hosts a carnival when the city celebrates with fireworks and everyone wears spectacular masks.

SOCCER FANS
Italians are crazy about soccer and fanatically follow the performance of teams such as Juventus, AC Milan, Inter, and Roma. Italian teams frequently win major European competitions, and the national team has won the World Cup four times—in 1934, 1938, 1982, and 2006.

SLOVENIA
AUSTRIA
CROATIA

Brenner Pass
4508ft
(1374m)

Trieste
Tarvisio
Cortina d'Ampezzo
Gemona del Friuli
Udine
Montalcone
Venice (Venezia)
Gulf of Venice
Bressanone
Dolomites
Merano
Bolzano
Trento
Pordenone
Portogruaro
Mestre
Chioggia
Foci del Po
Edolo
Arco
Lake Garda
Bassano del Grappa
Vicenza
Padova
Monselice
Rovigo
Ferrara
Comacchio
Lake Como
Como
Lombardy
(Lombardia)
Bergamo
Brescia
Verona
Mantova
Po
Ostiglia
Carpi
Imola
Ravenna
Forlì
Faenza
Cesena
Rimini
SAN MARINO
SAN MARINO
Pesaro
Fano
Falconara Marittima
Ancona
Civitanova Marche
Fermo
Ascoli Piceno
Giulianova
Teramo
Pescara

SWITZERLAND
Mont Blanc
15,771ft
(4807m)
Great St.-Bernard Pass 8,100ft (2469m)
Little St.-Bernard Pass 7178ft (2188m)
Gran Paradiso 13,323ft (4061m)
Rhône

Alps
Aosta
Susa
Rivoli
Piemonte
Po
Moncalieri
Savigliano
Cuneo
Mondovì
Finale Ligure
Imperia
San Remo
Ventimiglia
MONACO
FRANCE

Lake Maggiore
Varese
Monza
Sesto San Giovanni
Rho
Milan (Milano)
Novara
Vercelli
Asti
Alessandria
Casteggio
Pavia
Piacenza
Parma
Reggio nell'Emilia
Modena
Bologna
Cremona
Po Valley
Appennino Ligure
Genoa (Genova)
Savona
Gulf of Genoa
La Spezia
Carrara
Massa
Viareggio
Lucca
Pisa
Livorno
Cecina
Piombino
Portoferraio
Isola d'Elba
Archipelago Toscano

Turin (Torino)

Marche
Umbro-Marchigiano
Appennino
Perugia
Foligno
Todi
Terni
L'Aquila
Sansepolcro
Arezzo
Florence (Firenze)
Prato
Pistoia
Arno
Chianti
Siena
Tuscany (Toscana)
Lago Trasimeno
Lago di Trasimeno
Grosseto
Orbetello
Viterbo
Lago di Bolsena
ITALY

Corsica
Pescara

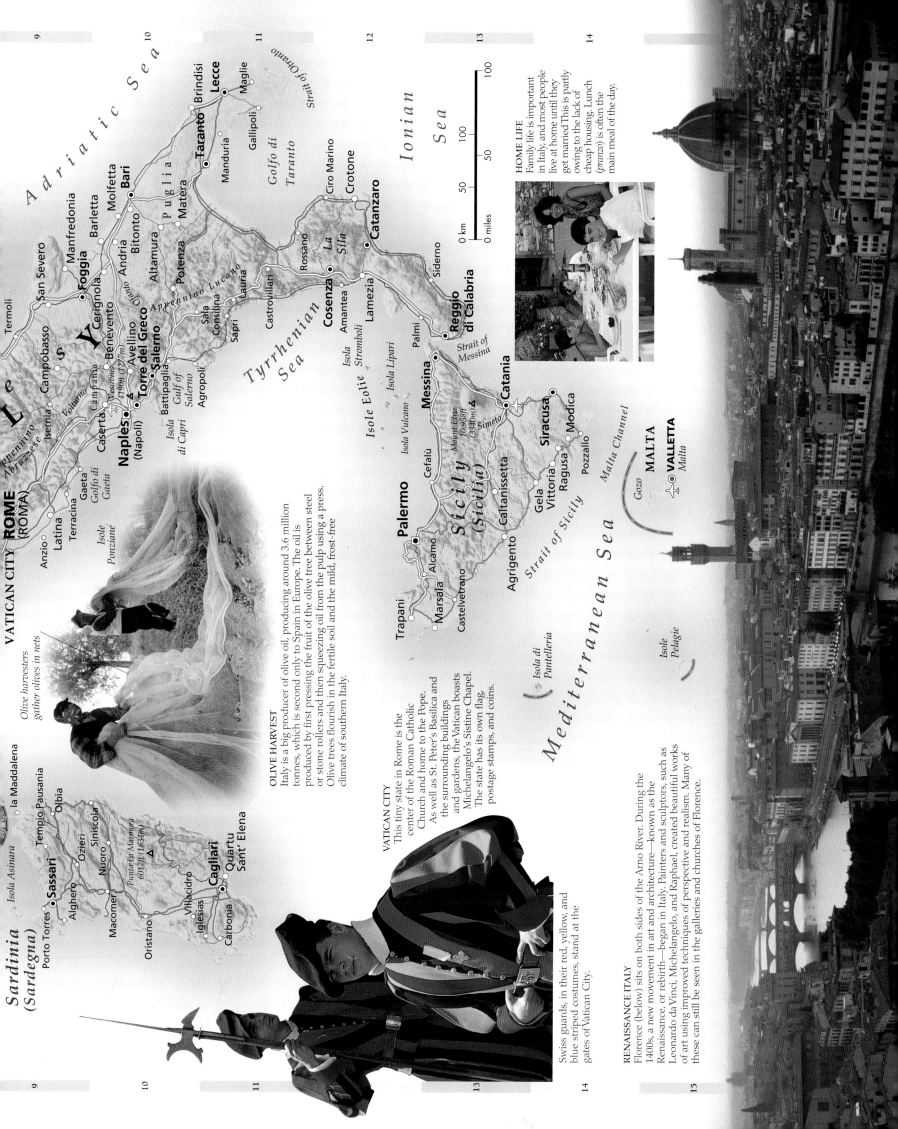

Adriatic Sea

Termoli
San Severo
Campobasso
Isernia
Gaeta
Terracina
Latina
Anzio
Isole Ponziane

Foggia
Cerignola
Benevento
Avellino
Caserta
Torre del Greco
Salerno
Battipaglia
Agropoli

Vesuvius 4190m (1277m)

Naples (Napoli)
Isola di Capri
Gulf of Gaeta
Golfo di Gaeta

VATICAN CITY
ROME
(ROMA)

A p p e n n i n o   A b r u z z e s e

Volturno

Campania

Gulf of Salerno

Manfredonia
Barletta
Molfetta
Andria
Bitonto
Altamura
Bari
Matera
Potenza

P u g l i a

Ofanto (127m)

Appennino Lucano

Sala Consilina
Sapri
Lauria
Castrovillari
Rossano

Brindisi
Lecce
Maglie
Gallipoli

Strait of Otranto

Taranto
Manduria

Golfo di Taranto

Ciro Marino
Crotone

La Sila

Cosenza
Amantea
Lamezia

Catanzaro

Siderno

I o n i a n   S e a

Palmi
Reggio di Calabria

Isola Stromboli
Isole Eolie
Isola Lipari
Isola Vulcano

Strait of Messina

Messina
Cefalù

Catania

Tyrrhenian Sea

Trapani
Marsala
Alcamo
Castelvetrano
Palermo

Mount Etna 10,958ft (3340m)
Simeto

Siracusa
Modica
Pozzallo
Ragusa
Vittoria
Gela
Caltanissetta
Agrigento

S i c i l y (S i c i l i a)

Strait of Sicily

Isola di Pantelleria

M e d i t e r r a n e a n   S e a

Malta Channel

Gozo
MALTA
✪ **VALLETTA**
Malta

Isole Pelagie

Sardinia (Sardegna)

Isola Asinara
la Maddalena
Porto Torres
Sassari
Tempio Pausania
Olbia
Alghero
Ozieri
Siniscola
Nuoro
Macomer
Oristano
Iglesias
Carbonia
Villacidro
Quartu Sant' Elena
Cagliari

Punta La Marmora 6017ft (1834m)

0 km   50   100
0 miles   50   100

OLIVE HARVEST

Italy is a big producer of olive oil, producing around 3.6 million tonnes, which is second only to Spain in Europe. The oil is produced by first pressing the fruit of the olive tree between steel or stone rollers and then squeezing oil from the pulp using a press. Olive trees flourish in the fertile soil and the mild, frost-free climate of southern Italy.

Olive harvesters gather olives in nets

VATICAN CITY

This tiny state in Rome is the center of the Roman Catholic Church and home to the Pope. As well as St. Peter's Basilica and the surrounding buildings and gardens, the Vatican boasts Michelangelo's Sistine Chapel. The state has its own flag, postage stamps, and coins.

Swiss guards, in their red, yellow, and blue striped costumes, stand at the gates of Vatican City.

RENAISSANCE ITALY

Florence (below) sits on both sides of the Arno River. During the 1400s, a new movement in art and architecture—known as the Renaissance, or rebirth—began in Italy. Painters and sculptors, such as Leonardo da Vinci, Michelangelo, and Raphael, created beautiful works of art using improved techniques of perspective and realism. Many of these can still be seen in the galleries and churches of Florence.

HOME LIFE

Family life is important in Italy, and most people live at home until they get married. This is partly owing to the lack of cheap housing. Lunch (*pranzo*) is often the main meal of the day.

Central Europe

FOUR COUNTRIES LIE at the heart of central Europe—
Poland, the Czech Republic, Slovakia, and Hungary. The
region is typically composed of wide plains broken up by
gentle hills and the Carpathian mountain range in the south.
In the late 1980s, these countries broke away from years of
communist rule. The new democratic governments were
faced with the problems of trying to modernize their nations.
These changes are ongoing, but in some of the countries,
such as the Czech Republic, there are signs of improvement
and a rise in living standards.

TRADITIONAL TRADES
The countries of central Europe, except
Slovakia, are heavily industrialized. Huge
coal mines, steelworks (above), and
engineering works dominate the urban
landscape. Although some of these sites are
old and poorly equipped, these countries
are trying to update the machinery and
introduce measures to improve standards
of environmental pollution.

FAMILY FARMS
Poland has one of the largest agricultural sectors
in Europe, with more than one fourth of the work
force employed in farming. Most farms are still
small, family-run businesses, growing grains, beets,
and potatoes. Large numbers of pigs and other
animals are also raised.

GOLDEN PRAGUE
Prague, the capital of the Czech Republic,
is one of Europe's most beautiful cities. It
contains many old buildings with golden
roofs and grand squares. Unlike other
central European cities, Prague escaped
serious damage during both world wars,
and thus retains a lot of its charm.

Part of Prague's colorful history
is preserved in buildings around
the Old Town Square.

RELIGION
The Roman Catholic
Church is very strong
throughout central
Europe. Attending
mass on Sunday and
observing religious
holidays, such as
Christmas and Easter,
are important features
of family life.

BELARUS

KALININGRAD
(to Russian Federation)

POLAND

GERMANY

Baltic Sea

Gulf of Danzig
Vistula Lagoon

Pomeranian Bay

Szczecin Lagoon

Oder (Odra)

Warta

Wisła

Narew

Bug

Noteć

Sudeten

Śnieżka
5,256ft
(1602m)

Wyżyna Lubelska

Małopolska

Śląsk

WARSAW
(WARSZAWA)

Goldap
Suwałki
Augustów
Kuźnica
Sokółka
Białystok
Łapy
Bielsk Podlaski
Siemiatycze
Biała Podlaska
Międzyrzec Podlaski
Radzyń Podlaski
Włodawa
Chełm
Krasnystaw
Zamość
Łężajsk
Tomaszów Lubelski
Mielec
Tarnobrzeg
Stalowa Wola
Sandomierz
Ostrowiec
Świętokrzyski
Skarżysko-Kamienna
Starachowice
Kielce
Jędrzejów
Zawiercie
Chorzów
Gliwice
Bytom
Kędzierzyn-Koźle
Opole
Brzeg
Ząbkowice Śląskie
Świdnica
Wałbrzych
Legnica
Jelenia Góra
Bolesławiec
Zgorzelec
Zielona Góra
Świebodzin
Krosno Odrzańskie
Nowa Sól
Głogów
Lubin
Rawicz
Leszno
Gorzów Wielkopolski
Międzyrzecz
Sulechów
Żagań
Lubsko
Szprotawa
Bytów
Szczecinek
Człuchów
Wałcz
Piła
Oborniki
Gniezno
Poznań
Września
Konin
Koło
Kalisz
Ostrów Wielkopolski
Pleszew
Kępno
Kłobuck
Częstochowa
Lubliniec
Kluczbork
Radomsko
Bełchatów
Sieradz
Zgierz
Łódź
Pabianice
Piotrków Trybunalski
Tomaszów Mazowiecki
Radom
Skierniewice
Zduńska
Grójec
Góra Kalwaria
Garwolin
Ryki
Puławy
Lublin
Kraśnik
Lublin
Łuków
Siedlce
Wyszków
Pułtusk
Ostrołęka
Ostrów Mazowiecka
Zambrów
Łomża
Grajewo
Ełk
Giżycko
Kętrzyn
Gołdap
Suwałki
Pisz
Szczytno
Olsztyn
Mrągowo
Dobre Miasto
Biskupiec
Warmiński
Lidzbark
Braniewo
Elbląg
Malbork
Gdynia
Gdańsk
Rumia
Wejherowo
Władysławowo
Słupsk
Lębork
Kościerzyna
Chojnice
Tczew
Starogard
Świecie
Tuchola
Grudziądz
Kwidzyn
Iława
Ostróda
Nidzica
Działdowo
Mława
Ciechanów
Płońsk
Płock
Włocławek
Kutno
Toruń
Inowrocław
Mogilno
Żnin
Bydgoszcz
Chodzież
Trzcianka
Czarnków
Wągrowiec
Nowy Dwór Mazowiecki
Pruszków
Pabianice
Łęczyca
Turek
Ozorków
Żyrardów
Rypin
Brodnica
Chełmża
Chełmno
Świnoujście
Kołobrzeg
Koszalin
Białogard
Szczecinek
Świdwin
Nowogard
Goleniów
Szczecin
Stargard Szczeciński
Choszczno
Myślibórz
Pyrzyce
Ustka
Sławno
Słupsk
Rumia
Kołobrzeg
Wrocław
Oleśnica
Trzebnica
Oława
Kalisz
Ostrzeszów
Wieluń
010
PRAGUE
Ústí nad Labem
Teplice
Most
Chomutov
Karlovy Vary
Děčín
Liberec
Turnov
Lovosice

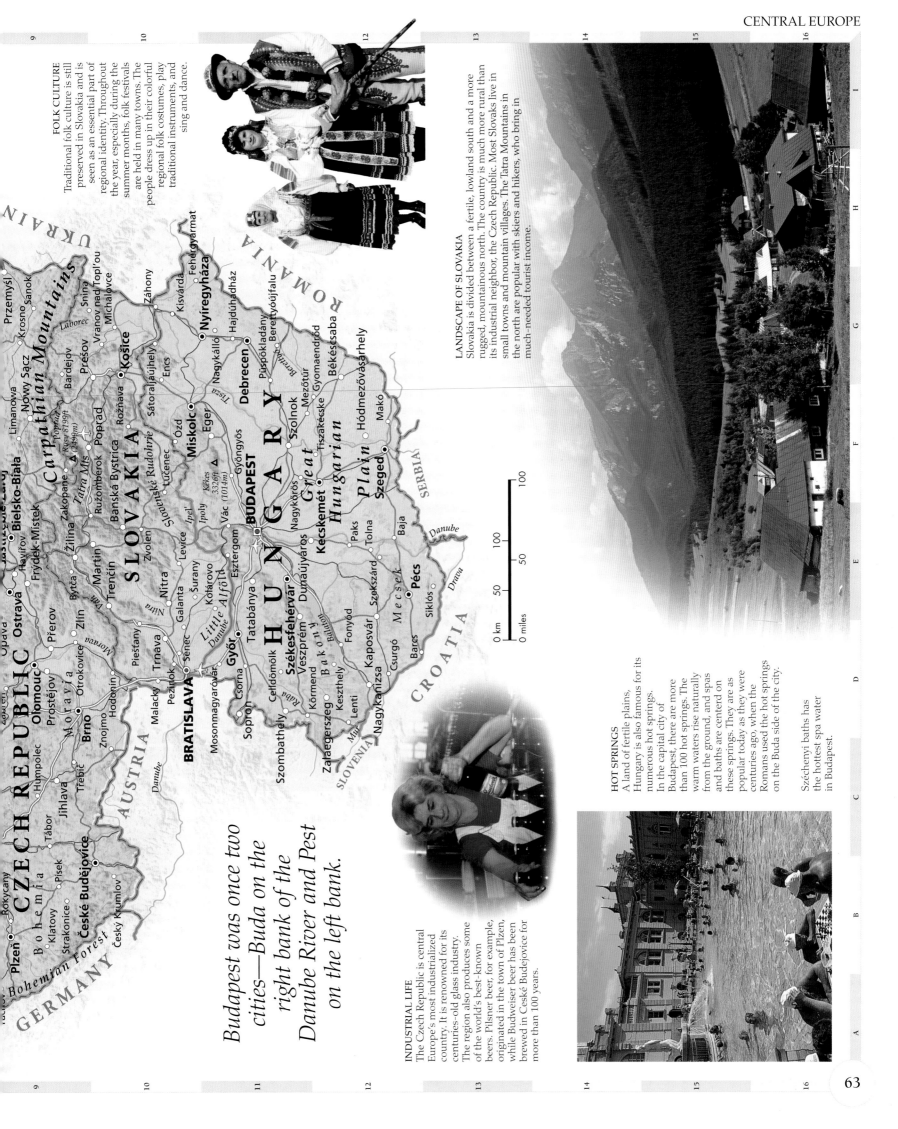

FOLK CULTURE

Traditional folk culture is still preserved in Slovakia and is seen as an essential part of regional identity. Throughout the year, especially during the summer months, folk festivals are held in many towns. The people dress up in their colorful regional folk costumes, play traditional instruments, and sing and dance.

LANDSCAPE OF SLOVAKIA

Slovakia is divided between a fertile, lowland south and a more rugged, mountainous north. The country is much more rural than its industrial neighbor, the Czech Republic. Most Slovaks live in small towns and mountain villages. The Tatra Mountains in the north are popular with skiers and hikers, who bring in much-needed tourist income.

HOT SPRINGS

A land of fertile plains, Hungary is also famous for its numerous hot springs. In the capital city of Budapest, there are more than 100 hot springs. The warm waters rise naturally from the ground, and spas and baths are centerd on these springs. They are as popular today as they were centuries ago, when the Romans used the hot springs on the Buda side of the city.

Széchenyi baths has the hottest spa water in Budapest.

Budapest was once two cities—Buda on the right bank of the Danube River and Pest on the left bank.

INDUSTRIAL LIFE

The Czech Republic is central Europe's most industrialized country. It is renowned for its centuries-old glass industry.

The region also produces some of the world's best-known beers. Pilsner beer, for example, originated in the town of Plzeň, while Budweiser beer has been brewed in České Budějovice for more than 100 years.

Southeast Europe

UNTIL 1991, CROATIA, Bosnia and Herzegovina, Serbia, Montenegro, and Macedonia were all part of Yugoslavia. Ethnic tensions between the Serbs and other peoples in Yugoslavia caused a series of bloody wars that broke up the country. Peace was eventually restored in 1999, but all five countries have suffered from intense economic problems as a result. So, too, has Albania ever since its communist government collapsed. The six nations do, however, have huge potential, with considerable agricultural and mineral resources. In the north, the Danube River is an important trade route for both Croatia and Serbia, while Croatia has a flourishing tourist industry along its beautiful Adriatic coast.

THE ADRIATIC
The long Adriatic coastline of Croatia is one of the most beautiful in Europe. The wooded hillsides, pretty beaches, such as Markarska (right), islands, and historic towns once attracted tourists from all over Europe. Now that the country is no longer involved in the war, tourists are returning, contributing vital income to the national economy.

GROWING FOOD
The most fertile area in this region lies along the Danube River in northern Serbia and eastern Croatia. Here, vegetables, fruit, corn, and cereals are grown, as well as grapes for winemaking. Most farms are small-scale family businesses that grow a wide range of crops.

Family-run allotments

DIFFERENT SCRIPTS
The Croatian and Serbian languages are very similar, but the people of Croatia, a predominantly Roman Catholic country, write in Roman script, as do Bosnians. Serbians are mostly Eastern Orthodox and write using both Roman and Russian Cyrillic scripts.

Magazine with Roman script

Magazine with Cyrillic script

The Dalmatian dog is named after the coastal region of Dalmatia in Croatia, its first known home.

SPORTING ACHIEVEMENT
Croatia is a great sports nation. Skier Janica Kostelic is not only Croatia's first triple Olympic champion, but she is also the most successful female Alpine skier of all time, winning three gold medals at the 2002 Winter Olympics and another gold and silver medal in 2006.

Janica Kostelic

Map labels

ROMANIA

HUNGARY

SERBIA

CROATIA

BOSNIA &

HERZEGOVINA

SLOVENIA

REPUBLIKA SRPSKA

FEDERACIJA BOSNA I HERCEGOVINA

Dinara

Velebit

Istra

Adriatic

Subotica
Kanjiža
Senta
Ada
Kikinda
Tisza
Bečej
Temerin
Zrenjanin
Mužlja
Vršac
Bela Crkva
Smederevo
Požarevac
Danube (Duna)
Velika Morava
Pančevo
BELGRADE (BEOGRAD)
Zemun
Mladenovac
Smederevska Palanka
Arandelovac
Gornji Milanovac
Bačka Topola
Vojvodina
Vrbas
Srbobran
Bačka Palanka
Novi Sad
Indija
Stara Pazova
Ruma
Batajnica
Futog
Sombor
Beli Manastir
Borovo
Vukovar
Sremska Mitrovica
Šabac
Drina
Loznica
Apatin
Osijek
Đakovo
Vinkovci
Županja
Valjevo
Slatina
Drava
Virovitica
Slavonska Požega
Bosanska Gradiška
Slavonski Brod
Bosanski Šamac
Derventa
Gradačac
Brčko
Modriča
Bijeljina
Zvornik
Srebrenica
Koprivnica
Bjelovar
Papuk
Nova Gradiška
Bosanski Brod
Doboj
Zavidovići
Tuzla
Maglaj
Zenica
Čakovec
Kutina
Kozara
Banja Luka
BOSNIA
Travnik
Varaždin
Sisak
Sava
Sana
Jajce
Visoko
SARAJEVO
Sesvete
Glina
Bosanska Dubica
Prijedor
Bosanski Novi
Kozara
Ključ
Livno
ZAGREB
Križevci
Petrinja
Karlovac
Cazin
Bihać
Una
Sana
Knin
Sinj
Samobor
Kolpa
Ogulin
Gospić
Troglav 6276ft (1913m)
Šibenik
Crikvenica
Senj
Zadar
Rijeka
Krk
Pag
Dugi Otok
Opatija
Cres
Lošinj
Kvarner
Poreč
Rovinj
Pula

ЗАБАВНИК

AMA

The remains of an impressive temple still stands in Apollonia, Albania.

APOLLONIA

About 8 miles (13 km) outside the city of Fier, Albania, lie the ruins of an ancient city called Apollonia. Founded in 588 BCE by Greeks from Corinth, it is one of 30 cities named after the Greek god Apollo. Austrian archaeologists began excavating the site during World War I, and French archaeologists continued digging in the 1930s. However, most of the city still remains buried in the surrounding hills.

Eel

An Albanian family

LIFE IN ALBANIA

Albania is one of the poorest countries in Europe. Most people are ethnic Albanian, with a sizable Greek minority in the south of the country. Loyalty to one's family or clan is more important than national identity, and married sons often live with their parents and look after them in old age.

Lake Prespa

GREAT LAKES

Macedonia contains two huge lakes—Ohrid and Prespa. The latter has clear water fed by underground streams and is a popular tourist destination. In 2002, the first Prespa boat regatta took place here. Both lakes have substantial fish stocks, especially of trout and eel, which are used to make local dishes.

DUBROVNIK

The medieval walled city of Dubrovnik, at the southern tip of Croatia on the Adriatic Sea, is one of the architectural gems of Europe. In 1991, Serb troops shelled the city, causing immense damage. The city was restored after the end of the war. Other historic cities damaged during the fighting, notably Sarajevo and Mostar in Bosnia and Herzegovina, have yet to be fully restored.

BULGARIA

GREECE

MONTENEGRO

North Albanian Alps

KOSOVO (disputed)

PRISTINA

SKOPJE

MACEDONIA

ALBANIA

TIRANA (TIRANË)

PODGORICA

Balkan Mountains

Niš
Zaječar
Knjaževac
Pirot
Paraćin
Aleksinac
Kruševac
Kruševac
Prokuplje
Vlasotince
Surdulica
Južna Morava
Leskovac
Vranje
Bujanovac
Preševo
Kumanovo
Kočani
Štip
Radoviš
Strumica
Gevgelija
Kavadarci
Vardar
Bregalnica
Veles
Prilep
Bitola
Kopaonik
Kraljevo
Ibar
Priboj
Prijepolje
Pljevlja
Bijelo Polje
Novi Pazar
Sjenica
Berane
Mitrovicë
Podujevë
Vushtrri
Fushë Kosovë
Gjilan
Ferizaj
Prizren
Pejë
Rahovec
Gjakovë
Dinara
Tetovo
Gostivar
Kičevo
Debar
Ohrid
Struga
Lake Ohrid
Pogradec
Lake Prespa
Korçë
Crna Reka
Lumi i Drinit
Black Drin
Bajram Curri
Kukës
Peshkopi
Burrel
Lezhë
Krujë
Laç
Lumi i Shkumbini
Elbasan
Lumi i Devollit
Berat
Lumi i Osumit
Tepelenë
Lumi i Vjosës
Gjirokastër
Sarandë
Konispol
Durrës
Kavajë
Lushnjë
Fier
Kuçovë
Vlorë
Corfu (Kérkyra)
Strait of Otranto
Podgorica
Nikšić
Cetinje
Kotor
Bar
Shkodër
Lake Scutari
Dubrovnik
Trebinje
Mostar
Metković
Ploče
Mljet
Korčula
Hvar
Vis
Neretva
Drina

8720ft (2658m)

0 km   50   100
0 miles 50 100

Bulgaria and Greece

FOR MORE THAN 400 YEARS, Bulgaria and Greece were ruled by the Ottoman Turks. Bulgaria gained independence in 1908, while southern Greece became independent in 1832 and was joined by northern Greece in 1913. After World War II, Bulgaria became a communist state. Both states are now democracies and members of the European Union (EU). Bulgaria remains relatively poor while in 2010, it emerged that Greece had a huge national deficit owing to spending more than it had been collecting in taxes. The EU lent Greece 112 billion euros (146.6 billion dollars) to restore its economy. Although they border each other, Bulgaria and Greece are quite different; the Greek mainland is mountainous, with only one third of the land suitable for cultivation. By contrast, Bulgaria is more fertile, with a strong agricultural tradition. Tourism is an important source of income to both countries, with visitors flocking to the Black Sea resorts in Bulgaria, to the Greek mainland to see the ancient ruins, and to the Greek islands in search of sandy beaches.

First held in Athens in 1896, the modern Olympic Games were staged there again in 2004.

BULGARIAN AGRICULTURE

Wheat, corn, and other cereals grow in the fertile Danube River valley in the north of the country. Tobacco (right) grows in the Maritsa River valley in the southeast, while grapes for the wine industry flourish on the slopes of the Balkan Mountains. The festival of Kukerov Den, with traditional processions, celebrates the start of the agricultural year.

CITY LIFE

Bulgarians make up about 85 percent of the total population of the country. The rest are Turkish, Macedonian, or Roma. Most people live in apartment buildings in the main towns and cities. They are more likely to use public transportation as not all households have a car.

Trams provide an efficient way for people to get around the city of Sofia.

ARCHITECTURE

Bulgaria contains many beautiful old churches, monasteries, and mosques, despite the damage done to the country during World War II. Rila Monastery (above) was founded by a hermit monk who took to the mountains in search of solitude in 927 CE. After a fire in 1833, Rila was rebuilt, and the magnificent church now boasts three fine domes, a museum, and 1,200 frescoes.

LANGUAGE

The 24 characters in the Greek alphabet date from the 700s BCE, when the first texts were written in classical Greek. Since then the language has evolved and is now spoken by 11 million people around the world.

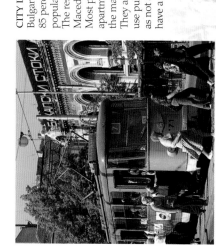

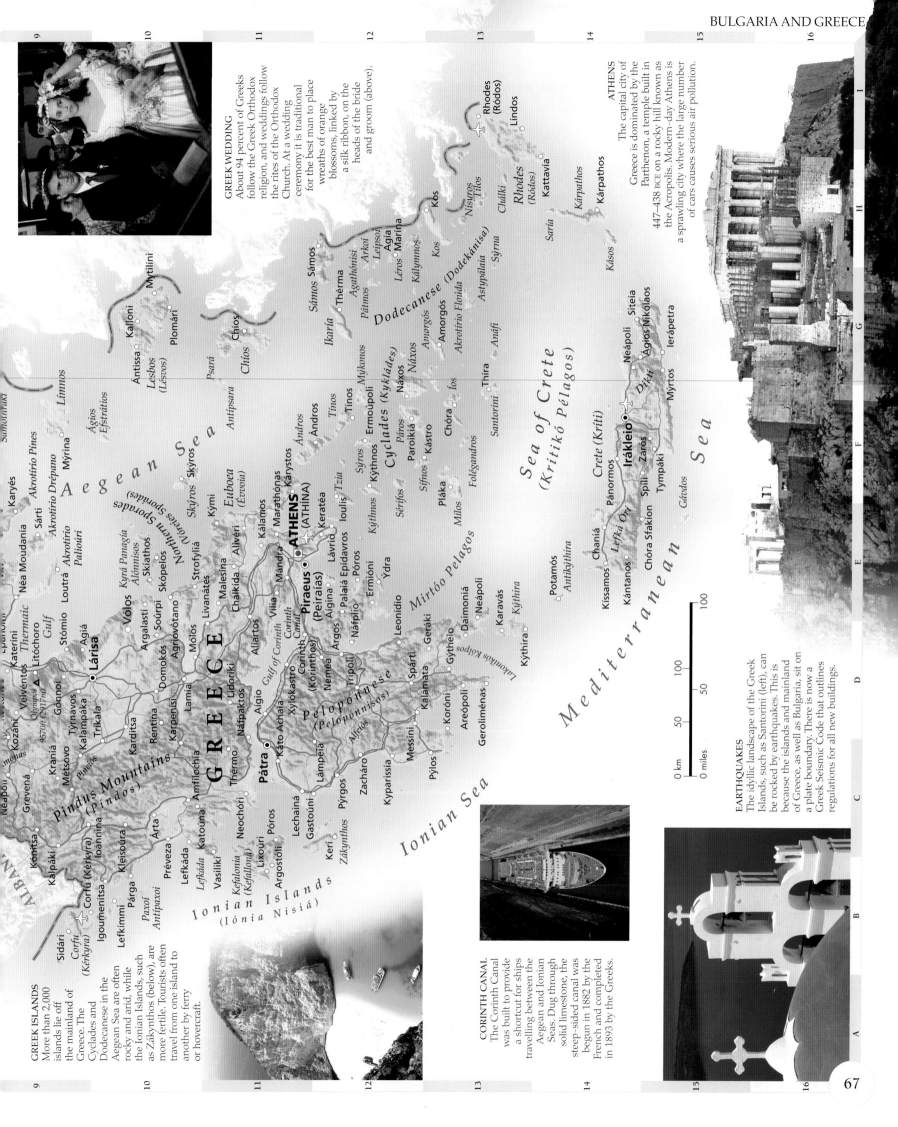

GREEK WEDDING

About 94 percent of Greeks follow the Greek Orthodox religion, and weddings follow the rites of the Orthodox Church. At a wedding ceremony it is traditional for the best man to place wreaths of orange blossoms, linked by a silk ribbon, on the heads of the bride and groom (above).

ATHENS

The capital city of Greece is dominated by the Parthenon, a temple built in 447–438 BCE on a rocky hill known as the Acropolis. Modern-day Athens is a sprawling city where the large number of cars causes serious air pollution.

GREEK ISLANDS

More than 2,000 islands lie off the mainland of Greece. The Cyclades and Dodecanese in the Aegean Sea are often rocky and arid, while the Ionian Islands, such as Zákynthos (below), are more fertile. Tourists often travel from one island to another by ferry or hovercraft.

CORINTH CANAL

The Corinth Canal was built to provide a shortcut for ships travelling between the Aegean and Ionian Seas. Dug through solid limestone, the steep-sided canal was begun in 1882 by the French and completed in 1893 by the Greeks.

EARTHQUAKES

The idyllic landscape of the Greek Islands, such as Santoríni (left), can be rocked by earthquakes. This is because the islands and mainland of Greece, as well as Bulgaria, sit on a plate boundary. There is now a Greek Seismic Code that outlines regulations for all new buildings.

GREECE

Aegean Sea

Ionian Sea

Ionian Islands (Iónia Nisiá)

Mediterranean Sea

Sea of Crete (Kritikó Pélagos)

Mirtóo Pelagos

Pindus Mountains (Pindos)

Peloponnese (Pelopónnisos)

Northern Sporades (Vóreies Sporádes)

Cyclades (Kykládes)

Dodecanese (Dodekánisa)

Crete (Kriti)

Lakonikós Kólpos

Gulf of Corinth

ALBANIA

ATHENS (ATHÍNA)
Piraeus (Peiraiás)
Lárisa
Vólos
Pátra
Rhodes (Ródos)
Irákleio

0 km 50 100
0 miles 50 100

67

Ukraine, Moldova, & Romania

THROUGHOUT MOST OF THE PAST CENTURY, Ukraine and Moldova formed part of the Soviet Union, while Romania was ruled for 20 years by the dictator Nicolae Ceausescu. In 1989, Ceausescu was overthrown, while Ukraine and Moldova became independent in 1991. Today, the three countries are struggling to come to terms with their communist inheritance and transform themselves into modern democracies. All three lack modern technology and face serious economic and environmental problems arising from outdated industry. They also face increasing ethnic tensions with their minority populations—Hungarians in Romania, as well as Russians left behind in Ukraine and Moldova after the collapse of the Soviet Union.

CITY LIFE
Romania has many cities and towns, with a mix of old and new buildings. Sibiu (left) was founded in the 1100s and, at one time, had 19 guilds—each representing a different craft—within its city walls. Most remains from this colorful history, especially in the painted buildings of the old town.

FOLK CUSTOMS
Despite years of communist rule, folk customs thrived in the rural areas of Romania and Ukraine. In Ukraine, singers perform *dumas*, historical epics that tell of slavery under the Turks. One of the traditional instruments is a bandura (left), a stringed instrument that sounds like a harpsichord.

DRACULA'S CASTLE
Situated in Transylvania, Bran Castle is a favourite tourist destination. This is where author Bram Stoker's fictional blood-drinking Count Dracula lived. The story is probably based on a 15th-century Romanian prince, Vlad Dracula, who reigned for less than 10 years but caused more than 50,000 deaths.

The word Transylvania means "land beyond the forests."

EASTER BREAD
In Romania, Easter is celebrated with a meal of roast lamb served with a bread called *cozonac*. This is made by pounding nuts, raisins, and even cocoa into the dough.

INDUSTRY IN THE UKRAINE
Ukraine is the world's eighth-largest producer of steel and has a large coal industry, as well as reserves of oil and gas. Today, however, most of its industry is out of date and inefficient. Most of the heavy industry is situated in the central Dnieper River valley.

Liquid iron ore

VACATIONS BY THE SEA
The Black Sea resorts of the Crimea, in southern Ukraine, were once a favorite vacation destination for Russians heading south for the summer sun. Today, resorts such as Yalta (below), are growing again in popularity, sometimes as a budget alternative to Mediterranean destinations. The quality of facilities is improving as tourist numbers increase.

PEOPLE OF ROMANIA
Romanians speak Romanian—a language closely related to French, Italian, and Spanish. The country also has sizable Hungarian and Roma minorities, which have both been discriminated against in recent years. Most Hungarian speakers live in the region of Romania known as Transylvania.

Children of the Maramures region of Transylvania

RICH SOIL OF MOLDOVA
Moldova consists of partially wooded plains intercut with rivers and streams. About 75 percent of the land is rich in chernozem (black) soil, which is very fertile. Wine and sunflower production are important here. Fruit and vegetables, such as pumpkins (left), also grow well.

RUSSIAN FEDERATION

0 km 50 100
0 miles 50 100

Black Sea

Sea of Azov

Gulf of Taganrog

Baltic States & Belarus

T HE THREE BALTIC STATES—Estonia, Latvia, and Lithuania—all share a small stretch of coast on the Baltic Sea. Belarus lies between Poland, Ukraine, and the Russian Federation. Following independence from the Soviet Union in 1991, all of these countries faced problems such as price rises, food shortages, and pollution. However, the Baltic States have since tried to reform their societies and economies along Western lines. Belarus has kept close links with Russia and has been the slowest to reform. This mostly rural country remains isolated from the rest of Europe and, with few natural resources, remains one of its poorest nations.

SINGING REVOLUTION
Estonia is known for its classical music tradition—most notably its choirs. This love of music was most powerful when people raised their voices during the Singing Revolution in 1988 (right), part of their move toward independence.

Political rally in Tallinn

TALLINN'S OLD TOWN
With its colorful buildings, turreted walls, and gabled roofs, Tallinn is one of the best-preserved capital cities in Europe. All of the winding, cobbled streets lead to Town Square (left).

AMBER
Two thirds of the world's amber—the fossilized resin of pine trees—is washed up from the seabed along the Baltic coast. Amber is used to make jewelry, among other items.

Belarus used to be known as Belorussia, a name that means "White Russia."

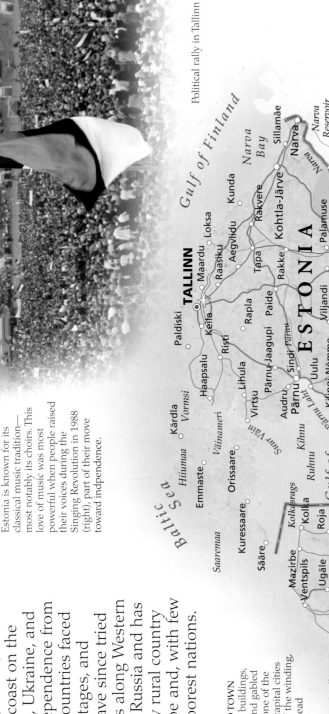

Map

RUSSIAN FEDERATION

Gulf of Finland

Narva Bay

Narva Reservoir

Narva

Sillamäe
Kohtla-Järve
Kallaste
Lake Peipus
Lake Pskov
Rakvere
Kunda
Loksa
Maardu
Aegviidu
Tapa
Rakke
Paide
Rapla
Kehra
Keila
TALLINN
Paldiski
Haapsalu
Risti
Lihula
Virtsu
Pärnu-Jaagupi
Audru
Pärnu
Sindi
Uulu
Kilingi-Nõmme
Viljandi
Mõisaküla
Rõngu
Tõrva
Otepää
Põlva
Võru
Tartu
Võnnu
Rapina
Puurmani
Palamuse
ESTONIA
Emajõgi
Valga
Valka
Smiltene
Ape
Alūksne
Gulbene
Balvi
Vilaka
Gaizina Kalns 1043ft (311m)
St799t
Munamägi 1043ft (318m)
Apa
Rūjiena
Staicele
Aloja
Burtnieku Ezers
Valmiera
Cēsis
Limbaži
Ainaži
Salacgrīva
Saulkrasti
Gauja
Jaunpiebalga
Madona
Varakļāni
Lubāns Ezers
Jēkabpils
Līvāni
Spogi
Daugavpils
Dagda
Krāslava
Rēzekne
Malta
Ludza
Kārsava
Dagda
Viļāni
Plaviņas
Rugāji
LATVIA
Kolkasrags
Kolka
Roja
Mērsrags
Engure
Tukums
Jūrmala
RIGA
Jelgava
Iecava
Bauska
Aizkraukle
Ķegums
Viesīte
Nereta
Jēkabpils
Pļaviņas
Rokiškis
Pasvalys
Biržai
Aknīste
Obeliai
Zarasai
Anykščiai
Utena
Visaginas
Ignalina
Rūjiena
Hiiumaa
Kärdla
Emmaste
Vormsi
Vänamäri
Orissaare
Kuressaare
Saaremaa
Sāre
Muhu
Baltic Sea
Suur Väin
Kihnu
Ruhnu
Gulf of Riga
Mazirbe
Ventspils
Ugāle
Talsi
Usmas Ezers
Kuldīga
Kandava
Saldus
Brocēni
Engures Ezers
Pāvilosta
Liepāja
Grobiņa
Durbe
Venta
Kurzeme
Skuodas
Mažeikiai
Papilė
Joniškis
Radviliškis
Pakruojis
Šiauliai
Kelmė
Raseiniai
Naujamiestis
Panevėžys
Subačius
Ukmergė
Kaišiadorys
Jonava
VILNIUS
Neris
Širvintos
Salantai
Plungė
Telšiai
Gargždai
Kretinga
Klaipėda
Priekulė
Nida
Šilutė
Neman
Tauragė
Jurbarkas
Skaudvilė
Šilalė
Žemaičių Aukštumas
Kuršėnai
Šalčininkai
Šalčininkai
Vilkaviškis
Marijampolė
Kalvarija
Alytus
Prienai
Rūdiškės
Trakai
Merkinė
Varėna
Druskininkai
Veisiejai
LITHUANIA
Kaunas
Kernavė
Rudamina
Primorsk
Pionerskiy
Zelenogradsk
Baltiysk
Gvardeysk
KALININGRAD (to Russian Federation)
Kaliningrad
Chernyakhovsk
Gusev
Mamonovo
Bagrationovsk
Zheleznodorozhnyy
Courland Lagoon
POLAND
Navapolatsk
Polatsk
Harany
Drysa
Western Dvina
Yukhavichy
Vyerkhnyadzvinsk
Bihosava
Vidzy
Giedraičiai
Vyetryna
Myadzyel
Hlybokaye
Pastavy
Ashmyany
Vetrino
Viliya
Neris
Yezyaryshcha
Sarochyna
Harany

MINSK
The capital of Belarus, Minsk, was destroyed during World War II and then rebuilt in a starkly modern style. Minsk is the country's economic center. Cars, lorries and tractors, chemicals, timber products, and a range of high-tech goods are all produced here. Farm produce (above) is also sold in markets.

TEXTILES
The development of the textile industry (above) in these countries is strong, with foreign investment from several other European countries helping growth. Clothes, bedding, curtains, and towels are just some of the items made for export.

FARMING
The fertile soil and flat landscape make this region good for farming. The Baltic States, especially Latvia (left), have large dairy farms. Belarus is a major producer of flax, which is used to make linen and other products. Potatoes—used to make vodka—beets, and other root crops are also grown here.

LITHUANIAN DRESS
In some Lithuanian villages, people still wear traditional folk costumes, especially for festive occasions. Women's clothing is generally colorful (left) and might include a white linen shirt, a skirt, and an apron. The decoration and style of the costume shows which region of Lithuania the wearer comes from.

GYMNASTICS
The former Soviet Union worked its young athletes and gymnasts extremely hard in order to win Olympic medals and thus national glory. Many of the most famous gymnasts came from Belarus, notably Olga Korbut and, more recently, Svetlana Boginskaya (right), who has won three gold, one silver, and one bronze Olympic medals.

FORESTS AND LAKES
All four countries are lowlying, with many moors, bogs, unspoiled lakes, and fir and pine forests. Forestry is an important industry, providing wood pulp for papermaking and timber for furniture and houses.

Ferns thrive in this Latvian forest

RUSSIAN FEDERATION

BELARUS

POLAND

UKRAINE

Vitsyebsk
Lyozna
Chashniki
Bahushewsk
Sava
Horki
Shklow
Orsha
Mahilyow
Harbavichy
Khodasy
Klimavichy
Kastsyukovichy
Baron'ki
Talachyn
Krupki
Kruhlaye
Byalynichy
Dashkawka
Cherykaw
Kryehaw
Slawharad
Krasnaye
Plyeshchanitsy
Zhodzina
Barysaw
Byerezino
Chervyen'
Pukhavichy
Tal'ka
Yalizava
Chachevichy
Abidavichy
Babruysk
Rahachow
Zhlobin
Buda-Kashalyova
Uvaravichy
Kastsyukowka
Dobrush
Tsyerakhowka
MINSK
Minskaya Wzvyshsha
Horka
Mar"ina
Rudzyensk
Shyshchytsy
Asipovichy
Brozha
Shchadryn
Aktsyabrski
Svyetlahorsk
Kalinkavichy
Mazyr
Rechytsa
Homyel'
Khoyniki
Loyew
Byval'ki
Shatsk
Ptsich
Shyichy
Narowlya
Valozhyn
Shchuchyn
Masty
Vawkavysk
Novy Dvor
Ruzhany
Pruzhany
Zhabinka
Kobryn
Damachava
Makrany
Brest
Bug
Orlya
Zel'va
Slonim
Navahrudak
Baranavichy
Abrova
Hantsavichy
Lyusina
Drahichyn
Ivanava
Pinsk
Luninyets
Bastyn'
Lyel'chytsy
Milashavichy
Yel'sk
Dabryn
Simanichy
Tonyezh
Pripet
Pripet Marshes
Yasyel'da
Byelaruskaya Hrada
Lyakhavichy
Kapyl'
Nyasvizh
Syemyezhava
Salihorsk
Starobin
Kaptsevichy
Pyetrykaw
Mikashevichy
Zhytkavichy
Slutsk
Stowbtsy
Staryya Darohi
Kapyl'
Shyshchytsy
Ivatsevichy
Haradzyets
Iatsevichy

Dnieper
Dniester
Ptsich

0 km   50   100
0 miles   50   100

71

European Russia

SEPARATED FROM ASIAN RUSSIA by the Ural Mountains, European Russia is so large that it spans four time zones. The climate and landscape range from cold desert and frozen tundra in the north to the warm coast of the Black Sea in the southwest. Forests and grassy steppes cover huge areas. More than 100 million people—two thirds of the total Russian population—live in European Russia, most of them in cities such as the capital, Moscow. Since the collapse of communism in 1991, many Russians have experienced a decline in their standard of living. Shortages of food and manufactured goods occurred, and crime and unemployment rates rose. As a result, Russia was the only European country in which life expectancy dropped. As the country recovered, it was hit by deep recession in 2009.

ST. PETERSBURG
Once Russia's capital, St. Petersburg was built in the 1700s by Czar Peter the Great as a "window on the west." Today, it is a popular tourist destination, full of grand palaces and extravagant architecture (left). The city spreads over some 40 islands, linked by a network of canals and rivers.

The Church of Our Savior on Spilled Blood marks the spot where Czar Alexander II was murdered in 1881.

BALLET
Russia is famous for its ballet companies, such as the Bolshoi Ballet of Moscow and the Kirov Ballet of St. Petersburg. Most of the ballets performed are classics, such as Swan Lake and Sleeping Beauty. Developed in Europe in the 1800s, ballet became a popular form of art and entertainment in the 1900s.

Sleeping Beauty is performed here by dancers from the Kirov Ballet.

EDUCATION
Children attend school here from the age of 7 through 17. Although the state education system is free, education declined after the fall of communism owing to chronic underfunding. Major efforts are now raising standards in state schools, but private schools are becoming increasingly popular.

Map labels

0 km   150   300
0 miles   150   300

Kara Sea
(Karskoye More)

Novaya
Zemlya

Ostrov
Vaygach

Proliv Karskiye Vorota

Pechorskoye
More

Pomorskiy Proliv

Barents
Sea

Ostrov
Kolguyev

White Sea
(Beloye More)

Kola Peninsula
(Kol'skiy Poluostrov)

NORWAY

FINLAND

ESTONIA

LATVIA

BELARUS

Severnyy
Vorkuta
Promyshlennyy
Bol'shezemel'skaya Tundra
Nar'yan-Mar
Inta
Usa
Usinsk
Pechora
Pechora
Malozemel'skaya Tundra
Nizhniy Odes
Yarega
Ukhta
Kama
Berezniki
Solikamsk
Kirovo-Chepetsk
Zuyevka
Kirov
Koryazhma
Syktyvkar
Yemva
Mikun'
Luza
Kotlas
Sukhona
Uren'
Timanskiy Kryazh
Mezen'
Pinega
Northern Dvina
Onega
Archangel (Arkhangel'sk)
Novodvinsk
Onega
Severodvinsk
Medvezh'yegorsk
Plesetsk
Nyandoma
Vel'sk
Konosha
Belozersk
Sokol
Vologda
Kostroma
Kineshma
Ivanovo
Cherepovets
Rybinsk
Yaroslavl'
Murmansk
Severomorsk
Olenegorsk
Nikel'
Zapolyarnyy
Polyarnyy
Murmashi
Monchegorsk
Apatity
Kandalaksha
Zelenoborskiy
Ozero
Topozero
Kem'
Belomorsk
Nadvoitsy
Segezha
Kondopoga
Suoyarvi
Petrozavodsk
Lake
Onega
Savinskiy
Lake
Ladoga
Olonets
Sortavala
Vyborg
Gulf of Finland
Saint Petersburg
(Sankt-Peterburg)
Gatchina
Kolpino
Petrodvorets
Kirishi
Volkhov
Tikhvin
Babayevo
Borovichi
Uglovka
Valday
Velikiy Novgorod
Luga
Sol'tsy
Porkhov
Pskov
Ostrov
Opochka
Velikiye Luki
Zapadnaya Dvina
Rzhev
Torzhok
Tver'
Zelenograd
Smolensk
Volkhov
RUSSIAN FEDERATION

Ural'skiye Gory (Ural'skiye Gory)
Mountains

RURAL LIFE
Rural life has become extremely tough since the economic collapse of large-scale farms in the 1990s, with many people living in poverty. Smaller cooperatives and farms (above) have sprung up, and the agricultural industry is going through a painful period of reform. Due to the harsh climate, only 10 percent of the land is suitable for agriculture.

Icons, common in the Russian Orthodox Church, are religious images painted on wooden panels.

THE TATARS
Russia's largest ethnic minority, the Tatars (below) are an Islamic people descended from the Mongols. Their largest population lives in the Tatarstan Republic, halfway between Moscow and the Urals.

The title czar, once used for Russian rulers, means "emperor" and comes from the ancient Roman title "Caesar."

THE RUSSIAN CHURCH
The main religion in Russia is the Russian Orthodox Church. Under communism, all religion was banned. The new freedom means that many Russians now attend church services on a regular basis. New churches are being built, old ones restored, and seminaries reopened to train new priests.

MOSCOW SUBWAY
Not many underground trains can claim to be tourist attractions, but Moscow's subway can. Built in the 1930s, many of its stations are decorated with beautiful chandeliers, mosaics, paintings, and sculptures. One of the busiest, most efficient subway systems in the world, it is used by more than 7 million people daily.

POLLUTION
The communists invested heavily in industry, but their outdated methods of production have affected the environment. Rivers such as the Volga are badly polluted, and many cities are covered in a permanent and poisonous smog. Chest infections and other diseases related to air pollution are common.

Industrial smog casts a haze over Moscow.

ASIA

The vast continent of Asia is dominated by two giant nations—China and India each with more than one billion people and a rich and colorful history. Both are being transformed by rapid economic growth, and so are many other Asian countries, listed below in order of size. Yet in some regions of central Asia, life has barely changed in thousands of years.

China
- 3,705,387 sq miles
  9,596,961 sq km
- 1,350,000,000
- Beijing
- Mandarin, Wu, Cantonese, Hsiang, Min, Hakka, Kan

Iran
- 636,368 sq miles
  1,648,195 sq km
- 74,200,000
- Tehran
- Farsi, Azeri, Luri, Gilaki, Mazandarani, Kurdish, Turkmen, Arabic, Balochi

Afghanistan
- 251,826 sq miles
  652,230 sq km
- 28,100,000
- Kabul
- Pashto, Tajik, Dari, Farsi, Uzbek, Turkmen

Iraq
- 169,234 sq miles
  438,317 sq km
- 30,700,000
- Baghdad
- Arabic, Kurdish, Turkic languages, Armenian, Assyrian

Philippines
- 115,830 sq miles
  300,000 sq km
- 92,000,000
- Manila
- Filipino, English, Tagalog, Cebuano, Ilocano, Hiligaynon, many other local languages

Nepal
- 56,827 sq miles
  147,181 sq km
- 29,300,000
- Kathmandu
- Nepali, Maithili, Bhojpuri

India
- 1,269,212 sq miles
  3,287,263 sq km
- 1,200,000,000
- New Delhi
- Hindi, English, Urdu, Bengali, Marathi, Telugu, Tamil, Bihari, Gujarati, Kannada.

Mongolia
- 603,905 sq miles
  1,564,116 sq km
- 2,670,000
- Ulan Bator
- Khalkha Mongolian, Kazakh, Chinese, Russian

Yemen
- 203,848 sq miles
  527,968 sq km
- 23,600,000
- Sanaak
- Arabic

Japan
- 145,913 sq miles
  377,915 sq km
- 127,000,000
- Tokyo
- Japanese, Korean, Chinese

Laos
- 91,428 sq miles
  236,800 sq km
- 6,320,000
- Vientiane
- Lao, Mon-Khmer, Yao, Vietnamese, Chinese, French

Bangladesh
- 55,598 sq miles
  143,998 sq km
- 162,000,000
- Dhaka
- Bengali, Urdu, Chakma, Marma (Magh), Garo, Khasi, Santhali, Tripura, Mru

Kazakhstan
- 1,052,084 sq miles
  2,724,900 sq km
- 15,600,000
- Astana
- Kazakh, Russian, Ukrainian, German, Uzbek, Tatar, Uyghur

Pakistan
- 307,372 sq miles
  796,095 sq km
- 181,000,000
- Islamabad
- Punjabi, Sindhi, Pashtu, Urdu, Balochi, Brahui

Thailand
- 198,116 sq miles
  513,120 sq km
- 67,800,000
- Bangkok
- Thai, Chinese, Malay, Khmer, Mon, Karen, Miao

Vietnam
- 127,880 sq miles
  331,210 sq km
- 88,100,000
- Hanoi
- Vietnamese, Chinese, Thai, Khmer, Muong, Nung, Miao, Yao, Jarai

Kyrgyzstan
- 77,201 sq miles
  199,951 sq km
- 5,480,000
- Bishkek
- Kyrgyz, Russian, Uzbek, Tatar, Ukrainian

Tajikistan
- 55,251 sq miles
  143,100 sq km
- 6,950,000
- Dushanbe
- Tajik, Uzbek, Russian

Saudi Arabia
- 829,995 sq miles
  2,149,690 sq km
- 25,700,000
- Riyadh
- Arabic

Turkey
- 302,533 sq miles
  783,562 sq km
- 74,800,000
- Ankara
- Turkish, Kurdish, Arabic, Circassian, Armenian, Greek, Georgian, Ladino (Judaeo-Spanish)

Turkmenistan
- 188,455 sq miles
  488,100 sq km
- 5,110,000
- Ashgabat
- Turkmen, Uzbek, Russian, Kazakh, Tatar

Malaysia
- 127,354 sq miles
  329,847 sq km
- 27,500,000
- Kuala Lumpur
- Bahasa Malaysia, Malay, Chinese, Tamil, English

Syria
- 71,498 sq miles
  185,180 sq km
- 21,900,000
- Damascus
- Arabic, French, Kurdish, Armenian, Circassian, Turkic languages, Assyrian, Aramaic

North Korea
- 46,540 sq miles
  120,538 sq km
- 23,900,000
- Pyongyang
- Korean

Indonesia
- 735,354 sq miles
  1,904,569 sq km
- 230,000,000
- Jakarta
- Javanese, Sundanese, Madurese, Bahasa Indonesia, Dutch

Myanmar (Burma)
- 261,227 sq miles
  676,578 sq km
- 50,000,000
- Nay Pyi Taw
- Burmese, Shan, Karen, Rakhine (Arakanese), Chin, Yangbye, Kachin, Mon

Uzbekistan
- 172,741 sq miles
  447,400 sq km
- 27,500,000
- Tashkent
- Uzbek, Russian, Tajik, Kazakh

Oman
- 119,498 sq miles
  309,500 sq km
- 2,850,000
- Muscat
- Arabic, Balochi, Farsi, Hindi, Punjabi

Cambodia
- 69,898 sq miles
  181,035 sq km
- 14,800,000
- Phnom Penh
- Khmer, French, Chinese, Vietnamese, Cham

South Korea
- 38,502 sq miles
  99,720 sq km
- 48,300,000
- Seoul
- Korean

Jordan
- 34,495 sq miles
  89,342 sq km
- 6,320,000
- Amman
- Arabic

Sri Lanka
- 25,332 sq miles
  65,610 sq km
- 20,200,000
- Colombo
- Sinhala, Tamil, Sinhala-Tamil, English

Azerbaijan
- 33,436 sq miles
  86,600 sq km
- 8,830,000
- Baku
- Azerbaijani, Russian

Bhutan
- 14,824 sq miles
  38,394 sq km
- 697,300
- Thimphu
- Dzongkha, Nepali, Assamese

Israel
- 8,019 sq miles
  20,770 sq km
- 7,170,000
- Jerusalem
- Hebrew, Arabic, Yiddish, German, Russian, Polish, Romanian, Persian

Qatar
- 4,473 sq miles
  11,586 sq km
- 1,410,000
- Doha
- Arabic

United Arab Emirates
- 32,278 sq miles
  83,600 sq km
- 4,600,000
- Abu Dhabi
- Arabic, Farsi, Indian and Pakistani languages, English

Taiwan
- 13,892 sq miles
  35,980 sq km
- 23,000,000
- Taipei
- Amoy Chinese, Mandarin Chinese, Hakka Chinese

Kuwait
- 6,880 sq miles
  17,818 sq km
- 2,990,000
- Kuwait City
- Arabic, English

Lebanon
- 4,015 sq miles
  10,400 sq km
- 4,220,000
- Beirut
- Arabic, French, Armenian, Assyrian

Bahrain
- 286 sq miles
  741 sq km
- 791,500
- Manama
- Arabic

Seychelles
- 176 sq miles
  455 sq km
- 84,600
- Victoria
- French Creole, English, French

Georgia
- 26,911 sq miles
  69,700 sq km
- 4,260,000
- T'bilisi
- Georgian, Russian, Azeri, Armenian, Mingrelian, Ossetian, Abkhazian

Armenia
- 11,484 sq miles
  29,743 sq km
- 3,080,000
- Yerevan
- Armenian, Azeri, Russian

East Timor
- 5,743 sq miles
  14,874 sq km
- 1,130,000
- Dili
- Tetum (Portuguese/Austronesian), Bahasa Indonesia, Portuguese

Brunei
- 2,226 sq miles
  5,765 sq km
- 399,700
- Bandar Seri Begawan
- Malay, English, Chinese

Singapore
- 269 sq miles
  697 sq km
- 4,740,000
- Singapore
- Mandarin, Malay, Tamil, English

Maldives
- 115 sq miles
  298 sq km
- 309,400
- Malé
- Dhivehi (Maldivian), Sinhala, Tamil, Arabic

75

Turkey and the Caucasus

TURKEY LIES IN BOTH ASIA and Europe—separated by the Bosphorus—and was once part of the powerful Ottoman Empire. Although Turks are 99 percent Muslim, modern Turkey is a country with no official religion. Western Turkey is relatively industrialized, with a tourist industry along the Mediterranean coast that brings in considerable income. Many farmers and herders in the center and east, however, struggle to make a living in the arid environment. To the northeast lie the Caucasus countries of Georgia, Azerbaijan, and Armenia. Once part of the U.S.S.R., they are now independent.

ISTANBUL
The different faces of Turkey can be seen in its former capital, Istanbul, which lies on both sides of the Bosphorus waterway. Churches, mosques, and ancient buildings in both European and Islamic styles sit side by side with modern stores and offices. Bridges link the two parts of the city. In 1923, Ankara became the new capital.

TURKISH FOOD
Turkey is self-sufficient in food, and grows specialized crops such as eggplants, peppers, figs, and dates. A typical Turkish meal might consist of spiced lamb, often grilled on a skewer with onion and tomato to make a shish kebab. This would be served with rice or cracked wheat.

EPHESUS
Tourism is one of Turkey's major industries. As well as beach resorts, the country has many ancient sites. One of these is the ancient Greek city of Ephesus, which lies 35 miles (56 km) south of modern-day Izmir on the Aegean coast. The city was famous for its Temple of Artemis, which was considered one of the seven wonders of the world.

Visitors to Ephesus admiring the remains of the Library of Celsus

FATHER OF THE TURKS
Mustafa Kemal Atatürk (1881–1938), the founder of the modern Turkish state, became its first president in 1923. He introduced many reforms, including more equality for women and better education for all. He also declared that Islam was no longer the official religion.

TURKISH REPUBLIC OF NORTHERN CYPRUS
(recognized only by Turkey)

CYPRUS

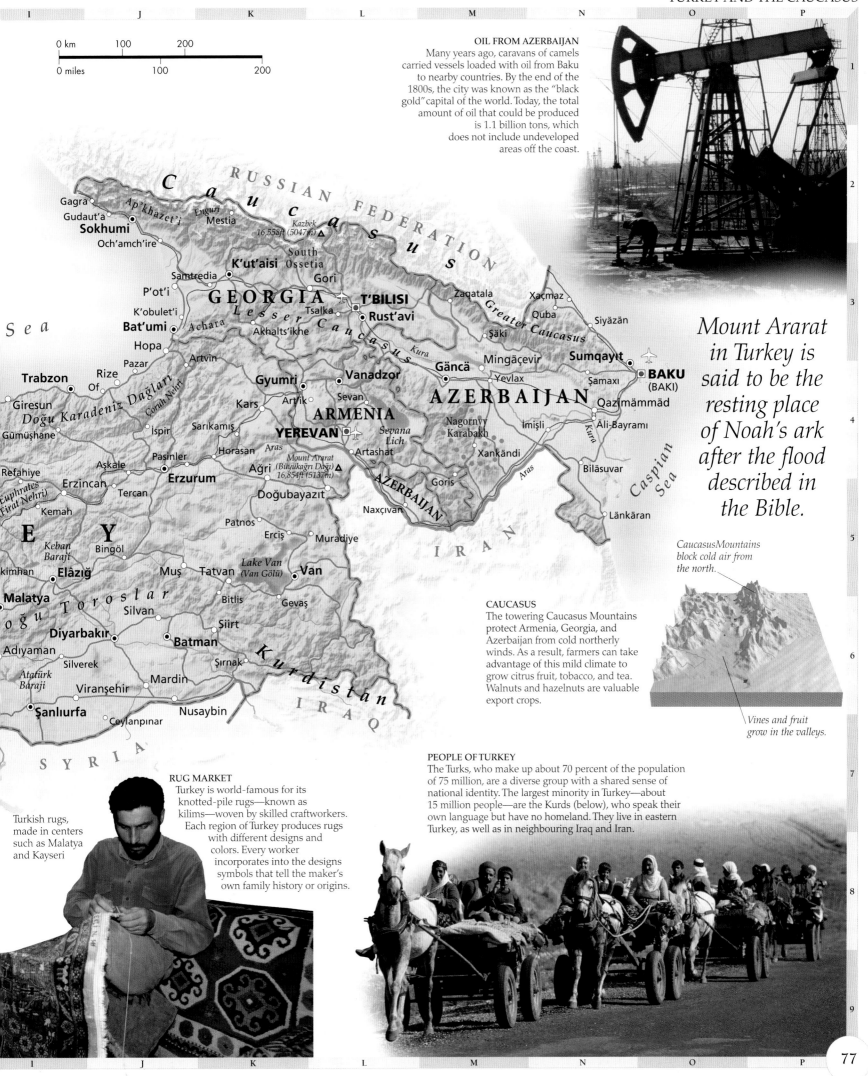

0 km 100 200
0 miles 100 200

OIL FROM AZERBAIJAN
Many years ago, caravans of camels carried vessels loaded with oil from Baku to nearby countries. By the end of the 1800s, the city was known as the "black gold" capital of the world. Today, the total amount of oil that could be produced is 1.1 billion tons, which does not include undeveloped areas off the coast.

Mount Ararat in Turkey is said to be the resting place of Noah's ark after the flood described in the Bible.

CaucasusMountains block cold air from the north.

CAUCASUS
The towering Caucasus Mountains protect Armenia, Georgia, and Azerbaijan from cold northerly winds. As a result, farmers can take advantage of this mild climate to grow citrus fruit, tobacco, and tea. Walnuts and hazelnuts are valuable export crops.

Vines and fruit grow in the valleys.

RUG MARKET
Turkey is world-famous for its knotted-pile rugs—known as kilims—woven by skilled craftworkers. Each region of Turkey produces rugs with different designs and colors. Every worker incorporates into the designs symbols that tell the maker's own family history or origins.

Turkish rugs, made in centers such as Malatya and Kayseri

PEOPLE OF TURKEY
The Turks, who make up about 70 percent of the population of 75 million, are a diverse group with a shared sense of national identity. The largest minority in Turkey—about 15 million people—are the Kurds (below), who speak their own language but have no homeland. They live in eastern Turkey, as well as in neighbouring Iraq and Iran.

Russia and Kazakhstan

THE RUSSIAN FEDERATION is the biggest country in the world, almost twice as big as either the USA or China. It extends halfway around the world, crosses two continents, and spans 11 time zones. The vast region of Siberia alone is larger than Canada. Kazakhstan lies to its south and is a large but sparsely populated country. From 1917 to 1991, both countries were part of the Union of Soviet Socialist Republics (U.S.S.R.), the world's first communist state. When the U.S.S.R. collapsed, Russia, Kazakhstan, and the 13 other member republics gained independence. Since then, Russia and Kazakhstan have begun to transform themselves from communist states into democratic nations. Both countries have a lot of fertile land, huge mineral deposits, and many other natural resources. However, Russia still has a very low life expectancy compared to other industrialized countries.

Lake Baikal is up to 6,365 ft (1,940 m) deep and contains more than 20 percent of the world's freshwater supply.

Kazakh man hunting with a trained golden eagle

KAZAKH CULTURE
The majority of people in Kazakhstan are Kazakh Muslims. They were once a nomadic people who traveled around on horseback, herding their sheep. Although most Kazakhs live in rural areas of the country, retaining a strong loyalty to their clans and families, the new, modern capital city of Astana is growing quickly, due to wealth generated by oil and gas.

Coal miners in Siberia

NATURAL WEALTH
Siberia contains almost one third of the world's natural gas reserves and has huge deposits of oil, as well as abundant minerals such as coal and precious metals including gold. However, many of these resources are inaccessible or in remote places, and the extreme winters make it difficult to extract them.

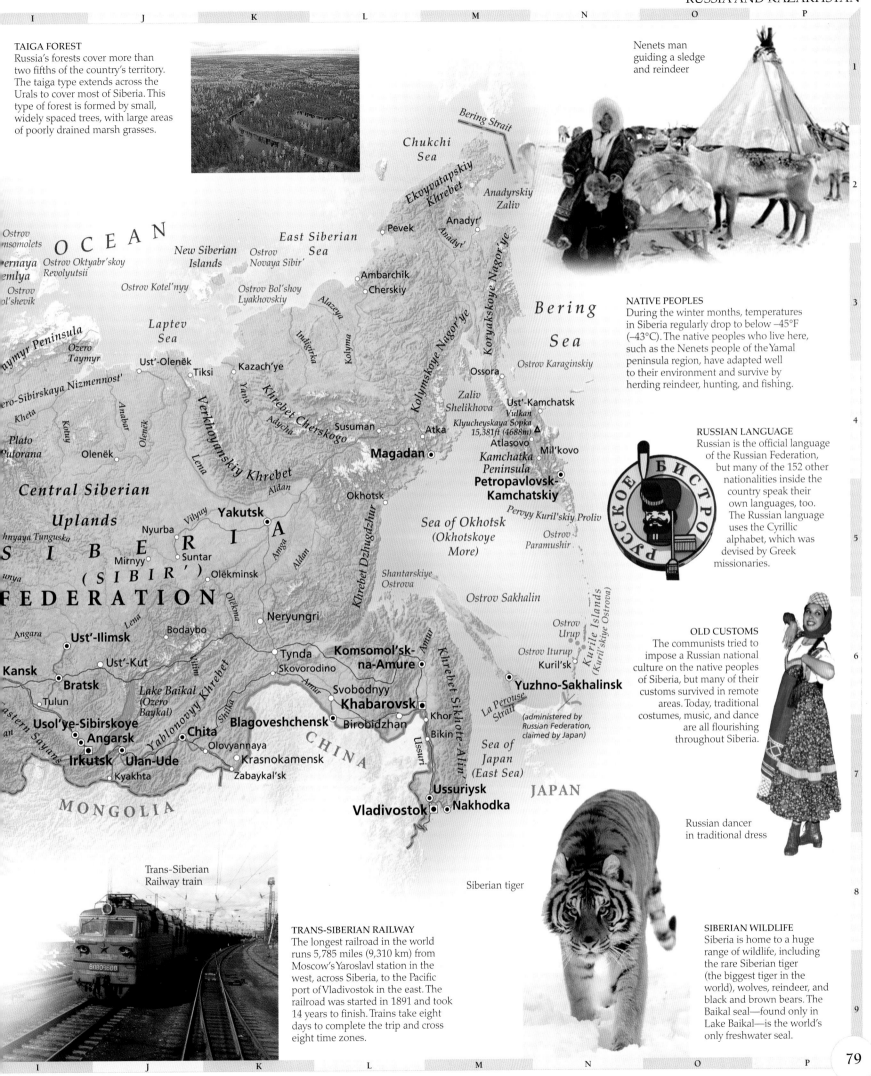

TAIGA FOREST
Russia's forests cover more than two fifths of the country's territory. The taiga type extends across the Urals to cover most of Siberia. This type of forest is formed by small, widely spaced trees, with large areas of poorly drained marsh grasses.

Nenets man guiding a sledge and reindeer

Chukchi Sea

Bering Strait

OCEAN

East Siberian Sea

Ostrov Omsomolets

Severnaya Zemlya

Ostrov Oktyabr'skoy Revolyutsii

New Siberian Islands

Ostrov Novaya Sibir'

Ekvyvatapskiy Khrebet

Anadyrskiy Zaliv

Ostrov Bol'shevik

Ostrov Kotel'nyy

Ostrov Bol'shoy Lyakhovskiy

Pevek

Anadyr

Anadyr'

Bering Sea

NATIVE PEOPLES
During the winter months, temperatures in Siberia regularly drop to below –45°F (–43°C). The native peoples who live here, such as the Nenets people of the Yamal peninsula region, have adapted well to their environment and survive by herding reindeer, hunting, and fishing.

Laptev Sea

Ambarchik

Cherskiy

Koryakskoye Nagor'ye

Ozero Taymyr

Taymyr Peninsula

Zapadno-Sibirskaya Nizmennost'

Kheta

Ust'-Oleněk

Tiksi

Kazach'ye

Indigirka

Alazeya

Kolyma

Kolymskoye Nagor'ye

Ossora

Ostrov Karaginskiy

Anabar

Oleněk

Yana

Adycha

Susuman

Atka

Zaliv Shelikhova

Vulkan Klyucheyskaya Sopka 15,381ft (4688m) △

Ust'-Kamchatsk

Plato Putorana

Oleněk

Lena

Verkhoyanskiy Khrebet

Aldan

Magadan

Okhotsk

Atlasovo

Kamchatka Peninsula

Mil'kovo

RUSSIAN LANGUAGE
Russian is the official language of the Russian Federation, but many of the 152 other nationalities inside the country speak their own languages, too. The Russian language uses the Cyrillic alphabet, which was devised by Greek missionaries.

Central Siberian Uplands

Nizhnyaya Tunguska

Yakutsk

Nyurba

Vilyuy

Anga

Aldan

Petropavlovsk-Kamchatskiy

Pervyy Kuril'skiy Proliv

Sea of Okhotsk (Okhotskoye More)

Ostrov Paramushir

SIBERIA (SIBIR')

Mirnyy

Suntar

Oleěkminsk

Anga

Shantarskiye Ostrova

Podkamennaya Tunguska

Angara

Khrebet Dzhugdzhur

Ostrov Sakhalin

FEDERATION

Lena

Ust'-Ilimsk

Bodaybo

Olěkma

Neryungri

Vitim

Amur

Kurile Islands (Kuril'skiye Ostrova)

Ostrov Urup

OLD CUSTOMS
The communists tried to impose a Russian national culture on the native peoples of Siberia, but many of their customs survived in remote areas. Today, traditional costumes, music, and dance are all flourishing throughout Siberia.

Kansk

Ust'-Kut

Bratsk

Tulun

Lake Baikal (Ozero Baykal)

Tynda

Skovorodino

Komsomol'sk-na-Amure

Ostrov Iturup

Kuril'sk

Eastern Sayans

Usol'ye-Sibirskoye

Angarsk

Irkutsk

Ulan-Ude

Yablonovyy Khrebet

Chita

Shilka

Svobodnyy

Khabarovsk

Blagoveshchensk

Birobidzhan

Amur

Khor

Bikin

Yuzhno-Sakhalinsk

Khrebet Sikhote-Alin'

La Perouse Strait

(administered by Russian Federation, claimed by Japan)

Sea of Japan (East Sea)

Russian dancer in traditional dress

Kyakhta

Olovyannaya

Krasnokamensk

Zabaykal'sk

CHINA

Ussuri

JAPAN

MONGOLIA

Ussuriysk

Vladivostok

Nakhodka

Siberian tiger

Trans-Siberian Railway train

TRANS-SIBERIAN RAILWAY
The longest railroad in the world runs 5,785 miles (9,310 km) from Moscow's Yaroslavl station in the west, across Siberia, to the Pacific port of Vladivostok in the east. The railroad was started in 1891 and took 14 years to finish. Trains take eight days to complete the trip and cross eight time zones.

SIBERIAN WILDLIFE
Siberia is home to a huge range of wildlife, including the rare Siberian tiger (the biggest tiger in the world), wolves, reindeer, and black and brown bears. The Baikal seal—found only in Lake Baikal—is the world's only freshwater seal.

79

The Near East

ISRAEL, JORDAN, SYRIA, AND LEBANON are the countries collectively known as the Near East. This is a land that is dominated by deserts but also has fertile coastal plains. Lack of water is a constant problem here, although Israel has introduced computerized irrigation systems to extend the land suitable for agriculture. The creation of the Jewish state of Israel in 1948, in what was previously Arab-dominated Palestine, has led to almost continuous conflict in the region. Arabs and Israelis have fought four major wars that have cost many lives. The Mediterranean island of Cyprus has also suffered a violent recent history.

The map on Cyprus's flag is copper colored because Cyprus means "island of copper".

SYRIAN MARKET
Damascus is one of the oldest inhabited cities in the world. At its center is a huge souk (bazaar) where the streets are full of stalls and small stores selling everything from rugs, textiles, and jewelry to household goods and fresh produce.

DAILY LIFE
Even in a war-torn country such as Israel, people continue to live as normal a life as possible. Children listen to rock music and watch their favorite sports stars, either live or on Television. In a peaceful break, these Palestinian boys play football in a Jerusalem street.

LEBANON REBUILT
Beirut, the capital of Lebanon, was once the commercial and banking center of the Arab world but was devastated by the civil war that ravaged the country from 1975 to the early 1990s. Today, the country is largely at peace, and Beirut is regaining much of its former glory. Lebanon remains dominated, however, by its two powerful neighbors—Syria and Israel.

CYPRUS
Cyprus became independent from Great Britain in 1960. However, conflict between Greeks and Turks caused Turkey to invade the island in 1974. Since then, Cyprus has been divided between a Turkish-Cypriot north and a Greek-Cypriot south. Most Cypriots make a living from farming grapes, citrus fruit, and olives. Women often sell handmade lace items to tourists.

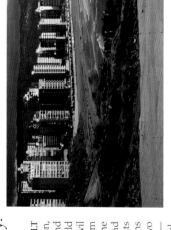

Scale:
0 km 50 100
0 miles 50 100

IRAQ

TURKEY

SYRIA

IRAQ

Mediterranean Sea

Al Mālikīyah
Al Qāmishlī
Al Ḩasakah
Al Jazīrah
Ash Shadādah
Aş Şuwār
Al Manāşif
Subaykhān
Abū Ḩardān
Abū Kamāl
Ra's al 'Ayn
Jabal 'Abd al 'Azīz
Al Mayādīn
Al 'Ashārah
Dayr az Zawr
At Tibnī
At Sabkhah
Ar Raqqah
As Sabkhah
Jabal Bishrī
As Sukhnah
Tudmur (Palmyra)
At Tall al Abyaḑ
Nahr Balīkh
Madīnat ath Thawrah
Lake Assad (Buḩayrat al Asad)
Sabkhat al Jabbūl
Al Bāridah
Manbij
Jarābulus
Euphrates
Aleppo (Ḩalab)
Al Bāb
A'zāz
Afrīn
Idlib
Ḩārim
Ariḩā
Ma'arrat an Nu'mān
Abū aḑ Ḑuhūr
Ḩamāh
Salamiyah
Ar Rāmi
Ḩimş (Homs)
Al Qusayr
Jibāl as Sāḩilīyah
Maşyāf
Bāniyās
Tarţūs
Tall Kalakh
Qoubaīyāt
Jablah
Lādhiqīyah (Latakia)
El Mina
Batroūn
Tripoli
Jebel Liban

TURKISH REPUBLIC OF NORTHERN CYPRUS
(recognized only by Turkey)
Agialoúsa (Yenierenköy)
Ammóchostos (Gazimağusa) (Famagusta)
Kerýneia (Girne)
Kythréa (Değirmenlik)
NICOSIA
Dekéleia
Sovereign Base Area (to U.K.)
Lárnaka
Lápithos (Lapta)
Mórfou (Güzelyurt)
Troódos
CYPRUS
Limassol (Lemesós)
Pólis
Páfos
Sovereign Base Area (to U.K.)
Akrotírion

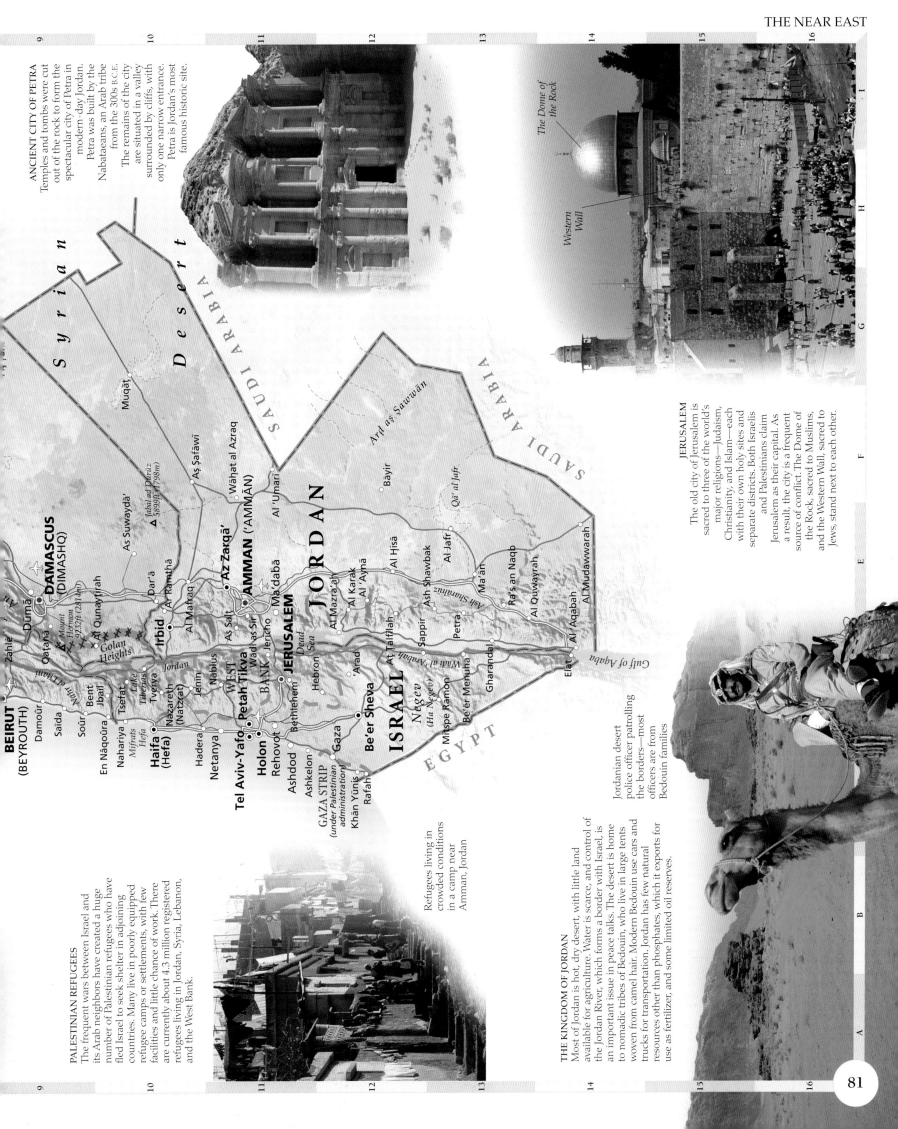

ANCIENT CITY OF PETRA
Temples and tombs were cut out of the rock to form the spectacular city of Petra in modern-day Jordan. Petra was built by the Nabataeans, an Arab tribe from the 300s B.C.E. The remains of the city are situated in a valley surrounded by cliffs, with only one narrow entrance. Petra is Jordan's most famous historic site.

The Dome of the Rock

Western Wall

JERUSALEM
The old city of Jerusalem is sacred to three of the world's major religions—Judaism, Christianity, and Islam—each with their own holy sites and separate districts. Both Israelis and Palestinians claim Jerusalem as their capital. As a result, the city is a frequent source of conflict. The Dome of the Rock, sacred to Muslims, and the Western Wall, sacred to Jews, stand next to each other.

Jordanian desert police officer patrolling the borders—most officers are from Bedouin families

PALESTINIAN REFUGEES
The frequent wars between Israel and its Arab neighbors have created a huge number of Palestinian refugees who have fled Israel to seek shelter in adjoining countries. Many live in poorly equipped refugee camps or settlements, with few facilities and little chance of work. There are currently about 4.3 million registered refugees living in Jordan, Syria, Lebanon, and the West Bank.

Refugees living in crowded conditions in a camp near Amman, Jordan

THE KINGDOM OF JORDAN
Most of Jordan is hot, dry desert, with little land available for agriculture. Water is scarce, and control of the Jordan River, which forms a border with Israel, is an important issue in peace talks. The desert is home to nomadic tribes of Bedouin, who live in large tents woven from camel hair. Modern Bedouin use cars and trucks for transportation. Jordan has few natural resources other than phosphates, which it exports for use as fertilizer, and some limited oil reserves.

81

The Middle East

THE MIDDLE EAST IS HOME to the world's oldest civilizations, which developed in the Tigris and Euphrates river valleys of present-day Iraq more than 6,000 years ago. The world's first towns and cities were built here. Since then, many powerful empires have dominated the region, all leaving a wealth of buildings and monuments behind them. Today, the Middle East is at the center of the Islamic world. The population of every country is Arab and speaks Arabic, except Iran, where half the population are Farsi-speaking Persians.

DESERT WARS
Most international boundaries in the Middle East are simply lines drawn in the sand by former European colonial powers and have often caused conflicts. Iraq and Iran fought a bitter eight-year war along their common border from 1980. Since then, further conflicts between Iraq and international forces have caused a lot of suffering.

IRANIANS
About half the total population of Iran are Persians, who live in the center and north of the country. Large numbers of Azeris live in the northwest, while Kurds live in the west and Baluchi live in the southeast. The official language of Iran is Farsi, but many other languages are also spoken.

The Persian language is written in Arabic script

ROLE OF WOMEN
Family life is important throughout the Muslim world. The role of women varies from country to country—traditionally, women stay at home and look after the family, but some now work. In public, many cover their head or whole body with a burqa.

OIL PRODUCTION
The Middle East is the world's major oil producer—Saudi Arabia alone produces more than 10 percent of the world's supply. Oil has brought great wealth to the region, in particular to Saudi Arabia and the Gulf States.

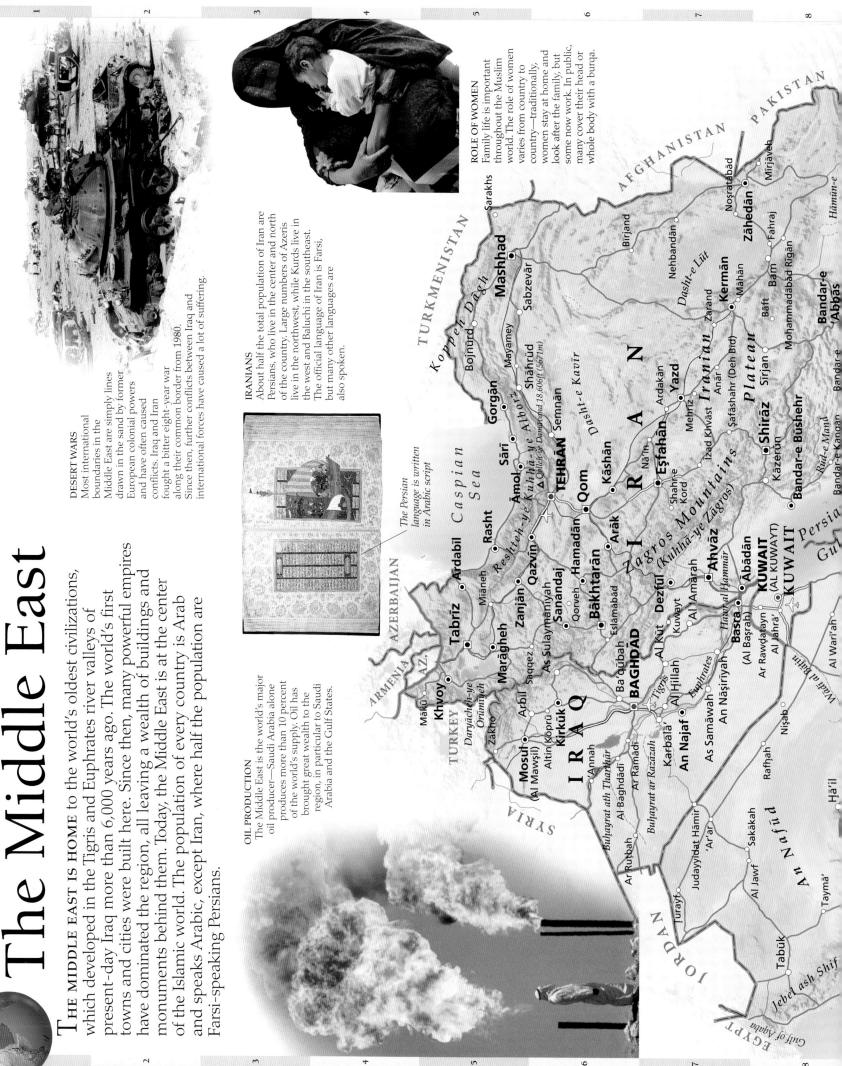

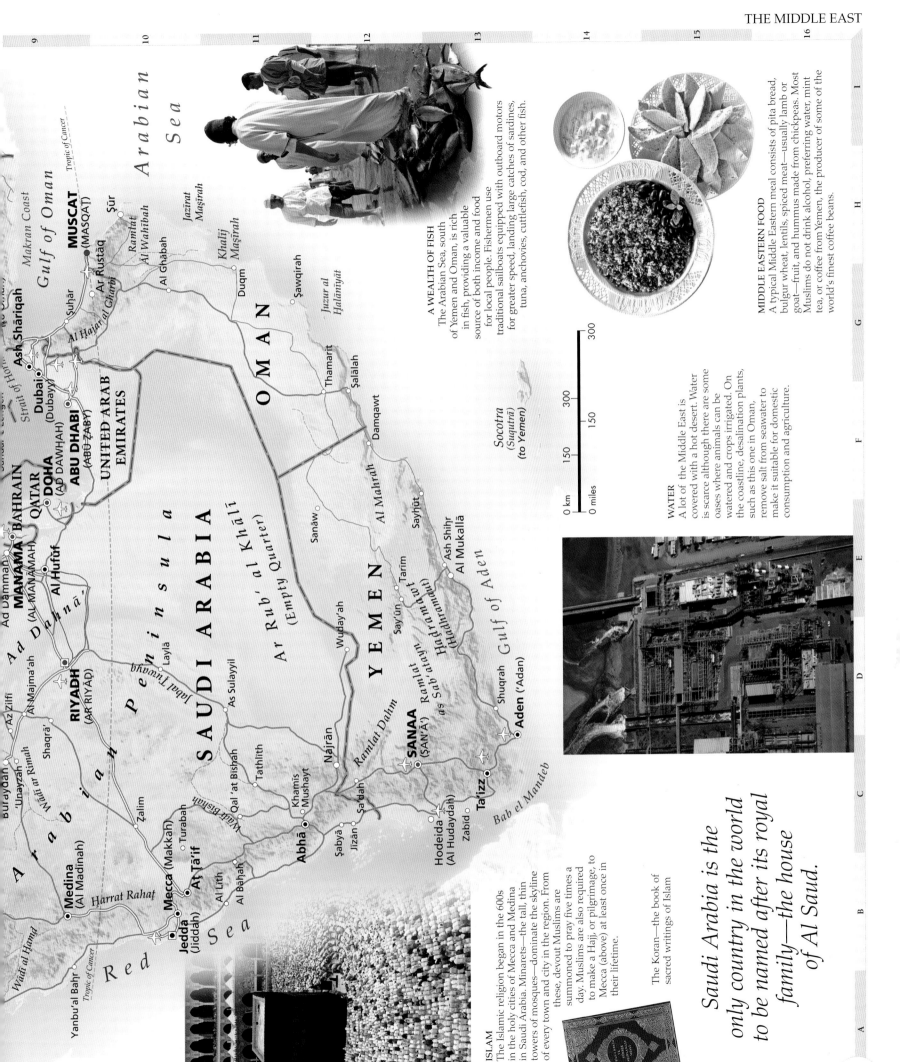

A WEALTH OF FISH
The Arabian Sea, south of Yemen and Oman, is rich in fish, providing a valuable source of both income and food for local people. Fishermen use traditional sailboats equipped with outboard motors for greater speed, landing large catches of sardines, tuna, anchovies, cuttlefish, cod, and other fish.

MIDDLE EASTERN FOOD
A typical Middle Eastern meal consists of pita bread, bulgur wheat, lentils, spiced meat—usually lamb or goat—fruit, and hummus made from chickpeas. Most Muslims do not drink alcohol, preferring water, mint tea, or coffee from Yemen, the producer of some of the world's finest coffee beans.

WATER
A lot of the Middle East is covered with a hot desert. Water is scarce although there are some oases where animals can be watered and crops irrigated. On the coastline, desalination plants, such as this one in Oman, remove salt from seawater to make it suitable for domestic consumption and agriculture.

ISLAM
The Islamic religion began in the 600s in the holy cities of Mecca and Medina in Saudi Arabia. Minarets—the tall, thin towers of mosques—dominate the skyline of every town and city in the region. From these, devout Muslims are summoned to pray five times a day. Muslims are also required to make a Hajj, or pilgrimage, to Mecca (above) at least once in their lifetime.

The Koran—the book of sacred writings of Islam

Saudi Arabia is the only country in the world to be named after its royal family—the house of Al Saud.

Map labels

Arabian Sea

Gulf of Oman

Makran Coast

Tropic of Cancer

Strait of Hormuz

MUSCAT (MASQAṬ)

Ṣūr

Ramlat Al Wahībah

Al Ghābah

Al Hajar al Gharbī

Suhār

Ar Rustāq

Ash Shāriqah

Dubai (Dubayy)

ABU DHABI (ABŪ ẒABY)

UNITED ARAB EMIRATES

Jazīrat Maṣīrah

Khalīj Maṣīrah

Duqm

O M A N

Ṣawqirah

Jazur al Ḥalānīyāt

Thamarīt

Ṣalālah

Damqawt

Socotra (Suquṭrā) (to Yemen)

DOHA (AD DAWḤAH)

QATAR

BAHRAIN

MANAMA (AL MANĀMAH)

Ad Dammām

Al Hufūf

Ad Dahnā'

A r a b i a n   P e n i n s u l a

S A U D I   A R A B I A

Ar Rub' al Khālī (Empty Quarter)

Al Mahrah

Sayḥūt

Sanāw

Al Mukallā

Ash Shiḥr

Ḥaḍramawt (Hadhramaut)

Gulf of Aden

Al Majma'ah

Az Zilfi

RIYADH (AR RIYĀḌ)

Laylā

Jabal Ṭuwayq

As Sulayyil

Wudạy'ah

Tarīm

Say'ūn

Ramlat as Sab'atayn

SANAA (ṢAN'Ā')

Y E M E N

Ramlat Dahm

Najrān

Aden ('Adan)

Shuqrah

Bab el Mandeb

'Unayzah

Buraydah

Wādī ar Rimah

Shaqrā'

Ẓalim

Tathlith

Qal 'at Bīshah

Khamīs Mushayt

Ṣa'dah

Taʿizz

Ṣabyā

Jīzān

Zabīd

Hodeida (Al Hudaydah)

Abhā

Wādī Bīshah

Turabah

Aṭ Ṭā'if

Mecca (Makkah)

Al Līth

Al Bāḥah

Medina (Al Madīnah)

Harrat Rahaṭ

Jedda (Jiddah)

Yanbu'al Baḥr

Wādī al Ḥamḍ

Tropic of Cancer

Red Sea

Thamarīt

Scale bar
0 km   150   300
0 miles   150   300

Central Asia

THE FIVE CENTRAL ASIAN NATIONS rise up from hot deserts in the west and south to cold, high mountain ranges in the east. The area has oil, gas, and mineral reserves, as well as other natural resources, but water is often scarce and agriculture is limited. The four northern nations were once part of the Soviet Union and are now independent nations. Afghanistan is a landlocked country, and three fourths of its land is inaccessible terrain. It was invaded by the Soviet Union in 1979, prompting a civil war that has lasted for more than 20 years. In 2002, American and other Western forces overthrew the fundamentalist Islamic regime in Afghanistan because of its support for international terrorism. The country, however, has been destroyed by these years of continuous warfare, making it one of the poorest and most deprived nations on Earth.

One of the world's largest gold mines is at Muruntau in the Kyzyl Kum desert in Uzbekistan.

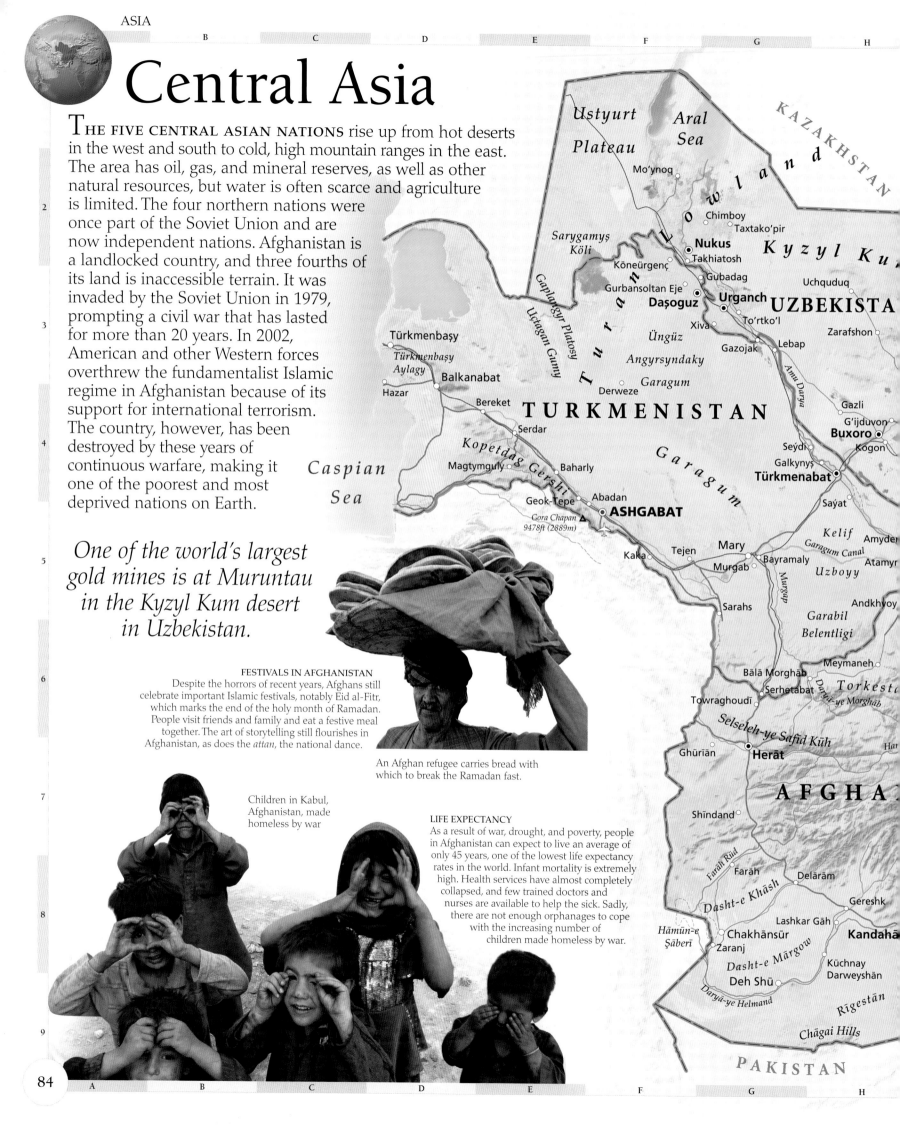

FESTIVALS IN AFGHANISTAN
Despite the horrors of recent years, Afghans still celebrate important Islamic festivals, notably Eid al-Fitr, which marks the end of the holy month of Ramadan. People visit friends and family and eat a festive meal together. The art of storytelling still flourishes in Afghanistan, as does the *attan*, the national dance.

An Afghan refugee carries bread with which to break the Ramadan fast.

Children in Kabul, Afghanistan, made homeless by war

LIFE EXPECTANCY
As a result of war, drought, and poverty, people in Afghanistan can expect to live an average of only 45 years, one of the lowest life expectancy rates in the world. Infant mortality is extremely high. Health services have almost completely collapsed, and few trained doctors and nurses are available to help the sick. Sadly, there are not enough orphanages to cope with the increasing number of children made homeless by war.

Ustyurt Plateau
Aral Sea
KAZAKHSTAN
Mo'ynoq
Turan Lowland
Chimboy
Taxtako'pir
Sarygamyş Köli
Nukus
Takhiatosh
Kyzyl Kum
Köneürgenç
Gubadag
Uchquduq
Gurbansoltan Eje
Urganch
UZBEKISTA
Daşoguz
Xiva
To'rtko'l
Gaplaňgyr Platosy
Türkmenbaşy
Üngüz
Zarafshon
Gazojak
Lebap
Uçajagan Gumy
Türkmenbaşy Aylagy
Balkanabat
Angyrsyndaky
Amu Darya
Gazli
Hazar
Bereket
Derweze
Garagum
G'ijduvon
Buxoro
TURKMENISTAN
Garagum
Seýdi
Kogon
Serdar
Galkynyş
Türkmenabat
Caspian Sea
Kopetdag Gershi
Baharly
Saýat
Magtymguly
Kelif
Amyder
Geok-Tepe
Abadan
Gora Chapan △ **ASHGABAT**
9478ft (2889m)
Garagum Canal
Mary
Atamyr
Kaka
Tejen
Murgab
Bayramaly
Uzboýy
Murgap
Sarahs
Garabil Belentligi
Andkhvoy
Bālā Morghāb
Meymaneh
Serhetabat
Daryā-ye Morghāb
Torkesta
Towraghoudī
Selseleh-ye Safīd Kūh
Ghūrīān
Herāt
Har
AFGHA
Shīndand
Farāh Rūd
Farāh
Delārām
Gereshk
Dasht-e Khāsh
Lashkar Gāh
Hāmūn-e Şāberī
Chakhānsūr
Kandahā
Zaranj
Dasht-e Mārgow
Kūchnay Darweyshān
Deh Shū
Daryā-ye Helmand
Rigestān
Chāgai Hills
PAKISTAN

ARAL SEA

The vast inland Aral Sea, between Uzbekistan and Kazakhstan, was once a thriving freshwater lake full of fish. Over the years, the rivers flowing into it were diverted or drained to provide irrigation for crops. The sea has now shrunk to half of its original size, reducing the numbers of fish and leaving former fishing villages stranded inland.

The fishing village of Muynoq is now more than 30 miles (48 km) away from the Aral Sea

A man in front of his home, called a *yurt*, in western Pamir, Tajikistan

MOUNTAIN LIFE

The two small eastern republics of Kyrgyzstan and Tajikistan are both very mountainous and are subject to earthquakes and landslides. Only about six percent of Tajikistan can be used for agriculture, whereas Kyrgyzstan is more fertile.

LOCAL WEALTH

Uzbekistan, Turkmenistan, and Kyrgyzstan all grow considerable crops of cotton—Uzbekistan is the world's fifth-largest producer—as well as fruit and vegetables. The three countries are also rich in mineral deposits, such as gold, mercury, sulfur, and uranium, and have reserves of coal, oil, and natural gas.

Harvesting cotton in Uzbekistan

TAJIKS

The majority of people of Tajikistan are Iranian in origin and speak Tajik, which is related to Farsi. The minority Uzbeks are mostly made up of descendents of Turkic-speaking (related to Turkish) nomads. This division has led to ethnic tension between the two groups. Civil war between the government and Islamic rebels in the east of the country during the 1990s led to an exodus of Uzbeks and Russians, who had moved into the country when it was part of the Soviet Union.

Tajik horsemen in Pamir, Tajikistan

Tilla-Kari, a 17th-century Islamic religious school in Samarqand, Uzbekistan

THE SILK ROAD

The Silk Road is the ancient trade route that brought silks and other fine goods from China through central Asia and the Middle East to Europe. Many cities were built along its route, including Buxoro (Bukhara, Uzbekistan), an important place of pilgrimage for Muslims, and Samarqand, which contains some of the finest Islamic architecture in the world. Many of these cities are now UNESCO-designated World Heritage Sites.

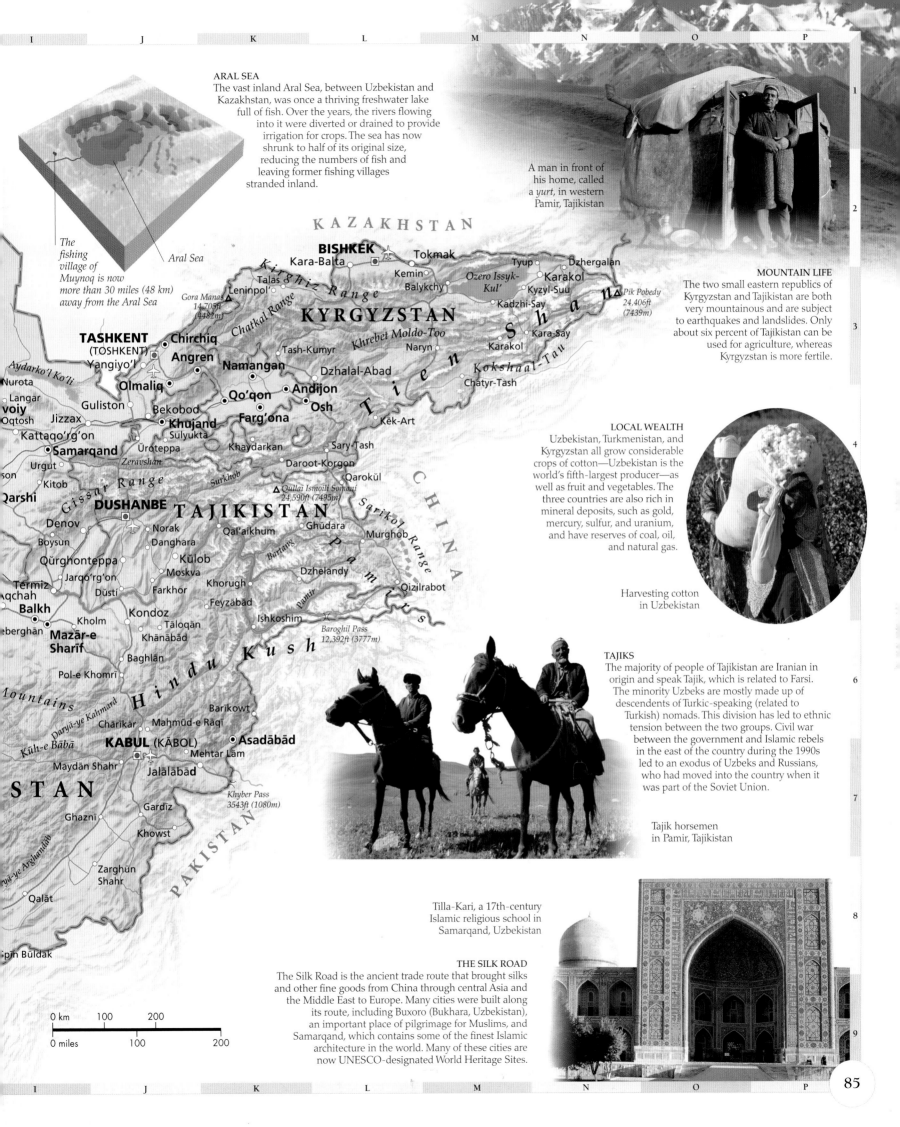

Map labels

KAZAKHSTAN

BISHKEK · Kara-Balta · Tokmak · Kemin · Tyup · Dzhergalan
Leninpol' · Talas · Balykchy · Ozero Issyk-Kul' · Karakol · Kyzyl-Suu
Kirghiz Range · Gora Manas 14,705ft (4482m) · Kadzhi-Say · Pik Pobedy 24,406ft (7439m)
KYRGYZSTAN · Kara-Say
TASHKENT (TOSHKENT) · Chirchiq · Chatkal Range · Tash-Kumyr · Khrebet Moldo-Too · Naryn · Kara-Say
Yangiyo'l · Angren · Namangan · Dzhalal-Abad · Tien Shan · Kokshaal-Tau
Aydarko'l Ko'li · Nurota · Olmaliq · Qo'qon · Andijon · Chatyr-Tash
Langar · Guliston · Bekobod · Farg'ona · Osh · Kёk-Art
voiy · Oqtosh · Jizzax · Khujand · Sulyukta · Khaydarkan · Sary-Tash
Kattaqo'rg'on · Samarqand · Ŭroteppa · Daroot-Korgon · Qarokŭl
Urgut · Zeravshan · Surkhob
Kitob · Gissar Range · Qullai Ismoili Somoni 24,590ft (7495m) · Sarikol Range · CHINA
Qarshi · DUSHANBE · TAJIKISTAN · Ghūdara · Murghob
Denov · Norak · Qal'aikhum · Bartang
Boysun · Danghara · Pamirs
Qŭrghonteppa · Jarqo'rg'on · Kŭlob · Moskva · Dzhelandy · Qizilrabot
Termiz · Dŭsti · Farkhor · Khorugh
qchah · Feyzābād · Ishkoshim · Pamir · Baroghil Pass 12,392ft (3777m)
Balkh · Kondoz · Tāloqān
eberghān · Kholm · Khānābād
Mazār-e Sharīf · Baghlān · Hindu Kush
Pol-e Khomrī
Mountains · Barīkowt
Kŭh-e Bāba · Darya-ye Kahmard · Chārīkār · Mahmūd-e Rāqī
KABUL (KĀBOL) · Asadābād · Mehtar Lām
Maydān Shahr · Jalālābād
STAN · Khyber Pass 3543ft (1080m)
Ghaznī · Gardīz
Khowst
Darya-ye Arghandāb · Zarghūn Shahr
Qalāt · Darya-ye Arghastān
pīn Būldak

Scale:
0 km 100 200
0 miles 100 200

Indian Subcontinent

SEPARATED FROM the rest of Asia by the Himalayas, the Indian subcontinent is home to almost one fourth of the world's population—a staggering 1.5 billion people. They have a long and complex history, form many different ethnic groups, speak a wide variety of languages, and worship many different gods. While some people in these countries are wealthy, many others live in poverty. Tensions between and within countries in this region have sometimes erupted into warfare. The Indian subcontinent is often affected by natural disasters, notably cyclones in the Bay of Bengal and earthquakes and floods in Pakistan. However, India, the most heavily populated nation and once prone to famine, is now more than self-sufficient in food. All but Nepal and Bhutan were once ruled by the British, whose legacy can be seen in the common language of English, the architecture, the vast railroad system, and in sports—most notably cricket.

MONSOON
From May/June to September, warm, moist southerly winds sweep up from the Indian Ocean and the Bay of Bengal across the subcontinent. Once these winds meet dry land, moisture falls as monsoon rainfall. Although this irrigates the land and replenishes the water supply, it can also cause severe flooding.

SRI LANKA
In 1983, civil war erupted in Sri Lanka between the Buddhist majority Sinhalese, who dominate the government, and the Hindu minority Tamils, who wanted to establish their own independent state in the north of the island. The civil war, which ended in 2009 when the government defeated the Tamil Tigers, has cost many lives and disrupted the island's economy. Yet Sri Lanka still has one of the highest literacy rates in the world and high levels of health care.

FAMILY LIFE IN PAKISTAN
Pakistanis have strong ties to their extended families, and often many generations live and work together in family-run businesses. Smaller family units, however, are becoming more common in urban areas. Although some women hold prominent positions in public and commercial life, such as Benazir Bhutto who was prime minister twice before she was assassinated in December 2007, most women do not work outside the home.

School child, Sri Lanka

0 km   150   300
0 miles   150   300

AFGHANISTAN
IRAN
PAKISTAN
Baluchistān
Chāgai Hills
Central Makrān Range
Kirthar Range
Toba Kākar Range
Sulaimān Range
Hindu Kush
Khyber Pass 3543ft (1080m)
Mingāora
Mardān
ISLĀMĀBĀD
Peshāwar
Wāh
Rāwalpindi
Jhelum
Jammu
Sargodha
Gujrāt
Gujrānw
Lahore
Amrits
Faisalābād
Ludhiā
Multān
Okāra
Chandīgar
Bathinda
Haryana
Bahāwalpur
Karna
Rahīmyār Khān
Delh
NEW DEL
Bīkāner
Alwar
Jaipur
Thar Desert
Rājasthān
Jaisalmer
Jodhpur
Beāwar
Kot
Pāli
Udaipur
Pālanpur
Rann of Kachchh
Gujarāt
Ahmadābād
Ratlām
Godhra
Indore
Vadodara
I
Jāmnagar
Rājkot
Porbandar
Bhāvnagar
Sūrat
Bhusāwal
Sātpura Ran
Daman
Manmād
Nāshik
Aurangāb
Kalyān
Godāvari
Mahārāshtra
D
Mumbai (Bombay)
Pune
Nānde
Bārāmati
Solāpur
Gulbar
Kolhāpur
Rāic
Belgaum
Gadag
Panaji
Hubli
Dāvange
Karnātaka
Shimoga
Udupi
Bangalore
Mangalore
Mysore
Kāsaragod
Kannur / Cannanore
Kozhikode / Calicut
Ero
Coimbatore
Ernākulam
Kochi / Cochin
Kollam / Quilon
Thiruvananthapuram / Trivandrum
Nāgerco
Arabian Sea
Quetta
Dera Ghāzi Khān
Kālat
Sibi
Jacobābād
Shikārpur
Lārkāna
Sukkur
Khairpur
Turbat
Nawābshāh
Hyderābād
Mīrpur Khās
Karāchi
Sujāwal
Mouths of the Indus
Tropic of Cancer
Gulf of Kachchh
Gāndhīdhām
Gulf of Khambhāt
Gwādar
Pasni
Sind
Indus
Sutlej
Chaman
P u n j a b
K2 28,25 (861
Hindu Kush Karakoram Ran
Indus
Pottwar Plateau
Vindhya Ran
Western Ghats
Kerala

J K L M N O P

A "line of control" was agreed between India and Pakistan in 1972

AKSAI CHIN administered by China, claimed by India)

DEMCHOK/ DÊMQOG (administered by China, claimed by India)

Jammu and Kashmir

THE HIMALAYAS
The highest chain of mountains in the world, the Himalayas have eight peaks that are more than 26,247 ft (8,000 m) high. Everest, the world's highest mountain at 29,035 ft (8,850 m), is on the border of Nepal and Tibet. Mountaineers come from far and wide to scale these massive peaks.

Bhutanese people

ARUNACHAI PRADESH (claimed by China)

BHUTAN
Hidden away in the Himalayas, the people of Bhutan are devoutly Buddhist and have little contact with the outside world. A minority of the population are Nepalese Hindus who came to the country in the first half of the 1900s. Most Bhutanese live in the fertile river valleys of the center and south of the country. Traditional dress—the *kira* for women and the *gho* for men—is widely worn.

The name Bhutan means "Land of the Thunder Dragon" in Dzongkha, the country's official language.

RELIGION
Two of the world's great religions—Hinduism and Buddhism—began in India more than 2,500 years ago. Most Pakistanis and Bangladeshis are Muslim, most Indians and Nepalese are Hindu, and most Sri Lankans and Bhutanese are Buddhist.

Hindus bathe in the Ganges River, which is considered sacred

BOLLYWOOD
More movies are produced in Mumbai (Bombay), India—more than 800 a year—than in the entire USA, turning "Bollywood," as it is known, into a major cultural center. Bollywood movies generally have historical, religious, or social themes and are famous for their song-and-dance routines and glamorous stars. These movies are an important export to central Asia, the Middle East, and Africa.

TEA IN SRI LANKA
Sri Lanka is the world's largest exporter of tea. The plantations are mostly located in the center of the island and they employ women to pick the delicate, green shoots of the bushes.

Map labels

Uttarakhand
Meerut
Bareilly
Uttar Pradesh
Agra
Lucknow
Gwalior
Jhansi
...puri
Sāgar
...pal
Jabalpur
...IA
Bilaspur
...Korba
Nāgpur
Gondia
Raipur
Chandrapur
...c
...an
...zāmābād
Karimnagar
Warangal
Hyderābād
...rishna
...urnool
...dpatri
uddapah
...du
...lem
...llore
Tiruchchirāppalli
Madurai
...uticorin
...Gulf of ...annar
...egombo

NEPAL
Sālyān
Annapurna 26,545ft (8091m)
Pokharā
KATHMANDU
Bhaktapur
Lalitpur
Faizābād
Gorakhpur
Chhapra
Dinājpur
Kānpur
Allahābād
Patna
Vārānasi
Gaya
Rajshahi
Pabna
Dhanbād
Āsānsol
Jessore
Khulna
Rānchi
Jamshedpur
Rāulakela
Kharagpur
Kolkata (Calcutta)
Sambalpur
Bāleshwar
Cuttack
Bhubaneshwar
Puri
Brahmapur
Jagdalpur
Vizianagaram
Visākhapatnam
Rājahmundry
Vijayawāda
Chīrāla
Ongole
Kāvali
Nellore
Chennai (Madras)
Kānchīpuram
Pondicherry

CHINA
Dibrugarh
Mount Everest 29,035ft (8850m)
Kula Kangri 24,783ft (7554m)
THIMPHU
BHUTAN
Bongaigaon
Jorhāt
Shiliguri
Guwāhāti
Kohima
Rangpur
Meghalaya
Imphāl
Jamalpur
Sylhet
Silchar
BANGLADESH
DHAKA
Comilla
Barisal
Chittagong

malayas

Himalayas

Bihār
Jharkhand
Madhya Pradesh
Chota Nāgpur
West Bengal
Chhattisgarh
Orissa
Mahānadi
Andhra Pradesh
Eastern Ghats
Godāvari
Krishna

Ganges
Brahmaputra
Assam

MYANMAR

Tropic of Cancer

Mouths of the Ganges
Bay of Bengal

North Andaman
Middle Andaman
Port Blair
Andaman Islands (to India)
South Andaman
Little Andaman
Nicobar Islands (to India)
Car Nicobar
Katchall Island
Little Nicobar
Great Nicobar
Indira Point
Andaman Sea

Palk Strait
Jaffna
SRI LANKA
Mannar
Trincomalee
Puttalam
Batticaloa
Kandy
COLOMBO
Sri Jayewardanapura Kotte
Kalutara
Galle
Matara

INDIAN OCEAN

J K L M N O P

1
3
4
5
8
9

Western China and Mongolia

CHINA IS A LAND of huge geographical diversity and amazing landscapes. More than 90 percent of the population are Han Chinese—descendents of people who settled here more than 5,000 years ago. This region includes western China, Mongolia, and Tibet. Mongolia gained its independence from China in 1911 and is now an independent democracy. Tibet is currently governed by China. Compared to eastern China, this region is sparsely populated and characterized by vast deserts, remote mountains, and extreme temperatures.

DESERT LANDS
The cold, rocky Gobi Desert (right) stretches for more than 400,000 sq miles (1,000,000 sq km) through Mongolia and northeast China. Many dinosaur bones and eggs have been found here, making it one of the richest dinosaur fossil regions in the world.

MONGOLIANS
Most of the people living in Mongolia are Khalkha Mongols. About half of these people now live in urban areas, but some still lead traditional lives as nomadic herders. They live in large felt tents called *yurts*. Smoke from the central iron stove escapes through a chimney in the roof.

In traditional Mongolian khoomi singing, men are able to sing several notes at once.

CHINESE WRITING
The Chinese alphabet is not made up of letters. Instead, separate symbols stand for individual words or parts of words. There are more than 40,000 characters in the Chinese language. The same symbols are used everywhere in China, and no matter what Chinese language or dialect people speak, they can all read the same script.

兒童百科全書

Chinese symbols, whose strokes have to be written in a certain order

MONASTERIES IN MONGOLIA
Under communism, Mongolians were forbidden to practice their traditional Buddhist faith, which was viewed as superstitious and unscientific. Since the democratic government was set up in 1990, about 100 monasteries have reopened. Most people, however, no longer follow any religion.

Map labels:

Hövsgöl Nuur
Uvs Nuur
Ulaangom
Ölgiy
Hyargas Nuur
Halban
Mörö
Har Us Nuur
Altay
Hovd
Har Nuur
Tsetserl
KAZAKHSTAN
Altai Mountains
Hangayn Nur
MON
Karamay
Gurbantünggüt Shamo
Altay
Bayanhong
Kuytun
Borohoro Shan
Shihezi
Fukang
Jimsar
Aj Bogd Uul 12,474ft (3802m)
Yining
Ürümqi
Qitai
Turpan
Atas Bogd 8842ft (2695m)
G
Tien Shan
△ Tomür Feng 7443m
Turpan Pendi
Hami
KYRGYZSTAN
Korla
Bosten Hu
Xingxingxia
GANSU
Kashi
Tarim He
Tarim Basin
Kuruktag
Yengisar
XINJIANG
Laojunmiao
Shache
Takla Makan Desert
Ruoqiang
Qilian Shan
Yecheng
Pishan
Altun Shan
Danghe Nanshan
TAJIKISTAN
(claimed by India)
Moyu
C H I N
Qing
GH.
Hotan
Qira
Karakoram Range
K2 28,251ft (8611m)
Kunlun Shan
Qaidam Pendi
Golmud
Dulan
AKSAI CHIN
Burhan Budai Shan
Anyêmaqên Shan
PAKISTAN
AKSAI CHIN (administered by China, claimed by India)
Plateau of Tibet (Qingzang Gaoyuan)
QINGHAI
INDIA
Rutog
Tongtian He
Bayan Har Shan
DEMCHOK/DÊMQOG (administered by China, claimed by India)
Indus
Gar Xincun
Zanda
Gozhê
Siling Co
Amdo
Yushu
Mekong
Tangra Yumco
Gyaring Co
Nam Co
Nagqu
Qamdo
Himalaya
Brahmaputra
Ngangzê Co
Damxung
Tanggula Shan
Salween
Nyainqêntanglha Shan
Lhazê
Xigazê
Maizhokunggar
Lhasa
NEPAL
Gonggar
Gyangzê
ARUNÁCHAL PRADESH (claimed by China)
Hengduan Shan
Mount Everest 29,035ft (8850m)
BHUTAN
INDIA
MYANMAR

A B C D E F G H

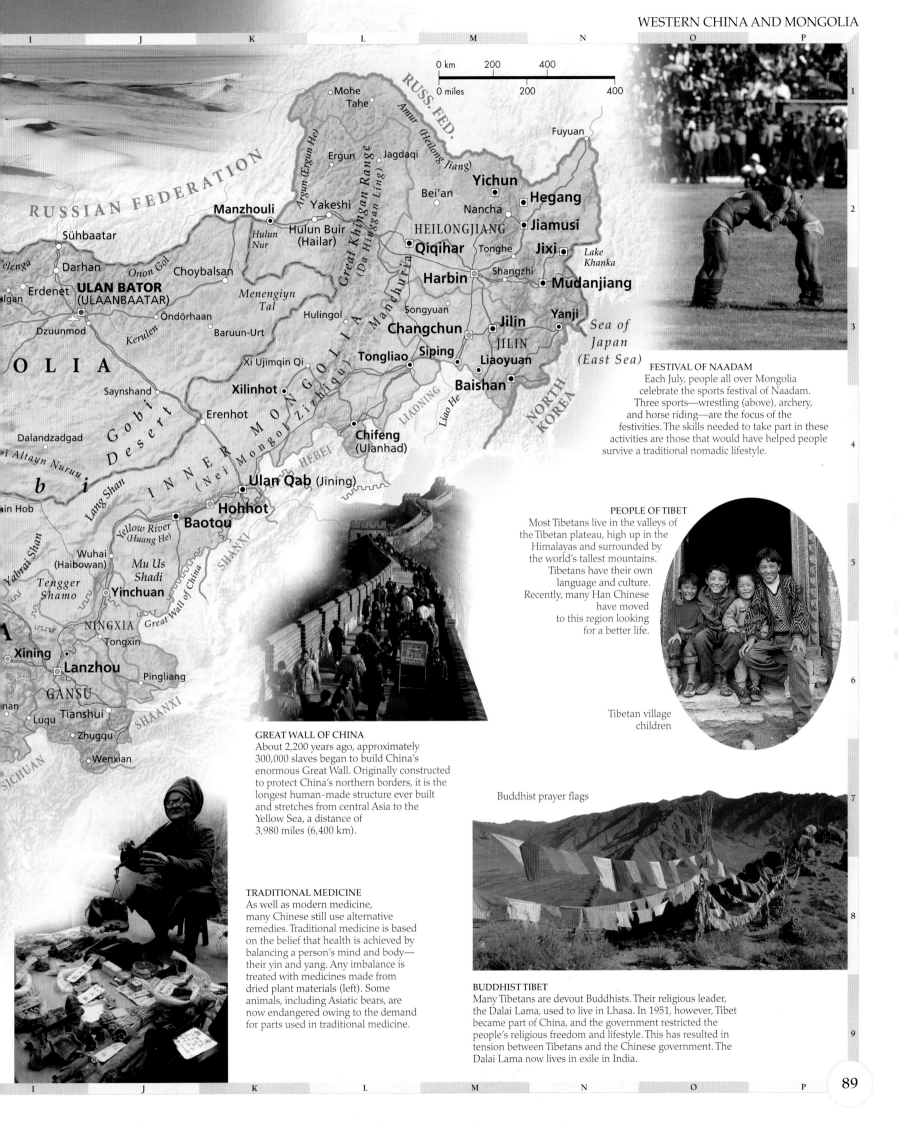

RUSS. FED.

RUSSIAN FEDERATION

Mohe
Tahe
Ergun
Jagdaqi
Argun (Ergun He)
Amur (Heilong Jiang)
Fuyuan
Sühbaatar
Manzhouli
Yakeshi
Bei'an
Yichun
Hegang
elenga
Darhan
Onon Gol
Choybalsan
Hulun Buir
(Hailar)
Nancha
Jiamusi
Erdenet
Hulun Nur
HEILONGJIANG
lgan
ULAN BATOR
(ULAANBAATAR)
Menengiyn Tal
Qiqihar
Tonghe
Jixi
Lake Khanka
Dzuunmod
Kerulen
Hulingol
Harbin
Shangzhi
Öndörhaan
Baruun-Urt
Songyuan
Mudanjiang
Xi Ujimqin Qi
Changchun
Jilin
Yanji
Sea of Japan (East Sea)
Saynshand
Tongliao
Siping
JILIN
Gobi Desert
Xilinhot
Liaoyuan
Erenhot
Baishan
i Altayn Nuruu
Dalandzadgad
Chifeng
(Ulanhad)
LIAONING
Liao He
NORTH KOREA
b i
Lang Shan
INNER MONGOLIA
(Nei Mongol Zizhiqu)
HEBEI
in Hob
Ulan Qab (Jining)
Hohhot
Yellow River
(Huang He)
Baotou
SHANXI
Wuhai
(Haibowan)
Mu Us Shadi
Tengger Shamo
Yinchuan
Yabrai Shan
NINGXIA
Great Wall of China
SHAANXI
Xining
Tongxin
Lanzhou
Pingliang
GANSU
nan
Tianshui
Luqu
Zhugqu
SICHUAN
Wenxian

FESTIVAL OF NAADAM

Each July, people all over Mongolia celebrate the sports festival of Naadam. Three sports—wrestling (above), archery, and horse riding—are the focus of the festivities. The skills needed to take part in these activities are those that would have helped people survive a traditional nomadic lifestyle.

PEOPLE OF TIBET

Most Tibetans live in the valleys of the Tibetan plateau, high up in the Himalayas and surrounded by the world's tallest mountains. Tibetans have their own language and culture. Recently, many Han Chinese have moved to this region looking for a better life.

Tibetan village children

GREAT WALL OF CHINA

About 2,200 years ago, approximately 300,000 slaves began to build China's enormous Great Wall. Originally constructed to protect China's northern borders, it is the longest human-made structure ever built and stretches from central Asia to the Yellow Sea, a distance of 3,980 miles (6,400 km).

Buddhist prayer flags

TRADITIONAL MEDICINE

As well as modern medicine, many Chinese still use alternative remedies. Traditional medicine is based on the belief that health is achieved by balancing a person's mind and body—their yin and yang. Any imbalance is treated with medicines made from dried plant materials (left). Some animals, including Asiatic bears, are now endangered owing to the demand for parts used in traditional medicine.

BUDDHIST TIBET

Many Tibetans are devout Buddhists. Their religious leader, the Dalai Lama, used to live in Lhasa. In 1951, however, Tibet became part of China, and the government restricted the people's religious freedom and lifestyle. This has resulted in tension between Tibetans and the Chinese government. The Dalai Lama now lives in exile in India.

Eastern China and Korea

CHINA HAS A LARGE population of more than 1.3 billion, with two thirds living in eastern China. For thousands of years, powerful emperors ruled China. During this period, Chinese civilization was very advanced, but most of the population lived in poverty. In 1949, after a communist revolution, the People's Republic of China was established. Food, education, and health care became available to more people, but there was also a loss of freedom. Today, Chinese people have more freedom, but the government still has tight control over their lives. The Korean peninsula is politically divided into north and south, and political tensions continue to exist between the two governments. Since 1949, Taiwan has been in dispute with China about who governs the mountainous island of Taiwan.

NEW-YEAR CELEBRATIONS

Chinese New Year, also known as the Spring Festival, is the country's most important festival. It is usually held in January or February. Good-luck messages decorate buildings, and there are feasts, fireworks, fairs, and processions. People wear red clothes for good luck and give gifts of coins to symbolize wealth.

Chinese New Year parade

HONG KONG

For 100 years, Hong Kong was a British colony. Then, in 1997, it was returned to China. These small islands are some of the most densely populated areas of the world. Most people live and work in skyscrapers. It has a prosperous economy at the heart of global finance, and the people there have one of the world's highest life expectancies.

Skyline of Hong Kong with a Chinese junk in the foreground

ONE-CHILD FAMILIES

Many Chinese children do not have brothers or sisters. This is owing to policies introduced by the Chinese goverment in 1979. To try to control the rising population, the government offers special benefits to couples with only one child. Although this has slowed down the rate of growth, China's population still grows by millions each year.

PADDY FIELDS

Rice forms the basis of most Chinese meals. It grows in paddy fields in the southeast of the country. During the growing season, fields are flooded so that farmers can grow more rice more quickly. In drier regions, wheat is grown and used to make noodles, buns, and dumplings. Rice or wheat is combined with local vegetables, meats, and spices to create regional dishes.

Tongchuar
Xianya
Baoji
Xi'an
GANSU
Hanzhong SHAAN
Hongyuan
NINGXIA
Bayan Har Shan
QINGHAI
Guangyuan
Yalong Jiang
SICHUAN Mianyang Wanyua
Nanchong
Luhuo
Chengdu Sichuan Wanzho
Pendi
Litang
TIBET
Ya'an C H I
Leshan Neijiang Lich
Hengduan Shan
Zigong Chongqing
CHONGQING SHI
Xichang
Zhongdian Tongzi
Zunyi
Huaih
Zhoatong GUIZHOU
Panzhihua Guiyang
Dali Anshun Kaili
Guanling Duyun
Baoshan Kunming Dushan
Xingxi
YUNNAN
Yuxi Liuzho
Kaiyuan Bose GUANGX
Wenshan
Gejiu
Tropic of Cancer Nanning
Jinghong VIETNAM
Qinzhou
LAOS Beihai

0 km   150   300
0 miles   150   300

Gulf of Tongking
Danzho
Dongfang
HAINA

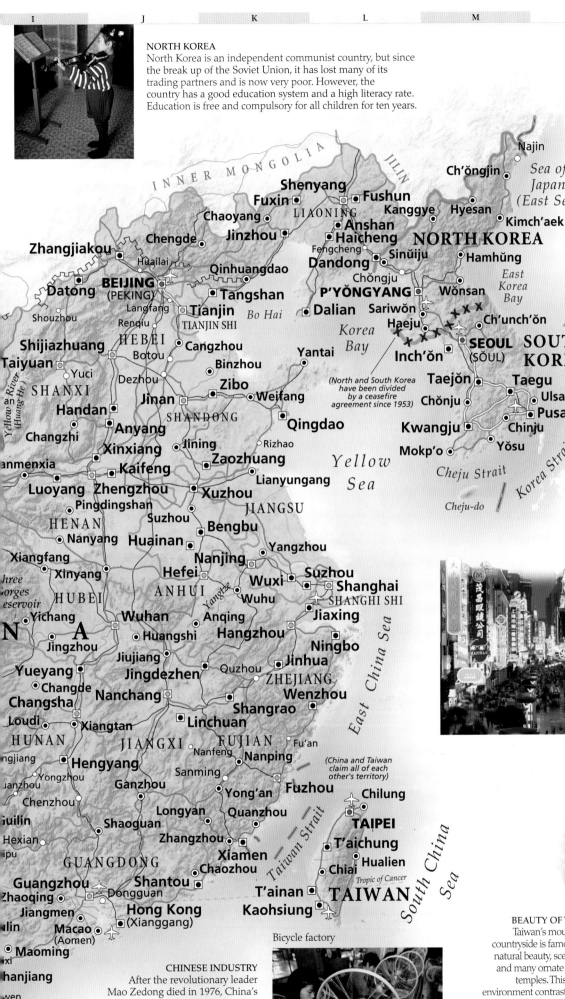

NORTH KOREA

North Korea is an independent communist country, but since the break up of the Soviet Union, it has lost many of its trading partners and is now very poor. However, the country has a good education system and a high literacy rate. Education is free and compulsory for all children for ten years.

SOUTH KOREA

South Korea is a democratic nation with a thriving electronics and machinery industry. One fourth of the population lives in or near the capital city, Seoul. The Internet has quickly developed in South Korea and plays an important role in work and leisure. The children below are using computers at an Internet café in the central city of Taejon.

The majority of the Chinese population lives in only 15 percent of the total land area.

MODERN SHANGHAI

China's largest city is Shanghai. More than 13 million people live in this wealthy east-coast port. International trade has recently transformed Shanghai's skyline, which is now crowded with skyscrapers and modern shopping malls. The center of town still has some old Western-style buildings that have survived from the days before the revolution.

BEAUTY OF TAIWAN

Taiwan's mountainous countryside is famous for its natural beauty, scenic lakes, and many ornate Buddhist temples. This peaceful environment contrasts sharply with Taiwan's capital city, Taipei, which is one of the fastest-growing cities in Asia.

Bicycle factory

CHINESE INDUSTRY

After the revolutionary leader Mao Zedong died in 1976, China's economy opened up. New industry is now encouraged, and many people are moving from the country to cities, where there are relatively well-paid jobs.

Japan

JAPAN IS SITUATED in the north Pacific Ocean off the coast of the Asian continent. It is made up of four main islands and more than 3,000 smaller ones. The Japanese people have a distinctive culture based on traditions built up over thousands of years. They have their own language and script. School children all learn to read and write both in the traditional script and using letters. Social rules in Japan are strict, and respect and politeness are considered very important. Most people bow when greeting one another, for example. Japan is a very modern country, however, with one of the world's most technologically advanced societies. Its economy is based on the development and production of cutting-edge electronics and vehicles, and most families have the latest consumer goods.

RELIGIONS OF JAPAN

Many Japanese people follow a mix of the Shinto and Buddhist religions, attending wedding ceremonies in Shinto shrines and funerals in Buddhist temples. Buddhism originated in India and arrived in Japan in the 500s, whereas the Shinto faith is native to Japan. Respect for nature is especially important in the Shinto religion. Many natural locations, such as Mount Fuji, are considered sacred.

EARTHQUAKES

The islands of Japan are situated in an area where four of Earth's tectonic plates meet. This causes frequent earthquakes. Japanese school children are taught how to stay safe during an earthquake by sheltering in a doorway or under a table.

OVERCROWDING

Most of the country's 127 million people live in cities in the flatter coastal areas. Tokyo and Osaka are very crowded, and homes here are usually very small and are designed to make the most of the limited space.

FASHION IN JAPAN

On regular days, Japanese people usually wear Western-style clothes. Most children have a school uniform. On festival days, such as Children's Day, many people prefer to wear the traditional kimono. Women's kimonos are often made of colorful silk, decorated with beautiful designs.

Traditional and modern dresses

La Perouse Strait

Rebun-tō
Rishiri-tō

Wakkanai

Sea of Okhotsk

Ostrov Kunashir

Ostrov Shikotan

Kurile Islands

(Kurile Islands administered by Russian Federation, claimed by Japan)

Nemuro

Akkeshi

Bekkai

Shari

Kushiro

Abashiri

Kitami

Shintoku

Obihiro

Monbetsu

△ Asahi-dake 7513ft (2290m)

Shirataki

Hokkaidō

Hiroo

△ Horoshiri-dake 6732ft (2052m)

Nakagawa

Nayoro

Shibetsu

Takikawa

Chitose

Tomakomai

Noboribetsu

Asahikawa

Ebetsu

Muroran

Uchiura-wan

Otaru

Sapporo

Iwanai

Setana

Esashi

Hakodate

Okushiri-tō

Fukushima

Tsugaru-kaikyō

Ishikari-wan

Mutsu -wan

Mutsu

Aomori

Goshogawara

Kuroishi

Towada

Hachinohe

Kuji

Fudi

Miyako

Iwate

Hirosaki

Odate

Morioka

Noshiro

Gojōme

Hanamaki

Kesennuma

Yokote

Shizugawa

Akita

Honjō

Shinjō

Ishinomaki

Yuzawa

Sakata

Furukawa

Tsuruoka

0 km   100   200   200

0 miles   100   200

Japanese Temple

Mount Fuji is a dormant volcano.

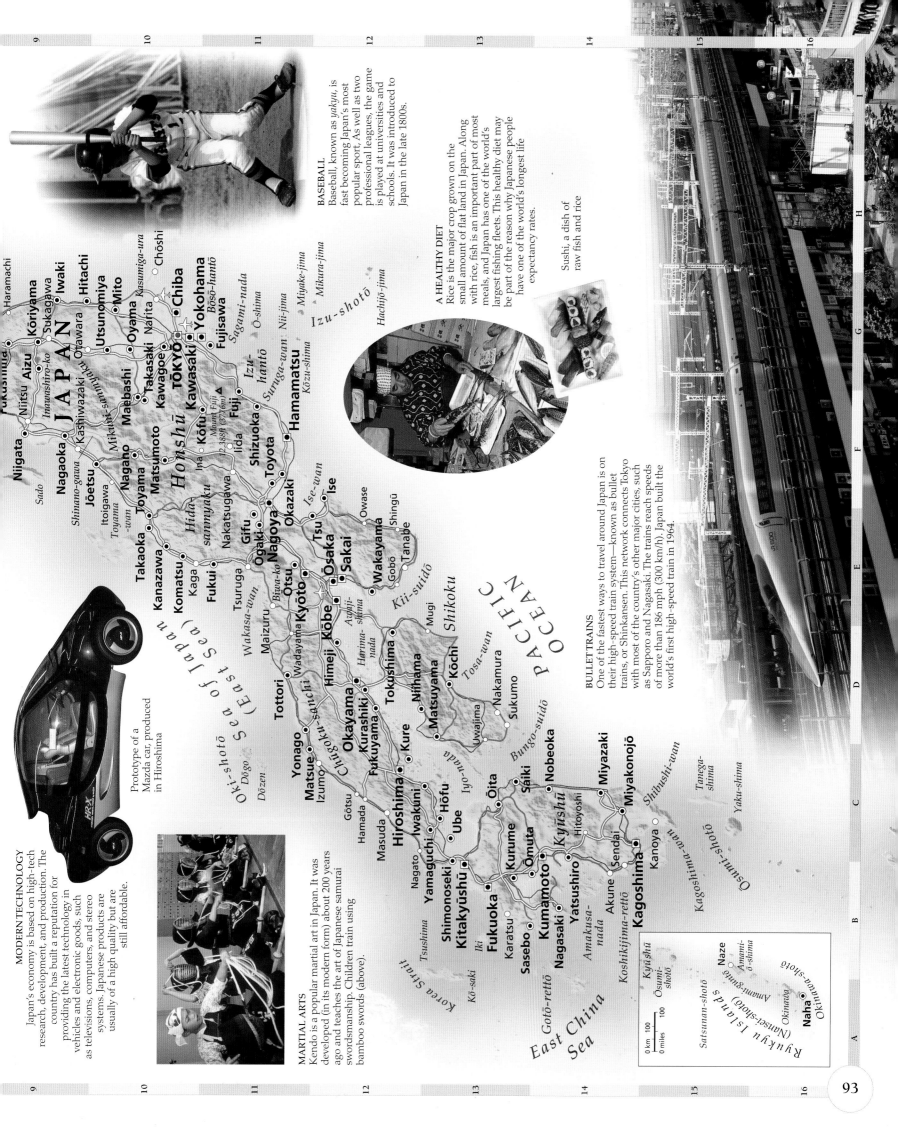

MODERN TECHNOLOGY

Japan's economy is based on high-tech research, development, and production. The country has built a reputation for providing the latest technology in vehicles and electronic goods, such as televisions, computers, and stereo systems. Japanese products are usually of a high quality but are still affordable.

Prototype of a Mazda car, produced in Hiroshima

MARTIAL ARTS

Kendo is a popular martial art in Japan. It was developed (in its modern form) about 200 years ago and teaches the art of Japanese samurai swordsmanship. Children train using bamboo swords (above).

BASEBALL

Baseball, known as *yakyu*, is fast becoming Japan's most popular sport. As well as two professional leagues, the game is played at universities and schools. It was introduced to Japan in the late 1800s.

A HEALTHY DIET

Rice is the major crop grown on the small amount of flat land in Japan. Along with rice, fish is an important part of most meals, and Japan has one of the world's largest fishing fleets. This healthy diet may be part of the reason why Japanese people have one of the world's longest life expectancy rates.

Sushi, a dish of raw fish and rice

BULLET TRAINS

One of the fastest ways to travel around Japan is on their high-speed train system—known as bullet trains, or Shinkansen. This network connects Tokyo with most of the country's other major cities, such as Sapporo and Nagasaki. The trains reach speeds of more than 186 mph (300 km/h). Japan built the world's first high-speed train in 1964.

Map labels

JAPAN

Honshū

Shikoku

Kyūshū

Ryūkyū Islands (Nansei-shotō)

PACIFIC OCEAN

Sea of Japan (East Sea)

East China Sea

Korea Strait

Haramachi
Iwaki
Hitachi
Sukagawa
Mito
Kōriyama
Aizu
Niigata
Niitsu
Imawashiro-ko
Utsunomiya
Otawara
Kashiwazaki
Kashiwazaki
Nagaoka
Jōetsu
Shinano-gawa
Sado
Toyama
Takaoka
Kanazawa
Komatsu
Kaga
Fukui
Tsuruga
Maizuru
Wakasa-wan
Tottori
Matsue
Izumo
Yonago
Gōtsu
Hamada
Masuda
Nagato
Yamaguchi
Shimonoseki
Kitakyūshū
Fukuoka
Karatsu
Sasebo
Nagasaki
Kumamoto
Yatsushiro
Akune
Kagoshima
Kanoya
Sendai
Miyakonojō
Miyazaki
Nobeoka
Saiki
Ōita
Hōfu
Ube
Iwakuni
Hiroshima
Kure
Fukuyama
Kurashiki
Okayama
Himeji
Kōbe
Ōsaka
Sakai
Kyōto
Ōtsu
Biwa-ko
Gifu
Ōgaki
Nagoya
Okazaki
Toyota
Shizuoka
Hamamatsu
Fuji
Kōfu
Matsumoto
Nagano
Maebashi
Takasaki
Kawagoe
Kawasaki
TŌKYŌ
Yokohama
Fujisawa
Chiba
Narita
Chōshi
Mito
Oyama
Hida sanmyaku
Mount Fuji 12,388ft (3776m)
Tsu
Ise
Wakayama
Gobō
Tanabe
Shingū
Owase
Nakamura
Sukumo
Uwajima
Matsuyama
Niihama
Kōchi
Tokushima
Kagawa
Nagato
Izu-shotō
Izu-hantō
Bōsō-hantō
Suruga-wan
Sagami-nada
Ō-shima
Nii-jima
Miyake-jima
Mikura-jima
Hachijō-jima
Kōzu-shima
Kii-suidō
Tosa-wan
Bungo-suidō
Iyo-nada
Harima-nada
Tsushima
Iki
Gotō-rettō
Amakusa-nada
Koshikijima-rettō
Ōsumi-shotō
Tanega-shima
Yaku-shima
Kagoshima-wan
Kagoshima-shotō
Ōsumi-shotō
Satsunan-shotō
Amami-shotō
Naze
Amami-ō-shima
Naha
Okinawa
Okinawa-shotō

0 km 100
0 miles 100

93

Mainland SE Asia

THE PENINSULA of Southeast Asia lies directly to the south of India and China, between the Pacific and Indian oceans. It is made up of Myanmar (Burma), Thailand, Vietnam, Cambodia, and Laos. Over thousands of years, the influence of people from nearby India, China, and Arabian countries has helped give this region a diverse mix of cultures and religions. Most of the land here is mountainous, with half of the region covered in forests. Most people live in coastal or lowland regions, where they can grow crops such as rice, raise cattle, and catch fish. In recent years, the electronics industry has also become an important part of southeast Asian economies, especially in Thailand.

ORPHANS IN CAMBODIA

Cambodia has a very high percentage of widows and orphans, mostly because many men were killed in civil wars in recent decades.

Cambodian orphanage

GROWING RICE

Rice is the most important crop in southeast Asia. It grows well in wet lowland areas, such as the Mekong River delta in Vietnam, where the plants can be grown in paddy fields. Most rice is planted and harvested by women.

RURAL LIVING

Most people in southeast Asia live in rural areas rather than cities, and farming is the most common occupation. The steep, mountainous regions are often unsuitable for growing crops or raising cattle, however, and many farming communities are based in the fertile river valleys and deltas. There are more than 200 villages on and around this lake (right) in Myanmar.

KAREN TRIBE

There are 600,000 tribespeople living in the northeastern hills of Thailand. The Karen are the largest hill tribe. They originated from Myanmar but moved into Thailand to escape political unrest.

Padaung women, who are part of the Karen tribe, wear distinctive gold neck rings.

| 0 km | 100 | 200 |
| 0 miles | 100 | 200 |

THAILAND

CAMBODIA

MALAYSIA

South China Sea

Gulf of Thailand

Andaman Sea

Mergui Archipelago

Mouths of the Irrawaddy

Mouths of the Mekong

Cities and places (map labels):

Đà Nẵng, Hội An, Tam Ky, Quang Ngai, Quy Nhon, Tuy Hoa, Nha Trang, Cam Ranh, Phan Rang-Thap Cham, Phan Thiết, Đà Lat, Di Linh, Pleiku, Virochey, Samakhixai, Salavan, Muang Khôngxédôn, Pakxé, Champasak, Ubon Ratchathani, Buriram, Surin, Roi Et, Nakhon Ratchasima, Nakhon Sawan, Lop Buri, Sara Buri, Ayutthaya, Srinagarind Reservoir, Nakhon Pathom, BANGKOK (KRUNG THEP), Samut Prakan, Chon Buri, Pattaya, Rayong, Ban Hua Hin, Ratchaburi, Phetchaburi, Ko Chang, Phumĭ Sâmraông, Phumĭ Kâmpóng Trâbêk, Stœ̆ng Trêng, Krâchéh, Kâmpóng Cham, Kâmpóng Chhnăng, Kâmpóng Spœ, Kâmpôt, Kâmpóng Saôm, Trâpeăng Vêng, Kralanh, Angkor Wat, Bătdâmbâng, Reăng Kesei, Moŭng Roessei, Chanthaburi, Chuŏr Phnum Krâvanh, Ódôngk, PHNOM PENH (PHNUM PÉNH), Suŏng, Svay Riêng, Biên Hoa, Hồ Chí Minh, Vung Tau, My Tho, Tra Vinh, Long Xuyên, Cần Tho, Sóc Trăng, Bac Liêu, Rach Gia, Ca Mau, Châu Đôc, Côn Dao, Vinh Rach Gia, Stœ̆ng Sên, Muang Không, Pouthisăt, Tônlé Srêpôk, Tônlé Sap, Chuŏr Phnum Dângrêk, Bilauktaung Range, Isthmus of Kra, Ranong, Chumphon, Lang Suan, Ko Phangan, Ko Samui, Surat Thani, Sichon, Nakhon Si Thammarat, Pak Phanang, Thung Song, Trang, Phatthalung, Thale Luang, Songkhla, Hat Yai, Pattani, Yala, Narathiwat, Ko Ta Ru Tao, Pulau Langkawi, Ko Lanta, Phang-Nga, Phuket, Ko Phra Thong, Ao Krung Thep, Daung Kyun, Letsôk-aw Kyun, Lanbi Kyun, Zadetkyi Kyun, Tenasserim, Myeik, Kadan Kyun, Mali Kyun, Ye, Dawei, Mudon, Kyaikkami, Bogale, Labutta, Great Coco Island, Little Coco Island, Mali Kyun, Ao Krung Thep, Ko Samui

ANGKOR

The impressive temple complex of Angkor in Cambodia attracts visitors interested in its history and architecture. This combination of temples and palaces was built in 1113 CE by the Khmer king Suryavarman II. The buildings, such as Angkor Wat, below, are made of stone and brick and are decorated with relief sculptures showing mythical scenes of Hindu gods and great royal processions. The complex was uncovered in 1861 by French naturalist Henri Mouhot, following stories of a "lost city" in the jungle.

Angkor Wat

MONASTIC LIFE

The main religion in mainland southeast Asia is Buddhism. Almost all Thai villages have their own temple, or wat, which is the center of village life. Most young men spend some time in a monastery, where they have few possessions and spend most of their time in meditation.

FLOATING MARKET

The capital of Thailand, Bangkok, is a busy, crowded city with more than nine million inhabitants. The city was built on an island in the river, and has many canals. Boats, known as sampans, (above) act as floating markets from which traders sell fresh fruit and vegetables.

A large, previously unknown mammal, the Vu Quang ox was only recently discovered in the forests of northern Vietnam.

THAI BEACHES

Tourism is now a major industry for Thailand. Popular destinations include the country's lively capital, Bangkok, and beautiful island beach resorts (below). Phuket, Thailand's largest island, is often referred to as the "Pearl of the South."

B   C   D   E   F   G   H

Maritime SE Asia

To the south of the Asian mainland lies maritime southeast Asia. It includes Malaysia, Indonesia, East Timor, Singapore, and the Philippines. Part of Malaysia is connected to the mainland, but the rest of the region is made up of more than 20,000 islands that stretch across the Pacific and Indian oceans. Lying near the Equator, the climate is mostly hot, wet, and humid. Most of the larger islands are mountainous and covered in dense forests, and many people live in villages near rivers or on the coast. Like the rest of southeast Asia, the population is made up of people from many different cultural backgrounds speaking hundreds of different languages. The most common religion is Islam, except in the Philippines, where most people are Roman Catholic.

GREAT APES
Orangutans are great apes that live only in Borneo and the northern corner of Sumatra. They spend most of their time in the trees, even building tree-top nests in which to sleep. Sadly, the orangutan is endangered because of deforestation.

PEOPLE OF MALAYSIA
Ethnic Malaysians make up 53 percent of the population and are known as bumiputera, meaning "son of the soil." Most Malaysians are Muslim. Ethnic Chinese form 26 percent of the population.

THE SULTAN OF BRUNEI
Brunei is ruled by a sultan who lives in the world's largest palace. The sultan is one of the wealthiest men in the world.

Ubadiah mosque, Malaysia

SINGAPORE
As the financial and industrial centre of southeast Asia, Singapore is one of the wealthiest countries in this region. It has a thriving high-tech industry and a high standard of living. There are strictly enforced laws forbidding littering and other petty crimes. The death penalty is imposed for drug smuggling. The government also controls the press and restricts the Internet.

Skyscrapers in Singapore's financial district

KITE FLYING
After the harvest, the people of Malaysia celebrate with the Wau (kite-flying) Festival, where skilled people demonstrate the traditional Malaysian sport.

A   B   C   D   E   F   G   H

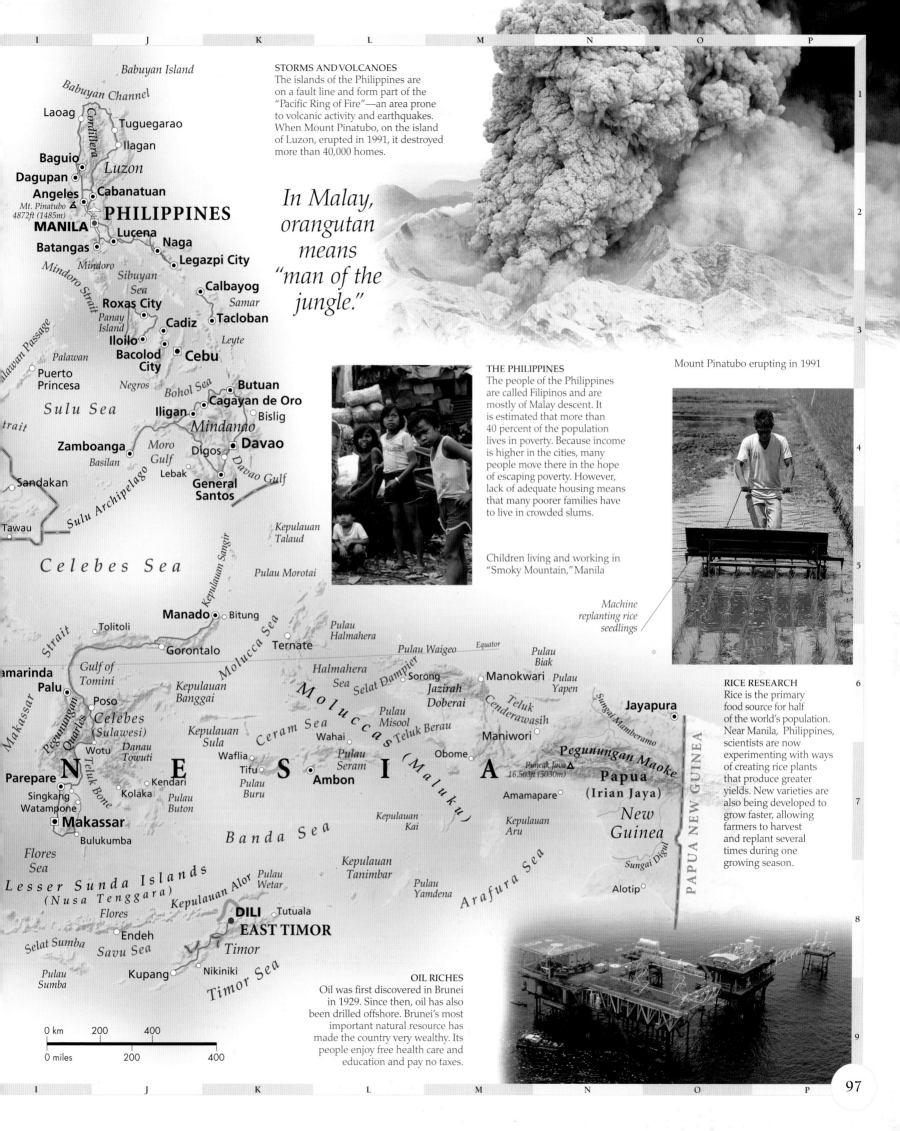

STORMS AND VOLCANOES
The islands of the Philippines are on a fault line and form part of the "Pacific Ring of Fire"—an area prone to volcanic activity and earthquakes. When Mount Pinatubo, on the island of Luzon, erupted in 1991, it destroyed more than 40,000 homes.

In Malay, orangutan means "man of the jungle."

Mount Pinatubo erupting in 1991

THE PHILIPPINES
The people of the Philippines are called Filipinos and are mostly of Malay descent. It is estimated that more than 40 percent of the population lives in poverty. Because income is higher in the cities, many people move there in the hope of escaping poverty. However, lack of adequate housing means that many poorer families have to live in crowded slums.

Children living and working in "Smoky Mountain," Manila

Machine replanting rice seedlings

RICE RESEARCH
Rice is the primary food source for half of the world's population. Near Manila, Philippines, scientists are now experimenting with ways of creating rice plants that produce greater yields. New varieties are also being developed to grow faster, allowing farmers to harvest and replant several times during one growing season.

OIL RICHES
Oil was first discovered in Brunei in 1929. Since then, oil has also been drilled offshore. Brunei's most important natural resource has made the country very wealthy. Its people enjoy free health care and education and pay no taxes.

Map labels

Babuyan Island
Babuyan Channel
Laoag
Tuguegarao
Ilagan
Cordillera
Baguio
Dagupan
Luzon
Angeles · Cabanatuan
Mt. Pinatubo
4872ft (1485m)
PHILIPPINES
MANILA
Lucena
Batangas · Naga
Legazpi City
Mindoro
Sibuyan Sea
Mindoro Strait
Calbayog
Roxas City
Samar
Panay Island
Cadiz · Tacloban
Iloilo
Leyte
Bacolod City · Cebu
Palawan
Negros
Bohol Sea
Butuan
Puerto Princesa
Iligan · Cagayan de Oro
Bislig
Sulu Sea
Mindanao
Zamboanga · Davao
Basilan · Moro Gulf · Digos
Sandakan
Lebak
General Santos · Davao Gulf
Tawau
Sulu Archipelago
Kepulauan Talaud
Celebes Sea
Kepulauan Sangir
Pulau Morotai
Manado · Bitung
Tolitoli · Molucca Sea
Gorontalo · Ternate
Pulau Halmahera
Pulau Waigeo · Equator
Pulau Biak
Samarinda
Gulf of Tomini
Halmahera Sea · Selat Dampier · Sorong
Manokwari · Pulau Yapen
Palu · Poso
Kepulauan Banggai
Moluccas (Maluku)
Jazirah Doberai
Jayapura
Celebes (Sulawesi)
Kepulauan Sula
Ceram Sea
Pulau Misool · Teluk Berau
Teluk Cenderawasih
Sungai Mamberamo
Pegunungan Quarles
Wotu
Danau Towuti
Wahai
Maniwori
Pegunungan Maoke
I N D O N E S I A
Waflia
Pulau Seram
Puncak Jaya
16,503ft (5030m)
Papua (Irian Jaya)
Parepare
Tifu · Ambon
Obome
Amamapare
New Guinea
Pulau Buru
Kendari
Kolaka
Pulau Buton
Teluk Bone
Singkang
Watampone
Kepulauan Kai
Kepulauan Aru
PAPUA NEW GUINEA
Makassar
Banda Sea
Bulukumba
Flores Sea
Kepulauan Tanimbar
Sungai Digul
Lesser Sunda Islands
(Nusa Tenggara)
Pulau Yamdena
Arafura Sea
Alotip
Kepulauan Alor · Pulau Wetar
Flores
DILI · Tutuala
EAST TIMOR
Endeh
Timor
Selat Sumba
Savu Sea
Kupang · Nikiniki
Pulau Sumba
Timor Sea

0 km   200   400
0 miles   200   400

Indian Ocean

THE THIRD-LARGEST ocean in the world, the Indian Ocean is bounded by Africa, Asia, Australasia, and Antarctica. The ocean contains some 5,000 islands. Madagascar and Sri Lanka are large, but most of the islands are small and ringed by coral reefs. The people of the Maldives have very mixed origins, incorporating Indian, Sinhalese, Arab, and African heritages, while two thirds of those living in Mauritius are Indian immigrants and their descendents. Altogether, about one fifth of the world's population live on this ocean's warm shores. Those along the northern coasts are often threatened by monsoon rain and tropical storms, which can cause severe flooding.

THE MALDIVES
The Maldives is a low-lying archipelago of 1,300 small coral islands, of which 202 are inhabited. The main industries are fishing—still carried out by traditional pole and line methods to conserve stocks—and tourism. Vacation resorts are on separate islands to those inhabited by locals, so as not to disturb the Maldive peoples' traditional Muslim lifestyles.

CORAL ISLANDS
Coral is a living organism formed in warm water by tiny sea creatures known as polyps. These creatures build limestone skeletons around themselves that accumulate over thousands of years. As sea levels change, this coral can be exposed as low-lying islands or submerged as reefs.

THE SEYCHELLES
The Seychelles consists of 115 islands—some are coral islands, while others are mountainous and made of granite. Most Seychellois people are Creoles—people of mixed African, Asian, and European ancestry. There are also small Chinese and Indian communities.

Market on the largest Seychelles island, Mahé

ENVIRONMENT
Beautiful shells are for sale on this beach in South Africa. If the trader collects only empty shells, no harm is done, but in many parts of the world, dealers hunt live shellfish, sea turtles, and rare species of starfish and sea urchins. Nations such as the Maldives take great care to protect the environment.

LIMITED TOURISM
The tropical climate, sandy beaches, beautiful coral reefs, and abundant marine life make both the Seychelles and the Maldives ideal tourist destinations. These same features also make them extremely attractive to scuba divers. However, the fragile environment of both island nations means that they have deliberately tried to make them exclusive, attracting only limited numbers of wealthy visitors, instead of pursuing mass tourism.

Mediterranean Sea

Arabian Peninsula

Red Sea

Gulf of Aden

Ethiopian Highlands

Horn of Africa

Andrew Tablemoun

AFRICA

Somali Bas

COMORO

MAYOTT (to France)

MADAGASCAR

Mozambique Channel

Davie Ridge

Mozambique Plateau

Natal Basin

Africana Seamount △

Agulhas Basin

Agulhas Plateau

Prince Edward Islands (to South Africa)

Aral Sea

Caspian Sea

Tien Shan

Gobi

A S I A

Himalayas

Iranian Plateau

Yellow Sea

Gulf of Oman   Indus Fan

Murray Ridge

Owen Fracture Zone

Arabian Sea

Ganges Fan

Bay of Bengal

PACIFIC OCEAN

...cotra (Yemen)

Arabian Basin

Laccadive Islands (to India)

Andaman Islands (to India)

SRI LANKA

...Ridge

Carlsberg Ridge

Chagos-Laccadive Plateau

Chagos Trench

MALDIVES
MALE'

Ceylon Plain

Nicobar Islands (to India)

Andaman Sea

Kepulauan Mentawai

Investigator Ridge

Gulf of Thailand

South China Sea

Sumatra

VICTORIA
·YCHELLES

BRITISH INDIAN OCEAN TERRITORY (to U.K.)

Mid-Indian Basin

Mid-Indian Ridge

Ninetyeast Ridge

Cocos Basin

Borneo

East Indies

Celebes

...scarene Basin

I N D I A N

COCOS ISLANDS (to Australia)

CHRISTMAS ISLAND (to Australia)

Java Sea

Java

Java Trench

...rene Plain

Argo Fracture Zone

Egeria Fracture Zone

North Australian Basin

MAURITIUS

RÉUNION (to France)

O C E A N

Wharton Basin

Exmouth Plateau

...adagascar Basin

Southwest Indian Ridge

East Indiaman Ridge

Cuvier Plateau

AUSTRALASIA & OCEANIA

Broken Ridge

Perth Basin

Naturaliste Plateau

Diamantina Fracture Zone

Crozet Basin

Amsterdam Island

St. Paul Island

South east Indian Ridge

...rozet ...ateau

FRENCH SOUTHERN & ANTARCTIC TERRITORIES (to France)

Crozet Islands

Kerguelen Plateau

Kerguelen

South Indian Basin

HEARD & MCDONALD ISLANDS (to Australia)

Ob' △

△ Lena Tablemount

Ba..zare Seamounts

...Tablemount

Enderby Plain

S O U T H E R N   O C E A N

A N T A R C T I C A

SALT FROM THE SEA
Salt is essential for life and has been traded here for centuries. People around the Indian Ocean make salt by flooding large flat areas with seawater. As the water evaporates in the sun, salt crystals are left behind. These are then collected, drained, and cleaned.

Collecting salt in the Maldives

MANGROVES
A lot of the coast in the tropical part of the Indian Ocean is fringed with mangrove forests. These amazing trees live in salty water and have long roots that trap sediment and protect the coast from erosion. Without these trees, settlements and land along the coast are in danger of being damaged by high tides and strong storms.

The moutia dance of the Seychelles was brought to the islands by African slaves in the 1700s.

INTERNATIONAL SEAWAYS
The Indian Ocean contains some of the busiest and most important shipping routes in the world. Smaller ships sail to and from the Mediterranean Sea and the ports of Europe and North America through the Red Sea and Suez Canal, while larger freighters and oil tankers from the Persian Gulf sail around the Cape of Good Hope at the southern tip of Africa.

Norwegian freighter

AUSTRALASIA OCEANIA

Unknown to the outside world before the 1600s, Australia is a still a sparsely inhabited land where most people live in cities. At its heart is a huge arid desert, in stark contrast to the islands of Oceania, where all of life revolves around the glittering ocean. The 3,000 named islands are grouped into nations, listed below in order of land area.

Australia
- 2,988,902 sq miles
  7,741,220 sq km
- 21,300,000
- Canberra
- English, Italian, Cantonese, Greek, Arabic, Vietnamese, Aboriginal languages

The thickly wooded Rock Islands of Palau near the Philippines are ancient reefs raised above sea level, fringed by coral sand beaches and blue lagoons.

Micronesia
- 271 sq miles
  702 sq km
- 110,700
- Palikir
- Trukese, Pohnpeian, Kosraean, Yapese, English

New Zealand
- 103,363 sq miles
  267,710 sq km
- 4,270,000
- Wellington
- English, Maori

Palau
- 177 sq miles
  459 sq km
- 20,400
- Melekeok
- Palauan, English, Japanese, Angaur, Tobi, Sonsorolese

Papa New Guinea
- 178,704 sq miles
  462,840 sq km
- 6,730,000
- Port Moresby
- Pidgin English, Papuan, English, Motu, 800 (est) native languages

Solomon Islands
- 11,157 sq miles
  28,896 sq km
- 523,200
- Honiara
- English, Pidgin English, Melanesian Pidgin, c. 120 other languages

Fiji
- 7,056 sq miles
  18,274 sq km
- 849,200
- Suva
- Fijian, English, Hindi, Urdu, Tamil, Telugu

Vanuatu
- 4,706 sq miles
  12,189 sq km
- 239,800
- Port-Vila
- Bislama (Melanesian Pidgin), English, French, other indigenous languages

Kiribati
- 313 sq miles
  811 sq km
- 99,482
- Bairiki (Tarawa Atoll)
- English, Kiribati

Samoa
- 1,093 sq miles
  2,831 sq km
- 178,800
- Apia
- Samoan, English

Tonga
- 288 sq miles
  747 sq km
- 104,000
- Nuku'Alofa
- English, Tongan

Marshall Islands
- 70 sq miles
  181 sq km
- 65,859
- Majuro
- Marshallese, English, Japanese, German

Sydney's iconic Opera House and Harbor Bridge symbolize this Australian city's role as a center of global culture.

The ancestors of today's Pacific Islanders reached their islands by crossing the ocean in giant canoes. Many islanders still rely on the ocean to make a living.

The colorfully named Champagne Pool is one of many hot springs in Rotorua, New Zealand— one of the most volcanically active countries in the world.

Tuvalu

🏛 10 sq miles
   26 sq km
👤 11,100
⬛ Fongafale (Funafuti Atol)
💬 Tuvaluan, Kiribati, English

Nauru

🏛 8 sq miles
   21 sq km
👤 9,800
⬛ None
💬 Nauruan, Kiribati, Chinese, Tuvaluan, English

SW Pacific

THE ISLANDS of the southwest Pacific Ocean are home to people of many different cultures and languages. These islands are divided into three general groups based on their location and the similarities between their peoples. The Polynesian islands to the east include Tonga, Samoa, the Cook Islands, and Tahiti. Melanesia includes Fiji, the Solomon Islands, and Vanuatu. The smallest group, Micronesia, includes the Marshall, Kiribati, and Caroline Islands. The first Europeans came to the southwest Pacific in the 1600s, several thousand years after the Melanesians, Micronesians, and Polynesians first arrived.

ISLAND VACATION
White sandy beaches and warm water makes this region ideal for tourists.

NORTHERN MARIANA ISLANDS
(to U.S.)
Saipan
Tinian
Rota
GUAM
(to U.S.)
HAGATÑA

MARSHALL ISLAND

Enewetak Atoll
Bikini Atoll
Rongelap Atoll
Ujelang Atoll
Ratak Cha
Ralik Cha
Kwajalein Atoll
Namu Atoll
Ailinglaplap Atoll

Micronesi

MICRONESIA

Yap
Babeldaob
MELEKEOK
PALAU

Chuuk Islands
PALIKIR
Pohnpei
Caroline Islands
Kosrae

Jaluit Atoll
Ebon Atoll

Equator

LAND OF MANY LANGUAGES
Historically, the mountainous landscape of Papua New Guinea made contact between villages difficult. As a result of many years of isolation, some villages developed their own individual languages. Nationwide, about 800 different languages evolved.

NAURU

Bana

INDONESIA

Admiralty Islands
St.Matthias Group
Bismarck Archipelago
Bismarck Sea
New Ireland

PAPUA NEW GUINEA

Madang
Central Range
New Guinea
Mount Wilhelm 14,793ft (4509m)
Lae
Owen Stanley Range
Gulf of Papua
PORT MORESBY

New Britain
Bougainville Island
Choiseul
Solomon Islands
Solomon Sea
New Georgia Islands
Santa Isabel
Malaita
HONIARA
Guadalcanal
D'Entrecasteaux Islands
Louisiade Archipelago
San Cristobal
Rennell

Mela

SOLOMON ISLANDS

Santa Cruz Islands

Men in Papua New Guinea wearing traditional makeup

A MIX OF RELIGIONS
Christianity is the dominant religion on most southwest Pacific islands. However Islam and Hinduism are also practiced. Many people also retain beliefs from traditional religions that existed before the islands were colonized by people from Europe and Asia.

Beads, shells, and feathers form part of the decoration.

Coral Sea

CORAL SEA ISLANDS
(to Australia)

Banks Islands

VANUATU

Espiritu Santo
Malekula
PORT-VILA

Maéwo
Pente
Ambr
Epi
Efaté

NEW CALEDONIA
(to France)
New Caledonia
NOUMÉA

Erromango
Tanna
Aneity
Ouvéa
Lifou
Maré
Iles Loyauté

Tropic of Capricorn

Vanuatu tribespeople dancing at a religious ceremony

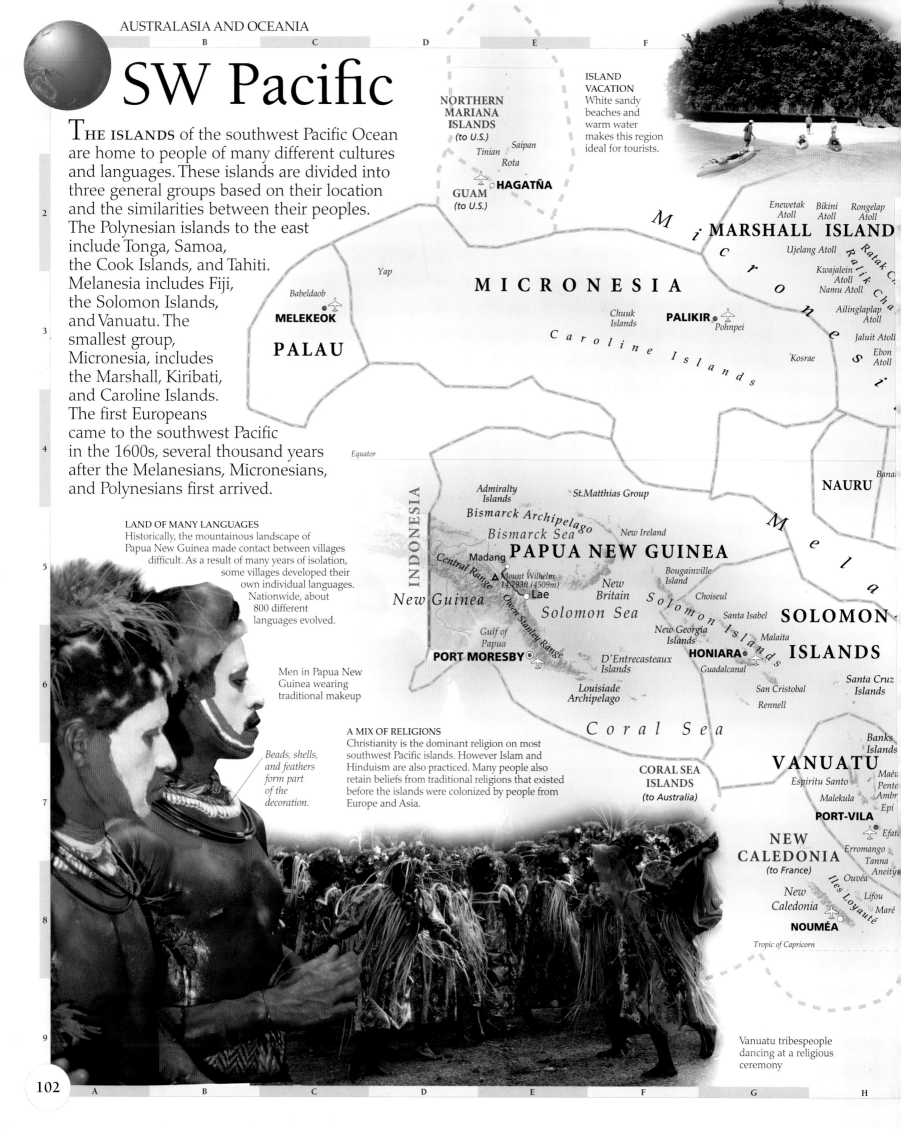

FOOD CROPS

Most Pacific Islanders live in small villages near the ocean. Inland areas are often mountainous, making farming difficult. Instead, people grow foods such as sweet potatoes, bananas, and coconuts in lowland areas. As well as providing milk, coconut flesh is used to produce copra, a substance for making soap and cosmetics.

Copra worker in Fiji scooping coconut kernels

THE KINGDOM OF TONGA

Tonga is the only Pacific nation never fully brought under foreign rule. Instead, it is run in the traditional way by its own king. All land is owned by the royal family and is allotted to households for their use. Now, some young, Westernized Tongans have started calling for more democracy.

The Royal Palace in Tonga

Cook Islands family

FAMILY LIFE

Many Pacific peoples live in extended family groups. Recently, however, some islanders have migrated to countries such as New Zealand and the United States in order to look for work.

Map labels

KINGMAN REEF (to U.S.)

PALMYRA ATOLL (to U.S.)

BAKER & HOWLAND ISLANDS (to U.S.)

JARVIS ISLAND (to U.S.)

Teraina
Tabuaeran
Kiritimati (Christmas Island)

BAIRIKI

elap Atoll
ro Atoll
i Atoll
kin
awa
nama
nouti

Beru
Nikunau
Tamana
Arorae

KIRIBATI

Tungaru

International Dateline

PACIFIC OCEAN

Kanton
Birnie Island
McKean Island
Nikumaroro
Orona
Manra

Enderbury Island

KIRIBATI
Phoenix Islands

Line Islands

Malden Island

KIRIBATI

Starbuck Island

Vostok Island
Millennium Island

Nuku Hiva

Marquesas Islands

Hiva Oa
Fatu Hiva

Nanumea Atoll
Niutao
Nanumaga
Nui Atoll
Nukufetau
Funafuti Atoll

FONGAFALE

Nukulaelae

TUVALU

Niulakita

Atafu Atoll
Nukunonu Atoll
Fakaofo Atoll

TOKELAU
(to New Zealand)

Penrhyn
Rakahanga
Manihiki

Northern Cook Islands

Flint Island

Polynesia

Tikehau
Takaroa
Fakarava
Makemo

Rotuma

WALLIS & FUTUNA
(to France)

MATĀ'UTU

Île Uvea

Île Futuna

SAMOA

APIA

Savai'i
'Upolu

AMERICAN SAMOA
(to U.S.)

PAGO PAGO
Ta'ū
Tutuila

COOK ISLANDS
(to New Zealand)

Raiatea

PAPEETE
Tahiti

Tuamotu Islands

Amanu
Tatakoto

FIJI
Cikobia
Vanua Levu

Nadi
Viti Levu

SUVA

Kadavu

Lau Group

Niuatoputapu

TONGA

Vava'u Group
Tofua
Ha'apai Group

International Dateline

NIUE
(to New Zealand)

ALOFI

Palmerston

Manuae

Southern Cook Islands
Takutea

AVARUA
Rarotonga
Mangaia

Archipel de la Société

FRENCH POLYNESIA
(to France)

Rurutu
Tubuai

Îles Australes

Raevavae

Vanavana

Tureia

Ahunui

Marutea

Tropic of Capricorn

Fangataufa

NUKU' ALOFA
Tongatapu
'Eua

Tongatapu Group

Marotiri

OUTRIGGER CANOES

Transportation between many islands has traditionally been by outrigger canoes. Floats attached to the sides provide extra stability, especially useful for the fishermen who stand in the boats to cast their nets.

Islanders net fishing in an outrigger off the coast of Ifalik, Micronesia

0 km	300	600
0 miles	300	600

Australia

A HUGE, GENERALLY FLAT COUNTRY, Australia has relatively few inhabitants. This is mostly because most of the land is hot, semiarid desert—known as the outback—unsuitable for towns or farms. In places where there is some vegetation or the land has been irrigated, sheep and cattle are grazed. Wheat is grown in the fertile south. The first people to live here were the Aborigines, who arrived from Asia at least 50,000 years ago. Today, most Australians are descendants of European immigrants, with a more recent addition of Asians.

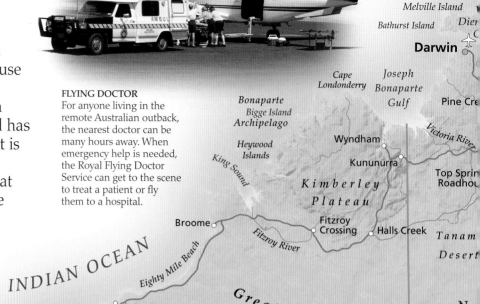

FLYING DOCTOR
For anyone living in the remote Australian outback, the nearest doctor can be many hours away. When emergency help is needed, the Royal Flying Doctor Service can get to the scene to treat a patient or fly them to a hospital.

AUSTRALIAN ABORIGINES
The original inhabitants of Australia had an intimate understanding of the environment. This connection to the land and its plants and animals affects every aspect of their culture. When Europeans started arriving in the late 1700s, only the Aborigines in remote areas escaped contact with the diseases they brought. Today, Aborigines rarely live off the land, but instead work in factories or on farms.

MINING
Australia has one of the world's most important mining industries, with resources including gold (left), coal, natural gas, iron ore, copper, and opals. However, damage to the environment—and Aboriginal claims over land used for mining—still need to be faced.

Scale:
0 km 200 400
0 miles 200 400

AUSTRALIAN FOOTBALL
A popular sport here is Australian Rules Football. One of the rules is that players can kick or punch the ball, but they must not throw it. Many Australians either play the game themselves or support their favorite team. As the name implies, the game originated in Australia, but it now has leagues in other countries, such as Great Britain and the U.S.

OUTDOOR SPORTS
A warm climate, with easy access to beaches and wilderness areas, has made outdoor activities an important part of modern Australian life. Watersports, such as swimming, sailing, and surfing, are especially popular. Because of the danger of exposure to strong sunlight, people are told to cover up and always use sunscreen.

Map labels

Melville Island
Bathurst Island
Dier
Darwin
Cape Londonderry
Joseph Bonaparte Gulf
Pine Cre
Bonaparte
Bigge Island
Archipelago
Heywood Islands
Wyndham
Kununurra
Victoria River
Top Sprin
Roadhou
Kimberley Plateau
King Sound
Fitzroy Crossing
Halls Creek
Tanam
Broome
Fitzroy River
Desert
INDIAN OCEAN
Eighty Mile Beach
Great Sandy Desert
N
Barrow Island
Dampier
Port Hedland
Marble Bar
Percival Lakes
Exmouth Gulf
Fortescue River
Onslow
T E
Exmouth
Hamersley Range
Newman
Lake Mackay
Ashburton River
W E S T E R N
Tropic of Capricorn
Barlee Range
Lake Disappointment
Maca
A U S T
Gibson Desert
Lake Amadeus
Bernier Island
Gascoyne River
Uluru
(Ayers Rock)
2844ft (867m)
Dorre Island
Carnarvon
Shark Bay
Dirk Hartog Island
Denham
Murchison River
Robinson Range
Lake Carnegie
Lake Wells
Musgrave Range
Meekatharra
A U S T R A L I A
Kalbarri
Mount Magnet
Great Victoria
Geraldton
Lake Carey
Desert
Lake Barlee
Lake Moore
Lake Rebecca
Moora
Kalgoorlie
Zanthus
Reid
Southern Cross
Coolgardie
Nullarbor Plain
Gingin
Merredin
Lake Cowan
Eucla
Perth
Northam
Norseman
Fremantle
Brookton
Balladonia
Mandurah
Narrogin
Bunbury
Wagin
Collie
Katanning
Esperance
Great Australian Bight
Busselton
Manjimup
Augusta
Albany

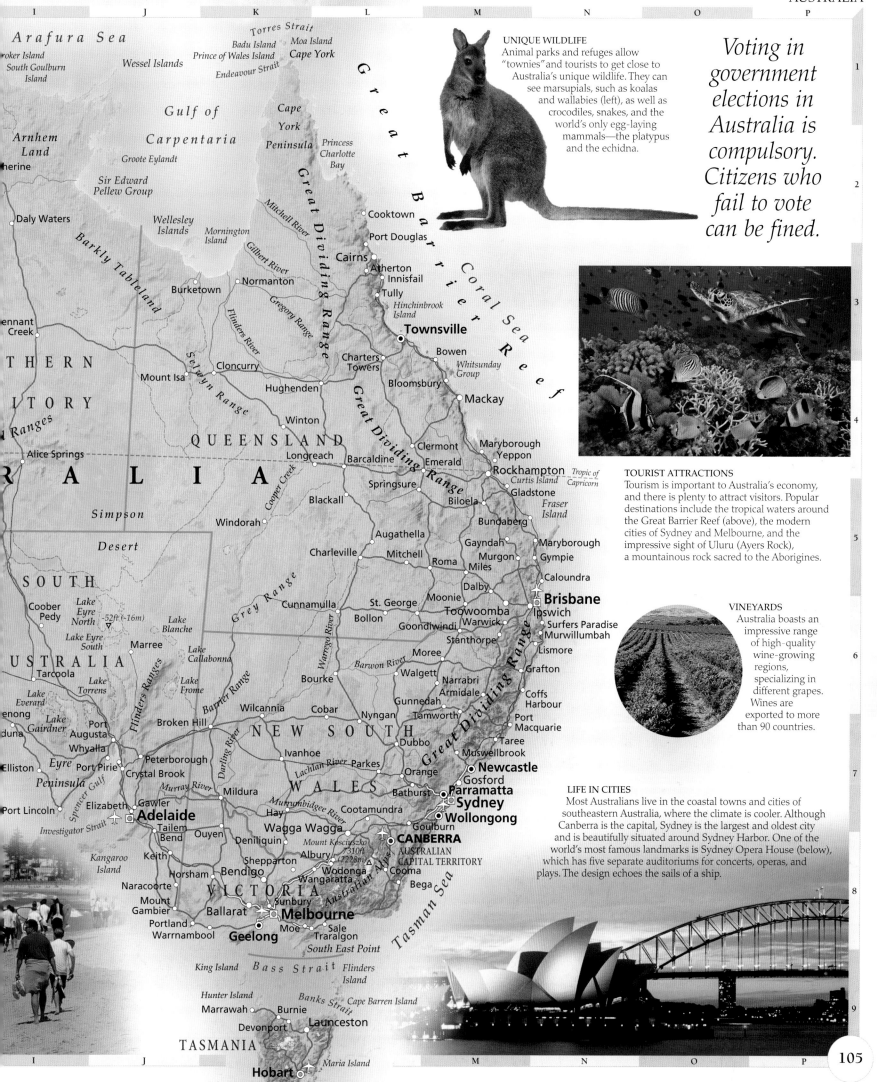

UNIQUE WILDLIFE
Animal parks and refuges allow "townies" and tourists to get close to Australia's unique wildlife. They can see marsupials, such as koalas and wallabies (left), as well as crocodiles, snakes, and the world's only egg-laying mammals—the platypus and the echidna.

Voting in government elections in Australia is compulsory. Citizens who fail to vote can be fined.

TOURIST ATTRACTIONS
Tourism is important to Australia's economy, and there is plenty to attract visitors. Popular destinations include the tropical waters around the Great Barrier Reef (above), the modern cities of Sydney and Melbourne, and the impressive sight of Uluru (Ayers Rock), a mountainous rock sacred to the Aborigines.

VINEYARDS
Australia boasts an impressive range of high-quality wine-growing regions, specializing in different grapes. Wines are exported to more than 90 countries.

LIFE IN CITIES
Most Australians live in the coastal towns and cities of southeastern Australia, where the climate is cooler. Although Canberra is the capital, Sydney is the largest and oldest city and is beautifully situated around Sydney Harbor. One of the world's most famous landmarks is Sydney Opera House (below), which has five separate auditoriums for concerts, operas, and plays. The design echoes the sails of a ship.

Arafura Sea
Broker Island
South Goulburn Island
Arnhem Land
Katherine
Daly Waters
Tennant Creek
NORTHERN TERRITORY
Alice Springs
Ranges
AUSTRALIA
Simpson Desert
SOUTH AUSTRALIA
Coober Pedy
Lake Eyre North
-52ft (-16m)
Lake Blanche
Lake Eyre South
Marree
Lake Callabonna
Tarcoola
Lake Torrens
Lake Frome
Lake Everard
Lenong
Lake Gairdner
Tailem
Elliston
Eyre Peninsula
Port Augusta
Whyalla
Port Pirie
Peterborough
Crystal Brook
Port Lincoln
Elizabeth
Gawler
Adelaide
Investigator Strait
Kangaroo Island
Keith
Naracoorte
Mount Gambier
Portland
Warrnambool

Torres Strait
Badu Island
Prince of Wales Island
Moa Island
Cape York
Endeavour Strait
Wessel Islands
Gulf of Carpentaria
Groote Eylandt
Sir Edward Pellew Group
Wellesley Islands
Mornington Island
Barkly Tableland
Burketown
Normanton
Gilbert River
Gregory Range
Mitchell River
Flinders River
Selwyn Range
Mount Isa
Cloncurry
Cape York Peninsula
Princess Charlotte Bay
Great Barrier Reef
Great Dividing Range
Cooktown
Port Douglas
Cairns
Atherton
Innisfail
Tully
Hinchinbrook Island
Townsville
Charters Towers
Bowen
Whitsunday Group
Bloomsbury
Coral Sea
Hughenden
Winton
QUEENSLAND
Mackay
Longreach
Barcaldine
Clermont
Emerald
Maryborough
Yeppon
Rockhampton
Curtis Island
Tropic of Capricorn
Springsure
Gladstone
Blackall
Biloela
Windorah
Fraser Island
Augathella
Bundaberg
Charleville
Mitchell
Roma
Gayndah
Murgon
Miles
Maryborough
Gympie
Cooper Creek
Cunnamulla
Dalby
Moonie
Caloundra
St. George
Toowoomba
Brisbane
Bollon
Goondiwindi
Warwick
Ipswich
Surfers Paradise
Stanthorpe
Murwillumbah
Moree
Lismore
Grey Range
Barwon River
Walgett
Grafton
Warrego River
Bourke
Narrabri
Armidale
Coffs Harbour
Barrier Range
Flinders Ranges
Broken Hill
Wilcannia
Cobar
Gunnedah
Tamworth
Port Macquarie
Darling River
NEW SOUTH WALES
Nyngan
Dubbo
Taree
Muswellbrook
Ivanhoe
Parkes
Orange
Newcastle
Gosford
Lachlan River
Bathurst
Parramatta
Sydney
Mildura
Hay
Cootamundra
Wollongong
Murray River
Murrumbidgee River
Wagga Wagga
Goulburn
Ouyen
Deniliquin
Albury
CANBERRA
AUSTRALIAN CAPITAL TERRITORY
Shepparton
Wodonga
Cooma
Keith
Bendigo
Wangaratta
Mount Kosciuszko 7310ft (2228m)
Australian Alps
Bega
Horsham
VICTORIA
Sunbury
Ballarat
Melbourne
Tasman Sea
Moe
Sale
Geelong
Traralgon
South East Point
King Island
Bass Strait
Flinders Island
Hunter Island
Banks Strait
Cape Barren Island
Marrawah
Burnie
Devonport
Launceston
TASMANIA
Maria Island
Hobart

105

New Zealand

MADE UP OF TWO MAIN ISLANDS and several smaller ones, New Zealand is one of the most isolated countries in the world. Located in the southern Pacific, the country has a mild climate, with warm summers and cool, wet winters. Both main islands have mountains, short, swift-flowing rivers, forests, and fertile farmland. Until the Europeans arrived, most of the landscape was covered in dense forest known as native bush. Today, although forests remain, most has been cleared for farming. Most New Zealanders live on North Island, which is warmer and less mountainous. Although New Zealanders are of mostly British descent, the Maoris—a people of Polynesian origin—were the first to arrive about 1,000 years ago. Today, non-Maori Polynesians and Asians are adding to the ethnic mix. The country has a liberal, clean, "green" image and a high standard of living.

MAORI CULTURE

Maoris make up almost 16 percent of the population, with most living on North Island. Before the coming of the *Pakeha* (white man), Maori history was orally passed on to succeeding generations. This included many legends and *waiata* (songs). Their carvings in wood (left) and stone (right) were another way in which they recorded and remembered events. In recent years, interest in Maori culture has increased, and schoolchildren are now taught the Maori language.

Greenstone (jade) carving, an example of Maori art

AUCKLAND

With its safe harbor and nearby scenic islands, Auckland is known as the "city of sails". It boasts more pleasure boats per person than anywhere else in the world. The water that separates the bigger islands is home to dolphins, families of blue penguins, and the occasional whale.

In 1893, New Zealand was the first country to give women the vote.

PACIFIC OCEAN

North Island

Mount Ruapehu 9177ft (2797 m)

Mount Taranaki (Mount Egmont) 8261ft (2518m)

Tasman Sea

Map labels:
Three Kings Islands, Cape Reinga, North Cape, Te Kao, Great Exhibition Bay, Ninety Mile Beach, Kaitaia, Okaihau, Kaikohe, Hokianga Harbour, Kerikeri, Paihia, Hikurangi, Whangarei, Ruawai, Kaipara Harbour, Dargaville, Wellsford, Helensville, Warkworth, Takapuna, Auckland, Waiuku, Pukekohe, Papakura, Manurewa, Huntly, Morrinsville, Hamilton, Cambridge, Te Kuiti, Otorohanga, Te Awamutu, Taumarunui, Ohura, New Plymouth, Waitara, Stratford, Hawera, Patea, Wanganui, Marton, Feilding, Palmerston North, Woodville, Dannevirke, Waipukurau, Waipawa, Havelock North, Hastings, Napier, Wairoa, Havke Bay, Taihape, Waiouru, Raetihi, Turangi, Lake Taupo, Taupo, Tokoroa, Rotorua, Kawerau, Murupara, Lake Waikaremoana, Opotiki, Whakatane, Bay of Plenty, Tauranga, Matamata, Katikati, Paeroa, Thames, Coromandel, Whitianga, Mayor Island, Gisborne, Poverty Bay, Mahia Peninsula, Ruatoria, East Cape, Raukumara Range, Rangitikei, Great Barrier Island, Little Barrier Island, Coville Channel, Hauraki Gulf, North Taranaki Bight, South Taranaki Bight, Cape Egmont, Cape Farewell, Waitoa, Lake Rotorua, Cape Farewell

Scale:
0 km 50 100
0 miles 50 100

AN AGRICULTURAL NATION

Agriculture is of prime importance, and it accounts for more than half of national export earnings. Orchards produce a wide range of fruit, from apples (above) to kiwi fruit (below). Cereals and other crops, such as sunflowers, add color and variety to the landscape. Traditional sheep and cattle farming has expanded to include deer, goats, and even ostrich.

VOLCANIC ACTIVITY

A fault line runs through New Zealand, where two major tectonic plates meet. It has caused devastating earthquakes but has also helped create breathtaking scenery. This includes South Island's Southern Alps and many smaller volcanic mountains, hot springs, and geysers on North Island.

Lady Knox geyser, North Island

UNIQUE WILDLIFE

New Zealand has many unique and endangered animal species, especially birds. There were no mammal predators before humans introduced them, so many animal species have few means of defense, and some birds, such as the kiwi, cannot fly. Conservation programs are now in place to protect endangered species.

Flightless Kiwi bird

GREEN ENERGY

Most of the country's electricity comes from hydroelectric power. It is generated by river water gushing through turbines inside dams at power plants. New Zealand also has geothermal energy, using heat taken from inside Earth.

FILM INDUSTRY

New Zealand has a well-established film industry. Today, thanks to the acclaimed Tolkien trilogy *Lord of the Rings* (above), the country has become increasingly popular with international studios for location work. The country offers an unusually wide range of scenery, as well as technical experts.

ADVENTURE-SPORTS PARADISE

New Zealand offers a huge range of adventure sports and outdoor activities, from white-water rafting (below) to bungee jumping. The latter originated in Queenstown on South Island. The town is billed as the country's top adventure-tourism destination because its surrounding lakes, mountains, and rivers—and its mostly dry climate—are ideal for outdoor pursuits.

NEW ZEALAND

WELLINGTON
Masterton
Lower Hutt
Porirua
Cape Palliser
Cape Campbell
Blenheim
Seddon
Picton
Nelson
Clarence
Wairau
Richmond
Motueka
Richmond Range
Mount Owen 6,171ft (1,875m)
Kaikoura
Hanmer Springs
Springs Junction
Reefton
Waipara
Pegasus Bay
Kaiapoi
Christchurch
Lyttelton
Banks Peninsula
Rangiora
Lake Ellesmere
Cook Strait
Karamea Bight
Seddonville
Westport
Cape Foulwind
Runanga
Greymouth
Hokitika
Ross
Abut Head
Whataroa
Fox Glacier
Otira
Arthur's Pass 3,018ft (920m)
Oxford
Darfield
Mayfield
Ashburton
Hinds
Canterbury Bight
Canterbury Plains
Geraldine
Temuka
Timaru
Studholme
Waimate
Oamaru
Southern Alps
New
South
Island
Horaki (Mt. Cook) 12,283ft (3744m)
Mount Cook
Haast
Lake Pukaki
Lake Tekapo
Fairlie
Waitaki
Hampden
Dunedin
Otago Peninsula
Lake Wanaka
Lake Hawea
Wanaka
Cromwell
Alexandra
Clutha
Taieri
Mosgiel
Milton
Balclutha
Lake Wakatipu
Queenstown
Lumsden
Mataura
Gore
Milford Sound
George Sound
Caswell Sound
Fiordland
Lake Te Anau
Te Anau
Lake Manapouri
Winton
Riverton
Invercargill
Mataura
Tokanui
Resolution Island
West Cape
Lake Hauroko
Ta Waewae Bay
Livingstone Mts.
Eyre Mts.
Waiau
Foveaux Strait
Toetoes Bay
Ruapuke Island
Codfish Island
Halfmoon Bay
Stewart Island
South West Cape
Muttonbird Islands

107

Pacific Ocean

THE LARGEST OCEAN ON EARTH, the Pacific covers one third of Earth's surface. The island nations of Japan, Indonesia, Australia, New Zealand, and many others are completely surrounded by this enormous ocean, which stretches from the Arctic in the north to the Antarctic in the south. The Pacific is also the world's deepest ocean—its greatest known depth is in the Mariana Trench, off Guam, which plunges steeply for 36,198 ft (11,033 m). Within the Pacific, there are many smaller seas that lie near land. These include the Tasman Sea, the South China Sea, and the Bering Sea. There are more than 30,000 islands in the Pacific. Most are too small or barren to be inhabited, but others are home to people of many different cultures and religions. The native island peoples fall into three main groups—Polynesians, Melanesians, and Micronesians. Although the word *pacific* means "peaceful," strong currents, tropical storms, and tsunamis can all make this ocean far from peaceful.

HAWAII
This chain of eight volcanic islands and 124 islets forms the 50th state of the United States of America, and was admitted to the union in 1959. The dramatic landscape and palm-fringed beaches make Hawaii a popular destination for tourists. Today, native Hawaiians are a minority in their own land.

Hawaiian conch shells, once blown to sound a warning

Marine iguana on black volcanic rocks, Galápagos Islands

GALÁPAGOS ISLANDS
When British naturalist Charles Darwin (1809–1882) traveled to the Galápagos Islands, he found many unusual animals. He also noticed differences between animals of the same species living elsewhere. This led him to believe that, over time, animals adapt, or evolve, to suit their habitats.

TSUNAMI
Earthquakes beneath the Ocean may cause giant waves called tsunamis. These can travel great distances across the ocean, building into a huge wall of water as they approach the coast. They can leave immense damage in their wake.

SURFING
The Hawaiian sport of surfing ranks as the oldest sport in the USA. It was first practiced by the nobility as a form of religious ceremony until the 1820s, when missionaries, who thought it was immoral, tried to ban it. Today, surfing is one of the most popular watersports and can be enjoyed all over the world, from Australia to the U.K.

Black smoker chimney

Large red tube worms

DEEP-SEA VENTS
Underwater exploration has revealed some amazing places deep in the Pacific. Large vents, formed by solidified minerals, act as chimneys for super-hot steam and gas that stream up from the sea bed. These vents are known as black smokers. Scientists have found a variety of new creatures living in this hostile environment.

ASIA

Yellow Sea

Sea of Japan (East Sea)

Japan

Japan Trench

East China Sea

Ryukyu Trench

Shikoku Basin

Emperor Seamounts

Taiwan

Philippine Sea

Philippine Basin

NORTHERN MARIANA ISLANDS (to U.S.)

Mariana Trench

South China Basin

Philippines

GUAM (to U.S.)

Challenger ▽ Deep 36,201ft (11,034m)

South China Sea

PALAU

Caroline Islan

MICRO

Celebes Sea

Borneo

Celebes

Me

East Indies

New Guinea

Java Sea

Banda Sea

Java

Arafura Sea

Torres Strait

Timor

Timor Sea

Co Great B Reef

INDIAN OCEAN

AUSTRALASIA & OCEANIA

Great Australian Bight

South Australian Basin

Bass St

Tasma

The Pacific is larger than Earth's entire land surface.

ARCTIC OCEAN

Sea of
Okhotsk

Bering Strait

Bering
Aleutian   Sea
Basin

Kurile
Islands

Kurile Trench

Aleutian Islands

Aleutian Trench

Gulf of
Alaska

Northwest Pacific
Basin

Chinook Trough

Cascadia
Basin

Rocky Mountains

NORTH
AMERICA

Mendocino Fracture Zone

MIDWAY
ISLANDS
(to U.S.)

Murray Fracture Zone

Hawaiian Ridge

Molokai Fracture Zone

Gulf of
Mexico

WAKE ISLAND
(to U.S.)

HAWAII
(U.S. STATE)

Gulf of California

Mid-Pacific Mountains

JOHNSTON ATOLL
(to U.S.)

Clarion Fracture Zone

Middle America Trench

Caribbean Sea

MARSHALL
ISLANDS

PACIFIC

Central

Pacific

Basin

KINGMAN REEF
(to U.S.)

Clipperton Fracture Zone

CLIPPERTON
ISLAND
(to France)

Guatemala
Basin

Cocos Ridge

Micronesia

Melanesian
Basin

PALMYRA
ATOLL

JARVIS ISLAND
(to U.S.)

NAURU

OCEAN

BAKER &
HOWLAND ISLANDS
(to U.S.)

Galápagos Fracture Zone

Galápagos Islands
(to Ecuador)

SOUTH
AMERICA

Gallego
Rise

Marquesas
Islands

Bauer
Basin

TUVALU

TOKELAU
(to N.Z.)

KIRIBATI

Marquesas Fracture Zone

Galápagos
Rise

Peru-Chile Trench

SOLOMON
ISLANDS

WALLIS & FUTUNA
(to France)

Polynesia

Mendaña Fracture Zone

North Fiji
Basin

AMERICAN
SAMOA
(to U.S.)

Tiki
Basin

VANUATU

SAMOA

Tahiti

Nazca Ridge

FIJI

COOK
ISLANDS
(to N.Z.)

FRENCH
POLYNESIA
(to France)

Austral
Fracture Zone

Peru
Basin

Andes

NEW CALEDONIA
(to France)

TONGA

NIUE
(to N.Z.)

East Pacific Rise

South
Fiji
Basin

Îles Gambier

PITCAIRN
ISLANDS
(to U.K.)

Sala y Gomez
(to Chile)

Isla San Ambrosio
(to Chile)

NORFOLK
ISLAND
(to Australia)

Horizon Deep

Ozbourn Seamount

Kermadec
Islands
(to N.Z.)

Îles Australes

Easter Island
(to Chile)

Isla San Félix
(to Chile)

Tonga Trench

Southwest
Pacific
Basin

Islas Juan Fernández
(to Chile)

Chile Basin

New Caledonia Basin

Lord Howe Rise

North Island

Louisville Ridge

Challenger Fracture Zone

Chile Rise

Tasman
Sea

South
Island

NEW
ZEALAND

Chatham Rise

Agassiz Fracture Zone

Tasman
Basin

Bounty
Trough

Chatham Islands
(to N.Z.)

Mornington
Abyssal
Plain

Campbell
Plateau

Eltanin Fracture Zone

Pacific-Antarctic Ridge

Southeast
Pacific Basin

Amundsen Plain

SOUTHERN OCEAN

EASTER ISLAND
Easter Island in the Pacific lies more than
2,000 miles (3,218 km) from the nearest
populated land. It is best known for the
gigantic stone figures known as Moai that
were carved from volcanic rock and erected
facing the ocean. It is thought that the people
who built the statues were of Peruvian descent.

EL NIÑO
Every few years, winds off the
South American coast weaken,
causing an unusually warm ocean
current known as El Niño. This kills
off plankton that provide food for
fish such as anchovies. Scientists
use heat-sensitive cameras to map
ocean temperatures and keep track
of El Niño. The warmest waters are
shown in orange/red (above).

SOUTH PACIFIC FISH
Fish stocks in the south Pacific are an important
food source for the island countries and a
major source of employment. Migratory tuna
are the most important fish. However, it is
becoming clear that the industry needs to be
effectively managed in order to avoid the
dangers of overfishing and the collapse
of fish stocks.

Tuna fishing needs
to be carefully
monitored.

Antarctica

THE FROZEN CONTINENT OF ANTARCTICA is covered by a vast icecap, many thousands of years old, and surrounded by the freezing waters of the Southern Ocean. It is the only continent with no permanent inhabitants—the only people who come here are scientists or tourists. Although the land is rich in oil and minerals, mining is prohibited under the laws of the Antarctic Treaty. This Treaty, agreed by 45 countries, made Antarctica a "continent for science" to be used for peaceful purposes only.

DAYTRIPPERS
Tourists visit Antarctica in the summer. There are no hotels, so visitors generally stay on small cruise ships. When they come ashore, people have to wear insulated clothing and goggles to protect their eyes from the glare off the ice.

OZONE HOLE
High up in the atmosphere, ozone (a gas) forms a natural shield that protects us from the Sun's ultraviolet rays. Scientists at both poles have found holes in the ozone layer, caused by chemicals known as CFCs, once used in aerosols, fridges, and plastic packaging.

RESEARCH
The only people who live in Antarctica are scientists. They come to study the climate, weather, and geology. By taking ice samples, for example, they can learn about changes in the world's climate over time.

Scientist checking an ice core

KRILL
Tiny, shrimplike creatures, krill are the primary food source for a large number of Antarctic animals. These include whales, seals, penguins, squids, and fish.

Emperor penguins huddling for warmth

FLOATING ICE
Icebergs are giant chunks of floating ice that break away, or calve, from ice sheets or glaciers. Most of their mass lies hidden below sea level.

Antarctica is actually a desert.

PENGUINS
Penguins walk awkwardly on land but can swiftly swim to catch fish. Waterproof feathers and a thick layer of fat help keep them warm.

Map labels

SOUTHERN OCEAN

Orcadas (Argentina)
South Orkney Islands
Signy (U.K.)
Drake Passage
South Shetland Islands
Esperanza (Argentina)
Capitán Arturo Prat (Chile)
Palmer (U.S.)
Graham Land
Antarctic Peninsula
Palmer Land
Rothera (U.K.)
San Martín (Argentina)
Weddell Sea
Ronne Ice Shelf
Berkner Island
Sanae (South Africa)
Georg von Neumayer (Germany)
Novolazarevskaya (Russian Federation)
Dronning Maud Land
Halley (U.K.)
Coats Land
Belgrano II (Argentina)
Lützow Holmbukta
Syowa (Japan)
Molodezhnaya (Russian Federation)
Enderby Land
Mawson (Australia)
Cape Darnley
Mackenzie Bay
Prydz Bay
Princess Elizabeth Land
Davis (Australia)
Bellingshausen Sea
PETER I ISLAND (to Norway)
Ellsworth Land
West Antarctica
Vinson Massif 16,066ft (4897m)
ANTARCTICA
Transantarctic Mountains
Amundsen-Scott (U.S.)
South Pole
East Antarctica
Mirny (Russ. Fed.)
Vostok (Russian Federation)
Shackleton Ice Shelf
Amundsen Sea
Marie Byrd Land
Mount Siple 10,171ft (3100m)
Mount Sidley 13,717ft (4181m)
Mount Kirkpatrick 14,856 ft (4528m)
Mount Markham 14,275ft (4351m)
Ross Ice Shelf
Roosevelt Island
Scott Base (N.Z.)
McMurdo Base (U.S.)
Mount Erebus 12,448ft (3794m)
Ross Sea
Victoria Land
Wilkes Land
Casey (Australia)
Cape Poinsett
Terre Adélie
Dumont d'Urville (France)
South Geomagnetic Pole
SOUTHERN OCEAN
Cape Adare
Leningradskaya (Russian Federation)
George V Land
Antarctic Circle
Balleny Islands

0 km   500
0 miles   500

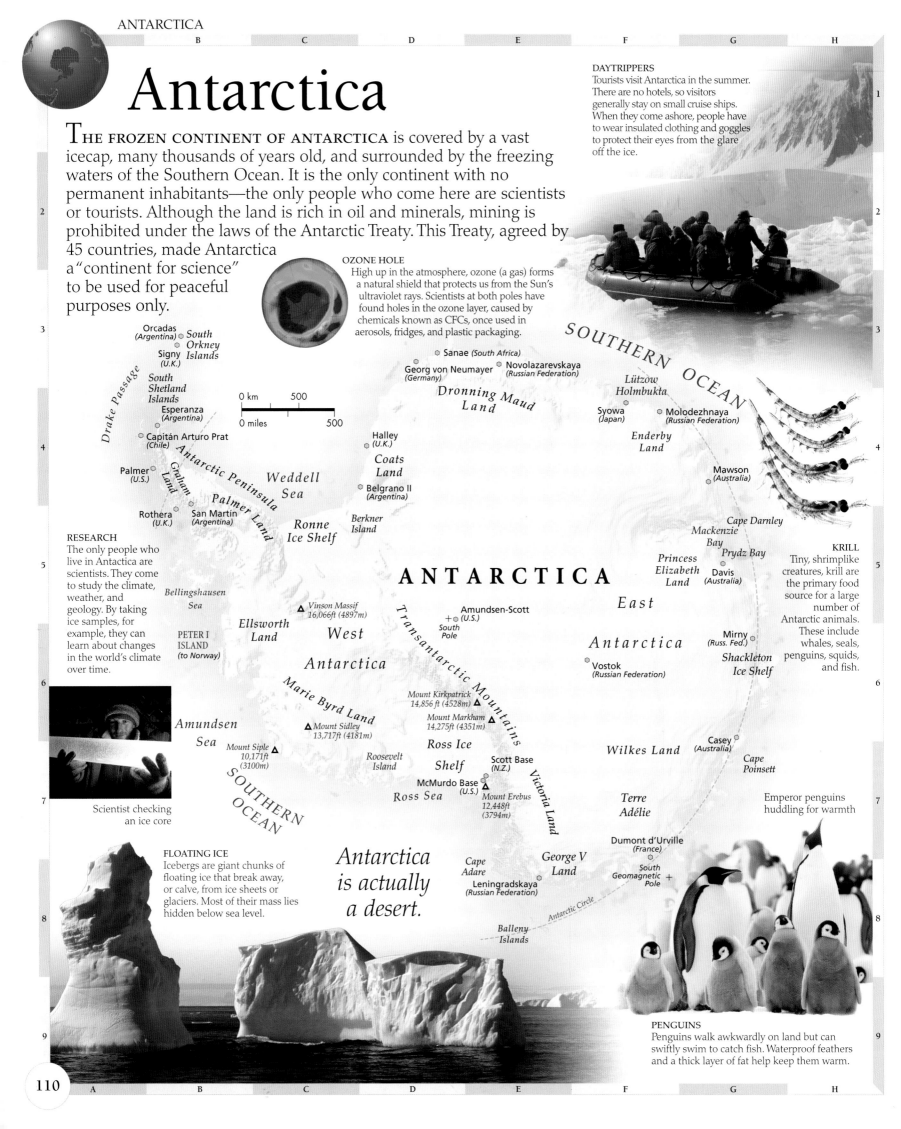

Arctic Ocean

THE SMALLEST OF THE WORLD'S oceans, the Arctic is almost completely surrounded by the northern edges of North America, Europe, and Asia. For most of the year, its waters are covered by a thick sheet of ice, although warmer currents from the Pacific and Atlantic oceans melt the ice along the continental coasts for a short time in the summer. Despite the harsh conditions, the region is home to a range of wildlife, such as reindeer, musk oxen, foxes, and wolves. Some people, including the Inuit of Canada and the Sami of northern Scandinavia, have also adapted to this tough environment.

LONG DAYS
Seasons at the poles are extreme. Polar summers are short, but there can be sunshine for 24 hours a day as the Sun never dips below the horizon (above). This is because Earth rotates at an angle to the Sun.

ALASKAN OIL
Reserves of oil and gas in the Beaufort Sea, off the coast of Alaska, have attracted interest. However, the introduction of ships and oil platforms brings problems. In a bid to protect the area, several environmental organizations are actively working to prevent drilling for more oil in this area.

Walrus breed off the Arctic coasts.

NORTHERN LIGHTS
In midwinter, the north polar skies are sometimes lit up by dramatic curtains of red and green light. Known as the northern lights, these special effects are caused by disturbances in the upper atmosphere. The same happens near Antarctica, where the effect is called the southern lights.

ARCTIC SURVIVORS
Polar bears live along the Arctic coasts of Canada, Greenland, and Russia. They hunt seals and fish at points where the sea ice melts. With so much Arctic ice having melted away in recent years, the polar bear's habitat is slowly disappearing. An insulating layer of fat called blubber helps the bears survive the cold. Their white fur also provides essential camouflage on the ice.

Map labels

Bering Strait
Arctic Circle
Chukchi Sea
Ostrov Vrangelya
East Siberian Sea
Novosibirskiye Ostrova
Laptev Sea
RUSSIAN FEDERATION
Amundsen Gulf
Beaufort Sea
Banks Island
Victoria Island
Melville Island
CANADA
Queen Elizabeth Islands
Lancaster Sound
A R C T I C
North Geomagnetic Pole
North Pole
Severnaya Zemlya
Kara Sea
O C E A N
Ellesmere Island
Lincoln Sea
Nares Strait
Knud Rasmussen Land
Kap Morris Jesup
Franz Josef Land
Baffin Bay
Wandel Sea
Kong Frederik VIII Land
SVALBARD (to Norway)
Spitsbergen
LONGYEARBYEN
GREENLAND (to Denmark)
Greenland Sea
Bjørnøya (to Norway)
Barents Sea
NUUK
Kong Christian IX Land
Norwegian Sea
JAN MAYEN (to Norway)
Denmark Strait
Arctic Circle
ICELAND
REYKJAVÍK

0 km 250 500
0 miles 250 500

Gazetteer

HOW TO USE THE GAZETTEER

This gazetteer is a selection of the names in *Children's World Atlas*, and can be used to help you find places on the maps. For example, to find the city of Lisbon in Portugal, look up its name in the gazetteer. The entry reads:

Lisbon *Capital* Portugal 58 E6

The first number, 58, tells you that Lisbon appears on the map on page 58. The second number, E6, shows that it is in square E6. Turn to page 58. Trace down from the letter E along the top of the grid (or up from the letter E on the bottom of the grid), and then across from the number 6 on the side of the grid. You will find Lisbon in the area where the letter and number meet.

A

Aachen *Town* Germany 56 B7
Aalborg *Town* Denmark 49 B11
Aalen *Town* Germany 57 E9
Aalst *Town* Belgium 53 D11
Aalter *Town* Belgium 53 C10
Äänekoski *Town* Finland 48 G8
Aba *Town* Nigeria 41 L8
Aba *Town* Democratic Republic of Congo 42 I8
Ābādān *Town* Iran 82 E7
Abakan *Town* Russian Federation 78 H7
Abbeville *Town* France 54 E5
Abéché *Town* Chad 42 F6
Abengourou *Town* Côte d'Ivoire 41 I8
Aberdeen *Town* South Dakota, USA 12 G4
Aberdeen *Town* Maryland, USA 9 H8
Aberdeen *Town* Scotland, UK 50 F5
Aberystwyth *Town* Wales, UK 51 E10
Abhā *Town* Saudi Arabia 83 C11
Abidjan *Town* Côte d'Ivoire 40 H8
Abilene *Town* Texas, USA 17 K5
Åbo *see* Turku
Abomey *Town* Benin 41 J7
Abrantes *Town* Portugal 58 F6
Abu Dhabi *Capital* United Arab Emirates 83 F9
Abu Hamed *Town* Sudan 38 E6
Abuja *Capital* Nigeria 41 L7
Abū Kamāl *Town* Syria 80 I7
Abū Ẓaby *see* Abu Dhabi
Acapulco *Town* Mexico 19 J9
Acarigua *Town* Venezuela 26 D5
Accra *Capital* Ghana 41 I8
Aconcagua, Cerro *Mountain* Argentina 30 D7
A Coruña *Town* Spain 58 E2
Açu *Town* Brazil 29 M3
Adamawa Highlands *Mountain range* Cameroon 42 D8
'Adan *see* Aden
Adana *Town* Turkey 76 G6
Adapazari *Town* Turkey 76 E4
Ad Dahnā' *Desert* Saudi Arabia 83 E9
Ad Dakhla *Town* Western Sahara 36 C7
Ad Dammān *Town* Saudi Arabia 83 E9
Ad Dawhah *see* Doha
Addis Ababa *Capital* Ethiopia 39 F9

Adelaide *Town* South Australia, Australia 105 J7
Aden *Town* Yemen 83 D13
Aden, Gulf of Indian Ocean 83 E13
Adirondack Mountains New York, USA 8 H4
Ādīs Ābeba *see* Addis Ababa
Adiyaman *Town* Turkey 76 H6
Adrar *Town* Algeria 36 G6
Aegean Sea Greece 67 F9
Afghanistan *Country* 84 H7
Afmadow *Town* Somalia 39 G11
Afyon *Town* Turkey 76 E5
Agadez *Town* Niger 41 L4
Agadir *Town* Morocco 36 E5
Agen *Town* France 55 D10
Agialoúsa *Town* Cyprus 80 B7
Āgra *Town* India 87 I3
Aǧri *Town* Turkey 77 K4
Agrigento *Town* Sicily, Italy 61 E13
Agropoli *Town* Italy 61 F10
Aguachica *Town* Colombia 26 C5
Agua Prieta *Town* Mexico 18 F3
Aguascalientes *Town* Mexico 19 I7
Aguaytía *Town* Peru 27 B10
Aguilas *Town* Spain 59 J8
Aguililla *Town* Mexico 19 I8
Ahaggar *Mountain range* Algeria 37 I7
Ahlen *Town* Germany 56 C7
Ahmadābād *Town* India 86 G4
Ahuachapán *Town* El Salvador 20 E5
Ahvāz *Town* Iran 82 E7
Aiken *Town* South Carolina, USA 11 J4
Ailigandí *Town* Panama 21 N7
'Aïn Ben Tili *Town* Mauritania 40 G2
Aiquile *Town* Bolivia 27 E12
Aïr, Massif de l' *Mountain range* Niger 41 L4
Aix-en-Provence *Town* France 55 G11
Aizu *Town* Japan 93 G9
Ajaccio *Town* France 55 I13
Ajo *Town* Arizona, USA 16 E5
Akchâr *Desert* Mauritania 40 E3
Akhalts'ikhe *Town* Georgia 77 K3
Akhisar *Town* Turkey 76 C5
Akhtubinsk *Town* Russian Federation 73 D11
Akita *Town* Japan 92 F8
Akjoujt *Town* Mauritania 40 E3
Akkeshi *Town* Japan 92 H5
Akron *Town* Ohio, USA 13 M6
Akrotírion *Town* Cyprus 80 A8
Aksai Chin *Administrative region* China 88 D6
Aksaray *Town* Turkey 76 F5
Akşehir *Town* Turkey 76 E5
Aktau *Town* Kazakhstan 78 D6
Aktobe *Town* Kazakhstan 78 E6
Aktsyabrski *Town* Belarus 71 F11
Akula *Town* Democratic Republic of Congo 43 F9
Akune *Town* Japan 93 B14
Alabama *State* USA 10 G5
Alabama River Alabama, USA 10 G6
Al 'Amārah *Town* Iraq 82 D7
Alamo *Town* Nevada, USA 14 H7
Alamogordo *Town* New Mexico, USA 16 H5
Åland *Island group* Finland 49 F9
Alanya *Town* Turkey 76 E7
Al 'Aqabah *Town* Jordan 81 D14
Alaşehir *Town* Turkey 76 D5
Alaska *Province* Canada 4 E5
Alaska, Gulf of Alaska, USA 4 E6
Alaska Range *Mountain Range* Alaska, USA 4 E5
Albacete *Town* Spain 59 J6
Alba Iulia *Town* Romania 68 E6
Albania *Country* 65 F12
Albany *River* Ontario, Canada 6 F5
Albany *Town* Western Australia, Australia 104 E7
Albany *Town* Georgia, USA 10 H6
Albany *Town* New York, USA 9 I5
Al Bāridah *Town* Syria 80 F8
Al Başrah *Town* Iraq 82 D7
Alberta *Province* Canada 4 H7
Albert, Lake Democratic Republic of Congo 43 I9
Albuquerque *Town* New Mexico, USA 16 H4
Alcañiz *Town* Spain 59 K5

Alcoy *Town* Spain 59 K7
Alderney *Island* Channel Islands, UK 51 G13
Aleksin *Town* Russian Federation 73 C9
Alençon *Town* France 54 D7
Alenquer *Town* Brazil 29 I2
Aleppo *Town* Syria 80 E6
Alessandria *Town* Italy 60 C5
Aleutian Islands *Island Group* Alaska, USA 4 B5
Alexander Archipelago *Island* British Colombia, Canada 4 E7
Alexandria *Town* Louisiana, USA 10 E6
Alexandria *Town* Egypt 38 D4
Alexandria *Town* Romania 68 F7
Alexandroúpoli *Town* Greece 66 G8
Alga *Town* Kazakhstan 78 E6
Algarve *Region* Spain 58 E8
Algeciras *Town* Spain 58 G9
Alger *see* Algiers
Algeria *Country* 36 H5
Al Ghābah *Town* Oman 83 G10
Algiers *Capital* Algeria 36 H3
Algona *Town* Iowa, USA 12 H5
Al Ḩasakah *Town* Syria 80 H5
Al Ḩillah *Town* Iraq 82 D7
Al Hudaydah *see* Hodeida
Al Hufūf *Town* Saudi Arabia 83 E9
Alíartos *Town* Greece 67 E11
Alicante *Town* Spain 59 L7
Alice Springs *Town* Northern Territory, Australia 105 I4
Aliquippa *Town* Pennsylvania, USA 8 E7
Al Ismā'īlīya *Town* Egypt 38 E4
Al Jafr *Town* Jordan 81 E13
Al Jaghbūb *Town* Libya 37 N5
Al Jahrā' *Town* Kuwait 82 D8
Al Jawf *Town* Saudi Arabia 82 B8
Al Jazīrah *Physical region* Syria/Iraq 80 I5
Al Karak *Town* Jordan 81 E12
Al Khums *Town* Libya 37 K4
Alkmaar *Town* Netherlands 52 E7
Al Kufrah *Town* Libya 37 N7
Al Kūt *Town* Iraq 82 D7
Al Kuwayt *see* Kuwait
Allahābād *Town* India 87 I4
Allegheny Plateau Pennsylvania/New York, USA 8 F6
Allentown *Town* Pennsylvania, USA 9 H7
Al Līth *Town* Saudi Arabia 83 B11
Alma-Ata *see* Almaty
Al Madīnah *see* Medina
Al Mafraq *Town* Jordan 81 E10
Al Majma'ah *Town* Saudi Arabia 83 D9
Al Mālikīyah *Town* Syria 80 I4
Al Manāmah *see* Manama
Almansa *Town* Spain 59 K7
Al Marj *Town* Libya 37 M4
Almaty *Town* Kazakhstan 78 G8
Al Mawşil *see* Mosul
Al Mayādīn *Town* Syria 80 H6
Almelo *Town* Netherlands 52 G8
Almere *Town* Netherlands 52 F8
Almería *Town* Spain 59 J8
Al'met'yevsk *Town* Russian Federation 73 F9
Al Minyā *Town* Egypt 38 D4
Almirante *Town* Panama 21 K8
Al Mukallā *Town* Yemen 83 E13
Alofi *Capital* Niue 103 K7
Alotip *Town* Indonesia 97 N8
Alpena *Town* Michigan, USA 13 L4
Alpine *Town* Texas, USA 17 I7
Alps *Mountain range* Central Europe 57 D12
Al Qāmishlī *Town* Syria 80 I4
Al Qunayţirah *Town* Syria 81 D9
Altai Mountains *Mountain range* Mongolia/ Russian Federation 88 F4
Altamaha River Georgia, USA 11 I5
Altamira *Town* Brazil 29 J2
Altamura *Town* Italy 61 H10
Altar, Desierto de *Desert* Mexico 18 D2
Altay *Town* China 88 F3
Altay *Town* Mongolia 88 H3
Altin Köprü *Town* Iraq 82 C6
Altiplano *Physical region* Bolivia 27 E13
Altoona *Town* Pennsylvania, USA 9 F7
Altun Ha *Ancient site* Belize 20 F2
Altun Shan *Mountain range* China 88 G5

Al 'Umarī *Town* Jordan 81 F11
Al 'Uwaynāt *Town* Libya 37 J6
Alupka *Town* Ukraine 69 K7
Alva *Town* Oklahoma, USA 17 L3
Al Wajh *Town* Saudi Arabia 83 A9
Alwar *Town* India 86 H3
Al Wari'ah *Town* Saudi Arabia 82 D8
Alytus *Town* Lithuania 70 G9
Amamapare *Town* Indonesia 97 N7
Amantea *Town* Italy 61 G12
Amarapura *Town* Myanmar 94 B6
Amarillo *Town* Texas, USA 17 J4
Amazon *River* Brazil 29 J2
Amazon Basin Brazil 28 G3
Ambanja *Town* Madagascar 45 M4
Ambarchik *Town* Russian Federation 78 L3
Ambato *Town* Ecuador 26 A8
Amboasary *Town* Madagascar 45 L7
Ambon *Town* Indonesia 97 K7
American Samoa *Dependent territory* USA, Pacific Ocean 103 K6
Amersfoort *Town* Netherlands 52 F8
Amfilochía *Town* Greece 67 C10
Amherst *Town* Nova Scotia, Canada 7 K7
Amiens *Town* France 54 E6
Amman *Capital* Jordan 81 E11
'Ammān *see* Amman
Ammóchostos *Town* Cyprus 80 B8
Āmol *Town* Iran 82 F5
Amos *Town* Québec, Canada 6 H6
Amritsar *Town* India 86 H2
Amstelveen *Town* Netherlands 52 F8
Amsterdam *Capital* Netherlands 52 E8
Am Timan *Town* Chad 42 F6
Amundsen Gulf Canada 4 H4
Amundsen-Scott *Research station* Antarctica 110 E6
Amundsen Sea Southern Ocean 110 B7
Amuntai *Town* Indonesia 96 H7
Amur *River* China 89 L2
Amyderýa *River* Uzbekistan 84 G4
Anadyr' *Town* Russian Federation 78 M2
Anamur *Town* Turkey 76 F7
Anápolis *Town* Brazil 29 K5
Anatolia *Plateau* Turkey 76 E6
Anchorage *Town* Alaska, Canada 4 E5
Ancona *Town* Italy 60 F7
Andalucía *Region* Spain 58 H8
Andaman Islands *Island group* India 87 M8
Andaman Sea Indian Ocean 87 M8
Anderson *Town* Indiana, USA 13 K6
Andes *Mountain range* South America 26–27, 30–31
Andijon *Town* Uzbekistan 85 K4
Andkhvoy *Town* Afghanistan 84 H5
Andorra *Country* 55 D12
Andorra la Vella *Capital* Andorra 55 D12
Andreanof Islands *Island Group* Alaska, USA 4 A4
Andrews *Town* Texas, USA 17 J5
Andria *Town* Italy 61 H10
Andros Island Bahamas 22 F2
Andros Town Bahamas 22 F2
Angarsk *Town* Russian Federation 79 I7
Angeles *Town* Philippines 97 I2
Angel Falls *Waterfall* Venezuela 26 F6
Ångermanälven *River* Sweden 48 E7
Angers *Town* France 54 C7
Angkor Wat *Ancient site* Cambodia 95 F10
Anglesey *Island* Wales, UK 51 E9
Angola *Country* 44 E3
Angola Basin *Undersea feature* Atlantic Ocean 33 M6
Angoulême *Town* France 55 D9
Angren *Town* Uzbekistan 85 J3
Anguilla *Dependent territory* UK, Atlantic Ocean 23 N5
Anhui *Administrative region* China 91 J5
Ankara *Capital* Turkey 76 F4
Annaba *Town* Algeria 37 I3
An Nafūd *Desert* Saudi Arabia 82 B8
'Annah *Town* Iraq 82 C6
An Najaf *Town* Iraq 82 C7
Annamitique, Chaîne *Mountain range* Laos 94 F8
Annapolis *Town* Maryland, USA 8 G8
Ann Arbor *Town* Michigan, USA 13 L5

BARISAL – BREMEN

Barisal *Town* Bangladesh 87 L4
Barisan, Pegunungan *Mountain range* Indonesia 96 D7
Barkly Tableland *Plateau* Northern Territory, Australia 105 J3
Bârlad *Town* Romania 68 G6
Barlee Range *Mountain range* Western Australia, Australia 104 E4
Barletta *Town* Italy 61 H10
Barnaul *Town* Russian Federation 78 H6
Barnstaple *Town* England, UK 51 E11
Baron'ki *Town* Belarus 71 H11
Barquisimeto *Town* Venezuela 26 D5
Barrancabermeja *Town* Colombia 26 C5
Barranquilla *Town* Colombia 26 B4
Barreiras *Town* Brazil 29 L4
Barreiro *Town* Portugal 58 E7
Barrow-in-Furness *Town* England, UK 50 F8
Barstow *Town* California, USA 14 H8
Bartlesville *Town* Okahoma, USA 17 M3
Bartoszyce *Town* Poland 62 F5
Barysaw *Town* Belarus 71 F9
Basarabeasca *Town* Moldova 68 H6
Basel *Town* Switzerland 57 C11
Basque Country, The *Region* Spain 59 I3
Basra *see* Al Başrah
Bassano del Grappa *Town* Italy 60 E5
Basse-Terre *Island* Guadeloupe 23 N6
Basse-Terre *Capital* Guadeloupe 23 N6
Basseterre *Capital* Saint Kitts & Nevis 23 N6
Bassikounou *Town* Mauritania 40 H5
Bass Strait Australia 105 K9
Bata *Town* Equatorial Guinea 43 C9
Batangas *Town* Philippines 97 I2
Bătdâmbâng *Town* Cambodia 95 E10
Bath *Town* England, UK 51 F11
Bath *Town* Maine, USA 8 K4
Bathinda *Town* India 86 H2
Bathurst *Town* New South Wales, Australia 105 L7
Batman *Town* Turkey 77 J6
Batna *Town* Algeria 37 I3
Baton Rouge *Town* Louisiana, USA 10 E6
Batticaloa *Town* Sri Lanka 87 J9
Bat'umi *Town* Georgia 77 J3
Batu Pahat *Town* Malaysia 96 E5
Bauchi *Town* Nigeria 41 L6
Bauska *Town* Latvia 70 E6
Bavaria *Region* Germany 57 E10
Bayamo *Town* Cuba 22 G4
Bayan Har Shan *Mountain range* China 88 H7
Bay City *Town* Michigan, USA 13 L5
Baydhabo *Town* Somalia 39 H10
Bayeux *Town* France 54 D6
Bāyir *Town* Jordan 81 F12
Baykal, Ozero *see* Lake Baikal
Bayreuth *Town* Germany 56 E8
Baytown *Town* Texas, USA 17 N7
Beaufort Sea Arctic Ocean 111 L4
Beaumont *Town* Texas, USA 17 N6
Beauvais *Town* France 54 E6
Beāwar *Town* India 86 H3
Béchar *Town* Algeria 36 G5
Bedford *Town* England, UK 51 H10
Bedford *Town* Pennsylvania, USA 8 F8
Be'er Sheva *Town* Israel 81 D12
Bei'an *Town* China 89 M2
Beihai *Town* China 90 H9
Beijing *Capital* China 91 J3
Beilen *Town* Netherlands 52 G7
Beira *Town* Mozambique 45 J5
Beirut *Capital* Lebanon 81 D9
Beja *Town* Portugal 58 F7
Békéscsaba *Town* Hungary 63 G12
Bekobod *Town* Uzbekistan 85 J4
Belarus *Country* 71 E9
Bełchatów *Town* Poland 62 E7
Belcher Islands *Island group* Canada 6 G3
Beledweyne *Town* Somalia 39 H10
Belém *Town* Brazil 29 K2
Belén *Town* Nicaragua 20 H6
Belfast *Town* Northern Ireland, UK 50 D7
Belfield *Town* North Dakota, USA 12 E3
Belfort *Town* France 54 H8
Belgaum *Town* India 86 G6
Belgium *Country* 53 D11
Belgorod *Town* Russian Federation 73 B10
Belgrade *Capital* Serbia 64 G7
Belgrano II *Research station* Antarctica 110 D4
Belize *Country* 20 F2
Belize City *Town* Belize 20 F2
Belle Isle, Strait of Québec, Canada 7 M5
Bellevue *Town* Washington, USA 14 G2
Bellingham *Town* Washington, USA 14 G1
Bello *Town* Colombia 26 C6
Bellville *Town* South Africa 44 F9
Belmopan *Capital* Belize 20 F2
Belogradchik *Town* Bulgaria 66 D5
Belo Horizonte *Town* Brazil 29 L6
Belomorsk *Town* Russian Federation 72 D6
Beloretsk *Town* Russian Federation 73 G10
Bemaraha *Mountain range* Madagascar 45 L5
Benavente *Town* Spain 58 G4
Bend *Town* Oregon, USA 14 G3
Bendigo *Town* Victoria, Australia 105 K8
Benevento *Town* Italy 61 F10
Bengal, Bay of Indian Ocean 87 L5
Bengbu *Town* China 91 J5
Benghazi *Town* Libya 37 M4
Bengkulu *Town* Indonesia 96 E7
Benguela *Town* Angola 44 D3
Benidorm *Town* Spain 59 K7
Beni-Mellal *Town* Morocco 36 F4
Benin *Country* 41 J7
Benin, Bight of *Coastal feature* Nigeria 41 J8
Benin City *Town* Nigeria 41 K8
Beni Suef *Town* Egypt 38 D4
Ben Nevis *Mountain* Scotland, UK 50 E5
Benson *Town* Arizona, USA 16 F6
Bent Jbaïl *Town* Lebanon 81 D10
Benton *Town* Arkansas, USA 10 E4
Benue *River* Nigeria 41 L7
Benue *River* Nigeria 41 L7
Beograd *see* Belgrade
Berat *Town* Albania 65 F12
Berbera *Town* Somalia 39 H9
Berbérati *Town* Cameroon 42 D8
Berdyans'k *Town* Ukraine 69 L6
Berdychiv *Town* Ukraine 68 H3
Berezhany *Town* Ukraine 68 F3
Berezniki *Town* Russian Federation 72 G8
Bergamo *Town* Italy 60 D5
Bergen *Town* Norway 49 A9
Bergen *Town* Germany 56 F4
Bergerac *Town* France 55 D10
Bering Sea Russian Federation 79 N3
Bering Strait Russian Federation/USA 79 M2
Berkeley *Town* California, USA 14 F6
Berlin *Capital* Germany 56 G6
Berlin *Town* New Hampshire, USA 9 J3
Bermuda *Dependent territory* UK, Atlantic Ocean 32 H3
Bern *Capital* Switzerland 57 C11
Berner Alps *Mountain range* Switzerland 57 C12
Bertoua *Town* Cameroon 42 D8
Besançon *Town* France 54 G8
Betafo *Town* Madagascar 45 M5
Bethlehem *Town* Israel 81 D11
Béticos, Sistemas *Mountain range* Spain 59 I8
Bétou *Town* Congo 43 E9
Beveren *Town* Belgium 53 D10
Beyrouth *see* Beirut
Béziers *Town* France 55 E11
Bhaktapur *Town* Nepal 87 J3
Bhāvnagar *Town* India 86 G5
Bhopāl *Town* India 86 H4
Bhubaneshwar *Town* India 87 K5
Bhusāwal *Town* India 86 H5
Bhutan *Country* 87 L3
Biała Podlaska *Town* Poland 62 H7
Białystok *Town* Poland 62 H6
Biarritz *Town* France 55 B11
Bicaz *Town* Romania 68 G5
Biel *Town* Switzerland 57 C11
Bielefeld *Town* Germany 56 D6
Bielsko-Biała *Town* Poland 63 E9
Biên Hoa *Town* Vietnam 95 G11
Bié, Planalto do *Plateau* Angola 44 F3
Bighorn Mountains Wyoming, USA 15 K3
Bighorn River Montana, USA 15 K3
Bignona *Town* Senegal 40 E5
Big Sioux River South Dakota, USA 12 G4
Bihać *Town* Bosnia & Herzegovina 64 C7
Bijelo Polje *Town* Montenegro 65 F9
Bīkāner *Town* India 86 G3
Bikin *Town* Russian Federation 78 M7
Bikini Atoll Marshall Islands 102 H2
Bilāspur *Town* India 87 J5
Biläsuvar *Town* Azerbaijan 77 N4
Bila Tserkva *Town* Ukraine 69 I3
Bilauktaung Range *Mountain range* Thailand 95 D11
Bilbao *Town* Spain 59 I3
Billings *Town* Montana, USA 15 J3
Bilma, Grand Erg de *Desert* Niger 41 M4
Biloxi *Town* Mississippi, USA 10 F6
Binghamton *Town* New York, USA 8 G6
Bingöl *Town* Turkey 77 J5
Bintulu *Town* Malaysia 96 G5
Binzhou *Town* China 91 K4
Birāk *Town* Libya 37 K6
Birao *Town* Central African Republic 42 G7
Birātnagar *Town* Nepal 87 K3
Bīrjand *Town* Iran 82 H6
Birkenfeld *Town* Germany 57 C9
Birkenhead *Town* England, UK 51 F9
Birmingham *Town* England, UK 50 G10
Birmingham *Town* Alabama, USA 10 G5
Birnin Konni *Town* Niger 41 K5
Birobidzhan *Town* Russian Federation 79 L7
Birsk *Town* Russian Federation 73 G9
Biržai *Town* Lithuania 70 E6
Biscay, Bay of Atlantic Ocean 33 L2
Bishkek *Capital* Kyrgyzstan 85 L2
Biskra *Town* Algeria 37 I4
Bislig *Town* Philippines 97 K4
Bismarck *Town* North Dakota, USA 12 F3
Bismarck Archipelago *Island chain* Papua New Guinea 102 E5
Bismarck Sea Pacific Ocean 102 E5
Bissau *Capital* Guinea-Bissau 40 E6
Bistripa *Town* Romania 68 F5
Bitlis *Town* Turkey 77 K5
Bitola *Town* Macedonia 65 G12
Bitonto *Town* Italy 61 H10
Bitterroot Range *Mountain range* Idaho, USA 15 I2
Bitung *Town* Indonesia 97 K6
Bizerte *Town* Tunisia 37 J3
Bjørnøya Norway 111 N8
Black Forest *Region* Germany 57 C10
Black Hills *Mountain range* South Dakota, USA 12 E4
Blackpool *Town* England, UK 50 F8
Black Range *Mountain range* New Mexico, USA 16 G5
Black Rock Desert Nevada, USA 14 G5
Black Sea Asia/Europe 69 I6
Black Sea Lowland Ukraine 69 J6
Black Volta *River* Ghana 41 I6
Blagoevgrad *Town* Bulgaria 66 E7
Blagoveshchensk *Town* Russian Federation 79 L7
Blanca, Bahía *Bay* Argentina 31 F10
Blanca, Costa *Coastal region* Spain 59 K7
Blanes *Town* Spain 59 M4
Blantyre *Town* Malawi 45 J4
Blida *Town* Algeria 36 H3
Bloemfontein *Capital* South Africa 44 H7
Bloomfield *Town* New Mexico, USA 16 G3
Bloomington *Town* Indiana, USA 12 H4
Bloomington *Town* Minnesota, USA 13 K7
Bloomsbury *Town* Queensland, Australia 105 M4
Bluefields *Town* Nicaragua 21 J6
Blue Nile *River* Sudan 38 E8
Blumenau *Town* Brazil 29 K8
Bo *Town* Sierra Leone 40 F7
Boa Vista *Town* Brazil 28 H1
Bobo-Dioulasso *Town* Burkina Faso 40 H6
Bocay *Town* Nicaragua 20 H4
Bocholt *Town* Germany 56 C6
Bochum *Town* Germany 56 C7
Bodaybo *Town* Russian Federation 78 J6
Boden *Town* Sweden 48 F6
Bodrum *Town* Turkey 76 C6
Bogale *Town* Myanmar 95 B9
Bogor *Town* Indonesia 96 F8
Bogotá *Capital* Colombia 26 C6
Bo Hai *Gulf* China 91 K3
Bohemia *Region* Czech Republic 63 B9
Bohemian Forest *Region* Germany 57 F10
Bohol Sea Philippines 97 J4
Boise *Town* Idaho, USA 14 H4
Boise City *Town* Okahoma, USA 17 J3
Bojnūrd *Town* Iran 82 G5
Boké *Town* Guinea 40 E6
Bolesławiec *Town* Poland 62 C7
Bolgatanga *Town* Ghana 41 I6
Bolivia *Country* 27 E11
Bologna *Town* Italy 60 E6
Bolton *Town* England, UK 51 F9
Bolu *Town* Turkey 76 E4
Bolzano *Town* Italy 60 E4
Boma *Town* Democratic Republic of Congo 43 D11
Bombay *see* Mumbai
Bonaire *Dependent territory* Netherlands, Atlantic Ocean 23 K8
Bonaparte Archipelago *Island group* Australia 104 F2
Bondoukou *Town* Côte d'Ivoire 41 I7
Bone, Teluk *Bay* Indonesia 97 I7
Bongaigaon *Town* India 87 L3
Bongo, Massif des *Mountain range* Central African Republic 42 G7
Bonifacio *Town* Corsica, France 55 I13
Bonifacio, Strait of Mediterranean Sea 61 B9
Bonn *Town* Germany 56 C8
Boppard *Town* Germany 56 C8
Borås *Town* Sweden 49 D11
Bordeaux *Town* France 55 D10
Bordj Omar Driss *Town* Algeria 37 I6
Børgefjellet *Mountain range* Norway 48 D6
Borgholm *Town* Sweden 49 E11
Borisoglebsk *Town* Russian Federation 73 D10
Borneo *Island* Indonesia 96 G6
Bornholm *Island* Denmark 49 D13
Borovan *Town* Bulgaria 66 E5
Borovichi *Town* Russian Federation 72 C7
Boryslav *Town* Ukraine 68 E3
Bose *Town* China 90 H8
Bosnia & Herzegovina *Country* 64 D8
Bosporus *River* Turkey 76 D3
Bossembélé *Town* Central African Republic 42 E8
Bossier City *Town* Louisiana, USA 10 D5
Boston *Town* Massachusetts, USA 9 K5
Bothnia, Gulf of Finland 48 F7
Botoşani *Town* Romania 68 G5
Botou *Town* China 91 J3
Botswana *Country* 44 G6
Bouar *Town* Central African Republic 42 E8
Bou Craa *Town* Western Sahara 36 D6
Bougouni *Town* Mali 40 G6
Boujdour *Town* Western Sahara 36 C6
Boulder *Town* Colorado, USA 15 K5
Boulogne-sur-Mer *Town* France 54 E5
Boundiali *Town* Côte d'Ivoire 40 H7
Bourges *Town* France 54 E8
Bourke *Town* New South Wales, Australia 105 L6
Bournemouth *Town* England, UK 51 G12
Bouvet Island *Dependent territory* Norway, Atlantic Ocean 33 L8
Boysun *Town* Uzbekistan 85 I5
Bozeman *Town* Montana, USA 15 J3
Bradford *Town* England, UK 50 G8
Brahmapur *Town* India 87 K5
Brahmaputra *River* Asia 87 L3
Brăila *Town* Romania 68 G7
Brampton *Town* Ontario, Canada 6 G8
Brandenburg *Town* Germany 56 F6
Brasília *Capital* Brazil 29 K5
Braşov *Town* Romania 68 F6
Bratislava *Capital* Slovakia 63 D10
Bratsk *Town* Russian Federation 79 I6
Braunschweig *Town* Germany 56 E6
Brava, Costa *Coastal region* Spain 59 N4
Brawley *Town* California, USA 14 H8
Brazil *Country* 28 G4
Brazzaville *Capital* Congo 43 D11
Brecon Beacons *Hills* Wales, UK 51 F10
Breda *Town* Netherlands 53 E9
Bregovo *Town* Bulgaria 66 D5
Bremen *Town* Germany 56 D5

D

Dalain Hob *Town* China 89 I5
Dalandzadgad *Town* Mongolia 89 I4
Đa Lat *Town* Vietnam 95 H11
Dalby *Town* Queensland, Australia 105 M5
Dali *Town* China 90 F7
Dalian *Town* China 91 K3
Dallas *Town* Texas, USA 17 M5
Dalmatia *Cultural Region* Croatia 64 C8
Damascus *Capital* Syria 81 E9
Dampier *Town* Western Australia, Australia 104 E4
Dampier, Selat *Strait* Indonesia 97 L6
Damqawt *Town* Yemen 83 F12
Danakil Desert Ethiopia 38 G8
Đà Nẵng *Town* Vietnam 95 H9
Dandong *Town* China 91 L3
Danube *River* Germany 57 D10
Danville *Town* Virginia, USA 11 J3
Danzhou *Town* Hainan, China 90 H9
Danzig, Gulf of Poland 62 E4
Dar'ā *Town* Syria 81 E10
Dardanelles *Strait* Turkey 76 B4
Dar es Salaam *Capital* Tanzania 39 G13
Darfur *Cultural region* Sudan 38 C8
Darhan *Town* Mongolia 89 I3
Darien, Gulf of Panama 21 O7
Darjiling *Town* India 87 K3
Darling River New South Wales, Australia 105 K7
Darlington *Town* England, UK 50 F8
Darmstadt *Town* Germany 56 D8
Darnah *Town* Libya 37 M4
Dartmoor *Physical region* England, UK 51 E11
Dartmouth *Town* Nova Scotia, Canada 7 L7
Darwin *Town* Northern Territory, Australia 104 H1
Daşoguz *Town* Turkmenistan 84 F3
Datong *Town* China 91 I3
Daugavpils *Town* Latvia 70 F7
Dāvangere *Town* India 86 H7
Davao *Town* Philippines 97 K4
Davao Gulf Philippines 97 K4
Davenport *Town* Iowa, USA 13 I6
David *Town* Panama 21 K8
Davis *Research station* Antarctica 110 G5
Dawei *Town* Myanmar 95 C10
Dayr az Zawr *Town* Syria 80 H6
Dayton *Town* Ohio, USA 13 J7
Daytona Beach *Town* Florida, USA 11 J7
Dead Sea Jordan 81 D11
Deán Funes *Town* Argentina 30 E7
Death Valley California, USA 14 H7
Debar *Town* Macedonia 65 F11
Dębica *Town* Poland 63 G9
Debrecen *Town* Hungary 63 G11
Decatur *Town* Illinois, USA 13 J7
Deccan *Plateau* India 85 I5
Děčín *Town* Czech Republic 62 B8
Deggendorf *Town* Germany 57 F9
Deh Bīd *see* Şafāshahr
Deh Shū *Town* Afghanisatan 84 G9
Dekéleia *Town* Cyprus 80 B8
Delārām *Town* Afghanistan 84 G9
Delaware *State* USA 8 H8
Delft *Town* Netherlands 53 D9
Delhi *Town* India 86 H3
Delicias *Town* Mexico 18 H4
Delmenhorst *Town* Germany 56 D5
Del Rio *Town* Texas, USA 17 K7
Deltona *Town* Florida, USA 11 J7
Dembia *Town* Central African Republic 42 G8
Demopolis *Town* Alabama, USA 10 G5
Denekamp *Town* Netherlands 52 G8
Den Helder *Town* Netherlands 52 E7
Denizli *Town* Turkey 76 D6
Denmark *Country* 49 B12
Denov *Town* Uzbekistan 85 I5
Denpasar *Town* Indonesia 96 H8
Denton *Town* Texas, USA 17 M5
Denver *Town* Colorado, USA 15 L5
Dera Ghāzi Khān *Town* Pakistan 86 G2
Derbent *Town* Russian Federation 73 D14
Derby *Town* England, UK 51 G9
De Ridder *Town* Louisiana, USA 10 E6
Derweza *Town* Turkmenistan 84 F4
Desē *Town* Ethiopia 38 G8
Des Moines *Town* Iowa, USA 12 H6

Dessau *Town* Germany 56 F7
Detroit *Town* Michigan, USA 13 L5
Deva *Town* Romania 68 E6
Deventer *Town* Netherlands 52 F8
Devon Island Nunavut, Canada 5 J3
Dezfūl *Town* Iran 82 E7
Dezhou *Town* China 91 J4
Dhaka *Capital* Bangladesh 87 L4
Dhanbād *Town* India 87 K4
Diamantina, Chapada *Mountain range* Brazil 29 L4
Dibrugarh *Town* India 87 M3
Dieppe *Town* France 54 E5
Digos *Town* Philippines 97 K4
Dijon *Town* France 54 G8
Dikhil *Town* Djibouti 38 G8
Dikson *Town* Russian Federation 78 H4
Dili *Capital* East Timor 97 K8
Di Linh *Town* Vietnam 95 H11
Dilolo *Town* Democratic Republic of Congo 43 G13
Dimashq *see* Damascus
Dimitrovgrad *Town* Russian Federation 73 E10
Dimitrovgrad *Town* Bulgaria 66 G7
Dinajpur *Town* Bangladesh 87 K4
Dinar *Town* Turkey 76 D6
Dinaric Alps *Mountain range* Bosnia & Herzegovina/Montenegro 64 C8
Dinguiraye *Town* Guinea 40 F6
Diourbel *Town* Senegal 40 E5
Dirē Dawa *Town* Ethiopia 39 G9
Divinópolis *Town* Brazil 29 L6
Divo *Town* Côte d'Ivoire 40 H8
Diyarbakir *Town* Turkey 77 J6
Djanet *Town* Algeria 37 J7
Djelfa *Town* Algeria 36 H4
Djibouti *Country* 38 G8
Djibouti City *Capital* Djibouti 38 G8
Dnieper *River* Ukraine 69 J6
Dnieper Lowland Ukraine 69 J3
Dniester *River* Ukraine 68 H4
Dniprodzerzhyns'k *Town* Ukraine 69 K4
Dnipropetrovs'k *Town* Ukraine 69 K4
Doba *Town* Chad 42 E7
Doboj *Town* Bosnia & Herzegovina 64 E7
Dobrich *Town* Bulgaria 66 H5
Dodecanese *Island group* Greece 67 G12
Dodekánisa *see* Dodecanese
Dodge City *Town* Kansas, USA 12 F7
Dodoma *Capital* Tanzania 39 F13
Doğubayazit *Town* Turkey 77 L4
Doha *Capital* Qatar 83 F9
Dokkum *Town* Netherlands 52 F6
Dôle *Town* France 54 G8
Dolisie *Town* Congo 43 D11
Dolni Chiflik *Town* Bulgaria 66 H6
Dolomites *Mountain range* Italy 60 E4
Dolores *Town* Uruguay 30 G8
Dolores *Town* Guatemala 20 E3
Dolores *Town* Argentina 31 G9
Dolores Hidalgo *Town* Mexico 19 J7
Dominica *Country* 23 O6
Dominican Republic *Country* 23 J4
Don *River* Russian Federation 73 D11
Doncaster *Town* England, UK 51 G9
Donegal *Town* Ireland 50 C7
Donets *River* Ukraine 69 L4
Donets'k *Town* Ukraine 69 M5
Dongguan *Town* China 91 J8
Đông Ho'i *Town* Vietnam 94 G7
Donostia-San Sebastián *Town* Spain 59 J2
Doolow *Town* Ethiopia 39 G10
Dordogne *River* France 55 D10
Dordrecht *Town* Netherlands 53 E9
Dortmund *Town* Germany 56 C7
Dos Hermanas *Town* Spain 58 G8
Douala *Town* Cameroon 42 C8
Douglas *Capital* Isle of Man 50 E8
Douglas *Town* Arizona, USA 16 F6
Dover *Town* Delaware, USA 8 H8
Dover *Town* England, UK 51 I11
Dovrefjell *Plateau* Norway 48 C8
Dra, Hamada du *Plateau* Algeria 36 E5
Drahichyn *Town* Belarus 71 C10

Drakensberg *Mountain range* South Africa 44 H8
Drake Passage Southern Ocean 110 A4
Dralfa *Town* Bulgaria 66 G5
Dráma *Town* Greece 66 E8
Drammen Norway 49 B10
Drava *River* Croatia 64 E6
Dresden *Town* Germany 56 G7
Drina *River* Bosnia & Herzegovina 65 E9
Drobeta-Turnu Severin *Town* Romania 68 D7
Drogheda *Town* Ireland 50 D8
Drummondville *Town* Québec, Canada 7 I7
Dryden *Town* Ontario, Canada 6 D5
Dubai *Town* United Arab Emirates 83 G9
Dubăsari *Town* Moldova 68 H5
Dubayy *see* Dubai
Dublin *Capital* Ireland 51 D9
Du Bois *Town* Pennsylvania, USA 8 F7
Dubrovnik *Town* Croatia 65 D10
Dubuque *Town* Iowa, USA 13 I5
Dudelange *Town* Luxembourg 53 F14
Duisburg *Town* Germany 56 C7
Duk Faiwil *Town* Sudan 39 E9
Dulan *Town* China 88 H6
Dulovo *Town* Bulgaria 66 H5
Duluth *Town* Minnesota, USA 13 I3
Dūmā *Town* Syria 81 E9
Dumont d'Urville *Research station* Antarctica 110 F7
Dumyāt *Town* Egypt 38 E4
Dunaújváros *Town* Hungary 63 E11
Dunav *River* Bulgaria 66 G5
Dunav *see* Danube
Dunavska Ravnina *Plain* Bulgaria 66 E5
Dundee *Town* South Africa 45 I7
Dundee *Town* Scotland, UK 50 F6
Dunedin *Town* New Zealand 107 C13
Dunfermline *Town* Scotland, UK 50 E6
Dunkerque *Town* France 54 F4
Dunkirk *Town* New York, USA 8 E6
Dún Laoghaire *Town* Ireland 51 D9
Duqm *Town* Oman 83 H11
Durango *Town* Mexico 18 H6
Durango *Town* Colorado, USA 15 K7
Durban *Town* South Africa 45 I8
Durham *Town* England, UK 50 G7
Durham *Town* North Carolina, USA 11 K3
Durrës *Town* Albania 65 E11
Dushan *Town* China 90 H7
Dushanbe *Capital* Tajikistan 85 J5
Düsseldorf *Town* Germany 56 C7
Dutch Harbor *Town* Alaska, USA 4 B5
Duyun *Town* China 90 H7
Dzerzhinsk *Town* Russian Federation 73 D9
Dzhalal-Abad *Town* Kyrgyzstan 85 L4
Dzhelandy *Town* Tajikistan 85 K5
Dzhergalan *Town* Kyrgyzstan 85 N3
Dzhusaly *Town* Kazakhstan 78 E7
Dzuunmod *Town* Mongolia 89 J3

E

East Antarctica *Region* Antarctica 110 F5
Eastbourne *Town* England, UK 51 H12
East Cape *Coastal feature* New Zealand 106 I6
East China Sea Pacific Ocean 91 L6
Easter Island Chile, Pacific Ocean 109 M7
Eastern Ghats *Mountain range* India 87 J6
Eastern Sayans *Mountain range* Russian Federation 79 I7
East Kilbride *Town* Scotland, UK 50 E6
East Korea Bay North Korea/South Korea 91 M3
Eastleigh *Town* England, UK 51 G11
East London *Town* South Africa 44 H8
East Pacific Rise *Undersea feature* Pacific Ocean 109 L7
East Sea Pacific Ocean 93 D10 *see also* Japan, Sea of
East Siberian Sea Arctic Ocean 111 N3
East Timor *Country* 97 K8
Eau Claire *Town* Wisconsin, USA 13 I4
Eberswalde-Finow *Town* Germany 56 G5
Ebetsu *Town* Japan 92 F5

Ebolowa *Town* Cameroon 43 C9
Ebro *River* Spain 59 J4
Ecuador *Country* 26 A8
Ed Damer *Town* Sudan 38 E7
Ed Debba *Town* Sudan 38 D7
Ede *Town* Nigeria 41 K7
Ede *Town* Netherlands 52 F8
Edéa *Town* Cameroon 42 C8
Edinburgh *Town* Scotland, UK 50 F6
Edirne *Town* Turkey 76 C3
Edmonton *Town* Alberta, Canada 4 H8
Edmundston *Town* New Brunswick, Canada 7 J6
Edna *Town* Texas, USA 17 M7
Edolo *Town* Italy 60 D4
Edremit *Town* Turkey 76 C4
Edward, Lake Democratic Republic of Congo 43 I10
Edwards Plateau Texas, USA 17 K7
Eemshaven *Town* Netherlands 52 G6
Effingham *Town* Illinois, USA 13 J7
Eger *Town* Hungary 63 F11
Egypt *Country* 38 D5
Eidfjord *Town* Norway 49 B9
Eindhoven *Town* Netherlands 53 F10
Eivissa *see* Ibiza
Elat *Town* Israel 81 D14
Elâzığ *Town* Turkey 76 H5
Elbasan *Town* Albania 65 F12
Elbe *River* Germany/Czech Republic 56 E5
Elbląg *Town* Poland 62 E5
El'brus *Mountain* Russian Federation 73 C13
El Cajon *Town* California, USA 14 H8
El Callao *Town* Venezuela 26 F5
Elche *Town* Spain 59 K7
Elda *Town* Spain 59 K7
El Dorado *Town* Venezuela 26 F6
Eldoret *Town* Kenya 39 F11
Elektrostal' *Town* Russian Federation 72 C8
El Fasher *Town* Sudan 38 C8
El Geneina *Town* Sudan 38 C8
Elgin *Town* Illinois, USA 13 J5
El Goléa *Town* Algeria 36 H5
Elista *Town* Russian Federation 73 C11
El-Jadida *Town* Morocco 36 E4
Elk *Town* Poland 62 G5
El Khârga *Town* Egypt 38 D5
Ellesmere Island Nunavut, Canada 5 J2
Ellsworth Land *Region* Antarctica 110 C6
El Mahbas *Town* Western Sahara 36 E6
El Mina *Town* Lebanon 80 D8
Elmira *Town* New York, USA 8 G6
El Mreyyé *Desert* Mauritania 40 G3
Elmshorn *Town* Germany 56 D5
El Muglad *Town* Sudan 38 D8
El Obeid *Town* Sudan 38 D8
El Oued *Town* Algeria 37 I4
Eloy *Town* Arizona, USA 16 E5
El Paso *Town* Texas, USA 16 H6
El Porvenir *Town* Panama 21 M7
El Progreso *Town* Honduras 20 G3
El Salvador *Country* 20 E5
El Sáuz *Town* Mexico 18 G4
El Tigre *Town* Venezuela 26 E5
Emba *Town* Kazakhstan 78 E6
Emden *Town* Germany 56 C5
Emerald *Town* Queensland, Australia 105 L4
Emmen *Town* Netherlands 52 G7
Empalme *Town* Mexico 18 F4
Empty Quarter *see* Ar Rub' al Khālī
Encarnación *Town* Paraguay 30 H6
Encs *Town* Hungary 63 G10
Endeh *Town* Indonesia 97 J8
England *National Region* UK 51 G9
English Channel UK/France 51 H12
Enid *Town* Oklahoma, USA 17 L3
En Nâqoûra *Town* Lebanon 81 D10
Enschede *Town* Netherlands 52 G8
Ensenada *Town* Mexico 18 C3
Entebbe *Town* Uganda 39 E11
Enugu *Town* Nigeria 41 L7
Eolie, Isole *Island* Italy 61 F12
Épinal *Town* France 54 H7
Equatorial Guinea *Country* 43 C9
Erdenet *Town* Mongolia 89 I3
Ereğli *Town* Turkey 76 F6
Erenhot *Town* China 89 K4

Erfurt *Town* Germany 56 E7
Ergun *Town* China 89 L2
Erie *Town* Pennsylvania, USA 8 E6
Erie, Lake Canada/USA, 13 M5
Eritrea *Country* 38 F7
Erlangen *Town* Germany 57 E9
Ernākulam *Town* India 86 H8
Erode *Town* Pakistan 86 H8
Er-Rachidia *Town* Morocco 36 F5
Erzincan *Town* Turkey 76 H4
Erzurum *Town* Turkey 77 J4
Esbjerg Denmark 49 B12
Escondido *Town* California, USA 14 H8
Escuinapa *Town* Mexico 18 H6
Escuintla *Town* Mexico 19 N9
Escuintla *Town* Guatemala 20 D4
Eşfahān *Town* Iran 82 F7
Eskişehir *Town* Turkey 76 E4
Eslāmābād *Town* Iran 82 D6
Esmeraldas *Town* Ecuador 26 A7
Esperance *Town* Western Australia,
  Australia 104 G7
Esperanza *Research station* Antarctica
  110 B4
Esperanza *Town* Mexico 18 F4
Espiritu Santo *Island* Vanuatu 102 H7
Espoo *Town* Finland 49 G9
Essaouira *Town* Morocco 36 E4
Essen *Town* Belgium 53 E10
Essen *Town* Germany 56 C7
Estância *Town* Brazil 29 M4
Estonia *Country* 70 G4
Ethiopia *Country* 39 G9
Ethiopian Highlands *Upland* Ethiopia 39 F9
Etna, Mount *Volcano* Italy 61 F13
Eucla *Town* Western Australia,
  Australia 104 H6
Euclid *Town* Ohio, USA 13 M5
Eugene *Town* Oregon, USA 14 F3
Euphrates *River* Turkey/Syria/Iraq 76 H4
Eureka *Town* Montana, USA 15 I2
Evanston *Town* Wyoming, USA 15 J5
Evanston *Town* Illinois, USA 13 J5
Evansville *Town* Indiana, USA 13 K8
Everest, Mount *Mountain* Nepal/
  China 87 K3
Everett *Town* Washington, USA 14 G2
Everglades, The *Wetlands* Florida, USA 11 J8
Évora *Town* Portugal 58 F7
Exeter *Town* England, UK 51 E12
Extremadura *Region* Portugal 58 G6
Eyre North, Lake South Australia,
  Australia 105 J6
Eyre Peninsula South Australia,
  Australia 105 I7
Eyre South, Lake South Australia,
  Australia 105 J6

F

Fabens *Town* New Mexico, USA 16 H6
Fada *Town* Chad 42 F5
Fada-Ngourma *Town* Burkina Faso 41 J6
Faenza *Town* Italy 60 E6
Faeroe Islands *Dependent territory* Denmark,
  Atlantic Ocean 33 K1
Fahraj *Town* Iran 82 H8
Fairbanks *Town* Alaska, USA 4 E5
Fairfield *Town* California, USA 14 F6
Faisalābād *Town* Pakistan 86 G2
Faizābād *Town* India 87 J3
Falkland Islands *Dependent territory* UK,
  Atlantic Ocean 33 I8
Falun *Town* Sweden 49 D9
Famagusta *see* Ammóchostos
Fano *Town* Italy 60 F7
Farewell, Cape *Coastal feature*
  New Zealand 106 D8
Fargo *Town* North Dakota, USA 12 G3
Farg'ona *Town* Uzbekistan 85 K4
Farkhor *Town* Tajikistan 85 J5
Fastiv *Town* Ukraine 69 I3
Faya *Town* Chad 42 E4
Fayetteville *Town* North Carolina, USA 11 K4
Fdérik *Town* Mauritania 40 F3

Fear, Cape *Coastal feature* North Carolina,
  USA 11 K4
Federacija Bosna I Hercegovina
  Administrative region Bosnia & Herzegovina
  64 D8
Feijó *Town* Brazil 28 F4
Feilding *Town* New Zealand 106 G8
Feira de Santana *Town* Brazil 29 M5
Felipe Carrillo Puerto *Town* Mexico 19 O7
Felixstowe *Town* England, UK 51 I10
Fengcheng *Town* China 91 L3
Ferrara *Town* Italy 60 E6
Ferreñafe *Town* Peru 27 A9
Ferizaj *Town* Kosovo 65 G10
Ferrol *Town* Spain 58 F2
Fès *Town* Morocco 36 F4
Fezzan *Cultural region* Libya 37 L6
Fianarantsoa *Town* Madagascar 45 M6
Figuig *Town* Algeria 36 G4
Fiji *Country* 103 I7
Filiaşi *Town* Romania 68 E7
Filipstad *Town* Sweden 49 D10
Findlay *Town* Ohio, USA 13 L6
Finland *Country* 48 G7
Finland, Gulf of Finland/Estonia 49 G10
Finnmarksvidda *Physical region*
  Norway 48 F4
Fiordland *Physical region* New Zealand
  107 A13
Firenze *see* Florence
Flagstaff *Town* Arizona, USA 16 E4
Flensburg *Town* Germany 56 D4
Flinders Ranges *Mountain range*
  Australia 105 J6
Flint *Town* Michigan, USA 13 L5
Florence *Town* Italy 60 D7
Florencia *Town* Colombia 26 B7
Flores *Town* Guatemala 20 E2
Flores Sea Indonesia 97 I8
Floriano *Town* Brazil 29 L3
Florianópolis *Town* Brazil 29 K8
Florida *State* USA 11 J8
Florida Keys *Island group* Florida, USA 11 J9
Florida, Straits of USA/Bahamas 11 K9
Florissant *Town* Missouri, USA 13 I7
Focşani *Town* Romania 68 G6
Foggia *Town* Italy 61 G9
Foligno *Town* Italy 60 E8
Folkestone *Town* England, UK 51 I11
Fongafale *Capital* Tuvalu 103 J5
Fonseca, Gulf of El Salvador 20 F5
Fontainebleau *Town* France 54 F7
Fonyód *Town* Hungary 63 D12
Forlì *Town* Italy 60 E6
Formosa *Town* Argentina 30 G5
Formosa, Serra *Mountain range* Brazil 29 I4
Fort Albany *Town* Ontario, Canada 6 G5
Fortaleza *Town* Bolivia 27 E10
Fortaleza *Town* Brazil 29 M3
Fort Collins *Town* Colorado, USA 15 L5
Fort-de-France *Capital* Martinique 23 O7
Fort Frances *Town* Ontario, Canada 6 D6
Fort Lauderdale *Town* Florida, USA 11 J8
Fort Myers *Town* Florida, USA 11 J8
Fort Nelson *Town* British Columbia,
  Canada 4 G7
Fort Severn *Town* Ontario, Canada 6 F3
Fort-Shevchenko *Town* Kazakhstan 78 D6
Fort Smith *Town* Arkansas, USA 10 D3
Fort Smith *Town* Arkansas, USA 10 D3
Fort Stockton *Town* Texas, USA 17 J6
Fort Vermilion *Town* Alberta, Canada 4 H7
Fort Wayne *Town* Indiana, USA 13 K6
Fort William *Town* Scotland,UK 50 E5
Fort Worth *Town* Texas, USA 17 L5
Foumban *Town* Cameroon 42 C8
Foveaux Strait New Zealand 107 B14
France *Country* 54 E8
Francistown *Town* Botswana 44 H5
Frankfurt am Main *Town* Germany 56 D8
Frankfurt an der Oder *Town* Germany 56 G6
Fransisco Escárcega *Town* Mexico 19 N7
Fraser Island *Island* Australia 105 N5
Fredericton *Town* New Brunswick,
  Canada 7 J7
Fredrikstad Norway 49 C10
Freeport *Town* Texas, USA 17 N7

Freeport *Town* Bahamas 22 F1
Freetown *Capital* Sierra Leone 40 E7
Freiburg im Breisgau *Town* Germany 57 C10
Fremantle *Town* Western Australia,
  Australia 104 E7
French Guiana *Dependent territory* 26 H6
French Polynesia *Dependent territory* France,
  Pacific Ocean 103 N8
Fresnillo *Town* Mexico 19 I6
Fresno *Town* California, USA 14 G7
Frías *Town* Argentina 30 E6
Friedrichshafen *Town* Germany 57 D11
Frisian Islands, East *Island group*
  Germany 56 C5
Frisian Islands, North *Island group*
  Germany 56 C4
Frontera *Town* Mexico 19 N7
Frýdek-Místek *Town* Czech Republic 63 E9
Fu'an *Town* China 91 K7
Fudi *Town* Japan 92 G7
Fuerte Olimpo *Town* Paraguay 30 G4
Fuji *Town* Japan 93 F11
Fujian *Administrative region* China 91 K7
Fuji, Mount *Mountain* Japan 93 F11
Fujisawa *Town* Japan 93 G11
Fukui *Town* Japan 93 E11
Fukuoka *Town* Japan 93 B13
Fukushima *Town* Japan 93 G9
Fukushima *Town* Japan 92 F6
Fukuyama *Town* Japan 93 D12
Fulda *Town* Germany 56 D8
Fundy, Bay of Canada 7 K7
Fürth *Town* Germany 57 E9
Furukawa *Town* Japan 92 G8
Fushun *Town* China 91 L2
Fuyuan *Town* China 89 N1
Fuxin *Town* China 91 K2
Fuzhou *Town* China 91 K7

G

Gaalkacyo *Town* Somalia 39 H9
Gabès *Town* Tunisia 37 J4
Gabon *Country* 43 C10
Gaborone *Capital* Botswana 44 G6
Gabrovo *Town* Bulgaria 66 F6
Gadag *Town* Sri Lanka 86 H7
Gafsa *Town* Tunisia 37 J4
Gagnoa *Town* Côte d'Ivoire 40 H8
Gagra *Town* Georgia 77 J2
Gaillac *Town* France 55 E11
Gainesville *Town* Texas, USA 17 M5
Gainesville *Town* Florida, USA 11 I7
Galanta *Town* Slovakia 63 E10
Galápagos Islands *Island group* Ecuador,
  Pacific Ocean 109 M5
Galapi *Town* Romania 68 G6
Galesburg *Town* Illinois, USA 13 I6
Galicia *Region* Spain 58 F3
Galle *Town* India 87 I9
Gallup *Town* New Mexico, USA 16 G4
Galtat-Zemmour *Town* Western Sahara
  36 D6
Galveston *Town* Texas, USA 17 N7
Galway *Town* Ireland 51 B9
Gambell *Town* Alaska, USA 4 D3
Gambia *Country* 40 E5
Gambia *River* Senegal 40 F5
Gäncä *Town* Azerbaijan 77 M3
Gandajika *Town* Democratic Republic of
  Congo 43 G12
Gander *Town* Newfoundland & Labrador,
  Canada 7 M5
Gāndhīdhām *Town* India 86 F4
Ganges *River* Asia 87 K4
Ganges, Mouths of the *Coastal feature* India/
  Bangladesh 87 L5
Gansu *Administrative region* China 88 H5
Ganzhou *Town* China 91 J7
Gao *Town* Mali 41 J5
Garagum *Desert* Turkmenistan 84 F4
Garagum Canal Turkmenistan 84 H5
Garland *Town* Texas, USA 17 M5
Garonne *River* France 55 D10
Garoua *Town* Cameroon 42 D7

Garsen *Town* Kenya 39 G12
Gar Xincun *Town* China 88 D7
Gary *Town* Indiana, USA 13 K6
Garzón *Town* Colombia 26 B7
Gaspé *Town* Québec, Canada 7 K6
Gaspé, Péninsule de *Peninsula*
  Newfoundland & Labrador, Canada 7 K6
Gatchina *Town* Russian Federation 72 C7
Gatineau *Town* Québec, Canada 6 H7
Gāvbandī *Town* Iran 82 F8
Gavere *Town* Belgium 53 D11
Gävle *Town* Sweden 49 E9
Gaya *Town* India 87 J4
Gaza *Town* Israel 81 C12
Gaza Strip *Disputed region* Near East 81 C11
Gaziantep *Town* Turkey 76 H6
Gazimağusa *see* Ammóchostos
Gazli *Town* Uzbekistan 84 H4
Gdańsk *Town* Poland 62 E5
Gdynia *Town* Poland 62 E4
Gedaref *Town* Sudan 38 F8
Gediz *Town* Turkey 76 D5
Geelong *Town* Victoria, Australia 105 K8
Gejiu *Town* China 90 F8
Gela *Town* Sicily, Italy 61 E13
Gembloux *Town* Belgium 53 E11
Gemena *Town* Democratic Republic Congo
  43 F9
General Alvear *Town* Argentina 30 D8
General Eugenio A.Garay *Town*
  Paraguay 30 F4
General Santos *Town* Philippines 97 K4
Geneva *Town* Switzerland 57 B12
Geneva, Lake Switzerland 57 B12
Genève *see* Geveva
Genk *Town* Belgium 53 F11
Genoa *Town* Italy 60 C6
Genoa, Gulf of Italy 60 C6
Genova *see* Genoa
Gent *see* Ghent
George Town *Capital* Cayman Islands 22 D5
George Town *Town* Bahamas 22 G3
George Town *Town* Malaysia 96 D4
Georgetown *Capital* Guyana 26 G6
Georgetown *Town* South Carolina,
  USA 11 K5
Georgia *Country* 77 K3
Georgia *State* USA 11 I5
Georg von Neumayer *Research station*
  Antarctica 110 D3
Gera *Town* Germany 56 F7
Gerede *Town* Turkey 76 F4
Germany *Country* 56 D7
Gerona *see* Girona
Gerpinnes *Town* Belgium 53 E12
Gerze *Town* Turkey 76 G3
Getafe *Town* Spain 59 I5
Gevaş *Town* Turkey 77 K5
Gevgelija *Town* Macedonia 65 H12
Ghana *Country* 41 I7
Ghardaïa *Town* Algeria 36 H4
Ghaznī *Town* Afghanistan 85 J7
Ghent *Town* Belgium 53 D10
Ghŭdara *Town* Tajikistan 85 K5
Gibraltar *Dependent territory* UK 58 H9
Gibraltar, Strait of Spain/Morocco 58 G9
Gibson Desert Western Australia,
  Australia 104 G5
Giessen *Town* Germany 56 D8
Gifu *Town* Japan 93 E11
Gijon *Town* Spain 58 H2
Gillette *Town* Wyoming, USA 15 K4
Giresun *Town* Turkey 76 H4
Girona *Town* Spain 59 M4
Gisborne *Town* New Zealand 106 I7
Gissar Range *Mountain range* Tajikistan 85 I5
Giulianova *Town* Italy 60 F9
Giurgiu *Town* Romania 68 F8
Giza *Town* Egypt 38 D4
Glace Bay *Town* Nova Scotia, Canada 7 L6
Glåma *River* Norway 49 C9
Glasgow *Town* Scotland, UK 51 E6
Glazov *Town* Russian Federation 72 F8
Glendale *Town* Arizona, USA 16 E5
Glens Falls *Town* New York, USA 9 I5
Gliwice *Town* Poland 62 E8
Globe *Town* Arizona, USA 16 F5

GŁOGÓW – HOLON

Głogów *Town* Poland 62 D7
Gloucester *Town* England, UK 51 F10
Gniezno *Town* Poland 62 D6
Gobi *Desert* Mongolia 89 I4
Godāvari *River* India 86 H5
Godhra *Town* India 86 G4
Godoy Cruz *Town* Argentina 30 D8
Goes *Town* Netherlands 53 D10
Goiânia *Town* Brazil 29 K6
Göksun *Town* Turkey 76 H6
Golan Heights *Mountain range* Syria 81 D10
Goldsboro *Town* North Carolina, USA 11 K3
Goleniów *Town* Poland 62 C5
Golmud *Town* China 88 G6
Goma *Town* Democratic Republic of Congo 43 H10
Gombi *Town* Nigeria 41 M6
Gómez Palacio *Town* Mexico 18 H5
Gonaïves *Town* Haiti 23 I5
Gonder *Town* Ethiopia 38 F8
Gondia *Town* India 87 I5
Good Hope, Cape of *Coastal feature* South Africa 44 F9
Goor *Town* Netherlands 52 G8
Göppingen *Town* Germany 57 D9
Gorakhpur *Town* Pakistan 87 J3
Goraâde *Town* Bosnia & Herzegovina 65 E9
Gorē *Town* Ethiopia 39 F9
Gorgān *Town* Iran 82 F5
Gori *Town* Georgia 77 L3
Görlitz *Town* Germany 56 G7
Gorontalo *Town* Indonesia 97 J6
Gorzów Wielkopolski *Town* Poland 62 C6
Gosford *Town* New South Wales, Australia 105 M7
Goshogawara *Town* Japan 92 F7
Göteborg *see* Gothenburg
Gotel Mountains Nigeria 41 M7
Gotha *Town* Germany 56 E7
Gothenburg *Town* Sweden 49 C11
Gotland *Island* Sweden 49 E11
Gōtsu *Town* Japan 93 C12
Göttingen *Town* Germany 56 D7
Gouda *Town* Netherlands 53 E9
Governador Valadares *Town* Brazil 29 L6
Gradaús, Serra dos *Mountain range* Brazil 29 J4
Grafton *Town* New South Wales, Australia 105 N6
Grafton *Town* North Dakota, USA 12 G2
Grampian Mountains Scotland, UK 50 E5
Granada *Town* Spain 59 I8
Granada *Town* Nicaragua 20 H6
Gran Chaco *Plain* Paraguay 30 G4
Grand Bahama Island Bahamas 22 F1
Grand Canyon Arizona, USA 16 E3
Grand Cayman *Island* West Indies 22 E5
Grande, Bahía *Bay* Argentina 31 E13
Grand Erg Occidental *Desert* Algeria 36 G5
Grand Erg Oriental *Desert* Algeria 37 I5
Grande, Rio *River* Mexico/USA 16 G5
Grand Forks *Town* North Dakota, USA 12 G2
Grand Rapids *Town* Minnesota, USA 12 H3
Grand Rapids *Town* Michigan, USA 13 K5
Grand-Santi *Town* French Guiana 26 H6
Grants Pass *Town* Oregon, USA 14 F4
Grayling *Town* Alaska, USA 4 D4
Graz *Town* Austria 57 H11
Great Australian Bight *Sea feature* Australia 104 G7
Great Barrier Island New Zealand 106 G4
Great Barrier Reef *Coral reef* Australia 105 L3
Great Basin Nevada, USA 14 H6
Great Bear Lake Northwest Territories, Canada 4 H5
Great Dividing Range *Mountain range* Queensland/New South Wales, Australia 105 L4
Greater Antilles *Island group* Caribbean Sea 22 G5
Greater Caucasus *Mountain range* Asia/Europe 77 M3
Great Falls *Town* Montana, USA 15 J2
Great Hungarian Plain Hungary 63 F12
Great Inagua *Island* Bahamas 23 I4
Great Karoo *Plateau* South Africa 44 F8
Great Khingan Range *Mountain range* China 89 L3
Great Rift Valley Africa 39 F12
Great Sand Sea *Desert* Egypt 38 C4
Great Sandy Desert Western Australia, Australia 104 G4
Great Slave Lake Northwest Territories, Canada 4 H6
Great Victoria Desert Western Australia/ South Australia, Australia 104 G6
Great Wall of China *Ancient monument* China 89 J5
Great Yarmouth *Town* England, UK 51 I9
Greece *Country* 67 D11
Greeley *Town* Colorado, USA 15 L5
Green Bay *Town* Wisconsin, USA 13 J4
Greenfield *Town* Massachusetts, USA 9 J5
Greeneville *Town* Tennessee, USA 11 I3
Greenland *Dependent territory* Denmark, Atlantic Ocean 111 C8
Greenland Sea Arctic Ocean 111 M7
Green Mountains Vermont, USA 9 I5
Greenock *Town* Scotland, UK 50 E6
Greensboro *Town* North Carolina, USA 11 J3
Greenville *Town* Mississippi, USA 10 F5
Greenville *Town* South Carolina, USA 11 I4
Greifswald *Town* Germany 56 F4
Grenada *Country* 23 O8
Grenadines, The *Island group* St Vincent & The Grenadines 23 O8
Grenoble *Town* France 55 G10
Gresham *Town* Oregon, USA 14 F3
Grevenmacher *Town* Luxembourg 53 G13
Greymouth *Town* New Zealand 107 D10
Grey Range *Mountain range* New South Wales/Queensland, Australia 105 K6
Griffin *Town* Georgia, USA 10 H5
Grimsby *Town* England, UK 51 H9
Grise Fiord *Town* Nunavut, Canada 5 J3
Grójec *Town* Poland 62 F7
Groningen *Town* Netherlands 52 G6
Grootfontein *Town* Namibia 44 F5
Grosseto *Town* Italy 60 D8
Groznyy *Town* Russian Federation 73 D14
Gubkin *Town* Russian Federation 73 C10
Grudziądz *Town* Poland 62 E5
Gryazi *Town* Russian Federation 73 C10
Guadalajara *Town* Spain 59 I5
Guadalajara *Town* Mexico 19 I7
Guadalcanal *Island* Solomon Islands 102 G6
Guadalupe *Town* Mexico 19 I6
Guadeloupe *Dependent territory* France, Atlantic Ocean 23 O6
Guaimaca *Town* Honduras 20 G4
Gualeguaychú *Town* Argentina 30 G8
Guam *Dependent territory* USA, Pacific Ocean 102 D2
Guamúchil *Town* Mexico 18 G5
Guanabacoa *Town* Cuba 22 D3
Guanajuato *Town* Mexico 19 J7
Guanare *Town* Venezuela 26 D5
Guangdong *Administrative region* China 91 J8
Guangxi *Administrative region* China 90 H8
Guangyuan *Town* China 90 H5
Guangzhou *Town* China 91 I8
Guantánamo *Town* Cuba 22 H4
Guantánamo Bay *Territory* USA, Cuba 22 H5
Guasave *Town* Mexico 18 G5
Guatemala *Country* 20 D3
Guatemala City *Capital* Guatemala 20 D4
Guayaquil *Town* Ecuador 26 A8
Guaymas *Town* Mexico 18 E4
Guéret *Town* France 55 E9
Guernsey *Island* Channel Islands, UK 51 F13
Guerrero Negro *Town* Mexico 18 D4
Guiana Highlands *Mountain range* Colombia/Venezuela/Brazil26 F7
Guider *Town* Cameroon 42 D7
Guildford *Town* England, UK 51 G11
Guilin *Town* China 91 I7
Guinea *Country* 40 F6
Guinea-Bissau *Country* 40 E6
Guinea, Gulf of Atlantic Ocean 33 M5
Guiyang *Town* China 90 H7
Guizhou *Administrative region* China 90 G7
Gujrānwāla *Town* Pakistan 86 H2
Gujrāt *Town* Pakistan 86 H2
Gulbarga *Town* India 86 H6
Gulbene *Town* Latvia 70 G6
Gulf, The Middle East 82 E6
see also Persian Gulf
Guliston *Town* Uzbekistan 85 J4
Gulu *Town* Uganda 39 E10
Gümüşhane *Town* Turkey 76 H4
Güney Doğu Toroslar *Mountain range* Turkey 76 H6
Gusau *Town* Nigeria 41 K6
Güstrow *Town* Germany 56 F5
Gütersloh *Town* Germany 56 D6
Guwāhāti *Town* India 87 L3
Guyana *Country* 26 G6
Gwādar *Town* Pakistan 86 D3
Gwalior *Town* India 87 I3
Gyomaendrőd *Town* Hungary 63 G11
Gyöngyös *Town* Hungary 63 F11
Győr *Town* Hungary 63 D11
Gyumri *Town* Armenia 77 K

H

Haarlem *Town* Netherlands 52 E8
Haast *Town* New Zealand 107 B11
Hachinohe *Town* Japan 92 G7
Hadera *Town* Israel 81 D10
Ha Đông *Town* Vietnam 94 G7
Haeju *Town* North Korea 91 L3
Hagåtña *Capital* Guam 102 E2
Hagerstown *Town* Maryland, USA 8 F8
Ha Giang *Town* Vietnam 94 G6
Hague, The *Capital* Netherlands 52 D8
Haicheng *Town* China 91 L2
Haifa *Town* Israel 81 D10
Haikou *Town* China 91 I9
Ḩā'il *Town* Saudi Arabia 82 C8
Hainan *Administrative region* China 90 H9
Hainan Dao *Island* China 91 I9
Hai Phong *Town* Vietnam 94 G7
Haiti *Country* 23 I5
Hajdúhadház *Town* Hungary 63 G11
Hakodate *Town* Japan 92 F6
Ḩalab *see* Aleppo
Halifax *Town* Nova Scotia, Canada 7 L7
Halle *Town* Germany 56 F7
Halle *Town* Belgium 53 D11
Halle-Neustadt *Town* Germany 56 F7
Halley *Research station* Antarctica 110 D4
Halmstad *Town* Sweden 49 C11
Hamadān *Town* Iran 82 E6
Ḩamāh *Town* Syria 80 E7
Hamamatsu *Town* Japan 93 F11
Hamar *Town* Norway 49 C9
Hamburg *Town* Germany 56 E5
Hamburg *Town* New York, USA 9 F5
Hamersley Range *Mountain range* Western Australia, Australia 104 F4
Hamhŭng *Town* North Korea 91 M3
Hami *Town* China 88 G4
Hamilton *Town* Scotland, UK 50 E6
Hamilton *Town* New Zealand 106 G6
Hamilton *Town* Ontario, Canada 6 G8
Hamm *Town* Germany 56 C7
Hanamaki *Town* Japan 92 G8
Handan *Town* China 91 J4
Ha Negev *see* Negev
Hangzhou *Town* China 91 K6
Hannover *Town* Germany 56 D6
Ha Nôi *Capital* Vietnam 94 F7
Hantsavichy *Town* Belarus 71 D10
Hanzhong *Town* China 90 H5
Haradok *Town* Belarus 70 H8
Harare *Capital* Zimbabwe 45 I4
Harbel *Town* Liberia 40 F8
Harbin *Town* China 89 M3
Hardangervidda *Plateau* Norway 49 B9
Hardenberg *Town* Netherlands 52 G7
Hārer *Town* Ethiopia 39 G9
Hargeysa *Town* Somalia 39 H9
Ḩārim *Town* Syria 80 D6
Harlingen *Town* Texas, USA 17 M9
Harlow *Town* England, UK 51 H10
Harper *Town* Liberia 40 G8
Harrisburg *Town* Pennsylvania, USA 9 G7
Harrogate *Town* England, UK 50 G6
Hârşova *Town* Romania 68 G7
Hartford *Town* Connecticut, USA 9 J6
Hartlepool *Town* England, UK 50 G7
Hasselt *Town* Belgium 53 E11
Hastings *Town* New Zealand 106 H8
Hastings *Town* England, UK 50 H11
Hapeg *Town* Romania 68 E6
Hatteras, Cape *Coastal feature* North Carolina, USA 11 L3
Hat Yai *Town* Thailand 95 D13
Haugesund *Town* Norway 49 A10
Havana *Capital* Cuba 22 D3
Havant *Town* England, UK 51 G11
Havelock *Town* North Carolina, USA 11 L4
Hawaiian Ridge *Undersea feature* Pacific Ocean 109 J4
Hawera *Town* New Zealand 106 F8
Haysyn *Town* Ukraine 68 H4
Hazar *Town* Turkmenistan 84 D4
Heard & McDonald Islands *Dependent territory* Australia, Indian Ocean 99 I8
Hearst *Town* Ontario, Canada 6 F6
Hebei *Administrative region* China 91 J3
Hebron *Town* Israel 81 D11
Heerlen *Town* Netherlands 53 F11
Hefa *see* Haifa
Hefei *Town* China 91 J5
Hegang *Town* China 89 M2
Heidelberg *Town* Germany 57 D9
Heidenheim an der Brenz *Town* Germany 57 E10
Heilbronn *Town* Germany 57 D9
Heilong Jiang *see* Amur
Heilongjiang *Administrative region* China 89 M2
Heimdal Sweden 48 D7
Hekimhan *Town* Turkey 76 H5
Helena *Town* Montana, USA 15 I3
Helmond *Town* Netherlands 53 F10
Helsingborg *Town* Sweden 49 C12
Helsinki *Capital* Finland 49 G9
Henan *Administrative region* China 91 I5
Henan *Town* Qinghai, China 89 I6
Hengduan Shan *Mountain range* China 90 E7
Hengelo *Town* Netherlands 52 G8
Hengyang *Town* China 91 I7
Henzada *Town* Myanmar 94 B8
Herāt *Town* Afghanisatan 84 G7
Herford *Town* Germany 56 D6
Hermosillo *Town* Mexico 18 E4
Hexian *Town* China 91 I8
Hidalgo del Parral *Town* Mexico 18 H5
Hida-sanmyaku *Mountain range* Japan 93 E10
High Point *Town* North Carolina, USA 11 J3
Hikurangi *Town* New Zealand 106 F4
Hildesheim *Town* Germany 56 D6
Hillsboro *Town* New Hampshire, USA 9 J5
Hilversum *Town* Netherlands 52 E8
Himalayas *Mountain range* Asia 87 I2
Himeji *Town* Japan 93 D12
Ḩimş *Town* Syria 80 E8
Hînceşti *Town* Moldova 68 H5
Hindu Kush *Mountain range* Afghanisatan/ Pakistan 85 J6
Hinthada *Town* Myanmar 94 B8
Hirosaki *Town* Japan 92 F7
Hiroshima *Town* Japan 93 C12
Hitachi *Town* Japan 93 G9
Hitoyoshi *Town* Japan 93 C14
Hjørring *Town* Denmark 49 B11
Hlobyne *Town* Ukraine 69 J4
Hlybokaye *Town* Belarus 70 F8
Hobart *Town* Tasmania, Australia 105 K10
Hobro *Town* Denmark 49 B11
Hô Chi Minh *Town* Vietnam 95 G11
Hodeida *Town* Yemen 83 C12
Hódmezővásárhely *Town* Hungary 63 F12
Hodonín *Town* Czech Republic 63 D10
Hof *Town* Germany 56 F8
Hōfu *Town* Japan 93 C13
Hohhot *Town* China 89 K5
Hokkaidō *Island* Japan 92 G5
Holguín *Town* Cuba 22 G4
Hollabrunn *Town* Austria 57 H10
Holmsund *Town* Sweden 48 F7
Holon *Town* Israel 81 D11

Myitkyina *Town* Myanmar 94 C5
Mykolayiv *Town* Ukraine 69 J5
Myrhorod *Town* Ukraine 69 K3
Mýrina *Town* Greece 67 F9
Myrtle Beach *Town* South Carolina, USA 11 K4
Mysore *Town* India 86 H8
My Tho *Town* Vietnam 95 G11
Mzuzu *Town* Malawi 45 J3

N

Naberezhnyye Chelny *Town* Russian Federation 73 F9
Nāblus *Town* Israel 81 D11
Nacala *Town* Mozambique 45 K4
Nadi *Town* Fiji 103 I7
Nadvirna *Town* Ukraine 68 F4
Nadym *Town* Russian Federation 78 G5
Naga *Town* Philippines 97 J2
Nagano *Town* Japan 93 F10
Nagaoka *Town* Japan 93 F9
Nagasaki *Town* Japan 93 B14
Nagato *Town* Japan 93 C12
Nāgercoil *Town* India 86 H9
Nagornyy Karabakh *Region* Azerbaijan 77 M4
Nagoya *Town* Japan 93 F11
Nāgpur *Town* India 87 I5
Nagqu *Town* China 88 G7
Nagykanizsa *Town* Hungary 63 D12
Nagykőrös *Town* Hungary 63 F11
Naha *Town* Ryukyu Islands 93 A16
Nā'īn *Town* Iran 82 F7
Nain *Town* Newfoundland & Labrador, Canada 7 K3
Nairobi *Capital* Kenya 39 F11
Najin *Town* North Korea 91 M2
Najrān *Town* Saudi Arabia 83 C12
Nakagawa *Town* Japan 92 F4
Nakamura *Town* Japan 93 D13
Nakatsugawa *Town* Japan 93 F11
Nakhodka *Town* Russian Federation 79 M7
Nakhon Ratchasima *Town* Thailand 95 E9
Nakhon Sawan *Town* Thailand 95 D9
Nakhon Si Thammarat *Town* Thailand 95 D12
Nakuru *Town* Kenya 39 F11
Nal'chik *Town* Russian Federation 73 C13
Nālūt *Town* Libya 37 J5
Namangan *Town* Uzbekistan 85 K3
Nam Đinh *Town* Vietnam 94 G7
Namib Desert Namibia 44 E5
Namibe *Town* Angola 44 D4
Namibia *Country* 44 E5
Nampa *Town* Idaho, USA 14 H4
Nampula *Town* Mozambique 45 K4
Namur *Town* Belgium 53 E12
Nanaimo *Town* British Colombia, Canada 4 G9
Nancha *Town* China 89 M2
Nanchang *Town* China 91 J6
Nanchong *Town* China 90 H6
Nancy *Town* France 54 H7
Nānded *Town* India 86 H6
Nanfeng *Town* China 91 J7
Nanjing *Town* China 91 K5
Nanning *Town* China 90 H8
Nanping *Town* China 91 K7
Nanterre *Town* France 54 E6
Nantes *Town* France 54 C8
Nantucket *Town* Massachusetts, USA 9 K6
Nantucket Island Massachusetts, USA 9 K6
Nanyang *Town* China 91 I5
Napa *Town* California, USA 14 F6
Napier *Town* New Zealand 106 H7
Naples *Town* Italy 61 F10
Napoli *see* Naples
Napo, Río *River* Peru 26 C8
Narathiwat *Town* Thailand 95 E13
Narita *Town* Japan 93 G10
Närpes *Town* Finland 48 F8
Närpiö *see* Närpes
Narva *Town* Estonia 70 H4
Narvik *Town* Norway 48 E4

Năsăud *Town* Romania 68 F5
Nāshik *Town* India 86 G5
Nashua *Town* New Hampshire, USA 9 J5
Nashville *Town* Tennessee, USA 10 G3
Nassau *Capital* Bahamas 22 G2
Nasser *Lake* Egypt 38 E6
Nata *Town* Botswana 44 H5
Natal *Town* Brazil 29 N3
Natitingou *Town* Benin 41 J6
Natzrat *see* Nazareth
Nauru *Country* 102 H4
Nauta *Town* Peru 27 C9
Navapolatsk *Town* Belarus 70 G8
Navassa Island *Dependent territory* USA, Atlantic Ocean 22 H5
Navoiy *Town* Uzbekistan 85 I4
Navojoa *Town* Mexico 18 F5
Nawābshāh *Town* Pakistan 86 F3
Nayoro *Town* Japan 92 F4
Nay Pyi Taw *Capital* Myanmar 94 C7
Nazareth *Town* Israel 81 D10
Nazca *Town* Peru 27 C11
Nazilli *Town* Turkey 76 D6
Nazrēt *Town* Ethiopia 39 G9
N'Dalatando *Town* Angola 44 E2
Ndélé *Town* Central African Republic 42 F7
Ndjamena *Capital* Chad 42 D6
Neagh, Lough *Lake* Northern Ireland, UK 50 D8
Neápoli *Town* Greece 67 G14
Neápoli *Town* Greece 67 C9
Near Islands *Island Group* Alaska, USA 4 A3
Nebraska *State* USA 12 F5
Necochea *Town* Argentina 31 G10
Neftekamsk *Town* Russian Federation 73 F9
Negēlē *Town* Ethiopia 39 G10
Negev *Desert* Israel 81 D12
Negombo *Town* Sri Lanka 87 I9
Negotin *Town* Serbia 64 H8
Negro, Rio *River* Brazil 28 G2
Neijiang *Town* China 90 G6
Nei Mongol Zizhiqu *see* Inner Mongolia
Neiva *Town* Colombia 26 B7
Nellore *Town* India 87 I7
Nelson *Town* New Zealand 107 E9
Nemuro *Town* Japan 92 H4
Nepal *Country* 87 J3
Neryungri *Town* Russian Federation 79 K6
Netanya *Town* Israel 81 D11
Netherlands *Country* 52 E7
Neubrandenburg *Town* Germany 56 F5
Neuchâtel *Town* Switzerland 57 C11
Neufchâteau *Town* Belgium 53 F13
Neumünster *Town* Germany 56 D4
Neunkirchen *Town* Germany 57 C9
Neuquén *Town* Argentina 31 D10
Neustadt an der Weinstrasse *Town* Germany 57 C9
Neu-Ulm *Town* Germany 57 E10
Neuwied *Town* Germany 56 C8
Nevada *State* USA 14 H6
Nevinnomyssk *Town* Russian Federation 73 C11
Nevşehir *Town* Turkey 76 G5
New Amsterdam *Town* Guyana 26 G6
Newark *Town* New Jersey, USA 9 I7
Newark *Town* New York, USA 8 G5
New Bedford *Town* Massachusetts, USA 9 K6
Newberg *Town* Oregon, USA 14 F3
New Britain *Island* Papua New Guinea 102 F5
New Caledonia *Island* New Caledonia 102 G8
New Caledonia *Dependent territory* France, Pacific Ocean 102 G7
Newcastle *Town* New South Wales, Australia 105 M7
Newcastle upon Tyne *Town* England, UK 50 F7
New Delhi *Capital* India 86 H3
Newfoundland *Island* Ontario, Canada 7 M5
Newfoundland & Labrador *Province* Canada 7 L4
Newfoundland Basin *Undersea feature* Atlantic Ocean 33 J2
New Glasgow *Town* Nova Scotia, Canada 7 L7

New Guinea *Island* Indonesia/ Papua New Guinea 102 D5
New Hampshire *State* USA 9 J4
New Haven *Town* Connecticut, USA 8 I6
New Iberia *Town* Louisiana, USA 10 E6
New Jersey *State* USA 9 I7
Newman *Town* Western Australia, Australia 104 E4
New Mexico *State* USA 17 I4
New Orleans *Town* Louisiana, USA 10 F6
New Plymouth *Town* New Zealand 106 F7
Newport *Town* Vermont, USA 9 I3
Newport *Town* Wales, UK 51 F11
Newport News *Town* Virginia, USA 11 L3
New Providence *Island* Bahamas 22 G2
Newquay *Town* England, UK 51 E12
Newry *Town* Northern Ireland, UK 50 D8
New Siberian Islands *Island group* Russian Federation 79 K3
New South Wales *State* Australia 105 L7
Newtownabbey *Town* Northern Ireland, UK 50 D7
New York *State* USA 8 G5
New York *Town* New York, USA 9 I7
New Zealand *Country* 107 E9
Ngaoundéré *Town* Cameroon 42 D7
Ngo *Town* Congo 43 D10
Nguigmi *Town* Niger 41 M5
Nha Trang *Town* Vietnam 95 H10
Niagara Falls *Town* Ontario, Canada 6 G8
Niagara Falls *Town* New York, USA 8 E5
Niagara Falls *Waterfall* Canada/USA 8 E6
Niamey *Capital* Niger 41 J5
Nia-Nia *Town* Democratic Republic of Congo 43 H9
Nicaragua *Country* 20 H5
Nicaragua, Lago de *Lake* Nicaragua 21 I6
Nice *Town* France 55 H11
Nicholls Town *Town* Bahamas 22 F2
Nicobar Islands *Island group* India 87 M8
Nicosia *Capital* Cyprus 80 B8
Nicoya *Town* Costa Rica 20 H7
Nicoya, Golfo de *Gulf* Costa Rica 21 I7
Nida *Town* Lithuania 70 C6
Nieuw-Bergen *Town* Netherlands 53 F9
Niğde *Town* Turkey 76 G6
Niger *Country* 41 K5
Niger *River* Niger/Nigeria 41 J6
Nigeria *Country* 41 M7
Niger, Mouths of the *Coastal feature* Nigeria 41 K8
Niigata *Town* Japan 93 F9
Niihama *Town* Japan 93 D12
Niitsu *Town* Japan 93 F9
Nijmegen *Town* Netherlands 53 F9
Nikiniki *Town* Indonesia 97 J8
Nikopol' *Town* Ukraine 69 K5
Nikšić *Town* Montenegro 65 E10
Nile *River* East Africa 38 E5
Nile Delta Egypt 38 E4
Nîmes *Town* France 55 F11
Ninetyeast Ridge *Undersea feature* Indian Ocean 99 K4
Ninety Mile Beach *Coastal feature* New Zealand 106 E3
Ningbo *Town* China 91 L6
Ningxia *Administrative region* China 89 J6
Niort *Town* France 54 D8
Nipigon, Lake Québec, Canada 6 E6
Niš *Town* Serbia 65 H9
Nişab *Town* Saudi Arabia 82 D8
Nitra *Town* Slovakia 63 E10
Niue *Dependent territory* New Zealand, Pacific Ocean 103 K7
Nizāmābād *Town* India 87 I6
Nizhnekamsk *Town* Russian Federation 73 F9
Nizhnevartovsk *Town* Russian Federation 78 G5
Nizhniy Novgorod *Town* Russian Federation 73 E9
Nizhniy Odes *Town* Russian Federation 72 G7
Nizhyn *Town* Ukraine 69 J2
Nkayi *Town* Congo 43 D11
Nkongsamba *Town* Cameroon 42 C8
Nobeoka *Town* Japan 93 C14

Noboribetsu *Town* Japan 92 F6
Nogales *Town* Arizona, USA 16 F6
Nogales *Town* Mexico 18 E3
Nokia *Town* Finland 48 G8
Nokou *Town* Chad 42 D5
Nong Khai *Town* Thailand 94 E8
Noordwijk aan Zee *Town* Netherlands 52 D8
Norak *Town* Tajikistan 85 J5
Norderstedt *Town* Germany 56 E5
Nordhorn *Town* Germany 56 C6
Nordkapp *see* North Cape
Norfolk *Town* Nebraska, USA 12 G5
Norfolk *Town* Virginia, USA 11 L3
Norfolk Island *Dependent territory* Australia, Pacific Ocean 109 I7
Noril'sk *Town* Russian Federation 78 H4
Norman *Town* Oklahoma, USA 17 L4
Normandy *Region* France 54 D6
Norrköping *Town* Sweden 49 E10
Norrtälje *Town* Sweden 49 E10
North Albanian Alps *Mountain range* Serbia/ Montenegro 65 F10
Northampton *Town* England, UK 51 G10
North Bay *Town* Ontario, Canada 6 G7
North Cape *Coastal feature* New Zealand 106 E3
North Cape *Coastal feature* Norway 48 G2
North Carolina *State* USA 11 K4
North Charleston *Town* South Carolina, USA 11 J5
North Dakota *State* USA 12 F3
Northern Cook Islands *Island group* Cook Islands 103 M6
Northern Dvina *River* Russian Federation 72 E7
Northern Ireland *Political region* UK 50 D7
Northern Mariana Islands *Dependent territory* USA, Pacific Ocean 102 D1
Northern Sporades *Island group* Greece 67 E10
Northern Territory *State* Australia 104 H4
North Island New Zealand 106 G7
North Korea *Country* 91 M3
North Little Rock *Town* Arkansas, USA 10 E4
North Sea Europe 50 G4
North West Highlands *Mountain range* Scotland, UK 50 E4
Northwest Pacific Basin *Undersea feature* Pacific Ocean 109 I3
Northwest Territories *Province* Canada 4 H6
Norway *Country* 48 B8
Norwegian Sea Arctic Ocean 111 M8
Norwich *Town* England, UK 51 H9
Noshiro *Town* Japan 92 F7
Noşratābād *Town* Iran 82 H7
Nottingham *Town* England, UK 51 G9
Nouâdhibou *Town* Mauritania 40 E3
Nouakchott *Capital* Mauritania 40 E4
Nouméa *Capital* New Caledonia 102 H8
Nova Iguaçu *Town* Brazil 29 L7
Novara *Town* Italy 60 C5
Novaya Zemlya *Island* Russian Federation 72 G4
Novi Sad *Town* Serbia 64 F7
Novocheboksarsk *Town* Russian Federation 73 E9
Novocherkassk *Town* Russian Federation 73 C11
Novodvinsk *Town* Russian Federation 72 E6
Novokuznetsk *Town* Russian Federation 78 H7
Novolazarevskaya *Research station* Antarctica 110 E3
Novomoskovs'k *Town* Ukraine 69 K4
Novomoskovsk *Town* Russian Federation 73 C9
Novorossiysk *Town* Russian Federation 73 B12
Novoshakhtinsk *Town* Russian Federation 73 C11
Novosibirsk *Town* Russian Federation 78 H6
Novotroyits'ke *Town* Ukraine 69 K6
Nowy Sącz *Town* Poland 63 F9
Noyon *Town* France 54 F6
Nsawam *Town* Ghana 41 I8

SANANDAJ – SILVAN

Sanandaj *Town* Iran 82 D6
San Andrés Tuxtla *Town* Mexico 19 L8
San Angelo *Town* Texas, USA 17 K6
San Antonio *Town* Chile 30 C8
San Antonio *Town* Texas, USA 17 L7
San Antonio Oeste *Town* Argentina 31 E10
Sanāw *Town* Yemen 83 E11
San Bernardino *Town* California, USA 14 G8
San Carlos de Bariloche *Town* Argentina 31 D10
San Cristóbal *Town* Venezuela 26 C5
San Cristóbal de Las Casas *Town* Mexico 19 N8
Sancti Spíritus *Town* Cuba 22 F3
Sandakan *Town* Malaysia 97 I4
Sand Hills *Mountain range* Nebraska, USA 12 E5
San Diego *Town* California, USA 14 G9
Sandpoint *Town* Idaho, USA 14 H2
Sandvika Norway 49 B9
Sandy City *Town* Utah, USA 15 I5
San Fernando *Town* Venezuela 26 E5
San Fernando *Town* Spain 58 G9
San Fernando *Town* Trinidad & Tobago 23 O9
San Fernando del Valle de Catamarca *Town* Argentina 30 E6
San Francisco *Town* California, USA 14 F6
San Francisco del Oro *Town* Mexico 18 H5
San Francisco de Macorís *Town* Dominican Republic 23 J5
San Ignacio *Town* Guatemala 20 E2
San Ignacio *Town* Mexico 18 E5
San Joaquin Valley California, USA 14 F7
San Jorge, Golfo *Gulf* Argentina 31 E12
San José *Town* Bolivia 27 F12
San José *Capital* Costa Rica 21 J7
San José *Town* Guatemala 20 D5
San Jose *Town* California, USA 14 F6
San Juan *Capital* Puerto Rico 23 L5
San Juan *Town* Argentina 30 D7
San Juan del Norte *Town* Nicaragua 21 J6
San Juan Mountains New Mexico/Colorado, USA 16 H3
Sankt Gallen *Town* Switzerland 57 E11
Sankt-Peterburg *see* Saint Petersburg
Sankt Pölten *Town* Austria 57 H10
Sankuru *River* Democratic Republic of Congo 43 G11
Şanliurfa *Town* Turkey 77 I6
San Luis *Town* Guatemala 20 E3
San Luis *Town* Argentina 30 E8
San Luis *Town* Mexico 18 D2
San Luis Potosí *Town* Mexico 19 J6
San Marcos *Town* Guatemala 20 D4
San Marino *Country* 60 E7
San Marino *Capital* San Marino 60 E7
San Martín *Research station* Antarctica 110 B5
San Matías *Town* Bolivia 27 G12
San Matías, Golfo *Gulf* Argentina 31 F10
Sanmenxia *Town* China 91 I4
San Miguel *Town* El Salvador 20 F5
San Miguel *Town* Mexico 19 I4
San Miguel de Tucumán *Town* Argentina 30 E6
San Miguelito *Town* Panama 21 M8
Sanming *Town* China 91 K7
San Pedro *Town* Belize 20 F2
San Pedro de la Cueva *Town* Mexico 18 F4
San Pedro de Lloc *Town* Peru 27 A9
San Pedro Mártir, Sierra *Mountain range* Mexico 18 D3
San Pedro Sula *Town* Honduras 20 F3
San Rafael *Town* Argentina 30 D8
San Remo *Town* Italy 60 B6
San Salvador *Capital* El Salvador 20 F5
San Salvador de Jujuy *Town* Argentina 30 E5
Sansanné-Mango *Town* Togo 41 J6
Sansepolcro *Town* Italy 60 E7
San Severo *Town* Italy 61 G9
Santa Ana *Town* California, USA 14 G8
Santa Ana *Town* El Salvador 20 E4
Santa Barbara *Town* California, USA 14 G8
Santa Clara *Town* Cuba 22 E3
Santa Cruz *Town* Bolivia 27 F12
Santa Fe *Town* New Mexico, USA 16 H3
Santa Fe *Town* Argentina 30 F7
Santa Maria *Town* Brazil 29 J8
Santa Marta *Town* Colombia 26 C4
Santander *Town* Spain 59 I2
Santarém *Town* Brazil 29 I2
Santa Rosa *Town* Argentina 31 E9
Santa Rosa *Town* California, USA 14 F6
Santa Rosa de Copán *Town* Honduras 20 F4
Santiago *Capital* Chile 30 D8
Santiago *Town* Dominican Republic 23 J5
Santiago *Town* Spain 58 F3
Santiago de Cuba *Town* Cuba 22 G5
Santiago del Estero *Town* Argentina 30 E6
Santo Domingo *Capital* Dominican Republic 23 J5
Santo Domingo de los Colorados *Town* Ecuador 26 A7
Santorini *Town* Greece 67 G13
Santos *Town* Brazil 29 K7
Santo Tomé *Town* Argentina 30 H6
San Vicente *Town* El Salvador 20 F5
São Fransisco, Rio *River* Brazil 29 L4
Sao Hill *Town* Tanzania 39 F13
São José do Rio Preto *Town* Brazil 29 K6
São Luís *Town* Brazil 29 L2
São Paulo *Town* Brazil 29 K7
São Roque, Cabo de *Coastal feature* Brazil 29 N3
São Tomé *Capital* São Tomé & Príncipe 43 B10
São Tomé & Príncipe *Country* 43 B9
Sapele *Town* Nigeria 41 K8
Sapporo *Town* Japan 92 F5
Saqqez *Town* Iran 82 D6
Sarajevo *Capital* Bosnia & Herzegovina 64 E8
Sarakhs *Town* Iran 82 H5
Saraktash *Town* Russian Federation 73 G11
Saran' *Town* Kazakhstan 78 F7
Saransk *Town* Russian Federation 73 E9
Saratov *Town* Russian Federation 73 D10
Sarawak *Cultural region* Malaysia 96 G6
Sardegna *see* Sardinia
Sardinia *Island* Italy 61 A9
Sargasso Sea Atlantic Ocean 33 I3
Sargodha *Town* Pakistan 86 G2
Sarh *Town* Chad 42 E7
Sārī *Town* Iran 82 F5
Sariwŏn *Town* North Korea 91 L3
Sark *Island* Channel Islands, UK 51 G13
Sarmiento *Town* Argentina 31 D12
Sarnia *Town* Ontario, Canada 6 F8
Sarny *Town* Ukraine 68 G2
Sasebo *Town* Japan 93 B13
Saskatchewan *River* Saskatchewan, Canada 5 I8
Saskatchewan *Province* Canada 5 I8
Saskatoon *Town* Saskatchewan, Canada 5 I8
Sasovo *Town* Russian Federation 73 D9
Sassari *Town* Sardinia, Italy 61 B9
Sātpura Range *Mountain range* India 86 H5
Sattanen *Town* Finland 48 G5
Satu Mare *Town* Romania 68 E4
Saudi Arabia *Country* 83 D10
Sault Ste. Marie *Town* Ontario, Canada 6 F7
Sava *River* Serbia 64 F8
Savá *Town* Honduras 20 H3
Savannah *Town* Georgia, USA 11 J5
Savannah River Georgia/South Carolina, USA 11 I5
Saverne *Town* France 54 H7
Savona *Town* Italy 60 C6
Savu Sea Indonesia 97 J8
Sawhāj *Town* Egypt 38 E5
Saxony *Region* Germany 56 G7
Saýat *Town* Turkmenistan 84 H4
Sayḩūt *Town* Yemen 83 F12
Saynshand *Town* Mongolia 89 J4
Say'ūn *Town* Yemen 83 E12
Scarborough *Town* England, UK 50 H8
Schaerbeek *Town* Belgium 53 D11
Schagen *Town* Netherlands 52 E7
Schefferville *Town* Newfoundland & Labrador, Canada 7 J4
Scheldt *River* Belgium 53 D10
Schenectady *Town* New York, USA 8 I5
Schwandorf *Town* Germany 57 F9
Schwaz *Town* Austria 57 F11
Schweinfurt *Town* Germany 56 E8
Schwerin *Town* Germany 56 E5
Schwyz *Town* Switzerland 57 D11
Scilly, Isles of *Island group* England, UK 51 D13
Scotland *Political region* UK 50 E5
Scott Base *Research station* Antarctica 110 E7
Scottsbluff *Town* Nebraska, USA 12 E5
Scottsdale *Town* Arizona, USA 16 E5
Scranton *Town* Pennsylvania, USA 8 H6
Seattle *Town* Washington, USA 14 G2
Sébaco *Town* Nicaragua 20 H5
Sedan *Town* France 54 G6
Sedona *Town* Arizona, USA 16 E4
Seesen *Town* Germany 56 E6
Segezha *Town* Russian Federation 72 D6
Ségou *Town* Mali 40 H5
Segovia *Town* Spain 58 H5
Séguédine *Town* Niger 41 M3
Seine *River* France 54 E6
Sekondi-Takoradi *Town* Ghana 41 I8
Selby *Town* South Dakota, USA 12 F4
Selwyn Range *Mountain range* Queensland, Australia 105 K4
Semarang *Town* Indonesia 96 G8
Semipalatinsk *Town* Kazakhstan 78 G7
Semnān *Town* Iran 82 F6
Sendai *Town* Japan 93 B14
Sendai *Town* Japan 92 G8
Sendai-wan *Bay* Japan 92 G8
Senegal *Country* 40 E5
Senegal *River* Senegal 40 E4
Senj *Town* Croatia 64 B6
Senlis *Town* France 54 E6
Sennar *Town* Sudan 38 E8
Sens *Town* France 54 F7
Seoul *Capital* South Korea 91 M3
Sept-Îles *Town* Québec, Canada 7 J5
Seraing *Town* Belgium 53 F11
Serang *Town* Indonesia 96 F7
Serbia *Country* 64 G8
Serhetabat *Town* Turkmenistan 84 G6
Seremban *Town* Malaysia 96 E5
Serov *Town* Russian Federation 78 F5
Serpukhov *Town* Russian Federation 73 C9
Sérres *Town* Greece 66 E8
Sesto San Giovanni *Town* Italy 60 C5
Setana *Town* Japan 92 F6
Sète *Town* France 55 F11
Sétif *Town* Algeria 37 I3
Setté Cama *Town* Gabon 43 C10
Setúbal *Town* Portugal 58 E7
Sevan *Town* Armenia 77 L4
Sevastopol' *Town* Ukraine 69 J7
Severn *River* England, UK 51 F11
Severnaya Zemlya *Island group* Russian Federation 79 I3
Severnyy *Town* Russian Federation 72 H5
Severodvinsk *Town* Russian Federation 72 E6
Severomorsk *Town* Russian Federation 72 E4
Sevilla *see* Seville
Seville *Town* Spain 58 G8
Sevlievo *Town* Bulgaria 66 F6
Seychelles *Country* 99 I5
Sfântu Gheorghe *Town* Romania 68 F6
Sfax *Town* Tunisia 37 J4
's-Gravenhage *see* Hague, The
Shaanxi *Administrative region* China 90 H5
Shanxi *Administrative region* China 91 I4
Shackleton Ice Shelf *Ice feature* Antarctica 110 G6
Shāhrūd *Town* Iran 82 F5
Shandong *Administrative region* China 91 J4
Shanghai *Town* China 91 L5
Shangrao *Town* China 91 K6
Shannon *River* Ireland 51 C9
Shan Plateau Myanmar 94 C6
Shantou *Town* China 91 J8
Shaoguan *Town* China 91 J7
Shar *Town* Kazakhstan 78 G7
Shari *Town* Japan 92 H4
Shchuchinsk *Town* Kazakhstan 78 F6
Sheberghān *Town* Afghanistan 85 I6
Sheboygan *Town* Wisconsin, USA 13 J5
Shebshi Mountains *Mountain range* Nigeria 41 M7
Sheffield *Town* England, UK 51 G9
Shelby *Town* Montana, USA 15 I2
Shenyang *Town* China 91 L2
Shepparton *Town* Victoria, Australia 105 K8
Sherbrooke *Town* Québec, Canada 7 I7
's-Hertogenbosch *Town* Netherlands 53 F9
Shetland Islands *Island group* Scotland, UK 50 F2
Shihezi *Town* China 88 F4
Shijiazhuang *Town* China 91 J3
Shikārpur *Town* Pakistan 86 F3
Shikoku *Island* Japan 93 E13
Shiliguri *Town* India 87 K3
Shimoga *Town* India 86 H7
Shimonoseki *Town* Japan 93 B13
Shīndand *Town* Afghanistan 84 G7
Shingū *Town* Japan 93 E12
Shintoku *Town* Japan 92 G5
Shinyanga *Town* Tanzania 39 E12
Shiprock *Town* New Mexico, USA 16 G3
Shirataki *Town* Japan 92 G4
Shīrāz *Town* Iran 82 F8
Shivpuri *Town* India 86 H4
Shizugawa *Town* Japan 92 G8
Shizuoka *Town* Japan 93 F11
Shkodër *Town* Albania 65 E11
Shouzhou *Town* China 91 I3
Shreveport *Town* Louisiana, USA 10 D5
Shrewsbury *Town* England, UK 51 F9
Shu *Town* Kazakhstan 78 F8
Shumen *Town* Bulgaria 66 H5
Shuqrah *Town* Yemen 83 D13
Shwebo *Town* Myanmar 94 B6
Shymkent *Town* Kazakhstan 78 F8
Šiauliai *Town* Lithuania 70 D6
Šibenik *Town* Croatia 64 C8
Siberia *Region* Russian Federation 79 J5
Sibi *Town* Pakistan 86 F2
Sibir' *see* Siberia
Sibiu *Town* Romania 68 F6
Sibolga *Town* Indonesia 96 D5
Sibut *Town* Central African Republic 42 E8
Sibuyan Sea Philippines 97 J3
Sichuan *Administrative region* China 90 F5
Sichuan Pendi *Depression* China 90 G6
Sicilia *see* Sicily
Sicily *Island* Italy 61 E13
Sicily, Strait of Mediterranean Sea 61 E14
Sidas *Town* Indonesia 96 G6
Sîdi Barrâni *Town* Egypt 38 C4
Sidi Bel Abbès *Town* Algeria 36 G4
Sidney *Town* Nebraska, USA 12 E6
Sidney *Town* Montana, USA 15 L2
Siedlce *Town* Poland 62 G7
Siegen *Town* Germany 56 C7
Siena *Town* Italy 60 D7
Sieradz *Town* Poland 62 E7
Sierra Leone *Country* 40 F7
Sierra Madre *Mountain range* Guatemala 20 D4
Sierra Madre Occidental *Mountain range* Mexico 18 G5
Sierra Madre Oriental *Mountain range* Mexico 19 J6
Sierra Nevada *Mountain range* Spain 59 I8
Sierra Nevada *Mountain range* California, USA 14 G6
Sierra Vieja *Mountain range* Texas, USA 17 I7
Sigli *Town* Indonesia 96 C4
Signy *Research station* Antarctica 110 B3
Siguiri *Town* Guinea 40 G6
Siirt *Town* Turkey 77 K6
Sikhote-Alin', Khrebet *Mountain range* Russian Federation 79 M6
Silchar *Town* India 87 L4
Silesia *Region* Poland 62 C7
Silifke *Town* Turkey 76 F7
Silistra *Town* Bulgaria 66 H5
Sillamäe *Town* Estonia 70 H4
Silvan *Town* Turkey 77 J5

Silverek *Town* Turkey 76 H6
Simferopol' *Town* Ukraine 69 K7
Simpson Desert Northern Territory/ Queensland/South Australia, Australia 105 J5
Sinai *Desert* Egypt 38 E4
Sincelejo *Town* Colombia 26 B5
Singapore *Country* 96 E6
Singida *Town* Tanzania 39 E12
Singkang *Town* Indonesia 97 I7
Singkawang *Town* Indonesia 96 F6
Siniscola *Town* Sardinia, Italy 61 C9
Sinnamary *Town* French Guiana 26 I6
Sinsheim *Town* Germany 57 D9
Sint Maarten *Island* Caribbean Sea 23 N5
Sint-Niklaas *Town* Belgium 53 D10
Sinŭiju *Town* North Korea 91 L3
Sioux City *Town* Iowa, USA 12 G5
Sioux Falls *Town* South Dakota, USA 12 G5
Siping *Town* China 89 M3
Siquirres *Town* Costa Rica 21 J7
Siracusa *Town* Sicily, Italy 61 F13
Sirjan *Town* Iran 82 G8
Şırnak *Town* Turkey 77 K6
Sirte, Gulf of Libya 37 L4
Sittoung *River* Myanmar 94 C8
Sittwe *Town* Myanmar 94 A7
Siuna *Town* Nicaragua 21 I4
Sivas *Town* Turkey 76 H4
Sjælland *Island* Denmark 49 C12
Skagerrak *Sea* Norway 49 B11
Skaudvilė *Town* Lithuania 70 D6
Skegness *Town* England, UK 51 H9
Skellefteå *Town* Sweden 48 F7
Skopje *Capital* Macedonia 65 G11
Skovorodino *Town* Russian Federation 78 K6
Slagelse *Town* Denmark 49 C12
Slatina *Town* Romania 68 E7
Slavonski Brod *Town* Croatia 64 E7
Sligo *Town* Ireland 50 B8
Sliven *Town* Bulgaria 66 G6
Slonim *Town* Belarus 71 D9
Slovakia *Country* 63 E10
Slovenia *Country* 57 G12
Slov''yans'k *Town* Ukraine 69 M4
Słupsk *Town* Poland 62 D5
Slutsk *Town* Belarus 71 E10
Smallwood Reservoir Nova Scotia, Canada 7 K4
Smara *Town* Western Sahara 36 D6
Smederevo *Town* Serbia 64 G8
Smolensk *Town* Russian Federation 72 B8
Snake River Idaho/Oregon, USA 14 H3
Snowdonia *Physical region* Wales, UK 51 F9
Sochi *Town* Russian Federation 73 B12
Société, Archipel de la *Island chain* French Polynesia 103 N7
Socotra *Island* Yemen 83 F13
Soc Trăng *Town* Vietnam 95 G12
Söderhamn *Town* Sweden 49 E9
Södertälje *Town* Sweden 49 E10
Sofia *Capital* Bulgaria 66 E6
Sofiya *see* Sofia
Sogamoso *Town* Colombia 26 C6
Sokal' *Town* Ukraine 68 F2
Sokhumi *Town* Georgia 77 J2
Sokodé *Town* Togo 41 J7
Sokone *Town* Senegal 40 E5
Sokoto *Town* Nigeria 41 K6
Solāpur *Town* Pakistan 86 H6
Sol, Costa del *Coastal region* Spain 58 H9
Soledad *Town* Colombia 26 B4
Solikamsk *Town* Russian Federation 72 G8
Solingen *Town* Germany 56 C7
Sollentuna *Town* Sweden 49 E10
Solok *Town* Indonesia 96 D6
Solomon Islands *Country* 102 H5
Solomon Islands *Island group* Papua New Guinea/Solomon Islands 102 F5
Solomon Sea Pacific Ocean 102 F5
Solwezi *Town* Zambia 44 H3
Sōma *Town* Japan 93 G9
Somalia *Country* 39 H10
Somaliland *Cultural region* Somalia 39 H9
Somerset *Town* Kentucky, USA 10 H3

Somme *River* France 54 E5
Somotillo *Town* Nicaragua 20 G5
Somoto *Town* Nicaragua 20 H5
Songea *Town* Tanzania 39 F14
Songkhla *Town* Thailand 95 D13
Sonoran Desert Arizona, USA 16 D5
Sonsonate *Town* El Salvador 20 E5
Sop Hao *Town* Laos 94 F7
Sopron *Town* Hungary 63 D11
Sorgun *Town* Turkey 76 G4
Soria *Town* Spain 59 J4
Sorong *Town* Indonesia 97 L6
Sortavala *Town* Russian Federation 72 C6
Sŏul *see* Seoul
Sousse *Town* Tunisia 37 J3
South Africa *Country* 44 G7
Southampton *Town* England, UK 51 F12
Southampton Island Nunavut, Canada 5 K5
South Australia *State* Australia 105 J6
South Bend *Town* Indiana, USA 13 K6
South Carolina *State* USA 11 J4
South China Sea Pacific Ocean 91 L8
South Dakota *State* USA 12 F4
Southeast Indian Ridge *Undersea feature* Indian Ocean 99 K7
Southend-on-Sea *Town* England, UK 51 H11
Southern Alps *Mountain range* New Zealand 107 C11
Southern Cook Islands *Island group* Cook Islands 103 L8
Southern Cross *Town* Western Australia, Australia 104 E6
Southern Ocean 110 G3
Southern Uplands *Mountain range* Scotland, UK 50 E7
South Georgia & The Sandwich Islands *Dependent Territory* UK, Atlantic Ocean 33 J8
South Island New Zealand 107 D11
South Korea *Country* 91 M4
South Orkney Islands *Island group* Antarctica 110 B3
South Shetland Islands *Island group* Antarctica 110 B4
South Shields *Town* England, UK 50 G7
Southwest Indian Ridge *Undersea feature* Indian Ocean 99 I6
Southwest Pacific Basin *Undersea feature* Pacific Ocean 109 K7
Soweto *Town* South Africa 44 H7
Spain *Country* 58 H5
Spanish Town *Town* Jamaica 22 G5
Spartanburg *Town* South Carolina, USA 11 I4
Spijkenisse *Town* Netherlands 53 D9
Spīn Būldak *Town* Afghanistan 85 I8
Spitsbergen *Island* Arctic Ocean 111 M7
Split *Town* Croatia 64 C8
Spokane *Town* Washington, USA 14 H2
Springfield *Town* Massachusetts, USA 8 J6
Springfield *Town* Illinois, USA 13 J7
Springfield *Town* Ohio, USA 13 L6
Springfield *Town* Missouri, USA 12 H8
Spring Hill *Town* Florida, USA 11 I7
Srbobran *Town* Serbia 64 F7
Srebrenica *Town* Bosnia & Herzegovina 64 F8
Sri Jayewardanapura Kotte *Town* Sri Lanka 87 I9
Sri Lanka *Country* 87 J9
Stafford *Town* England, UK 51 F9
Stakhanov *Town* Ukraine 69 M4
Stalowa Wola *Town* Poland 62 G8
Stamford *Town* Connecticut, USA 8 I6
Starachowice *Town* Poland 62 F8
Stara Zagora *Town* Bulgaria 66 G6
Stargard Szczeciński *Town* Poland 62 C5
Starobil's'k *Town* Ukraine 69 M4
Staryy Oskol *Town* Russian Federation 73 C10
State College *Town* Pennsylvania, USA 8 F7
Statesboro *Town* Georgia, USA 11 I5
Staunton *Town* Virginia, USA 11 K2
Stavanger *Town* Norway 49 A10
Stavropol' *Town* Russian Federation 73 C11

Steamboat Springs *Town* Colorado, USA 15 K5
Steinkjer *Town* Norway 48 C7
Sterling *Town* Illinois, USA 13 J6
Sterlitamak *Town* Russian Federation 73 G10
Stevenage *Town* England, UK 51 H10
Stevens Point *Town* Wisconsin, USA 13 J4
Stewart Island New Zealand 107 B14
Stillwater *Town* Okahoma, USA 17 L3
Stockholm *Capital* Sweden 49 E10
Stockton *Town* California, USA 14 F6
Stockton Plateau Texas, USA 17 J7
Stěng Trěng *Town* Cambodia 95 G10
Stoke-on-Trent *Town* England, UK 51 F9
Stonehenge *Ancient site* England, UK 51 G11
Stornoway *Town* Scotland,UK 50 D4
Storuman *Town* Sweden 48 E6
Stralsund *Town* Germany 56 F4
Strasbourg *Town* France 54 H7
Strelka *Town* Russian Federation 78 H6
Strumica *Town* Macedonia 65 H12
Stryy *Town* Ukraine 68 F3
Stuttgart *Town* Germany 57 D9
Subotica *Town* Serbia 64 F6
Suceava *Town* Romania 68 G5
Sucre *Capital* Bolivia 27 E12
Sudan *Country* 38 D8
Sudbury *Town* Ontario, Canada 6 G7
Sudd *Region* Sudan 39 D9
Sudeten *Region* Poland 62 C8
Suez *Town* Egypt 38 E4
Suez, Gulf of Egypt 38 E4
Sühbaatar *Town* Mongolia 89 I2
Suhl *Town* Germany 56 E8
Sujāwal *Town* Pakistan 86 F4
Sukabumi *Town* Indonesia 96 F8
Sukagawa *Town* Japan 93 G9
Sukkur *Town* Pakistan 86 F3
Sukumo *Town* Japan 93 D13
Sulawesi *see* Celebes
Sullana *Town* Peru 27 A9
Sulu Archipelago *Island chain* Philippines 97 I5
Sulu Sea Pacific Ocean 97 J4
Sumatera *see* Sumatra
Sumatra *Island* Indonesia 96 E7
Sumbawanga *Town* Tanzania 39 E13
Sumbe *Town* Angola 44 D3
Sumqayit *Town* Azerbaijan 77 N3
Sumy *Town* Ukraine 69 K2
Sunderland *Town* England, UK 50 F7
Sundsvall *Town* Sweden 48 E8
Sungaipenuh *Town* Indonesia 96 D7
Sunnyvale *Town* California, USA 14 F6
Suŏng *Town* Cambodia 95 G11
Superior *Town* Wisconsin, USA 13 I3
Superior, Lake Canada/USA, 13 I3
Suqutrā *see* Socotra
Şūr *Town* Oman 83 H10
Surabaya *Town* Indonesia 96 G8
Surakarta *Town* Indonesia 96 G8
Sūrat *Town* India 86 G5
Surat Thani *Town* Thailand 95 D12
Surdulica *Town* Serbia 65 H10
Surfers Paradise *Town* Queensland, Australia 105 N6
Surgut *Town* Russian Federation 78 G5
Suriname *Country* 26 G6
Surt *Town* Libya 37 L5
Surt, Khalij *see* Sirte, Gulf of
Susa *Town* Italy 60 B5
Susteren *Town* Netherlands 53 F10
Susuman *Town* Russian Federation 78 L4
Suva *Capital* Fiji 103 J7
Suwałki *Town* Poland 62 G5
Suzhou *Town* China 91 K5
Svalbard *Dependent Territory* Norway, Arctic Ocean 111 M7
Svartisen *Glacier* Norway 48 D5
Svenstavik *Town* Sweden 48 D8
Svilengrad *Town* Bulgaria 66 G7
Svobodnyy *Town* Russian Federation 79 L6
Svyetlahorsk *Town* Belarus 71 F11
Swansea *Town* Wales, UK 51 E11
Swaziland *Country* 45 I7

Sweden *Country* 48 D7
Świdnica *Town* Poland 62 D8
Świebodzin *Town* Poland 62 C7
Swindon *Town* England, UK 51 G11
Świnoujście *Town* Poland 62 B5
Switzerland *Country* 57 C11
Sydney *Town* New South Wales, Australia 105 M7
Syeverodonets'k *Town* Ukraine 69 M4
Syktyvkar *Town* Russian Federation 72 F7
Sylhet *Town* Bangladesh 87 L4
Syowa *Research station* Antarctica 110 F4
Syracuse *Town* New York, USA 8 G5
Syria *Country* 80 F7
Syrian Desert Jordan 81 G10
Syzran' *Town* Russian Federation 73 E10
Szczecin *Town* Poland 62 C5
Szeged *Town* Hungary 63 F12
Székesfehérvár *Town* Hungary 63 E11
Szolnok *Town* Hungary 63 F11
Szombathely *Town* Hungary 63 D11

T

Tabora *Town* Tanzania 39 E12
Tabrīz *Town* Iran 82 D5
Tabūk *Town* Saudi Arabia 82 A8
Täby *Town* Sweden 49 E10
Tacloban *Town* Philippines 97 K3
Tacoma *Town* Washington, USA 14 F2
Tacuarembó *Town* Uruguay 30 H7
Tademaït, Plateau du Algeria 36 H6
Tādpatri *Town* Bhutan 87 I7
Taegu *Town* South Korea 91 M4
Taejŏn *Town* South Korea 91 M4
Taganrog *Town* Russian Federation 73 B11
Taguatinga *Town* Brazil 29 K5
Tagus *River* Spain/Portugal 58 F6
Tahoua *Town* Niger 41 K5
T'aichung *Town* Taiwan 91 L8
T'ainan *Town* Taiwan 91 K8
Taipei *Capital* Taiwan 91 L7
Taiping *Town* Malaysia 96 D5
Taiwan *Country* 91 L8
Taiwan Strait China/Taiwan 91 L8
Taiyuan *Town* China 91 I4
Ta'izz *Town* Yemen 83 C13
Tajikistan *Country* 85 K5
Takaoka *Town* Japan 93 E10
Takapuna *Town* New Zealand 106 F5
Takasaki *Town* Japan 93 F10
Takikawa *Town* Japan 92 F5
Takla Makan Desert China 88 E5
Talamanca, Cordillera de *Mountain range* Costa Rica 21 J8
Talas *Town* Kyrgyzstan 85 K3
Talavera de la Reina *Town* Spain 58 H5
Talca *Town* Chile 30 C8
Talcahuano *Town* Chile 31 C9
Taldykorgan *Town* Kazakhstan 78 G8
Tallahassee *Town* Florida, USA 10 H6
Tallinn *Capital* Estonia 70 G3
Talnakh *Town* Russian Federation 78 H4
Talsi *Town* Latvia 70 E5
Talvik *Town* Norway 48 F3
Tamale *Town* Ghana 41 I7
Tamanrasset *Town* Algeria 37 I7
Tamazunchale *Town* Mexico 19 K7
Tambacounda *Town* Senegal 40 E5
Tambov *Town* Russian Federation 73 D10
Tampa *Town* Florida, USA 11 I7
Tampa Bay Florida, USA 11 I8
Tampere *Town* Finland 48 G5
Tampico *Town* Mexico 19 K6
Tamworth *Town* New South Wales, Australia 105 M6
Tana *Town* Norway 48 G3
Tanabe *Town* Japan 93 E12
Tanami Desert Northern Territory, Australia 104 H3
Tandil *Town* Argentina 31 G9
Tane Range *Mountain range* Thailand 94 D8
Tanezrouft *Desert* Algeria 36 H7
Tanga *Town* Tanzania 39 G12

Index

Acknowledgments

For the 2011 edition, Dorling Kindersley would like to thank:

Natalie Godwin for jacket design, Niki Foreman for proofreading, Matilda Gollon for editorial help, and Carron Brown for the index and for editorial help.

CD production team:

Senior digital graphic designer Nain Singh Rawat
Producer Lakshmi Rao
Technical manager Jay Prakash Pandey
Producer and data architect Archna Sharma
Technical coordinator Amit Verma
Assistant editor Suchi Smita
Assistant graphic designer Vikas Sachdeva
Assistant DTP designers Abhishek Verma, Rohit Rojal
Senior producer, digital content Briar Towers

The publisher would like to thank the following for their kind permission to reproduce their photographs: (Key: a-above; b-below/bottom; c-centre; f-far; l-left; r-right; t-top)

i Corbis: B.S.P.I. (bl); Steve Rayner (fbr). **Photoshot:** World Pictures (fbl, br). **ii Corbis:** Stephanie Maze (br). **Getty Images:** Jim Cummins / Stone (cra). **Science Photo Library:** 1995 Worldsat International, and J. Knighton (l). **iii Corbis:** Sergio Pitamitz (br). **Robert Harding Picture Library:** Robert Frerck (cl); Frans Lemmens (cra). **v Corbis:** Frans Lanting (clb); Ludovic Maisant (bl); Werner H. Mueller (cla/dunes). **vi Corbis:** Howard Davies (br). **viii Corbis:** Jacky Naegelen / Reuters (cra). **2 Corbis:** Alan Schein Photography (bl). **Robert Harding Picture Library:** John Miller (cra). **3 Corbis:** Peter M. Wilson (clb). **Science Photo Library:** 1995 Worldsat International, and J. Knighton (globe). **4 Alaska Stock:** (clb). **Corbis:** Gunter Marx Photography (bl); Charles O'Rear (tr). **Photoshot:** World Pictures (bc). **5 Corbis:** Staffan Widstrand (tc); Peter M. Wilson (br/mountain background). **NHPA / Photoshot:** T. Kitchin and V. Hurst (cra); Andy Rouse (fbr/bear). **6 Cephas Picture Library:** Fred R. Palmer (tr). **Corbis:** Benjamin Rondel (bl/Toronto). Press Association Images: Tony Marshall / EMPICS Sport; (bc). **7 Corbis:** William A. Bake (br); Richard J. Nowitz (cra). **Photoshot:** Egmont Strigl / imagebroker; (tr); World Pictures (tl). **8 Pictures Colour Library:** (ca). **Robert Harding Picture Library:** Stuart Pearce / Age Fotostock (bl). **9 Corbis:** Alan Schein Photography (br); Paul Barton (crb); Ralf-Finn Hestoft (tl); Farrell Grehan (c). **Robert Harding Picture Library:** Andy Caulfield / Panoramic Images (tr). **10 Corbis:** Owen Franken (crb). **Getty Images:** Andy Sacks (cla). **Redferns:** (bc). **Robert Harding Picture Library:** Peter Lilja / Age Fotostock (br). **11 Corbis:** Tony Arruza (br); Flip Schulke (cb). **Getty Images:** Matthew Stockman (tc). **12 Corbis:** Blaine Harrington III (cl/buffalo). **Dorling Kindersley:** American Museum of Natural History, London (fcl). **Rex Features:** Sipa Press (bc). **Robert Harding Picture Library:** Sergio Pitamitz (bl). **13 Corbis:** Philip Gould (br); Julie Habel (tl). **Getty Images:** Jim Cummins / Stone (crb). **14 Robert Harding Picture Library:** Liane Cary / age fotostock (bl); Melissa Farlow / National Geographic (tc). **15 Corbis:** Dean Conger (ca); Jong Beom Kim / TongRo (clb); Lester Lefkowitz (br). **Rex Features:** Sipa Press (bc). **Robert Harding Picture Library:** Louise Murray (tr). **Science Photo Library:** George Bernard (bl). **16 Corbis:** B.S.P.I. (br); Richard Ransier (ftr). **Dorling Kindersley:** Hopi Learning Centre (br/doll). **Getty Images:** Eric Schnakenberg / Photographer's Choice (tr). **Robert Harding Picture Library:** Tony Gervis (bl). **17 NASA:** (tr). **Robert Harding Picture Library:** Walter Rawlings (bl). **18 Corbis:** Keith Dannemiller (tr); Danny Lehman (br). **Robert Harding Picture Library:** Robert Frerck / Odyssey / Chicago (cl). **Still Pictures:** Julio Etchart (bl). **19 Corbis:** Macduff Everton (tr); Tim Thompson (tc). **Getty Images:** Bruce Stoddard / Stone (ftl). 20 Corbis: Stephen Frink (cl); Sergio Pitamitz (crb). **Eye Ubiquitous / Hutchison:** Robert Francis (br). Photoshot: World Pictures (bl). **21 Corbis:** Poisson d'avril / Photocuisine (ca); Arvind Garg (tl). **Eye Ubiquitous / Hutchison:** Robert Francis (clb). **Photoshot:** World Pictures / Intervision (tr). **Robert Harding Picture Library:** Jose Enrique Molina / age fotostock (cb). **22 Corbis:** Bill Gentile (cl). **Photoshot:** Martin Engelmann (bl). **23 Corbis:** Wolfgang Kaehler (cb); Peter Turnley (clb). **Eye Ubiquitous / Hutchison:** John Fuller (tl). **Photoshot:** World Pictures (ca). **Robert Harding Picture Library:** John Miller (tr). **24 Robert Harding Picture Library:** P. Narayan / Age Fotostock (cra). **South American Pictures:** Jason Howe (b). **25 Photoshot:** World Pictures (clb). **Science Photo Library:** 1995, Worldsat International and J. Knighton (globe). **26 Corbis:** Pablo Corral V (cla). **Photoshot:** World Pictures (cr). **South American Pictures:** (tl). **27 Dorling Kindersley:** British Museum (br). **Eye Ubiquitous / Hutchison:** H. Jelliffee (tr); Paul Seheult (tl); Eric Lawrie (cra). **Photoshot:** World Pictures (bl). **Robert Harding Picture Library:** Gavin Hellier (cr). **28 Corbis:** Yann Arthus-Bertrand (crb). **Eye Ubiquitous / Hutchison:** Dr Nigel Smith (br). **Robert Harding Picture Library:** (clb). **South American Pictures:** Jason Howe (bl). **29 Corbis:** Stephanie Maze (cra). **Photoshot:** (br). **Tomek Sierek:** (tr). **30 Corbis:** Tony Arruza (br). **Photoshot:** World Pictures (bc). **Robert Harding Picture Library:** Bildagentur Schuster / Gluske (cla); Ken Welsh / Age Fotostock (tl). **31 Corbis:** Fulvio Roiter (tr). **Photoshot:** World Pictures (cla). **Robert Harding Picture Library:** Victor Englebert (bl); P. Narayan / Age Fotostock (tl). **South American Pictures:** (br). **32 Corbis:** Carlos Dominguez (crb); Wolfgang Kaehler (br). **NHPA / Photoshot:** B. & C. Alexander (bl). **Robert Harding Picture Library:** (tr); Roy Rainford (cra); Adam Woolfitt (clb). **33 Corbis:** George D. Lepp (br); Hans Strand (tr). **35 Science Photo Library:** Tom Van Sant, Geosphere Project / Planetary Visions (t). **36 Eye Ubiquitous / Hutchison:** Mary Jelliffee (br). **Photoshot:** World Pictures (tr, cl). **37 Corbis:** Benjamin Lowy (b). **Dorling Kindersley:** British Museum (tc). **Getty Images:** Frans Lemmens / The Image Bank (crb). **Photoshot:** World Pictures (tr). **Robert Harding Picture Library:** T.D. Winter (tl). **38 Corbis:** Michael Hanson / National Geographic Society (tr). **Photoshot:** World Pictures (br). **Robert Harding Picture Library:** Nakamura (ca). **39 Corbis:** Karl Ammann (br). **Eye Ubiquitous / Hutchison:** (tr); Jeremy Horner (bl); Sarah Errington (bc). **40 Dorling Kindersley:** Barnabas Kindersley (bl). **Panos Pictures:** Teun Voeten; (br/diamond). **Robert Harding Picture Library:** J. Lightfoot (cla). **41 Corbis:** Charles & Josette Lenars (bl). **Eye Ubiquitous / Hutchison:** Crispin Hughes (cr, br). **Panos Pictures:** Clive Shirley (tl). **42 Corbis:** Skip Brown / National Geographic Society (tl). **Dorling Kindersley:** Powell Cotton Museum (bc). **Eye Ubiquitous / Hutchison:** Sarah Errington (br). **Photoshot:** World Pictures (tc). **43 Dorling Kindersley:** Natural History Museum, London (cra/copper). **Eye Ubiquitous / Hutchison:** (c); Trevor Page (br). **Getty Images:** Nicolas Cotto / AFP (tr); Per-Anders Pettersson / The Image Bank (bl). **44 Corbis:** Anthony Bannister (cla). **Photoshot:** (bl). **Robert Harding Picture Library:** Alain Evrard (bc). **45 Alamy Images:** AfriPics.com (br/buffalo background). **Corbis:** Peter Turnley (bl). **Dreamstime.com:** Eric Isselée (fbr/lion). **Eye Ubiquitous / Hutchison:** Sarah Errington (tl); Liba Taylor (tr); Crispin Hughes (tc). **Robert Harding Picture Library:** Chris Mattison / age fotostock (crb/lemur). **47 Photoshot:** World Pictures (cr). **Science Photo Library:** Tom Van Sant, Geosphere Project / Planetary Visions (t). **48 Corbis:** Charles & Josette Lenars (tl). **Photoshot:** Paul Thompson / World Pictures (br). **Robert Harding Picture Library:** Kim Hart (ftl). **49 Corbis:** Jean-Pierre Amet / Sygma (tl); Dave Bartruff (tr); Stephanie Maze (cla). **TopFoto.co.uk:** Francis Dean / Imageworks (crb). **50 Corbis:** David Paterson / WildCountry (tr); Michael St. Maur Sheil (br). **Pictures Colour Library:** (bc). **Robert Harding Picture Library:** Eye Ubiquitous (tc). **51 Corbis:** Tommy Hindley / NewSport (bc). **Eye Ubiquitous / Hutchison:** Philp Wolmouth (br). **Pictures Colour Library:** Charles Bowman (cr). **Robert Harding Picture Library:** Mark Mawson / Robert Harding World Imagery (tr). **52 Corbis:** Owen Franken (br). **Photoshot:** World Pictures (bc). **Robert Harding Picture Library:** Adam Woolfitt (tl). **53 Corbis:** Dave Bartruff (bl); Ray Juno (br); Owen Franken (tr, tl). **54 Corbis:** G. Bowater (cb); Roger Ressmeyer (ftl). **Photoshot:** (tl). **55 Corbis:** Pierre Perrin / Sygma (bl); Kim Sayer (br); Mike Powell (cra). **Photoshot:** Carol Pucci / Seattle Times / MCT (tl). **56 Corbis:** Arnd Wiegmann / akw / Reuters (tl). **Getty Images:** Michael Rosenfeld (bc). **Masterfile:** Didier Dorval (tl). **Rex Features:** Sipa Press (br). **57 Corbis:** Dominic Ebenbichler / Reuters (cr). **Getty Images:** Sylvain Grandadam (tr); Jess Stock (br). **58 Corbis:** Morton Beebe (bl). **Dreamstime.com:** Photooiasson (Álvaro Germán Vilela) (clb). **Robert Harding Picture Library:** Jesus Nicolas Sanchez / age fotostock (cla). **59 Corbis:** Patrick Ward (br). **Getty Images:** AFP (tr). **Panos Pictures:** David Constantine (cr). **Pictures Colour Library:** © FMGB Guggenheim Bilbao Museoa. Photo by Charles Bowman. All rights reserved. Total or partial reproduction is prohibited. (tl). **Robert Harding Picture Library:** Robert Frerck (bl). **60 Corbis:** Jörg Carstensen / DPA (cl). **Rex Features:** Enrica Scalfari (tr). **Robert Harding Picture Library:** R. Richardson (br). **61 Art Directors & TRIP:** (cra). **Eye Ubiquitous / Hutchison:** Trevor Page (bc). **Photoshot:** World Pictures (r). **Pictures Colour Library:** (clb). **62 Dreamstime.com:** Taratorki (Ewa Rejmer) (tr). **Panos Pictures:** David Constantine (cla). **Robert Harding Picture Library:** (tl). **63 Eye Ubiquitous / Hutchison:** Liba Taylor (cb). **Photoshot:** Rick Strange / World Pictures (tl); World Pictures (tr, br). **64 Eye Ubiquitous / Hutchison:** (ca). **Press Association Images:** Tony Marshall (bc). **Photoshot:** World Pictures (tl). **65 Corbis:** John Heseltine (cb). **Eye Ubiquitous / Hutchison:** David Watson (br). **Robert Harding Picture Library:** G. R. Richardson (tr); Phil Robinson (bl). **66 Corbis:** Marco Cristofori / Robert Harding World Imagery (tl). **Eye Ubiquitous / Hutchison:** Melanie Friend (crb, br). **Robert Harding Picture Library:** (tr). **67 Corbis:** Dallas & John Heaton / Free Agents Limited (cb); Clay Perry (tl). **Photoshot:** Lorraine Nicol / World Pictures (bl); World Pictures (tr); World Pictures / Mauritius Images (br). **68 Art Directors & TRIP:** P. Mercea (br). **Eye Ubiquitous / Hutchison:** Nick Haslam (clb). **Photoshot:** World Pictures (bl). **Pictures Colour Library:** (cla). **69 Art Directors & TRIP:** D. Mossienko (tr); N.& J. Wiseman (cr). **Corbis:** Barry Lewis (bl). **Eye Ubiquitous / Hutchison:** Liba Taylor (br). **70 Art Directors & TRIP:** T. Noorits (tl). **Robert Harding Picture Library:** Angelo Cavalli (bc). **71 Corbis:** Serge Attal / Sygma (bl); Dimitri Iundt / TempSport (tr); Niall Benvie (fcra); Nik Wheeler (tl); Staffan Widstrand (bc). **Photoshot:** Paul Thompson / World Pictures (br). **72 Corbis:** Robbie Jack (bc); Steve Rayner (tr). **Photoshot:** World Pictures (cla). **73 Art Directors & TRIP:** D. Iusupov (ca). **Corbis:** Gavin Hellier / Robert Harding World Imagery (br). **Dorling Kindersley:** Pitt Rivers Museum (tc). **Eye Ubiquitous / Hutchison:** Victoria Ivleva-Yorke (tr); Liba Taylor (bl, tl). **75 Science Photo Library:** Tom Van Sant / Geosphere Project / Planetary Visions (t). **76 Corbis:** Dave G. Houser (br); Lawrence Manning (cl); Adam Woolfitt (tr). **Photoshot:** Adina Amsel / World Pictures (bl). **77 Corbis:** Arne Hodalic (bl); David Turnley (tr); Nik Wheeler (br). **78 Corbis:** Peter Turnley (bc). **Eye Ubiquitous / Hutchison:** Sarah Errington (bl). **79 Alamy Images:** Arcticphoto (tr). **Corbis:** Wolfgang Kaehler (bl); Gregor Schmid (crb). **Pictures Colour Library:** (cr). **Robert Harding Picture Library:** Morales (br). **80 Corbis:** David Turnley (cla). **Photoshot:** José Nicolas / Hemis.fr / World Pictures (cb); Rick Strange / World Pictures (br); World Pictures (fcla). **81 Corbis:** Christine Osborne (fcrb/police officer). **Eye Ubiquitous / Hutchison:** Bernard Gerard (bl); James Henderson (tr). **Photoshot:** Jonathan Carlile / Imagebrokers (tl). **Robert Harding Picture Library:** Michael Short (br/landscape). **82 Dorling Kindersley:** British Library (c). **Eye Ubiquitous / Hutchison:** Bernard Gerard (b). **Getty Images:** Bruno Morandi (tc). **Rex Features:** Stuart Clarke (tl). **83 Dorling Kindersley:** Barnabas Kindersley (br). **Eye Ubiquitous / Hutchison:** John Nowell (crb). **Robert Harding Picture Library:** Mohamed Amin (bl); Walter Bibikow (tl). **84 Corbis:** S. Sabawoon (bl). **Getty Images:** Shah Marai / AFP (cb). **85 Corbis:** David Turnley (cr); Nevada Wier (cb, tr/mountains, tr). **Robert Harding Picture Library:** Ivan Vdovin (br). **86 Corbis:** Keren Su (br). **Eye Ubiquitous / Hutchison:** Sarah Errington (clb). **Getty Images:** Martin Puddy (cl). **87 Alamy Images:** Tibor Bognar (tr). **Eye Ubiquitous / Hutchison:** Horner (bl). **Pictorial Press Ltd:** (crb). **Robert Harding Picture Library:** David Beatty (tl); Frans Lemmens (clb). **88 Eye Ubiquitous / Hutchison:** Sarah Murray (b); Stephen Pem (cla). **88-89 Robert Harding Picture Library:** Philippe Michel (tc). **89 Eye Ubiquitous / Hutchison:** Melanie Friend (bl); Stephen Pern (tr). **Photoshot:** Rudi Pigneter (clb). **Robert Harding Picture Library:** G. Hellier (br); Doug Traverso (cr). **90 Corbis:** Douglas Peebles (tr). **Eye Ubiquitous / Hutchison:** Melanie Friend (cb); Jeremy Horner (bl). **Photoshot:** World Pictures (cla). **91 Corbis:** Michael S. Yamashita (bc). **Eye Ubiquitous / Hutchison:** Trevor Page (tl); Christine Pemberton (br). **Getty Images:** Kim Jae-Hwan / AFP (cra). **Photoshot:** World Pictures (crb). **92 Corbis:** Robert Holmes (tl). **Getty Images:** Paul Chesley / Stone (cl). **Photoshot:** World Pictures (br). **Pictures Colour Library:** (tr). **93 Corbis:** Michael S. Yamashita (bl). **Eye Ubiquitous / Hutchison:** Jon Burbank (tl); N. Haslam (clb). **Getty Images:** Panoramic Images (tr). **Robert Harding Picture Library:** Gavin Hellier (ca). **94 Corbis:** (cla). **Eye Ubiquitous / Hutchison:** Rene Giudicelli (tl). **Photoshot:** (tc); World Pictures (tr). **95 Eye Ubiquitous / Hutchison:** Norman Froggatt (cr). **Photoshot:** Stuart Pearce / World Pictures (br). **Robert Harding Picture Library:** (clb); Alain Evrard (tr). **96 Corbis:** (cl); Tom Brakefield (tr). **Eye Ubiquitous / Hutchison:** John Halt (br); Juliet Highet (bl). **Rex Features:** Tim Rooke (ca). **97 Corbis:** Dean Conger (br). **Eye Ubiquitous / Hutchison:** Michael Macintyre (ca); Dr Nigel Smith (cr). **Rex Features:** Sipa Press (tr). **98 Eye Ubiquitous / Hutchison:** Isabella Tree (tr). **Photoshot:** Josef Beck (cla); Hartmut Röder (cr); World Pictures (bl). **Still Pictures:** Roland Seitre (cb). **99 Corbis:** Theo Allofs (cra). **Photoshot:** Eye Ubiquitous / Hutchison (tl). **Rex Features:** Wilhemsen (br). **100 Corbis:** Sergio Pitamitz (bl); Keren Su (cra). **101 Corbis:** Wolfgang Kaehler (cl). **Getty Images:** Travel Pix (br). **Science Photo Library:** 1995, Worldsat International and J. Knighton (globe). **102 Corbis:** B.S.P.I. (tr). **Dorling Kindersley:** Mark O'Shea (bl). **Eye Ubiquitous / Hutchison:** Michael Macintyre (bc). **103 Corbis:** Wolfgang Kaehler (bl). Eye Ubiquitous / Hutchison: Nick Haslam (cra); Michael MacIntyre (tr). **Robert Harding Picture Library:** Upperhall Ltd (tl). **104 Corbis:** Penny Tweedie (cla). **Eye Ubiquitous / Hutchison:** N. Durrell McKenna (clb). **Getty Images:** Panoramic Images (cla/landscape background). **Press Association Images:** Phil Walter / EMPICS Sport (bc). **Robert Harding Picture Library:** Ken Gillham (tr). **105 Corbis:** Sergio Pitamitz (br). **Eye Ubiquitous / Hutchison:** Robert Francis (bl). **Getty Images:** Jeff Hunter / Photographer's Choice (cra). **Robert Harding Picture Library:** Neale Clark (crb). **106 Photoshot:** Rick Strange / World Pictures (crb); Paul Thompson / World Pictures (tl); World Pictures (br). **107 Photoshot:** Jeny McMillan (tr). **Rex Features:** Simon Runting (bl). **Robert Harding Picture Library:** Jeremy Bright (cb); Julia Thorne (tl). **108 Getty Images:** Andy Hall / Australian Defense Force (clb); Jeremy Woodhouse / Photodisc (cra). **Photolibrary:** Seiden Allan / Pacific Stock; ; (tr). **Robert Harding Picture Library:** Andoni Canela (bl). **Verena Tunnicliffe:** (crb). **109 Corbis:** Wolfgang Kaehler (tr); Stephanie Maze (br). **Robert Harding Picture Library:** Warren Finlay / International Stock (cra). **110 Eye Ubiquitous / Hutchison:** Isabella Tree (bl). **NASA:** (cla). **Robert Harding Picture Library:** Thorsten Milse (br); Geoff Renner (tr). **Still Pictures:** Marc Steinmetz / VISUM; (clb). **111 Corbis:** Composite Image / Alaska Stock LLC (tr); Tim Davis (br); Vince Streano (cla); Torleif Svensson (crb).

Jacket: *Front:* **Corbis:** Owen Franken (fcr), Stephen Frink (fbr), Richard Ransier (fcrb) (children in swimming pool), Peter M. Wilson (fbl); **Getty Images:** Keren Su / Stone (cr) (2 girls); **Masterfile:** Hans Blohm / ZEFA (crb); **Robert Harding Picture Library:** Lee Frost (bl); **Science Photo Library:** Planetary Visions Ltd (globe); *Back:* **Corbis:** Alan Schein Photography (fcrb) (Statue of Liberty), B.S.P.I. (crb), Dave Bartruff (clb), Tim Davis (clb) (penguins), Stephen Frink (fbr), Peter M. Wilson (fbl); **Getty Images:** Kevin Morris / Stone (fclb); **Robert Harding Picture Library:** Lee Frost (bl); **Science Photo Library:** Planetary Visions Ltd (globe); *Spine:* **Corbis:** Owen Franken (t) (top), Richard Ransier (t) (lower image).

For further information see: www.dkimages.com

Limit of summer pack ice

Greenland
Sea

Spitsbergen

Franz Josef
Land

Severnaya
Zemlya

New Siberian
Islands

Iceland

Denmark
Strait

Norwegian
Sea

Limit of winter pack ice

Novaya
Zemlya

Barents
Sea

Kara
Sea

Laptev Sea

Scandinavia

West
Siberian
Plain

Ob

Central
Siberian Plateau

Lena

Khrebet Cherskogo

British
Isles

North
Sea

Baltic Sea

Volga

Ural Mountains

ASIA

Lake Baikal

Siberia

Sea of
Okhots

Bay of
Biscay

EUROPE

Alps

Carpathian Mts

Danube

Black Sea

Caucasus

Caspian
Sea

Aral Sea

Lake
Balkhash

Altai
Mountains

Gobi

Amur

Sakhal

Iberian
Peninsula

Balkans Mts

Anatolia

Tien Shan

Manchurian
Plain

Hokkaid

Azores

Mediterranean Sea

Zagros Mountains

Pamirs

Kunlun Mountains

Yellow River

Sea of
Japan
(East Sea)

Honshu

Madeira

Atlas
Mountains

Iranian
Plateau

Hindu Kush

Plateau
of Tibet

Yellow
Sea

Japan

Kyushu

Bonin Trench

Canary
Islands

Sahara

Libyan Desert

Syrian
Desert

Indus

Himalayas

Yangtze

East
China
Sea

Ryukyu
Islands

Ahaggar

Nile

Red Sea

Persian
Gulf

Thar
Desert

Mount Everest
29,035ft
(8850m)

Ganges

Taiwan

Tibesti

Arabian
Peninsula

Deccan

Philippine
Sea

Mariana
Islands

AFRICA

Sahel

Niger

Ethiopian
Highlands

Gulf of Aden

Arabian Sea

Western Ghats

Eastern Ghats

Bay of
Bengal

Mekong

South
China
Sea

Philippine Trench

Philippine Islands

M Carolin
e I

Mariana

Cape Verde
Islands

Adamawa
Highlands

Horn of
Africa

Maldive
Islands

Andaman
Islands

Sri Lanka

Nicobar
Islands

Malay
Peninsula

Gulf of
Guinea

Congo

Congo
Basin

Great Rift Valley

Lake Victoria

Kilimanjaro
19,340ft
(5895m)

Somali
Basin

Seychelles

Borneo

Celebes

East Indies

New
Guinea

ATLANTIC

Ascension Island

Great Rift Valley

Lake
Tanganyika

INDIAN

Sumatra

Java Sea

Java

Timor
Sea

Arafura
Sea

Great Barrier R

Great D

OCEAN

Angola
Basin

St Helena

Zambezi

Lake
Nyasa

Mozambique Channel

Madagascar

Mauritius
Réunion

Ninetyeast Ridge

Java Trench

Mid-Atlantic Ridge

Namib Desert

Kalahari
Desert

OCEAN

Great
Sandy Desert

AUSTRALIA

Cape
Basin

Drakensberg

Cape of
Good Hope

Great
Victoria Desert

Nullarbor Plain

Darling

Tristan da Cunha
Gough Island

Southwest Indian Ridge

Southeast Indian Ridge

Bass St

Tasmania

Kerguelen

31901051041715

South Indian Basin

Limit of winter pack ice

SOUTHERN OCEAN

ANTARCTICA

Limit of summer pack ice